Routing in
the Internet,
2nd Edition

ISBN 0-13-022647-5

90000

9 780130 226471

Routing in the Internet,

2nd Edition

Christian Huitema

Prentice Hall PTR
Upper Saddle River, NJ 07458
www.phptr.com

Library of Congress Cataloging-in-Publication Data

```
Huitema, Christian
     Routing in the internet / Christian Huitema.—2nd ed.
       p. cm.
     Includes bibliographical references and index.
     ISBN 0-13-022647-5 (case)
        1. Internet (Computer network). 2. Computer network protocols.
     3. Computer network architectures. 4. Routers (Computer networks)
     I. Title.

TK5105.875.I57 H85 1999
004.6'2—dc21                                          99-049861
                                                          CIP
```

Editorial/production supervision: *BooksCraft, Inc., Indianapolis, IN*
Acquisitions editor: *Mary Franz*
Editorial assistant: *Noreen Regina*
Marketing manager: *Lisa Konzelmann*
Manufacturing manager: *Maura Goldstaub*
Cover design director: *Jerry Votta*
Cover designer: *Talar Agasyan*
Project coordinator: *Anne Trowbridge*

© 2000, 1995 by Prentice Hall PTR
Prentice-Hall, Inc.
Upper Saddle River, NJ 07458

Prentice Hall books are widely used by corporations and government agencies for
training, marketing, and resale.

The publisher offers discounts on this book when ordered in bulk quantities.
For more information, contact:

Corporate Sales Department
Prentice Hall PTR
One Lake Street
Upper Saddle River, NJ 07458
Phone: 800-382-3419   Fax: 201-236-7141
E-mail: corpsales@prenhall.com.

Printed in the United States of America

10   9   8   7   6   5   4   3   2   1

ISBN: 0-13-022647-5

Prentice-Hall International (UK) Limited, *London*
Prentice-Hall of Australia Pty. Limited, *Sydney*
Prentice-Hall Canada Inc., *Toronto*
Prentice-Hall Hispanoamericana, S.A., *Mexico*
Prentice-Hall of India Private Limited, *New Delhi*
Prentice-Hall of Japan, Inc., *Tokyo*
Pearson Education Asia Pte. Ltd., *Singapore*
Editora Prentice-Hall do Brasil, Ltda., *Rio de Janeiro*

Contents

Part I: Architecture and Protocols

Part II: Interior Routing Protocols

Part III: Exterior Routing Protocols

Part IV: New Developments

Introduction to Routing in the Internet

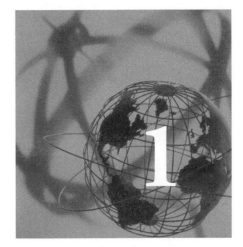

I first heard of the Internet in 1982. At that time, it was still centered around the Arpanet. Its access was reserved to a few research centers around the world. Our own research center, INRIA in France, could perhaps have joined its transatlantic extension, Satnet, but we never quite managed to convince the funding agencies of the usefulness of such a project. In fact, we were quite happy to acquire an indirect connection through the UNIX-based Usenet network a few years later. We had to wait until 1988 for a direct connection with the NSFnet, the interconnection network funded by the U.S. National Science Foundation.

1.1 The Worldwide Internet

The situation has changed a lot since that time. There were only a few hundred machines connected to the Internet by 1982: it was pretty much the playground for an elite group of computer scientists. That number had grown to 2.5 million connected computers on January 1, 1994, when the first edition of this book was being prepared. By the time of the second edition, in July 1999, there are about 60 million computer addresses registered in the domain name service. An estimated 20 million users had access to it, then. Nobody really knows how many users have access to the Internet now; estimates vary between 100 and 200 million. The initial core of experts has been joined by a variety of teachers and students, researchers and merchants, journalists and engineers. More than half of the connected computers in the United States already belonged to commercial companies in 1994, while academia only represents one-sixth of the network in 1999. The initial Internet was mostly a U.S.-only network, with a few appendices in a couple of friendly countries. By 1994, one could estimate that over half of the net was located in the United States, about one-third in Europe, with a growing presence in Asia and other continents. This figure has not changed much in 1999, as the North American networks have kept growing just as fast as the international networks. This rapid increase of the commercial and international participation is characteristic of the recent evolution and probably explains the amazing growth of the recent years: the net seems to double its size every year!

1.2 How Is It Organized?

The Internet is not "one network" in the common sense of the term: there is no such thing as one huge international company that would provide connections to users in various continents. Instead, the Internet is "a loose interconnection of networks," belonging to many owners. One usually distinguishes three levels of networks: organizational, regional, and transit.

The companies and institutions attached to the Internet generally manage an internal network. Its complexity can vary widely with the size of the organization. A typical example may be the research unit of INRIA in Sophia-Antipolis, where I used to work. The local network consisted of six Ethernet segments connecting about 300 workstations scattered in six buildings. The segments were connected to each other by a fiber-optic FDDI backbone that was directly attached to our supercomputers and service machines. Connection between the ring and the segments was assured by several specialized routers, using the Internet protocols. Indeed, this network was more complex than those of several small companies which often consist of one single Ethernet or token ring network. But large universities often have thousands of machines to connect, and multinational companies may have to manage a worldwide mesh of links between their different sites.

Most organizations' networks are connected to the Internet through a "regional" provider which manages a set of links covering a state, a region, or maybe a small country. These regional networks provide connectivity to their customers; they also render a number of related services, such as helping users to manage their networks or to get Internet addresses and providing mailboxes for isolated users. The regional nature of these providers is generally derived from these service relations: proximity helps. There is, however, no regional monopoly. Several companies may well compete in the same city or in the same region. There is also no restriction on the scope of the provider. Some companies that started in a limited geographic area are currently expanding their operations to other regions, maybe other countries. In fact, we are currently observing the burgeoning activity of a new industry. While the market grows, many new operators start their own activities. Some will succeed and become the giants of tomorrow. Some will remain small and concentrate on a particular corner of the market. Many others will probably be absorbed.

Being connected to other Internet users in the same city, even in the same state, is not quite sufficient. The purpose of the Internet is more ambitious: worldwide connectedness. This connectivity may be provided by a "transit" provider. The first network that clearly positioned itself as primarily a transit provider was the NSFnet. This successor of the Arpanet had a deliberate policy of allowing connection only through intermediate, regional providers. Another well-known transit system is the EBONE in Europe, which is operated in cooperation by several European regional networks. Such an interconnection is not adequate when the regional networks have grown so large that they already encompass many regions or many countries. In that case, bilateral or multilateral arrangements are preferred. The NSFnet has now been decommissioned, and the transit services are provided by a small number of very large international networks run by commercial organizations.

1.3 A Study of Routing

Many books have already been written on the Internet; yet another one would not be the most useful addition to the shelves of our libraries. This book, however, seeks to address one very specific topic: the organization of routing—the structure that glues together the worldwide Internet. It is divided into five parts. The first part includes three chapters: the general principles of the Internet architecture, the presentation of the Internet Protocol (IP) itself, and the presentation of IPv6, which has been designed as a replacement for IP. Each of the following chapters will present both the state of the art, based on the current version of IP (IPv4), and the provisions that are made for IPv6.

Three chapters cover the routing within organizations' networks. chapter 5 is devoted to RIP, the old Internet routing protocol. It is also an introduction to routing protocols in general, detailing the easy-to-understand "distance vector" technology. Then in chapter 6 we present the more modern Open Shortest Path First (OSPF) protocol, an example of the "link state" technology. chapter 7 completes this second part by discussing the other routing protocols in use in the Internet.

The interconnection between organizations' networks and providers requires another set of protocols, more concerned with the "management of connectivity" than with the dynamics of routing. Part 3 includes four chapters presenting the first "Exterior Gateway Protocol" (EGP), then the modern "Border Gateway Protocol" (BGP). chapter 10 is devoted to the recent development of "Inter-Domain Routing," while chapter 11 presents the general requirements of "policy-based routing."

The fourth part of the book is devoted to the recent advances in routing technology, with three chapters detailing the support of multicast transmission, mobile hosts, and real-time applications. This is a natural introduction to the last part of the book, which presents the transition to the new Internet Protocol. This transition will be necessary if we want to connect thousands of billions of hosts to the twenty-first century's Internet!

1.4 Acknowledgments

I would like to thank here the reviewers who helped me prepare the second edition of this book: Tony McAuley, Gary Mankin, Martha Streenstrup, and Jessica Yu. I would also like to thank Christophe Diot and Brian Levine for their revision of the multicast chapter, and Lixia Zhang for her review and revision of the real-time chapter. Finally, I would like to thank my wife, Neige Gil, and my son, Pedro Huitema, for bearing with me when I prepared this book in 1994, and again when I revised it in 1999.

Part I
Architecture and Protocols

The Internet Architecture

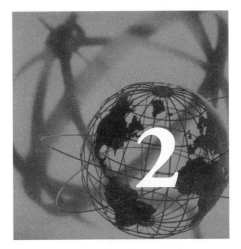

Many have often asked for a description of "the Internet architecture." As a former member of the Internet Architecture Board (IAB), I should be in a good position to describe this famed architecture, except for one small detail: the said architecture was not really written down. We had in fact to wait until 1996 to see a collection of architecture principles summarized in RFC-1958 [10].

2.1 Is There an Internet Architecture?

Prominent members of the community, including past chairs of the IAB, have often expressed largely dissenting opinions on what the architecture really is. "Architecture" implies that a network is built like a house: one should first draw the main lines and then detail the functional blocks and their relations. Careful planning guarantees that each building block has a well-defined role and well-defined interfaces, and that the details can then be worked out by independent teams. The Open Systems Interconnection (OSI) seven-layer model was an extremely formalized example of this approach.

Grand plans like this work better when a new design is started from scratch. Many object that a system as large as the Internet is more like a city than a house. Cities are very seldom erected from the ground up on an empty piece of land. More often, cities have grown through history, by a succession of adjunctions. Romulus and Remus probably had a bright idea of what a city should be when they founded Roma, but by the time of Julius Caesar that initial design was long lost. The followers of that approach believe that architectural principles are useful guidelines, but that the role of the architect is to study all the existing pieces and to make sure that the adjunctions will fit. In the networking world, this approach is characterized by the belief that "the architecture is in the protocols."

Both approaches can in fact be applied to the Internet. Important pieces of the design have been constantly reworked over time. One could hardly expect the system to double its size every year without needing constant improvements. But there are some very basic principles that have consistently guided this evolution and that are best captured by a small number of key phrases such as "the end-to-end principle," "IP over everything," or "connectivity is its own reward."

2.2 The End-to-End Argument

The end-to-end argument for the design of distributed systems was presented in a famous paper by J. H. Saltzer, D. P. Reed, and D. D. Clark [1]. David D. Clark, a senior scientist of the MIT Laboratory for Computer Science, was the "Internet Architect" and chaired the IAB from 1981 to 1990. He certainly used this principle a lot when he was in charge of the architecture of the Internet protocols [2]. Put simply, the argument is that the final decisions should always be made by the users themselves, that trying to supplement them by intelligence inside the network is redundant, and that the networking functions should thus be delegated as much as possible outside the network. This argument has implications in transmission control, in the management of interconnections, and in the design of applications.

2.2.1 Datagrams and Virtual Circuits

Who remembers now the heated debates of the 1970s between the partisans of "virtual circuits" and those of "datagrams"? The first packet switching networks (Arpanet, Cyclades) used a "letter" metaphor analogous to the "post office" service. When computers wanted to exchange data, they placed the data into packets inside an envelope (a packet header) that carried the destination address and "posted" the packet that the network would eventually deliver. The word "datagram" was coined by analogy to "telegram," probably to imply some faster service than "same-day delivery."

The first networks, however, proved somewhat untamed. Posting data whenever they are ready may be a very simple interface, but the independent decisions of dozens of computers would very easily generate the network equivalent of a traffic jam. The resulting congestions scared the public operators who were willing to provide a data service but wanted to retain control over their operations and ensure a smooth utilization of the resources. They rejected the datagram service and standardized on the virtual circuit model, following the X.25 protocol. In this model, the exchange of packets between the client's terminal and the first data switch is protected by the LAP-B procedure: each packet has to be acknowledged and repeated if the acknowledgment does not arrive before a "time-out" period. The computer that wishes to communicate must first send a call packet, which will be forwarded to the called party. During this initial forwarding, a virtual circuit will be set up and resources will be reserved for the circuit in the network. After the connection is set, data packets are simply pushed on this virtual circuit with minimal overhead—only the initial packets carry the called and calling addresses. The sending of packets is paced by a "credit mechanism," i.e., by the regular receptions of "rights to send" emitted by the network. In conditions of network overload, the operators can exert back pressure on the circuits that pass through a congested area and thus match the accepted traffic with the available capacities.

The scheme embodied in X.25 is often described as "hop-by-hop" control. IP follows a very different architecture: each packet is independent, there is no concept of circuit, and all the control is "end to end." There is no route set up; all IP datagrams carry a source and destination address; all are routed independently. There is no acknowledgment between the client's terminal and the network switch, nor any guarantee that the network will not lose packets: the packets must be acknowledged "end to end" by the remote Transport Control Protocol (TCP) process. If the TCP acknowledgment does not come back, the sending station will repeat the packet, which will travel all the way through the network again.

2.2.2 Should We Trust Networks?

The proponents of sophisticated virtual circuits like X.25 generally observe that X.25 and TCP have equivalent complexity. Both perform the same function, that of ensuring that packets get delivered correctly to the end user. The sole difference is in the implementation of the function—in the user's terminal for TCP, in the network for X.25. Basically, they present this as a mere design choice: the "transport" system should be seen as a "black box" by the user. Whether components are implemented in the network or in the station itself does not matter much. It is only a question of performance and engineering trade-offs. On the surface, this may seem a reasonable claim. When a datagram network drops a packet, it must be retransmitted from the initial sender to the final destination, while on a virtual circuit network it will only be retransmitted between two neighboring switches. Moreover, in cases of congestion, the virtual circuit network will simply pace down the senders, while the datagram network will have to rely on the "correct behavior" of its customers. So why should we really bother? Why not trade end-to-end retransmission for hop-by-hop procedures?

Well, the Internet architects believe it matters a lot, for in one case one has to trust the network while in the other case one merely has to trust oneself. My preferred example pictures a father and his son, walking in an orchard. The father spots a very red and very ripe apple on a fairly high branch. "Son," he says, "I would very much like to get this apple but I am not that slim anymore. Could you climb that tree and get it for me?" "But father," answers the son, "that branch is very high and looks a bit thin. I may break my neck." "Son, don't you trust your father? I tell you, you can do it, so just go and do it!" The boy climbs the tree, climbs over the branch, and almost reaches the apple, but the branch breaks. He falls and breaks his leg. He looks painfully at his father and reproaches him for his advice. The father says, "Son, this is a lesson for life. You should never trust anybody, not even your father!"

Obviously, if you are not going to trust your father, you should not trust a network either! The examples abound of those who, by doing so, broke their file systems, if not their legs. If one delegates the error discovery to a network, one is left without defense if the network somehow misbehaves, for example, because of a faulty memory board in a switch. Even one undetected error every so many million bits means an entirely polluted database after a few hundred transfers. Moreover, one may argue that even the best network cannot be trusted entirely: a link may break or a node may be powered out. Even if the network is making its best efforts to correct almost all errors, the responsible user will always perform end-to-end controls, using acknowledgments to check that the data arrived and checksums to verify their integrity. The "equivalent complexity" argument is thus fallacious. If the users always perform their own controls, the functions implemented by the network itself are redundant.

The only advantage of "local" error controls, between neighboring hosts, is that transmission errors will be corrected faster—we will not have to wait for the data to pass through the entire network. But there are very few transmission errors on modern networks. Well-tuned microwave channels generally exhibit less than one error per 10 million bits transmitted (10 to the –7 power), while the bit error rate of optical channels is often less than one in a billion (10 to the –9 power). Since the risk of losing a packet, due to a transmission error, is very low, a small difference in retransmission efficiency does not significantly impact the network's performance. One will always need end-to-end acknowledgments to be sure that the data have arrived at the final destination and have been processed. As these are always needed, it follows that sending hop-by-hop acknowledgments merely adds overhead and uses more transmission resources than the occasional end-to-end retransmission; in fact, implementing undue hop-by-hop procedures increases the cost of the intermediate nodes without really increasing the user services.

The Internet also includes some very noisy links, such as old telephone circuits or radio channels. Nothing prevents the managers of low-quality links from implementing a local error control procedure. These procedures will not guarantee that all errors are corrected; they will have to maintain the frequency of errors only within reasonable limits. A good design rule is that no link should exhibit a packet loss rate higher than 1%. If it does, then one should check the transmission equipment or install an error correction procedure.

We can also use end-to-end procedures to solve another problem—congestion control. Network congestion can be cured only by slowing down the senders. X.25 can achieve it by requesting a constant exchange of credits on each virtual circuit, but end-to-end solutions are also workable. On every TCP connection, "flow-control" credits are piggybacked in the end-to-end acknowledgment. If the network becomes congested, the flow of acknowledgment will be slowed down and so will the flow of credits. The senders will have to reduce their rate of transmission. We will analyze these flow-control procedures in detail in the "resource management" chapter; they have been well implemented in the Internet, thanks mostly to Van Jacobson, a famous network researcher of the Lawrence Berkeley Laboratories. As the TCP flow-control procedure is "piggybacked" in the end-to-end acknowledgments, which have to be transmitted in any case, one can argue that the flow of X.25 credits is merely an additional overhead. As congestion is caused by a lack of transmission capacity, consuming network resources without any good reason doesn't help much.

2.2.3 States and Fate-Sharing

There is another strong difference of philosophy between the end-to-end and the hop-by-hop approaches—the Internet architects describe this in terms of "network states." When an X.25 virtual circuit is set up, the state of the transit switches changes. From that moment, they must remember that a circuit exists, that some resources have been attached to it, and that it is associated with a path in the network. The state also changes when a packet is received and acknowledged upon a LAB-B connection. The switches must take care of the packet and guarantee that it will be properly relayed toward its destination. A side effect is known as "fate-sharing": if the end-to-end connection relies on state being kept in some other system, then it will share that other system's fate. If one of these systems fails and loses its memory, the connection will be broken.

This "stateful" approach contrasts with the "stateless" approach of IP. Since there is no circuit setup, the only task of the switches is to maintain up-to-date "routing tables." There is no guarantee that two packets sent to the same destination, on the same TCP connection, will follow the same path. At any time, users expect the network to compute the "best route" for any given destination. The first packet was sent on a route that was the best at that time; the next packet will follow another route, which will also be the best, but which will be different. Similarly, there is no guarantee that all packets will make their way to the destination. For example, packets may well be dropped if a link breaks, if a switch fails, or if an area becomes congested. This is not important, as they will be retransmitted by the TCP processes. The connection does not share the intermediate systems' fate.

Fighting over more or less efficiency in error control or congestion control is really a matter of details if one considers the gruesome effects of "state in the network" over interconnections. Linkage of X.25 networks is achieved through the X.75 protocol, a symmetric version of X.25 adapted for network-to-network transmissions. A virtual circuit that crosses several networks comes over several X.75 connections. At the end of each of these connections, a switch must associate a number of state variables with the circuit: where to relay the packets, how many credits to pass back, how many transit packets to relay. If one of these switches fails, the variables are lost and the circuit is broken. The client who relied on the virtual circuit will be strongly disappointed because, when the circuit breaks, the application terminates, the file transfer aborts, and the remote session ends. As a consequence, the smart clients use an end-to-end control program, much like TCP, in order to recover from these losses. They will have to reinstall a new circuit, retransmit the data, and resume the application. But then, they could as well have lived with a plain datagram network...

The interconnection of datagram networks, on the other hand, is much simpler and much more robust. There is no memory of connections, no trace of flow-control states. One simply has to know that this class of address can be reached by relaying packets over that connection. Should a particular node fail, its neighbors will simply recalculate their routing tables and pass the next packets through another path. In many cases, the application will not even notice the failure; at the worst, a few packets will be lost and will very naturally be retransmitted by the TCP program. One could indeed object that this simplicity and this robustness are obtained by trading less "state" complexity for more routing and processing requirements, as the switches have to perform address processing on a packet-per-packet basis, but even that is a false argument. If a connection exists, then there is a high chance that successive packets will all refer to the same address; if there are several connections, then they will refer to a reasonably small set of "active addresses." By caching the result of the route computation for these addresses, one can shortcut the processing requirements. In fact, IP switches are capable of sustaining very high speeds: hundreds of thousands of packets per second is not uncommon.

2.2.4 A Far-Reaching Argument

The end-to-end argument was first used in relation to security procedures. It was then applied to demonstrate the superiority of the stateless datagram approach over the stateful virtual circuit architecture. The main consequence for networking is that interconnections are much easier if only a "minimal set" of service is expected from the relays and if the "value-added" functions such as error correction or flow control are performed "end to end." But the argument goes far beyond the mere problem of relaying packets and is in fact at the heart of the Internet philosophy.

One can, for example, apply it to all "distributed system" procedures. Whatever the quality of the transmission, the information that data was duly processed and stored can come only from the end system itself, not from any sort of intermediate relay. One can also use it to demonstrate that intermediate translations of electronic mail (E-mail) messages are generally a bad idea because they will remove information that the end system will never be able to reconstruct. One can also apply it to the verification of records propagated in network databases: the checksums that protect these records should be computed by the originating application and checked by the recipients, certainly not recomputed by some intermediate storage or relay program.

2.3 IP over Everything

The end-to-end principle is attributed to Dave Clark and his colleagues at MIT. It describes the sharing of responsibilities between the network and its clients—one does the routing, the others do the control. The second paradigm of the Internet architecture is that the "Internetwork" is built by layering a unique "Internetworking protocol" on top of various network technologies in order to interconnect the various networks. This paradigm is due to Vint Cerf. Vint was the first president of the Internet Society; he has been associated with the development of the Internet since the very beginning, first as a researcher, then as the manager of the Internet program for DARPA or within the Corporation for Network Research Initiative [2]. He was in fact the co-inventor, with Bob Kahn, of the TCP-IP protocols. Vint is probably the only person who can wear a three-piece suit to a meeting of the Internet Engineering Task Force (IETF) without being frowned upon—and, in fact, the first time I saw him wearing a tee shirt instead of his famous grey suit, the phrase "IP over everything" was printed on it.

2.3.1 Interconnection of Networks

Historically, there have been two ways of interconnecting networks: translation and overlays. In the translation approach, each network has its own set of services, applications, and addressing format. To interconnect two networks, one must find a set of almost identical services and try to map them through a gateway. Such gateways are often designed for the mail application: one can find translators between the Internet mail and the X.400 "message handling system," or between these two and any number of mail packages sold by various companies.

The translation approach has some advantages. It is generally chosen when one cannot or doesn't wish to change the software used on the interconnected networks. It also has a number of disadvantages. Translations are never completely symmetric. Everybody knows a stock of old jokes about the first attempts at automatic translations of human speech, taking one colloquial English sentence, translating it into French, then back into English. "The spirit is strong but the flesh is weak" becomes "the alcohol is good but the meat is dull." Translating network protocols is prone to the same kind of surprises.

The approach chosen by the Internet is different. IP is layered on top of connecting networks such as Ethernet, token rings, and telephones. Each of these networks provides its own set of services, but IP uses only a very basic facility: being able to send packets from one point to a neighbor. That neighbor will "decapsulate" the IP packet from its local network envelope, examine the IP destination address, and, if needed, relay over another network.

2.3.2 IP and New Technologies

The overlay nature of IP, combined with the simplicity of design resulting from the end-to-end principle, makes it very simple to adopt new technologies in the Internet: one must merely define how to transfer packets and how to use the new network's switching capabilities.

Suppose that some brilliant researcher develops an optical switching network: one based on wavelength multiplexing, for example. The basic service here is probably the transmission of a sequence of bits over a light wave. We will have to define an "encapsulation" or "framing" protocol, explaining how IP packets should be inserted in the light wave and how their beginning and end should be signalled, perhaps devising a network-specific packet header to distinguish IP packets from other services available on the optical fabric. One will also have to translate the IP address into a "network address"—probably the wavelength of the receiver in our case. This translation is called "address resolution": deriving the local network address from the Internet address.

This approach has been successfully applied today to many technologies: IEEE-802 networks, point-to-point links, X.25 virtual circuits, and ATM channels.

2.3.3 Unique Addresses

One of the advantages of the "overlay" approach is that one can organize it solely for interconnection. The most salient need here is worldwide addressing—one must guarantee that each point in the Internet has a unique Internet address. Maintaining unique addresses has far-reaching consequences, the most important being to make addressing somewhat independent of the network topology. When new links are created or suppressed, the addresses of the stations accessed remain unchanged: the network adapts by modifying the routing. The very purpose of this book is to explain how this is done!

Another very interesting consequence of the unique addressing scheme is that the source of a packet can be identified independent of the network interface through which the packet is received. This is used by the transport control and application programs to associate packets to contexts. It can also be used by the security functions. It is easier to verify the origin of a packet when the source address is known.

2.3.4 What about Other Protocols?

From 1988 to 1992, the IAB maintained the view that the Internet protocol was only one of the many networking protocols used in the Internet, albeit the dominant one [3]. The Internet was then described as a "multiprotocol" network and many efforts were made to accommodate other protocols in parallel to IP, notably the Connection-Less Network Protocol (CLNP) defined by the International Organization for Standards (ISO).

The emphasis on multiprotocol has decreased in recent years, largely as a result of a cost-benefit analysis [4]. Running several protocols in parallel has a high cost: essentially, one multiplies the management efforts by the number of protocols that must be supported. Engineers must learn the different protocols, routing tables have to be maintained in parallel, and routers have to be programmed with many independent sets of software. That cost may well be justified in "corporate backbones" when there is a need to support applications that run only on one specific type of network (for example, mainframe applications that require IBM's SNA, personal computing applications that run best over Novell's IPX or Apple's Appletalk, and in fact many other vendor-specific protocols). Corporate backbones may be large, but they have a limited size and they usually fall under a single management. It will generally be a corporate decision to arbitrate between the high cost of managing several protocols and the benefits of enabling specific applications.

The cost of deploying a protocol suite parallel to IP on the whole Internet is even higher than on a corporate network as one must manage the interconnection of a large number of different networks. In practice, this is not done. The attempts to deploy CLNP have resulted in very little use—less than 0.01% of the network's usage according to NSFnet statistics. This is easily understandable since a simple alternative exists, that of running the foreign applications over IP, either by encapsulating the foreign network packets in IP packets or by porting the applications over the Internet's transport service, TCP. By and large, the Internet today is a single-protocol network and that protocol is IP; some day the only protocol that will be deployed in parallel to IP will be ... a new version of IP!

2.4 Connectivity Is Its Own Reward

The catch phrase that best describes the engine of the current Internet growth is due to Anthony Rutkowski, who was then the executive director of the Internet Society. He was amazed by the rapid increase in connectivity and usage and tried to find a rational explanation, which he summarized in a single phrase: connectivity is its own reward.

The Internet is almost doubling in size every year. There were about 1,250,000 machines connected in January 1993 and 2,500,000 in January 1994 and the trend continues. There were about 2,300 connected networks by January 1991; 4,500 by January 1992; 9,000 by January

1993; and 20,000 by January 1994. At the end of 1993, the Internet reached 62 countries; indirect access through electronic mail could be obtained in 75 others.

2.4.1 E-mail and the Internet

If so many people connect, there must be a reason. Indeed, the TCP-IP suite is loaded with interesting applications. It is a good support for the client-server applications on local networks. A rich set of routing and management protocols makes it easy to organize the corporate backbones. But then many vendors can provide local network software and local network interconnections using their own technologies. One has to go beyond the local networks' applications to find the magic.

What does it mean to be connected on the Internet? For most users, it means one extra line on their business card, listing an electronic mail address in addition to their phone and fax numbers. This is in fact the way to recognize an "internaut"—the word coined by Vint Cerf to designate an Internet user. Stating that my address is "huitema@inria.fr" means that whoever has "E-mail connectivity" can reach me by using that address. E-mail is a very powerful application. It allows you to compose a message on a computer screen and send it to your friends all over the world. If they are ready, they will receive it in a few seconds. If they are busy, the message will wait in their mailbox to be retrieved later. Actually, a fax has many of the same characteristics—which by the way explains much of its success. But E-mail has a couple of definitive advantages over fax. E-mail is personal: it arrives in *your* mailbox, on *your* computer screen. There is no such a thing as an E-mail basket through which various users have to browse to pick up their own fax. E-mail is digital: not only does it make the transmission process faster and more efficient than a fax, it also enables you to reuse the message. You can "cut and paste" the incoming text into another message, into a jointly edited report, or into a management application.

Looking at E-mail provides a clear explanation for the Internet's snowballing growth. There have been many electronic mail systems developed in several countries, and the Internet E-mail has long been only one of them. But E-mail users quickly realize that although some E-mail systems have a friendlier user interface or a richer and more complex set of functionalities, the only quality that really matters is connectivity. The more users I can send E-mail to, the more valuable my E-mail system is. In the last several years, the Internet has expanded beyond its initial realm of scholars and academics. The most popular estimation is that about 20 million users have access to the Internet E-mail service. This means that there is a great attraction for Jane Random to connect. She will immediately get the feeling of joining cyberspace. But then, the moment she joins, the reasons for Joe Follower to get a mailbox increase from 20 million to 20 million and one: mathematicians will recognize that the derivative of the size is proportional to the size itself. This is the exact recipe of exponential growth.

2.4.2 Connectivity Is More than E-mail

The following story was quite popular in France when I was in high school. It describes a legionnaire in the desert. He has lost his company and is trying to walk his way back to the barracks. But this is far away. His ordnance water bottle is now empty. He keeps walking but he is becoming very thirsty. He has already fallen several times in the desert's sand and his immediate future looks bleak. Suddenly, a dot in the sky grows larger and larger. It is a helicopter, painted red and white, which hovers over his head. The Coca-Cola logo is now clearly visible on the tail of the craft. It lands and a TV crew comes out to our legionnaire and starts to film him. The reporter moves to the guy and asks him: "What is your favorite drink?"

E-mail is just like that. When I had no direct Internet connectivity back in 1985, I was quite happy to have access to an E-mail relay allowing me at least to exchange documents in electronic form with others. But I am just as likely now to settle for E-mail only, even at a cheaper price, as our legionnaire would be to order a soft drink in the company's bar. Applications like file transfer, document retrieval, database browsing, and remote connections are all dependent on IP connectedness.

In fact, the snowballing paradigm applies just as much to these "connected" applications as to E-mail. According to the autumn 1993 issue of the *Internet Society's News*, the fastest growing applications on the Internet were the "browsing" tools called "Gopher" and "World Wide Web" with respective annual growth rates of 997% and 341%. These applications, which were created in 1991, accounted for nearly 4% of the Internet traffic by the end of 1993. We know now what happened to the web. Just like E-mail, this is an effect of connectivity. Information providers notice that there is a large number of customers and decide to set up new information servers. Once these servers are set, the network becomes more attractive for customers, who can now find more and more useful information. This means that more potential customers will join, attracting more providers, and on and on.

2.4.3 Cooperation between Network Providers

In the very old days, when the Internet was reserved for scientists and scholars, the networks were funded as "public goods," much like libraries or accelerators of nuclear particles. Each region, each nation, each university would contribute its own network, adding its own piece to the web of nets that gradually covered the planet. At that time, the idea of paying for your traffic was odd: the network was essentially free—it was paid by some "sugar daddy." There was no hindrance to connectedness. Since everything was free, why worry about accounting and compensations?

These days have gone. The free funding model is even disappearing from university networks. Community councils and regional ministries tend to look closely at such budget items. And the free funding model certainly cannot be applied when the network is used by private companies to conduct their business. Providing network connections is now an industry—a fast growing one, still in its infancy. New companies are founded every month, either as developments of classic telecommunication operators or as start-up enterprises by Internet visionaries. We have seen that before, in the early stages of railroads or just after the deregulation of airlines. Someday the market will probably mature. In between, all these new Internet providers benefit from the global connectivity.

Connectedness is clearly beneficial to all Internet subscribers. What's amazing is that connectedness is also beneficial to network providers, in other words, to the companies that provide these customers with network access. These providers are often competing for the same customers;

one could expect them not to be overly cooperative. But the value of each network increases with its connectedness, with the set of services that its customers can expect. A network provider that would decide to isolate itself from the Internet, or even from some part of it, would merely be shooting itself in the foot. The providers compete, but at the same time they must cooperate if they want to develop their common product, the Internet. They must interconnect.

This does not mean that interconnecting providers go without some negotiations. When a client of network A sends a packet to network B, it uses transmission resources of A and B but only pays the provider, A. In the simplest form of arrangement, usage of B by clients of A is compensated by the symmetric usage of A by clients of B. But the situation is not always symmetric. Network A may well rely on the resources of a third network, say C, to reach B. A will have to pay a compensation for this connectivity. Computing these compensations is nothing new in the telecommunication industry: telephone operators, or even the post offices, have been performing this kind of accounting for decades. This merely means that when a network's provider proposes a tariff, the fees must include not only its own operational costs but also the costs of the interconnections.

2.4.4 Be Liberal

In order to benefit fully from the Internet, users must acquire hardware and software products that implement the various Internet applications. There are many machines on the Internet, many "platforms." The days of academic users all using UNIX systems have passed. For all of these platforms, there are many sources of software, which are in principle developed in conformance with the Internet standards. There is a risk that some of these programs will not be entirely compatible, perhaps because one was written in conformity with an older specification, or because it did not implement a particular option.

The Internet approach is pragmatic. The goal is that the largest possible number of users be connected and able to communicate. The emphasis on connectedness leads to an interesting philosophy of protocol implementation, which was formalized by Jon Postel. Jon is one of the most famous figures of the Internet. He was the author of the Internet protocol's specifications and is now the editor of the RFC series, the archives of the net's wisdom. He is also the authority for number assignments that deliver, for example, protocol identifiers for new applications, and he is a long-term member of IAB. The philosophy is simple: "Be liberal with what you receive, conservative with what you send." When one writes a network program, one must expect that the program will receive all kinds of data packets. Sometimes, the syntax of these packets will be quite loose. "Be liberal" means that one must always try to understand what the partner meant, so that one could at least offer some kind of "default service." But loose syntax should not be encouraged. "Be conservative" means that one should do one's best and send only messages that strictly conform to the standards.

You might say, "So what?" Well, there were competing attempts to build "open system interconnections" (the OSI model) that relied on the precision of the documentation and the rigor of the testing. Their proponents thought that, if every protocol was specified down to the last bit and thoroughly tested, then the interconnection problems would disappear. There is no evidence that they succeeded. In fact, the "legalese" approach to interworking tends to produce quite the contrary. Implementors try to outperform others by conforming even more closely to the standard, so that they can reject competitors' messages and pinpoint their mistakes. In the Internet, on the contrary, such behaviors are frowned upon. The seasoned internaut will tell you that they are bad for your karma.

Bad karma? Such parlance is indeed a tribute to California and the Silicon Valley, a leftover of the early egalitarian and academic roots of the Internet, of the many researchers who developed the technology just after the 1960s. But the spirit remained. A large system like the Internet is always vulnerable. A user who behaves badly can do harm in many ways—for example, by sending abusive messages to popular E-mail distribution lists. But experience shows that these people will not do it twice because they are very likely to receive thousands of responses from angry internauts trying to educate them. Generally speaking, abusive behaviors are bad karma. And the aphorism on protocol development should also apply to the way everyone uses the net.

2.5 Developing the Internet Architecture

It is quite common in Europe to refer to the Internet Protocol by the name "DoD IP." This terminology is not entirely innocent: in a subtle way it infers that the Internet is not based on "international standards" and that its success should really be traced to massive subsidization by the U.S. Department of Defense (DoD). The same people who use the "DoD IP" terminology often classify the Internet protocols as "de facto" standards, in contrast to "truly international standards," "de jure," such as those produced by the ISO or by the International Telecommunications Union (ITU).

Reality is much more complex. The source of the Internet technology can certainly be traced back to the early packet-switching experiments funded by the DARPA, the agency of DoD in charge of advanced research projects. This research started in the late 1960s, and was conducted throughout the 1970s. The influence of the DARPA was prevalent during the early development of the technology. The IP standard itself, as published in 1978, 1979, and 1981, first through Internet Experiment Notes (IEN) [5, 6], and then as Request For Comment (RFC) [7], is mentioned as "specifying the DoD Standard Internet Protocol." However, it is fair to note that parallel research was conducted in several other countries. The Arpanet very soon developed international extensions through satellite links over the Atlantic; networks such as Cyclades in France also played a role in the development of the technology. In any case, the situation has changed radically since 1981.

DoD does not have much influence today on the evolution of the technology and certainly does not "own" it. This influence gradually disappeared as the "center of gravity" of the network shifted from computer science research to general academic usage in the 1980s, and then toward more and more commercial usage in the 1990s. The Internet has now grown so large that no single group can really pretend to dominate it. The technology is developed by a volunteer's organization, the IETF, and the standards are published by a nonprofit organization, the Internet Society.

2.5.1 From DARPA to the Internet Society

The Internet has its roots in the Arpanet, which was funded by DARPA in the 1970s. Throughout the 1980s, the development of Internet technology was the responsibility of the Internet Activities Board (later to become the Internet Architecture Board, or IAB) and its predecessors [3]. At the very beginning, the IAB was a consultative committee attached to the DARPA. As the Internet grew, the 12 IAB members sponsored the organization of a number of research groups in charge respectively of Internet engineering, end-to-end protocols, security, and privacy. In due military tradition, these groups were named "task forces." They were typically composed of interested researchers investigating specific projects that were needed to build up the Internet.

As more and more protocols had to be defined, the engineering task force grew and had to be organized into a set of independent working groups, each in charge of one particular topic. Very rapidly, the IAB discovered that it could not handle the day-to-day management of such a large organization, and it created the Internet Engineering Steering Group (IESG). The IESG is composed of area directors, each in charge of a set of working groups under the leadership of the IETF chair. The working groups prepare new Internet standards, which the IESG submits to the IAB for approval when they are ready.

This organization performed reasonably well for some years, but several stresses started to appear. First, the IAB was completely overloaded by the stream of standards that was coming out of the working groups (the IAB members are volunteers and perform this service in addition to their normal jobs). Approving standards requires that IAB members read and analyze them; with the various versions and stages of progress, IAB had to analyze a dozen specifications every month. This translated into backlogs and tension between the IAB and the working groups. Secondly, as the linkage with the DARPA and DoD had almost entirely disappeared, the IAB members realized that they were essentially publishing standards under their own personal authority. Suppose that a company discovers that its interests have been harmed by the way one particular standard was set—for example, because it gives an unfair advantage to the company's competitors. This company may decide to sue, and the prime target for litigation would be the IAB. Because the IAB is merely a set of individuals, these individuals could be held personally responsible and their personal properties could be seized. I was not too pleased when I learned it.

The Internet Society was founded in 1992. It is a not-for-profit organization, dedicated to developing the Internet and its technology. Its members are companies and users concerned with this development. Every year they elect a board of trustees, the government of the society. From the beginning, the idea was to attach the IAB and the Internet standards process to the Internet Society. But that move was precipitated by the events of 1992. The IAB members met in Kobe, Japan, during the first conference organized by the society. They were very concerned by the rapid pace at which Internet addresses were allocated to new users, as well as with the risk that the Internet would soon run out of addresses. It was necessary in their opinion to speed up the development of a new version of IP. At that time, the most credible alternative was the Connection-Less Network Protocol (CLNP), a copycat of IP that had been standardized by the ISO and that featured much larger addresses. The IAB was convinced that the CLNP addressing format should be the starting point of the new development. Shortly after the meeting, the IAB chair issued an announcement to that effect, which infuriated most of the IETF members for two reasons. It was thought to be technically incorrect by several prominent scientists, who observed that the ISO protocol was riddled with technical deficiencies and could never accommodate the new services that were emerging on the Internet. And the very idea of the IAB making a decision behind closed doors was perceived to be entirely undemocratic by some very active members of the IETF. It was time, they said, for a "new world order."

2.5.2 The IETF

The forum where the Internet standards are defined is the IETF [8]. The IETF is a volunteer organization. The only permanent staff is a small-size secretariat, subsidized by the U.S. federal government. The IETF is composed of working groups, grouped into areas; each area is supervised by one or two area directors. The area directors and the IETF chair form the IESG. There are currently eight areas: applications, user services, management, security, transport, routing, Internet, and operations. In the organization adopted in 1992, the IAB concentrates on long-term studies; it was renamed Internet Architecture Board to emphasize this new focus. Internet standards are approved directly by the IESG, without having to be submitted to the IAB; that board would only have to intervene in case of dispute, as a court of appeal.

Working groups are normally relatively short lived, typically from six months to two years. A working group is created to study and solve one particular problem; it ceases to exist when the corresponding standard has been adopted. A working group can be created only if there are a sufficient number of potential contributors interested in solving a problem; there must be a "constituency." A good way to test the existence of this constituency is to organize a "birds-of-a-feather" session during an IETF meeting. If there are enough participants and if they agree on the need to push the issue, the working group will be created. The next step is to write a working group charter, specifying the expected results and the calendar of the future working group. That charter is then reviewed. The IAB checks that the objectives and proposed solutions fit within the general architecture; the IESG assigns the working group to an area and nominates a working group chair. Occasionally, a working group proposal is turned down, generally because its technical objectives don't mix well with the general work of the Internet.

As should be expected from a networking body, most of the IETF discussions are conducted by E-mail through distribution lists. A major requirement is openness—all distribution lists are open to whoever wants to join, and all documents are placed in publicly accessible archives. The electronic discussions are complemented by face-to-face meetings. The IETF meets three times per year: in spring, summer, and fall. The same openness requirement applies here— whoever wants to register can participate in the meeting. Indeed, as an IETF meeting consists of a set of working group meetings, it does not make much sense to participate in the IETF if one is not actively participating in at least one working group. Participants are expected to have followed the E-mail discussions and to have read the electronically published documentation.

In the old organization, the members of the IAB were co-opted by their peers, and those of the IESG were nominated by the IETF chair. The new procedure is more democratic, although it stops short of going through formal elections. Each year a nominating committee is picked at random from volunteers within the IETF membership, and half of the IAB and IESG seats are open for nomination [9]. The committee is free to renominate old members or to pick new candidates. The nominations to IESG positions have then to be approved by the IAB, and the nominations to the IAB by the board of trustees of the Internet Society. This guarantees a chain of responsibilities. In theory, the responsibility of the standards process belongs to the Internet Society, which delegates it to the IESG through the IAB.

2.5.3   Rough Consensus and Running Code

The IETF is not the only organization that produces networking standards, but it has a distinctive flavor. As Dave Clark explained it during the 1992 discussions, "We reject kings, presidents, and voting; we believe in rough consensus and running code."

The part on kings and presidents relates to possible decision processes that were rejected by the IETF: neither an externally designated "king" nor an elected president could be accepted, because that would induce arbitrary or authoritarian decisions. A volunteer organization like the IETF just cannot cope with this form of authority. A decision that has not been agreed to by the working base will simply be rejected.

The IETF working groups generally don't vote. The goal of the process is to obtain a consensus of all participants; if your technical contribution cannot withstand technical criticism by your peers, it will simply be rejected. Voting occurs occasionally when there is a choice between two equally valid proposals, such as on the position of fields within a packet, but this is more a rational way to flip a coin than anything else. In fact, voting supposes counting voting rights, which supposes some formal membership—for example, one vote per country or one vote per member organization. This is almost contradictory with the open membership nature of the working groups which any interested individual can join. By avoiding votes, the IETF also avoids the "horse trading" that occurs in the last days preceding a vote in other organizations ("I will vote for your checksum algorithm if you vote for my address format"). Voting leads to compromises and overblown specifications that include every member's desires. This kind of compromise would not fly in the IETF. One has to get consensus through the excellence of the technical work. The search for consensus leads to technical elegance.

Consensus does not mean unanimity. There will always be some unconvinced minority. This is why the consensus is expected to be "rough." In fact, it can be so rough that two irreconcilable camps opt for two very different solutions. Trying to merge them would yield what is often derided as "a camel—a horse designed by a committee," where the bumps on the back reflect the diverse options. There are two famous examples of this situation, one in the management area (CMOT, derived from ISO's CMIP, versus SNMP) and one in the routing area (OSPF versus the adaptation of ISO's IS-IS). In both cases the problem was solved by letting two independent working groups pursue the two different options, producing two incompatible but self-consistent standards, and letting the market choose.

This is why the last part of the equation, running code, is important. An IETF specification can only progress from proposed standard to draft and then full standard if it is adopted by the market (if it is implemented and sold within networking products). A perfect specification that could not be implemented would just be forgotten; the document would be reclassified as "historical."

2.6 The Future of the Internet

The Internet is growing and changing; the commercial component is growing much faster than the initial academic core. But the roots that developed during the first years are strong and guarantee the harmonious growth of the network. The end-to-end principle, the emphasis on connectedness and on a unique "Internet" protocol, and the consensus-oriented standardization process are the key parts of the architecture.

The Internet protocol will probably change in the coming years to accommodate the exponential growth of international connectivity. The routing protocols that will be presented in this book are the result of the accumulated experience—OSPF was developed after RIP, BGP after EGP. This experience will, no doubt, be the basis for future evolution. But we have spent enough time dealing with generalities and should now start studying the protocols themselves!

References

1. J. H., Saltzer, D. P. Reed, and D. Clark, "End-to-End Arguments in System Design," *ACM Transactions on Computer Systems*, Vol. 2, No. 4, pp. 277–288.
2. G. Malkin, "Who's Who in the Internet Biographies of IAB, IESG and IRSG Members," RFC-1336, May 27, 1992.
3. V. Cerf, "The Internet Activities Board," RFC-1160, May 25, 1990.
4. B. Leiner and Y. Rekhter, "The MultiProtocol Internet," RFC-1560, December 23, 1993.
5. J. Postel, "Internetwork Protocol Specification—Version 4," IEN-41, June 1978.
6. J. Postel, "DOD Standard Internet Protocol," IEN-41, December 1979.
7. J. Postel, "Internet Protocol," RFC-791, September 1, 1981.
8. I. Architecture Board, I. Engineering Steer, C. Huitema, and P. Gross, "The Internet Standards Process—Revision 2," RFC-1602, March 24, 1994.
9. C. Huitema, I. Architecture Board, "Charter of the Internet Architecture Board (IAB)," RFC-1601, March 22, 1994.
10. B. Carpenter, "Architectural Principles of the Internet," RFC-1958, June 1996.

The Internet
Protocol

There would be no Internet without the Internet Protocol, which we will present in this chapter.

3.1 Model of Operation

IP runs over everything, as we explained in the previous chapter. The model of operation is very simple: networks are linked together by Internetwork programs. Each host on the Internet (each computer that wishes to run an Internet application) is expected to support an instance of this program. The applications generally access the Internetwork program through a transport program, TCP or the User Datagram Protocol (UDP), as illustrated by the following diagram:

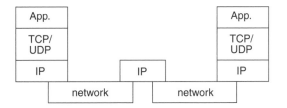

The diagram corresponds to two Internet hosts, say A and B, connected to two different networks, in this case two Ethernet segments that we will number 1 and 2. An Internet router, C, is connected to both networks.

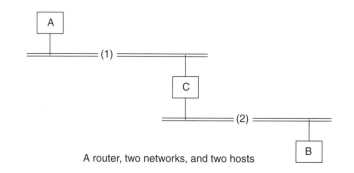

A router, two networks, and two hosts

The application program in A passes data to the local transport program. The program will encapsulate the data in one or several transport packets and will post the packets toward B through the Internet program. The Internet program formats an Internet header that specifies the Internet source and destination, and selects a "next hop": in our case, C. The Internet packet is then encapsulated in a local network packet and posted to C on this local network. When it leaves A, the packet contains the following information:

a1 $\rightarrow$ c1, IP	A $\rightarrow$ B, TCP	TCP header + data
Ethernet header	IP header	

The Ethernet header indicates that the packet is sent from A's port on network 1, which has the Ethernet number "a1," to the Ethernet address "c1," C's port on network 1. The Ethernet "payload type" indicates that this is an IP packet. After reception by C, it is thus passed to the Internet program on that router. The program will examine the IP header and find that the source is A and the destination B. By looking into the routing tables, it finds out that the packet must be relayed on network 2 toward B. It finds out the Ethernet address of B, say "b2," and posts the following packet on network 2:

c2 $\rightarrow$ b2, IP	A $\rightarrow$ B, TCP	TCP header + data
Ethernet header	IP header	

That packet will be received by B. The Internet program on B will recognize one of its own addresses, find out that the "protocol type" is "tcp," and pass the data to the TCP program that will eventually deliver the data to the application.

This is indeed a simplified example that only involves one relay and one single "network" technology. In today's Internet, the packet will often travel over several such relays: I count more than 20 relays between my workstation in France and the public archive server "ds.internic.net." These relays use many technologies: Ethernet, FDDI, various kinds of digital circuits, and optical fibers. In all cases, the same principle is maintained: the IP packet is encapsulated in order to cross one network, then "unencapsulated" and forwarded by an Internet program.

In this chapter, we will present the Internet addresses, the Internet protocol, and the control protocol associated to IP—the Internet Control Message Protocol (ICMP). Then, we will present the practical usage of IP by hosts and the most important applications of IP.

3.2 The Internet Addresses

Each Internet interface is identified by a 32-bit "Internet address." In this section, we will present the structure of Internet addresses, the relation between addresses and interfaces, and the particular addresses that have been defined for special purposes.

3.2.1 Address Formats

When IP was standardized in 1981, these addresses were defined as two-part objects: a "network identifier" and a "host number" within that network. There were three classes of network numbers, A, B, and C, corresponding to three address formats. A fourth class, D, was later defined for multicast addresses [1]. The remaining addresses constitute class E, reserved for experimental purposes.

High Order Bits	Format		Class
0	7 bits of net,	24 bits of host	A
10	14 bits of net,	16 bits of host	B
110	21 bits of net,	8 bits of host	C
1110	28 bits multicast group number		D
1111	reserved for experiments		E

Addresses are normally represented in text as four decimal numbers separated by dots. Each number represents one octet of the address. For example, the address of what used to be the ARPA "network information center" was 10.0.0.1, which corresponds to the four octets binary value 00001010 00000000 00000000 00000001.

The network numbers are assigned by the Internet numbering authorities: they are unique worldwide. The host numbers are assigned by each network manager. Uniqueness of host numbers within one network, combined with worldwide uniqueness of the network numbers, guarantee the worldwide uniqueness of the IP addresses.

The two-level hierarchy was sufficient in the early days of the Internet, when each organization's network was relatively simple—one local network for a single site was the norm. As local networks, work stations, and then personal computers became widespread, the network managers felt the need to structure their internal organization. In 1984, a third hierarchical level was added in the structure, the "subnet." A subnet is a division of the addressing space reserved to a network, so that the address format becomes:

network number	subnet	host

The subnet field can have any length—it is in fact specified by a 32-bit "mask." One determines that an address belongs to a subnet by a "comparison-under-mask" operation: all bits of the address for which the corresponding mask bit is null are zeroed and the result is compared to the subnet identifier.

Mask	Address	Net	Subnet	Host
0xFFFF0000	10.27.32.100	A: 10	27	32.100
0xFFFFFE00	136.27.33.100	B: 136.27	16 (32)	1.100
	136.27.34.141	136.27	17 (34)	0.141
0xFFFFFFC0	193.27.32.197	C: 193.27.32	3 (192)	5

—   examples of masks and addresses   —

Initially, there was no constraint on the form of the mask—one could for example use the low-order bits to identify the subnet and the middle bits to identify the host. But this liberty made the routing unnecessarily complex without much gain for network management. The specification has thus been updated: subnet masks must be "contiguous." They can have any length, provided it is larger than one.

The separation of network numbers into three classes was already an evolution. In the very early days of the Arpanet, one thought that 8 bits were more than enough for numbering all the networks that would be connected to the "experiment." The division into three classes identified by the most significant bits of the addresses was in fact a fix to this short-sighted initial design. But the practice showed that the three-class scheme was not adequate either. Most organizations requested a class B address because it left them with ample space to organize their subnetting. There are only 16,383 such addresses available, and they were "consumed" very fast. The alternative, which was to serve the organizations with several class C addresses, was not very satisfactory. We will see that the routing protocols carry one entry per network number. Assigning several numbers to a single organization increases the size of the routing tables and generally the cost of maintaining the routes. The Classless Inter-Domain Routing (CIDR) was designed as a fix to this last problem. Since there are not enough class B addresses available, organizations are served with a contiguous set of "class C" addresses. We will see in the CIDR chapter how the routing protocols are updated to aggregate these addresses in a single "mask."

3.2.2 Addresses and Interfaces

Internet addresses do not designate hosts. They are the identifiers of network interfaces. A host with several interfaces will have as many addresses. In Internet parlance, we say that such hosts are "multi-homed." This is often the case of important servers that wish to balance their transmission load over several connections for better performance or that want to maintain connectivity even if one of their interfaces fails. It is indeed also the case of routers that are designed to relay traffic from one network to the other.

Each of the interface addresses belongs to a subnet, which is generally contained within one single "network" (for example, one Ethernet cable, one token ring). The routing tables of the routers that belong to the IP network normally have one entry per subnet, indicating the fastest path toward that subnet; they may have specific entries for individual hosts.

Having one address per interface has two advantages over the alternative one address per host. It allows for precision routing. By specifying one specific interface address, one can indicate a preferred path for accessing a given host. It also allows for aggregation in the routing tables. If the address were not related to the topology at all, one would need to have one individual entry for every host in the router's tables. It indeed has a cost: one must list all the host addresses in the name server, and one must choose the "best" of the partner's addresses when making a connection. One must also select the appropriate source address when sending packets, as the path followed by the responses will be determined by that address.

3.2.3 Special Purpose Addresses

There are many cases where the host does not know its IP address or the IP address of its partner, e.g., when it is booting. Several addresses, or rather address forms, have been reserved for these purposes [2].

When the network number is unknown, a host can use 0 as a substitute. The special address "0.0.0.0" means "this host on this network." It can be used only as a source address—for example by a host that is booting. An address of the form "0.X.Y.Z" means "the host X.Y.Z on this network"; again, it can be used only as a source address—for example, by a host that is only partially initialized.

The special address "255.255.255.255" is the "limited broadcast" address. It can be used only as a destination address, to send a packet to all hosts on the local subnet. Packets sent to that address will never be relayed outside of the source's network.

An address of the form "A.255.255.255," "B.B.255.255," or "C.C.C.255" is a "directed broadcast" intended to reach all hosts in the class A network "A," or in the class B network "B.B," or in the class C network "C.C.C." If subnetting is used, an address where all "local" bits (the complement of the subnet mask) are set to 1 is the "directed broadcast" address for all hosts in that subnet.

A consequence of these conventions is that no subnet can have a null number or a number that is entirely expressed with binary ones. If one uses 3 bits for the subnet number, only the values 1 to 6 can be used. A further consequence is that a subnet number cannot have a size of only one bit!

The last special address is the "loopback" address. It is in fact a "loopback network number." The class A network 127 is reserved to that usage. Any address of the form "127.X.Y.Z" should be considered as local. Packets sent to that address will not be transmitted outside of the host.

In addition to these special addresses, the Internet numbering authorities have also reserved a number of "multicast" addresses for specific groups—for example, "224.0.0.1" for "All Systems on This Subnet" or "224.0.0.2" for "All Routers on This Subnet." Most of the assigned group numbers have been reserved for specific applications. IP multicasting will be detailed in a later chapter.

Address	Interpretation
0.0.0.0	Some unknown host (source)
255.255.255.255	Any host (destination)
129.34.0.3	Host number 3 in class B network 129.34
129.34.0.0	Some host in network 129.34 (source)
129.34.255.255	Any host in 129.34 (destination)
0.0.0.3	Host number 3 on "this network" (source)
127.0.0.1	This host (local loop)

—   examples of special addresses   —

3.3 The Internet Protocol

In this section, we present the Internet protocol itself, starting with its formats and explaining the various procedures that are part of IP: handling of types of services, fragmentation and reassembly, options.

3.3.1 The Internet Header

The Internet protocol header not only carries Internet source and destination addresses; it must also indicate a number of parameters that are essential for the operation of routers. The following diagram is copied from RFC-791, the definition of IP.

```
 0                   1                   2                   3
 0 1 2 3 4 5 6 7 8 9 0 1 2 3 4 5 6 7 8 9 0 1 2 3 4 5 6 7 8 9 0 1
+-+-+-+-+-+-+-+-+-+-+-+-+-+-+-+-+-+-+-+-+-+-+-+-+-+-+-+-+-+-+-+-+
| Version |  IHL  |  Type of Service  |         Total Length      |
+-------------------------------------+-------------------------+
|          Identification             | Flags |  Fragment Offset  |
+-------------------------------------+-------------------------+
|     Time to Live    |    Protocol    |      Header Checksum      |
+-------------------------------------+-------------------------+
|                       Source Address                           |
+----------------------------------------------------------------+
|                    Destination Address                         |
+-------------------------------------+-------------------------+
|                   Options                      |    Padding     |
+----------------------------------------------------------------+
```

The header comprises fixed fields present in every packet and several options. The header fields are generally aligned on a 32-bit boundary; each 32-bit world is transmitted with the most significant bit first—in other words, in "big endian" format, to use Danny Cohen's terminology [3]. The first header field is a "version" identifier. The current version of IP bears the version 4 which distinguishes it from previous versions (1 to 3), from the "stream" protocol ST-2 which is used in some real-time environments (version 5), and from the "new generation" protocols currently under evaluation (6 to 8). The next field is the Internet header's length (IHL) expressed as a number of 32-bit words. The length includes the fixed size and varies from 5, when no options are present, to 15. This allows for, at most, 40 octets of option. The type of service defines the packet's "precedence" and the desired type of routing; the type of service is detailed in section 3.2. The following field is the "total length"—the number of octets contained in the packet, including the IP header; this field is 16 bits long, which limits the packet size to 65,535 octets.

The identification, flags, and offset fields are used by the fragmentation and reassembly procedure which will be presented in detail later.

The "time to live" (TTL) was initially defined as an indication of the maximum lifetime of the packet in the network, expressed in seconds. A maximum TTL is a very helpful indication for transport protocols because it is an upper bound for various timers. For example, if one waits for the maximum TTL after the closure of a TCP connection, one is assured that no packets belonging to that connection are left in transit in the network. The connection context can thus be reused without any risk of mixing old and new packets. RFC-791 specifies that the routers should always decrement the TTL when relaying a packet, from one if the time spent in the queue and in the next hop is less than one second, from the estimated number of seconds otherwise. In practice, doing a precise estimate is very difficult. As the transit time on modern links is generally very low in any case, most routers just decrement the TTL by one. If the value reaches zero, the packet has lived too long and should be destroyed, not relayed. This is often an indication of a packet wandering on the wrong route or looping in the network.

The source and destination addresses are the fields that we mentioned in the "model of operation." When the packet has reached the final destination, the "protocol" field is used to determine the program to which the packet should be passed. The following table lists a few of the protocol numbers assigned by the Internet authorities [2].

Decimal	Keyword	Protocol
0		Reserved
1	ICMP	Internet Control Message
2	IGMP	Internet Group Management
3	GGP	Gateway-to-Gateway
4	IP	IP in IP (encapsulation)
5	ST	Stream
6	TCP	Transmission Control
8	EGP	Exterior Gateway Protocol
17	UDP	User Datagram
29	ISO-TP4	ISO Transport Protocol Class 4
38	IDPR-CMTP	IDPR Control Messager Transport Protocol
80	ISO-IP	ISO Internet Protocol (CLNP)
88	IGRP	IGRP
89	OSPF	Open Shortest Path First
255		Reserved

A transmission error on one of the header fields could have many undesirable consequences: delivery to the wrong destination, failure to kill a packet whose TTL has expired, reassembly of fragments not belonging to the same message. The "header checksum" is an attempt to protect IP against this type of misbehavior.

The checksum is computed "as the 16-bit one's complement of the one's complement sum of all 16-bit words in the header, after zeroing the checksum field itself." "Complement to one" refers to a particular binary representation of numbers in computer memories, where 0 can be represented as either 0000 or FFFF (in hexadecimal notation). Most computers use the "complement to 2" notation, where 0 can be represented only by the null binary value '0000.' If the numbers held in the 16-bit words were positive integers, one could obtain the "16-bit one complement sum" by adding all these numbers, then computing the rest of the division of this sum by 'FFFF' (65,535 in decimal notation). This is not a very strong protection; in particular, it does not protect against insertion of null words or permutation of words in the packets. However, experimental results show that this is an adequate balance between ease of computation and efficiency of error detection. The same algorithm is used by many other protocols, such as UDP, TCP, ICMP, and OSPF.

The header checksum is verified for each incoming packet. If the test fails, the packet must be discarded. Since some fields may vary (for example, the TTL), the checksum is computed again before any retransmission.

3.3.2 Precedence and Type of Service

The second octet of the packet header is called "type of service." It carries in fact two subfields, the "precedence" and the "type of service," which do not have quite the same function. The precedence is an indication of "priority," while the type of service is more an indication for routing. The precedence is carried on 3 bits, the type of service on the 5 other bits.

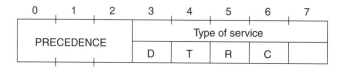

There are often several possible routes to the same destination, with very different characteristics: a telephone circuit will have a low delay but a very limited throughput; a satellite link may have a high throughput but suffers from a long delay; a radio channel may be very inexpensive but at the same time extremely noisy. Routing protocols normally attempt to compute the best route to a destination, but there are several definitions of best: cheapest, fastest, most reliable. We will see that several of them, notably OSPF and BGP, support routing by "type of service": they are capable of computing several routes according to the different type of services. By specifying a specific type of service, the application requests that its packets be routed according to its desires.

When IP was first specified in 1981, only three type-of-service bits were defined, indicating the relative emphasis on delay (bit 3, D), throughput (bit 4, T), and reliability (bit 5, R). Since that time, a new bit has been added, for low cost (bit 6, C). Setting the bit D was a way to request low delays, for example, by avoiding satellite links. Setting the bit T was a way to select the path with the highest throughput avoiding telephone links, for instance. Setting the bit R was a way to request a high reliability—such as by avoiding radio channels. Note that the bits should normally not be combined. The routing protocols are supposed to compute a default route (no bit set), a shortest route (bit D), a largest throughput route (bit T), a most reliable route (bit R), and a cheapest route (bit C). But the combination of C and T, for example, is not defined—in fact, it is illegal.

The "precedence" indicator does not affect routing but queuing—when several packets are waiting for transmission on the same channel, the one with the highest precedence should in theory be transmitted first. There are eight preference values:

```
111  —  Network Control
110  —  Internetwork Control
101  —  CRITIC-ECP
100  —  Flash Override
011  —  Flash
010  —  Immediate
001  —  Priority
000  —  Routine
```

The handling of preferences is in fact a very debatable point in network management, when most machines are simple PCs or workstations entirely under user control. Suppose that smart users find out that setting the precedence to some value actually increases their throughput or lowers their response times. It won't be long until those users start to use slightly modified programs that perform surprisingly better than the normal version.

RFC-791 contains a couple of caveats against the possible abuses of precedences. It states that precedence should be believed only within a network and that its use is the network's managers' responsibility. Precedence and type of service are currently being revisited by the IETF. The ongoing work will supercede the RFC-971 definitions and provide new semantics for the "Type of Service" byte, providing what is called "differentiated services" over the Internet. We will detail these extensions in chapter 14.

3.3.3 Fragmentation and Reassembly

The Internetworking programs are expected to relay packets between networks. These networks can indeed be dissimilar. They use different access methods, different transmission technologies, and different addressing schemes. All these differences are wiped out by the encapsulation technique. But the technology also implies a particular "maximum packet size." This size is typically related to the network data rate and to its expected error rate. If the network is slow, allowing very large packets may impose undue queuing delays—everybody must wait while a long packet is being transmitted. If the network is error prone, allowing long packets results in poor efficiency, because the probability of successful transmission decreases exponentially with the packet length. On the other hand, it is useful to increase the packet length on fast and reliable networks. This decreases the relative overhead of fixed header fields, reduces the interrupt rate and the CPU load in hosts, makes the link-sharing procedures less sensitive to propagation delays. This explains why the maximum packet size on a 10-Mbps (Megabits/second) Ethernet cable is 1,536 octets, 4,096 on a 100-Mbps FDDI ring, but can be much lower on a radio channel, for example. This maximum size is called the Media Transmission Unit (MTU).

Suppose now that a router just received a 4,000-octet packet from an FDDI ring and has to relay it to an Ethernet. It has only two choices: refuse to relay because the packet is too long, or chop it into adequately sized fragments. In the latter case, the fragments will be received separately by the destination Internetwork program which will have to concatenate them together before passing the whole packet to the application or to the transport protocol. The IP header includes specific fields to manage this fragmentation/reassembly process. These are the identification, flags, and offset fields.

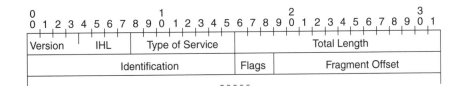

The flags field is composed of 3 bits, the first of which is reserved for future use and must be set to zero.

```
 0   1   2
┌───┬───┬───┐
│   │ D │ M │
│ 0 │ F │ F │
└───┴───┴───┘
```

The "don't fragment" bit (DF) indicates that the packet should not be fragmented. In our "FDDI to Ethernet" example, if this bit is set, the router should simply discard the packet and if possible send an ICMP error message back to the source address. If the bit is not set, fragmentation is allowed. In our example, a 4,000-octet packet will be chopped into three fragments.

	IP header fields				Data field
Incoming packet:	Id=X, L=4020,	DF=0,	MF=0,	offset=0	A‑ ‑ ‑AB‑ ‑ ‑BC‑ ‑ ‑C
Fragment 1:	Id=X, L=1520,	DF=0,	MF=1,	offset=0	A‑ ‑ ‑A
Fragment 2:	Id=X, L=1520,	DF=0,	MF=1,	offset=1500	B‑ ‑ ‑B
Fragment 3:	Id=X, L=1020,	DF=0,	MF=0,	offset=3000	C‑ ‑ ‑C

Each of the fragments has a complete IP header. Most fields of this header are directly copied from the incoming packet header, including the "identification" field. In fact, the only fields that are different are the length and offset, as well as the "more fragments" bit. The length indicates the complete fragment length, including the IP header; the offset indicates the relative position of the fragment within the complete packet. The more fragments bit is set in all packets, except the one containing the last fragment.

Fragmentation may occur at several stages of the transmission and may indeed occur recursively. Suppose, for example, that the fragments have to be relayed on a radio channel where the maximum length is only 520 octets. Each fragment will have to be fragmented again, as in the example below.

	IP header fields				Data field
Incoming Fragment 2:	Id=X, L=1520,	DF=0,	MF=1,	offset=1500	B‑ ‑ ‑B
Fragment 2a:	Id=X, L= 520,	DF=0,	MF=1,	offset=1500	B‑ ‑
Fragment 2b:	Id=X, L= 520,	DF=0,	MF=1,	offset=2000	‑ ‑ ‑
Fragment 2c:	Id=X, L= 520,	DF=0,	MF=1,	offset=2500	‑ ‑B

The offset and MF bits are always computed relative to the original packet.

The identification field is used by the reassembly procedure. In combination with the source address, it uniquely identifies the packet for the destination. The receiver must collect all fragments that bear the same identification (ID) and assemble them according to the "offset" value. The reassembly is complete when all fragments, including the last one (MF=0), have been received.

Indeed, one must observe that the reassembly procedure may well fail, for example, if a transmission error causes the loss of a fragment. The receiver should be careful to "time out" the partially reassembled packets. This is naturally done by decrementing the TTL of the received but unassembled fragments every second. If the TTL reaches zero before the packet is completely reassembled, all fragments will be destroyed and the corresponding memory resources will be freed. Linking reassembly with the TTL is in fact mandated by the definition of the identification field, which is only 16 bits long. A host cannot reuse an identifier for a new packet if there is a risk that the packet will be fragmented and that the new fragments will mix with the old ones. The only solution is to wait until all old fragments have disappeared from the network, in other words, to wait for the expiration of the TTL.

The fragmentation procedure is deprecated by modern network architects. In application of the reuse-of-identifiers rule, one can transmit at most 65,536 packets per TTL; if we associate this to the recommended 2 minutes TTL of TCP, we obtain a limit of 544 packets per second, or about 17 Mbps if the packet size is 4 Kilo-Octets (KO). This is clearly inadequate in the time of FDDI rings or T3 lines, let alone optical fiber interconnections! Another inconvenience is that it makes retransmission inefficient. As control procedures like TCP operate on top of IP, if a fragment is lost, the whole packet will have to be retransmitted. Also, a strange "buffer starvation" effect has been observed in some situations where many packets are being reassembled in parallel, requiring a lot of memory resources at the receiver. The loss of fragments causes all these parallel reassembly buffers to remain "in use" until the TTL expires, for very little benefit.

The correct principle is that transmission units (IP fragments) should have exactly the same size as control units (TCP packets). Modern versions of TCP achieve this by implementing the "path MTU discovery" algorithm. They start the connection with a large packet size, corresponding to the MTU of the local interface. The IP packets are transmitted with the "don't fragment" bit set. If they pass a gateway where fragmentation is needed, an error will occur and the packet will be lost. That loss will be detected, and the TCP will back off to a smaller packet length. After a period, the TCP will have computed a packet size that is acceptable for all media on the path. The packets will directly reach the recipient without ever needing to be fragmented. A side effect is that, as fragmentation is no longer required, there is no need to enforce the "unique identification" rule, so the limit of 65,536 packets per TTL is lifted.

3.3.4 IP Options

The IP options field was defined to carry specific functionalities, to request a particular routing for some packets. A packet may carry several optional parameters, concatenated to each other. Each parameter is identified by an "option-type" octet that contains several fields.

The "copied" flag (C) is set when the option must be copied in all fragments in case of fragmentation. If this is not set, the option need only be copied in the first fragment. The options are grouped by "class." Two option classes have been defined: 0 for "control" options and 2 for "debugging and measurement." Within the class, the number identifies the option. Several options are defined in RFC-791.

CLASS	NUMBER	LENGTH	DESCRIPTION
0	0	—	End of Option list. This option occupies only 1 octet; it has no length octet.
0	1	—	No Operation. This option occupies only one octet; it has no length octet.
0	2	11	Security. Used to carry Security, Compartmentation, User Group (TCC), and handling restriction codes compatible with DoD requirements.
0	3	var.	Loose Source Routing. Used to route the Internet datagram based on information supplied by the source.
0	9	var.	Strict Source Routing. Used to route the Internet datagram based on information supplied by the source.
0	7	var.	Record Route. Used to trace the route an Internet datagram takes.
0	8	4	Stream ID. Used to carry the stream identifier.
2	4	var.	Internet Timestamp.

Most options have a "variable length" encoding: the type octet is immediately followed by a length octet that counts the number of bytes necessary for the encoding, including the type and length themselves. The only exceptions are the "no operation" option, which is generally used to insert padding between separate options so that they begin on word boundaries, and the "end of option" list, which is used to indicate that the parsing of the option field should terminate there, even if the "IHL" field mentions that more room has been reserved for options. These two options are encoded on a single octet.

Options are rarely used now. Some of them are almost obsolete: the "stream ID" was used only in the Satnet experiment; the security option was defined for the needs of DoD as perceived at the end of the 1970s, and is generally not exercised in civilian networks. We will see in the next section that a program like "traceroute," which does not use options, provides the services for which "timestamps" and "route recording" were initially defined. In fact, the only two options that are in moderate use today are the "loose" and "strict" source-routing parameters.

Both source-routing options have the same syntax.

The "pointer" octet is followed by "length-3" octets of "route data" that contain a list of Internet addresses through which the packet must be relayed. The IP header "destination" field always indicates the next address toward which the packet must be routed. When that destination is reached, the option is examined. The pointer field contains an index, or an octet count starting from the beginning of the option; the minimal legal value is 4. If it is greater than the option's length, the packet has reached its final destination; otherwise, the header's destination address is replaced by the four octets following the pointer, or by the next address in the list. When the source routing is strict (type=137, '10001001'), this must be the address of an adjacent router; there is no constraint when the routing is loose (type=131, '10000011'). The address in the list must then be replaced by the local router's one and the pointer is incremented by 4; the option's length remains constant throughout the transmission of the packet.

3.3.5 Options and Header Processing

I mentioned previously that IP options are not used much in today's Internet. This remark is related to the processing cost of options and can be understood only if we explain the way modern IP routers are programmed.

A naive implementation of IP will perform a number of tests for every packet: verify the version field, the checksum, and the compatibility between the IP length and the information provided by the media; then it will parse the options, if any. Then one must look for the next hop for the destination address in the routing table and, taking into account the type of service, associate an interface and a media address to that next hop. All this can be quite long, maybe a few hundred instructions. If we want to perform gigabit-per-second networking, we must do better.

The classic way to speed up a computer program is to examine the most frequent path and optimize this path. Many router vendors have done precisely that, and the main path is quite simple—it corresponds to packets that have no options specified. In that case, the IP header has a fixed length. One can load its five 32-bit words in as many registers, which makes verifications much faster. This technique can be combined with the caching of most frequently used routes to reduce dramatically the cost of header processing for all "well-behaved" packets. Some high-performance routers are in fact already approaching the gigabit-per-second mark!

But the packets where options are specified do not benefit from these improvements. One must execute the "general purpose" part of the program instead of the fast path, which lowers the performance. Some routers have been programmed to limit the overall performance loss due to optioned headers by simply processing them with a lower priority than "normal" packets.

Because the use of options almost always entails a performance penalty, a number of alternatives to options have been developed. Perhaps the most typical is the replacement of source routing by a similar technique called "encapsulation." Instead of specifying a loose source route "from A to B through C," one simply encapsulates a packet "from A to B" in another packet "from A to C."

A $\rightarrow$ C, IP-IP	A $\rightarrow$ B, TCP	TCP header + data
IP header(1)	IP header(2)	

When C receives this packet, it examines the protocol type of the first header and discovers that this is an encapsulation of "IP in IP." It unwraps the header and forwards the inner packet.

A $\rightarrow$ B, TCP	TCP header + data
IP header(2)	

Now, consider the difference between the processing of these packets and the one of the loose "source route" option. The cost for C is probably comparable—parsing the option and unwrapping the header requires a similar number of instructions. But the cost for all the intermediate routers between A and C or C and B will be very different. All the encapsulated or unwrapped packets will be processed along the "fast path," while all optioned packets will have to be processed by the general program, perhaps at a lower priority. The intermediate routers will have to parse the option field to discover that it contains only a source route option that these intermediate routers do not have to process!

3.4 ICMP

IP is straightforward and simple: there is only one packet type, and the network has to do only its best to carry that packet toward the destination. But diagnosing error conditions would be extremely difficult if the network was not able to pass back some information.

The Internet Control Message Protocol (ICMP) carries this information exchange. Although layered on top of IP (protocol type 1), it is in fact an integral part of the IP requirement; all IP routers and hosts are expected to "speak" this protocol. Most ICMP packets are "diagnostic" information that is sent back to the source when a router destroys a packet, say, for example, because the destination is unreachable or the TTL expired; ICMP also defines an echo function that is used for testing connectivity.

The purpose of ICMP is not to make the IP datagram service more reliable, but merely to provide feedback about network problems. As ICMP messages are carried within IP datagrams, there is indeed always a risk that these packets will themselves be victims of errors or problems (for example, of local congestion). In order to avoid recursive avalanches, the rule is that no ICMP report is ever triggered by an ICMP message.

3.4.1 Diagnostics

All ICMP messages start with a common 32-bit ICMP header comprising a type field, a type specific code field, and a checksum.

The checksum is computed with the same algorithm used for protecting IP headers—the 16-bit one's complement of the one's complement sum of the ICMP message. It is used to detect any change in the transmission of the report. Several message types are defined [4, 5].

0	Echo Reply
3	Destination Unreachable
4	Source Quench
5	Redirect
8	Echo
9	Router Advertisement
10	Router Solicitation
11	Time Exceeded
12	Parameter Problem
13	Timestamp
14	Timestamp Reply
15	Information Request
16	Information Reply

—   ICMP message types   —

The most frequently used messages are those reporting "operational" problems that lead to the dropping of packets, such as "time exceeded," "destination unreachable," or "source quench." These packets all have the same format: the common ICMP header is followed by 32 bits of padding, then by the first bytes of the packet that triggered the problem. That excerpt is there so that the emitter can "audit" the packet and understand the problem. It includes the entire IP header and the first 8 octets of the content, sufficient information to identify the application that sent the packet.

 The most frequent ICMP message format —

The destination unreachable messages are sent when a router cannot forward a packet. The "code" field qualifies the error.

```
0 =   net unreachable
1 =   host unreachable
2 =   protocol unreachable
3 =   port unreachable
4 =   fragmentation needed and DF set
5 =   source route failed
```

The time exceeded messages are sent when a packet is destroyed because its TTL expired. The code field indicates whether this occurred in transit (code 0) or during reassembly (code 1).

The source quench messages can be sent by a router that detects a congestion. The source that receives such messages is supposed to reduce its sending rate. We will detail this, and the general problem of resource allocation, in a later chapter. The code field is not used in the source quench message and is always set to zero.

The "parameter problem" message is sent by a router that finds an error in the encoding of the IP header. Its format is quite similar to that of the destination unreachable or time expired message, except for the presence of a "pointer" field, which identifies the particular octet in the original datagram where the error was detected.

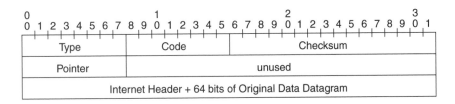

The "redirect," "router advertisement," and "router solicitation" messages are used to pass routing information to hosts and are described in the next section. The "echo," "information," and "timestamp" messages are used by simple management procedures that will be detailed in the next paragraphs.

3.4.2 Ping

ICMP includes a simple "echo" function. When a router or a host receives an ICMP message of type echo, it should respond by an "echo reply." Both the request and the reply have the same format.

The reply is very simply derived from the request by swapping the IP header's source and destination address, replacing the type ECHO (8) by the ECHO-REPLY (0), and then computing the new value of the IP and ICMP checksums. The data received in the echo request are returned unchanged in the echo reply.

The echo procedure is used by a very popular debugging program called "ping." This program tests the connectivity with a remote host by sending regularly spaced echo commands and then waiting for the corresponding replies. If it receives at least one echo, it can deduce that the remote host is still up and running:

```
ping ds.internic.net
ds.internic.net is alive
```

The program uses the "identifiers" and "sequence numbers" to match requests and replies, which enables the acquisition of simple statistics.

```
PING ds.internic.net: 100 data bytes
108  bytes   from    198.49.45.10:  icmp-seq=2.    time=173.    ms
108  bytes   from    198.49.45.10:  icmp-seq=0.    time=5048.   ms
108  bytes   from    198.49.45.10:  icmp-seq=1.    time=4410.   ms
108  bytes   from    198.49.45.10:  icmp-seq=3.    time=2461.   ms
108  bytes   from    198.49.45.10:  icmp-seq=8.    time=150.    ms
108  bytes   from    198.49.45.10:  icmp-seq=10.   time=191.    ms
108  bytes   from    198.49.45.10:  icmp-seq=11.   time=218.    ms
108  bytes   from    198.49.45.10:  icmp-seq=12.   time=210.    ms
108  bytes   from    198.49.45.10:  icmp-seq=13.   time=140.    ms
108  bytes   from    198.49.45.10:  icmp-seq=14.   time=270.    ms
108  bytes   from    198.49.45.10:  icmp-seq=15.   time=168.    ms
108  bytes   from    198.49.45.10:  icmp-seq=16.   time=152.    ms
108  bytes   from    198.49.45.10:  icmp-seq=17.   time=199.    ms
108  bytes   from    198.49.45.10:  icmp-seq=18.   time=220.    ms
─── ds.internic.net PING Statistics ───
20 packets transmitted, 14 packets received, 30% packet loss
round-trip (ms)        min / avg / max  = 140 / 1000 / 5048
```

Example of "ping" output

In our example, "ping" was used to test the connectivity between the author's workstation and the archive server "ds.internic.net." The program collects statistics by computing the time between the emission of each request and the corresponding reply; it is a very easy way to characterize the path between two hosts. In the Internet jargon, this is called "pinging" a host.

The original ICMP specification [4] also defines a simplified version of the ECHO messages—"information request" and "information reply" messages.

```
0                   1                   2                   3
0 1 2 3 4 5 6 7 8 9 0 1 2 3 4 5 6 7 8 9 0 1 2 3 4 5 6 7 8 9 0 1
+-+-+-+-+-+-+-+-+-+-+-+-+-+-+-+-+-+-+-+-+-+-+-+-+-+-+-+-+-+-+-+-+
|      Type       |      Code       |           Checksum        |
+-+-+-+-+-+-+-+-+-+-+-+-+-+-+-+-+-+-+-+-+-+-+-+-+-+-+-+-+-+-+-+-+
|            Identifier             |      Sequence Number      |
+-+-+-+-+-+-+-+-+-+-+-+-+-+-+-+-+-+-+-+-+-+-+-+-+-+-+-+-+-+-+-+-+
```

The sole difference between these and the echo messages is the absence of a data field.

3.4.3 Traceroute

The "traceroute" program is another very popular debugging tool built upon the IP and ICMP protocols. While "ping" attempts to characterize the end-to-end connectivity, "traceroute" tries to discover the various relays on the path. It works by sending regular IP packets toward the destination, progressively increasing the TTL field. The first packet is sent with a TTL of one; the first relay on the path will receive it, decrement the TTL to zero, destroy the packet, and send back a "TTL expired" ICMP message. The source address of this message identifies the first relay. The next message is sent with a TTL of 2; the response will identify the second relay. This will continue until the final destination is reached or until the point where the connectivity is broken has been identified.

```
traceroute to ds.internic.net (198.49.45.10)
 1    138.96.24.250      2 ms      2 ms      2 ms
 2    138.96.64.251      2 ms      2 ms      2 ms
 3    193.51.208.2       2 ms      2 ms      2 ms
 4    193.48.50.169      3 ms      3 ms      3 ms
 5    193.48.50.49       3 ms      3 ms      4 ms
 6    193.48.50.34      14 ms     10 ms      9 ms
 7    192.93.43.50      10 ms     10 ms     15 ms
 8    192.93.43.74      19 ms     17 ms     14 ms
 9    192.93.43.90      21 ms     20 ms     21 ms
10    192.93.43.17      21 ms     21 ms     32 ms
11    192.93.43.121     51 ms     39 ms     39 ms
12    192.121.156.226   69 ms     52 ms     58 ms
13    192.121.156.202  214 ms    211 ms    153 ms
14    192.157.65.122   233 ms    120 ms    160 ms
15    192.203.229.246  136 ms    191 ms    198 ms
16    140.222.58.2     125 ms       *      147 ms
17    140.222.56.222   229 ms       *        *
18    140.222.32.1     124 ms    138 ms       *
19    140.222.32.196   145 ms       *      255 ms
20    140.222.222.1    132 ms    150 ms    130 ms
21    198.49.45.10     128 ms    144 ms    142 ms
```

—   example of traceroute usage   —

Traceroute works by sending regular IP packets; in fact, it sends "User Datagram Protocol" (UDP) packets toward an unused UDP port. This is an interesting point of design: a major debugging function is performed by a side effect of a normal operation. There were in fact proposals to incorporate this function into the IP protocol itself, for example, by defining a "trace requested" IP option [6]. The routers that process a packet carrying that option would immediately send back a "trace" message to the packet's source. Such architecture will probably be more efficient because one single packet will suffice to trace all intermediate routers; the whole process will thus be completed in one exchange with the destination, instead of one exchange per relay with the regular traceroute. The specific IP option remains, however, experimental. It has not yet collected a large consensus because it would require an upgrade of all the existing routers and also because it is somewhat contradictory to the end-to-end principle. Why make all routers any more complex than necessary when the function can be efficiently accomplished by using the intelligence of the hosts?

3.4.4 Time Management

The "timestamp" and "timestamp reply" messages were designed in the original ICMP specification to facilitate the synchronization of clocks over the network. However, synchronized clocks are a very useful tool for managing a network. All routers normally collect logs of network conditions, statistics, and abnormal events. If the router's clocks are properly synchronized, it becomes easy to correlate the logs, for example, to reconstruct the history of a particular failure and to understand how it was propagated. On the contrary, if the clocks are not accurate enough, it becomes impossible to know which of router A or router B failed first!

```
 0                   1                   2                   3
 0 1 2 3 4 5 6 7 8 9 0 1 2 3 4 5 6 7 8 9 0 1 2 3 4 5 6 7 8 9 0 1
+-+-+-+-+-+-+-+-+-+-+-+-+-+-+-+-+-+-+-+-+-+-+-+-+-+-+-+-+-+-+-+-+
|      Type       |      Code       |           Checksum        |
+-+-+-+-+-+-+-+-+-+-+-+-+-+-+-+-+-+-+-+-+-+-+-+-+-+-+-+-+-+-+-+-+
|            Identifier             |       Sequence Number     |
+-+-+-+-+-+-+-+-+-+-+-+-+-+-+-+-+-+-+-+-+-+-+-+-+-+-+-+-+-+-+-+-+
|                    Originate Timestamp                        |
+-+-+-+-+-+-+-+-+-+-+-+-+-+-+-+-+-+-+-+-+-+-+-+-+-+-+-+-+-+-+-+-+
|                    Receive Timestamp                          |
+-+-+-+-+-+-+-+-+-+-+-+-+-+-+-+-+-+-+-+-+-+-+-+-+-+-+-+-+-+-+-+-+
|                    Transmit Timestamp                         |
+-+-+-+-+-+-+-+-+-+-+-+-+-+-+-+-+-+-+-+-+-+-+-+-+-+-+-+-+-+-+-+-+
```

—   format of timestamp requests and replies   —

A timestamp request-reply exchange enables a source to sample the difference between its clock and the one of the destination. The source sends a request that carries an "origination time"; the destination notes the "arrival time" of that request, prepares a reply by swapping the IP source and destination addresses and by setting the ICMP type to "timestamp response," and then sends it after filling in the "transmission time" and recomputing the IP and ICMP checksums. The originator will receive the packet and immediately note its reception time. All times are normally expressed as milliseconds since midnight "Universal time" (what used to be known as "Greenwich mean time"). When millisecond precision or UT reference are not available, the specification [4] allows an "escape" notation: the most significant bit in the timestamp is set.

Clock synchronization is a very complex topic. There are many ways that a clock can be "wrong": we can observe "phase" errors (too late or in advance) or "frequency" errors (too fast or too slow). The four time stamps provided by the exchange can be used to estimate the transmission delay and then the "phase error" between the two clocks. The transmission delay is normally estimated as one-half of the "round trip" delay—the difference between reception and origination times—minus the processing time at the destination—the difference between transmit and arrival time. Once the transmission time has been estimated, one can evaluate the phase error between the originator's and destination's clocks. Of course, all these measurements are subject to various kinds of errors; one must perform a statistical processing to eliminate random components, such as waiting delays within the network, and to estimate the difference between the clocks' frequencies. It is indeed important to implement the timestamp collection with extreme precision if one wants to tune the local clocks accurately. The origination stamp and transmission stamp must be filled in the packet as late as possible (just before transmission) while the arrival and reception stamps must be filled as early as possible after reception.

The design incorporated in ICMP [4] is based on the state of the art of 1981 [7]. The clock synchronization algorithm has been refined since and has evolved into an independent "Network Time Protocol" (NTP). Several versions of this protocol have been successively issued by Dave Mills between 1985 and 1993 [8, 9, 10, 11] together with several discussion papers [12, 13, 14, 15].

3.5 Sending IP Packets

The IP model distinguishes two kinds of systems: "hosts" and "routers." Most of this book will be devoted to routing, i.e., to the algorithms used by routers to find paths in the network and maintain IP connectivity. But IP is also used by hosts, such as systems that only send or receive IP packets but do not normally relay them. The host must find out the first relay to which an IP packet has to be sent. This may be another host on the same network—e.g., on the same Ethernet cable—or a router that will further relay the packet.

Finding the first relay is in fact a routing operation. In some very early implementations of IP, the hosts had to maintain their own routing tables for this. They generally did so by passively listening to the routing packets exchanged by the routers, but this approach has been deprecated for several years. It requires large resources from the hosts, which may not always have the processing capabilities or the memory capacities to handle complete routing tables. It also requires that the hosts know the details of the routing protocol, which supposes that the hosts know which routing protocol is used in the first place. This was practical when the routing tables were small and when the protocol in use was RIP, a very simple protocol that we will describe in a later chapter. It is impractical now; hosts are supposed to implement the "router discovery" protocol and to follow the "redirection" messages which we will detail in this section.

3.5.1 Sending Packets on the Network

When a host sends a packet, it must determine the next hop. Suppose first a host that has only one network connection, such as an Ethernet interface. An IP address has been assigned to that interface, and that address belongs to an IP subnet. The first test that the host performs is to determine whether the packet's destination address belongs to that subnet. This is performed by a "test under mask," i.e., testing whether the subnet masked bits of the destination address equal to those of the local address. If the test is "true," the destination belongs to the same subnet and the next hop's address is exactly the destination address. Otherwise, the destination is most probably remote and the next hop's address is the one of a router toward it.

Once the next hop's IP address has been determined, the host must find out the corresponding network address, which most modern documents call the "media address" to avoid the confusion between IP networks' addresses and local network addresses. In our Ethernet example, the host must find out the 48-bit Ethernet address of that next hop—the address of the destination itself if it is local or the address of a local router if the destination is remote. The translation between IP addresses and network or media addresses is performed by the "Address Resolution Protocol" defined in RFC-826 [16]. The host broadcasts an "ARP request" packet over the Ethernet. This will be received by all stations. One of them will recognize its IP address and reply by sending an "ARP response." Request and response have the same format.

Requests and responses are identified by the "operation code" (resp 1 and 2). The target's hardware address is indeed unknown when the request is sent; that field is initialized to zero and the destination field in the header is normally set to the "broadcast" address. Although designed for Ethernet, the protocol has been laid out with generality in mind—one can specify the type of "hardware" and "protocol" addresses and support more than just Ethernet and IP. One can also specify the addresses' lengths.

Performing the ARP translation for every packet would be extremely inefficient. The hosts are supposed to keep the result of the translation in a cache memory. If they have to send more packets to the same destination, they will simply look into that cache and copy the 48-bit address without having to resort to ARP.

Variants of the ARP have been defined for many networking technologies in addition to Ethernet. In fact, this is one of the two procedures that have to be defined before IP can be supported on any new technology, the other being the encapsulation technique. Defining the ARP procedure is very easy whenever the technology supports "broadcasting" or "multicasting." One can simply use the Ethernet technique of broadcasting the ARP query to all hosts in the subnet and waiting for a reply. In fact, the ARP defined for Ethernet [16] can be used over any of the IEEE-802 local area technologies, including token ring. Only minor adaptations are needed for ARCNET [17], HIPPI [18], FDDI [19], or even SMDS [20]. The problem is much harder to solve when the network supports only point-to-point transmission, which is the case of X.25, ISDN, Frame-Relay, or ATM. The most used solution is to consider these networks as providing quasi-permanent point-to-point connections. The address is then set by a management operation. This is the solution typically used for X.25, ISDN, or Frame-Relay [21, 22, 23]. Another solution is to use a centralized "ARP server"; this is being explored for ATM networks [24].

One should note that ARP replies do not necessarily come from the target itself. They might as well originate from a third party, e.g., a router that "knows" the target's address. This router can act as a "proxy" for the target; the process of third-party replies is known as "proxy ARP."

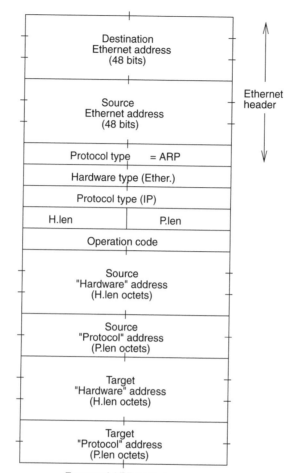

Format of ARP packets

3.5.2 Discovering the Local Router

When a destination is not local, the hosts should forward the IP datagram to a router. When there are several routers connected to the local network, the hosts should normally select the one that is the nearest to the destination. To do that, the hosts must first know the routers connected to the local network and second have sufficient routing information to elect the shortest path.

Discovering the addresses of the local routers may appear to be a very simple problem to many—why not just copy them in a file that will be read at start-up time? Well, this may look simple but it is really not. Somebody has to copy those files, most likely the "system manager." These files will have to be updated each time a new router is added or when the preferred router changes. A dynamic discovery procedure removes this administrative burden. The addresses are obtained from the network; they are always up to date; there is no need to learn as many administration procedures as there are different types of machines on the network.

Dynamic discovery could have been done by simply listening to the routing protocols, but this poses the problems that we have seen before. The format of messages or even their contents change with the protocol in use. There is a choice of many such protocols, some of which are not designed at all to enable easy eavesdropping. The official router discovery procedure is thus performed through specially designed ICMP messages [5]. The routers will announce their presence over the network by broadcasting "router advertisements" at regular intervals; the hosts may trigger the emission of these advertisements through a "solicitation." The router discovery procedure is not a routing protocol. The goal is simply to select one default router. It is assumed that, even if this router is not on the shortest path to the destination, it is capable of relaying the packets. We will see later how the redirection procedure can be used to inform hosts of more efficient routes.

The router advertisement messages contain the list of the router's addresses, together with a preference notation. The ICMP header specifies the type (9), a null code, the number of addresses in the list and the size of each entry (always two words in this version), and the "lifetime" of the announcement.

```
 0                   1                   2                   3
 0 1 2 3 4 5 6 7 8 9 0 1 2 3 4 5 6 7 8 9 0 1 2 3 4 5 6 7 8 9 0 1
+-+-+-+-+-+-+-+-+-+-+-+-+-+-+-+-+-+-+-+-+-+-+-+-+-+-+-+-+-+-+-+-+
|     Type      |     Code      |            Checksum           |
+---------------+---------------+-------------------------------+
|   Num Addrs   | Addr Entry Size|            Lifetime          |
+---------------+---------------+-------------------------------+
|                       Router Address[1]                       |
+---------------------------------------------------------------+
|                      Preference Level[1]                      |
+---------------------------------------------------------------+
|                       Router Address[2]                       |
+---------------------------------------------------------------+
|                      Preference Level[2]                      |
+---------------------------------------------------------------+
|                              .                                |
|                              .                                |
|                              .                                |
```

Routers may have several addresses to advertise, such as when they have several different interfaces connected to the same network or when several addresses have been assigned to the same interface (to serve two IP subnets that happen to share the same link). To each of these addresses is assigned a "preference" (an integer value). The preference values are encoded in "complement to 2" notation—the hexadecimal value 00000001 is 1, FFFFFFFF is –1. The highest values are preferred; the absolute lowest value, 80000000 (–214,783,648 in decimal notation), is used to report addresses of routers that are active but do not wish to receive "default" traffic. The preferences are normally set by the network administrator. The normal router will have a high preference, followed by the preferred backup, and so on.

Advertisements are normally sent on the "all hosts" multicast address—224.0.0.1—or on the "limited broadcast" address—255.255.255.255—if multicasting is not supported. They should be remembered for "lifetime" seconds and will normally be repeated at random intervals sizably shorter than "lifetime" in order to avoid the effects of transmission errors. However, periodic broadcasts are not a very desirable feature on a local network. Each packet must be processed by every host and thus consumes significant resources. Since all routers on the network should send such packets, the cumulative effect practically forbids the use of short lifetimes. The typical value of the lifetime is thus 30 minutes; advertisements are normally sent approximately every 7 minutes.

This long interval means that a host that just starts up may have to wait up to 7 minutes before being capable of sending packets out of the local network. This is a bit long in a world of "nanosecond" computing! Hosts that cannot wait so long will try to trigger the emission of router advertisement by sending a solicitation message.

Our example is a very simple ICMP message where only the type field (10) is significant. It is normally sent to the "all routers" address, 224.0.0.2, or to the "limited broadcast" address if multicasting is not available. The advertisements sent in response to such messages either can be sent directly to the soliciting host or multicast to all hosts, for instance, if the router was about to multicast an advertisement in any case.

The hosts will receive several router advertisements for many router addresses and preferences. They should ignore the router addresses that do not belong to their own subnet. This is done by a comparison with the local address under the subnet mask. If several addresses are acceptable, they select as default router the one that has the highest preference. In the absence of further information, all datagrams sent to addresses outside of the local subnet will be passed to that router.

3.5.3 Using Redirects

A default route is a nice way to establish connectivity but is not necessarily very efficient. Just suppose that we have a configuration where two routers, X and Y, are connected to host A's Ethernet segment. X is the default router; it manages the connectivity between that segment and the rest of the Internet. Y is another router that simply provides connectivity with another Ethernet segment to which host B is connected. Following default routing, all packets sent by A to the Internet just go through X and then are forwarded to their destination. This is quite satisfactory. But with the same rules, all packets sent by A to B first go to X, then from X to Y, then from Y to B. The packets cross the first Ethernet segment twice. This is slower than needed and also doubles the load of that segment, limiting the possible bandwidth.

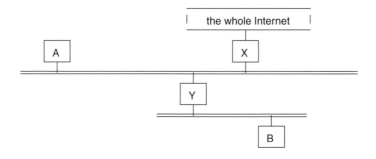

The "redirection" procedure allows routers and hosts to correct this misbehavior. The first packet bound to B will indeed be sent to X, but it will immediately trigger the emission of a "redirect" ICMP message from X to A. This message is formatted like classic ICMP error messages.

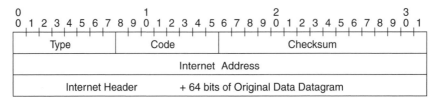

It contains a type (5), a code, and a copy of the first bytes of the packet that triggered the error. The second word of the packet encodes the IP address of a router that can reach the destination more efficiently than the default router. In our example, X will place here the address of Y. Upon reception of such messages, the hosts are supposed to retrieve the destination address to which the packet is being sent—it is present in the header field copied in the ICMP message. Then, the hosts are supposed to install an entry in a local routing table, noting that packets bound to that destination should be forwarded to the other router on the local network. The original ICMP specification lists several possible causes of redirection that could be encoded in the code field.

```
0  =  Redirect datagrams for the Network.
1  =  Redirect datagrams for the Host.
2  =  Redirect datagrams for the Type of Service and Network.
3  =  Redirect datagrams for the Type of Service and Host.
```

The "type of service" qualifier allows hosts to use different routes for different qualities of service. The network or host codes could be exploited to manage the host's routing table. If the redirection was for "all addresses within that network," the host could avoid transmitting packets bound to other destinations in the same network to the default router. There is however no way to specify a subnet mask within the redirection messages, which limits seriously the usefulness of managing network entries in the host tables.

3.5.4 Black Holes

Astronomers will tell you that a black hole is a "dead star" which has cooled down so much that it has eventually collapsed into a very dense kernel of material, so dense that gravity forces at its proximity will capture all nearby objects, even photons. This is why it is a black hole: whatever falls into it stays there; not even a particle of light comes out.

It is quite easy to build up the network equivalent of a black hole, for example, by wrongly setting the routing information and sending the data to a "dead router," a system that captures all packets sent to it and never sends any information back. We do indeed call these systems black holes. Detecting them and avoiding them is part of everyday networking life.

We will see that the routing protocols attempt to maintain connectivity by constantly checking and computing the paths between the routers. But the best computations would be useless if the host keeps choosing as first hop a dead router. Algorithms for detecting black holes are part of the "requirements for Internet hosts" [25]. Although not completely satisfactory, these algorithms rely on common sense and cumulated experience. The general principle is that a host should not keep sending data through a router without some feedback proving that the router is still operational.

Indeed, the definition of feedback varies. If the datagrams that are sent through the router belong to a TCP connection, the reception of a continuous stream of acknowledgment constitutes an ideal feedback. The TCP program should be capable of passing such information to the IP handlers. On the other hand, if the acknowledgments do not come back, something "suspect" might be happening, and the availability of the local router should be checked.

Other feedback besides TCP is possible, such as the fact that the router responds to ARP requests or that it is still periodically sending router advertisement—even if the preference factor within the advertisement is set to the minimal value. A host that does not receive this kind of feedback after a redirection may decide to revert to default routing. As long as the default router is operational, one may believe that its routing procedures will keep track of the conditions of the other routers and that it will not issue a new redirection toward a router that is not operational.

The advertisement procedure itself might prove too slow for adequately testing the default router; 6 to 7 minutes of silence might be long enough to break a connection. There are various ways to achieve better protection, such as by sending a fraction of the packets to other routers in order to minimize the consequences of one router's failure. If nothing else is available, the host may resort to "pinging" the default router—send an ICMP ECHO request and wait for the reply.

3.5.5 Some Reflections

The combined usage of IP, ARP, and ICMP which we have just described enables hosts to send packets with simple software and minimal configuration requirements. We could study a number of topics in addition to these simple procedures, e.g., the need for an initial configuration setup and the security risks associated with the redirection procedure.

All the procedures that we have described in this chapter suppose that the host knows its IP address. If the address is not configured, the host may possibly send packets using the conventional "unspecified source" address "0.0.0.0," but it cannot receive any packets except those sent to a broadcast address. The arguments that we used for the choice of the default router also apply here: we would very much like to avoid the "manual" administration of host addresses. Several responses have been proposed to this problem, notably the Reverse Address Resolution Protocol (RARP) [26] and the Bootstrap Protocol (BOOTP) [27]. RARP is an extension to ARP. It adds two new operation codes, 3 (request reverse) and 4 (reply reverse), for retrieving the IP address associated with a hardware address. BOOTP is a slightly more complex protocol, implemented on top of UDP. It performs the same function as RARP and also allows the station to "select a bootfile" that will be fetched later, e.g., through the "trivial file transfer protocol."

Both RARP and BOOTP were published in 1985. The emphasis at that time was on "diskless workstations," i.e., machines that for economy reasons had only volatile random access memory and no disk storage capacity. When such a machine was powered on, the memory was initialized to some random value. The only resilient memory was a small "read only memory" that contained a bootstrap code. The role of BOOTP in particular was to set up an IP address for these machines just after powering them up, then to fetch a less minimal bootstrap program through the network, and eventually to install the full system code in their memory.

The emphasis has now shifted away from diskless workstations. RARP or BOOTP do not remove the need for administration; they merely displace it. The administrator still has to allocate IP addresses, but, instead of having to manually install these data in each of the hosts, it suffices to administer a centralized RARP or BOOTP server. This is quite a distance from the goal of "plug and play" networking. In an ideal world, one would just take a station out of a box, plug in to the electricity and transmission networks, and power it on without any configuration whatsoever. There will probably not be a need for installing programs—even the smallest PC today has a disk, and it is quite reasonable to expect that it arrives from the factory with sufficient software already installed. What is needed is thus not so much bootstrapping as "autoconfiguration." The Dynamic Host Configuration Protocol (DHCP) [28] is a step in that direction.

Dynamic discovery through router advertisements, redirections, or even dynamic configuration by means of RARP, BOOTP, or DHCP do create a security risk. Suppose that a spy wants to listen to all of your packets or to capture your TCP-IP connections somehow. He can easily achieve this by sending a redirection command through his own IP station. The host that naively believes this command will send all its traffic to the spy. In fact, this is an example of a very generic problem, i.e., "should we believe networks?" In a very security-conscious environment, the answer is "certainly not." A secure station should in no way accept any data from the network without some proof of origin. Merely looking at fields in the packet, even source addresses or source ports, is not enough. Such information can be emulated very easily.

All of these procedures were in fact designed with the implicit assumption that the local network was secure—that only the "good guys" had access to machines in your subnet, on the same cable. This is reinforced by a couple of sanity checks on the redirect messages, for example, to accept only messages that suggest a redirection router located on the same subnet. Recent events have shown that "hackers" could in fact penetrate into remote subnets even without being physically able to access the machine. They would typically obtain an authorized user's password and from there on hack their way through the operating system's defenses ... and bugs. Nevertheless the general attitude is to try to increase the system's resistance to intrusion and to keep the simplicity of automatic configuration. As Vint Cerf once put it, users are ready to take amazing risks if it makes their lives simpler!

3.6 IP and Companion Protocols

IP is the Internet Protocol, but IP alone does not suffice in running the Internet. The Internet Protocol suite also comprises "transport control" protocols, notably TCP, and standard "applications" such as the "File Transfer Protocol" (FTP) or the "Simple Mail Transfer Protocol" (SMTP). Some of these applications are in fact part of the infrastructure and are used by other applications. This is the case of the "Domain Name Service" (DNS) and the "Simple Network Management Protocol" (SNMP).

The purpose of this book is to explain the Internet routing. Therefore, we will not invest much time in the study of the various transport protocols and applications. However, the transport protocols and the "infrastructure" applications are also used by routing protocols; we will thus briefly explain their broad characteristics.

3.6.1 TCP

IP provides a "best effort" service: most datagrams make their way to their destination, but there is no guarantee that all will. Local congestion may cause the discarding of queued packets; transmission errors may cause their loss. The nature of the datagram service may also result in "disordered delivery"—as packets are routed independently, they may be spread over parallel routes. If a datagram posted shortly after another takes a different and slightly shorter or slightly less loaded path, it will arrive first. In very rare cases of failure, the network may even "duplicate" a datagram and deliver several copies of it to the final destination.

The Transport Control Protocol was designed to hide these errors to the applications. TCP builds a reliable end-to-end "connection" on top of the datagram service. Each of the two communicating application programs can post a stream of octets over this "reliable pipe."

The TCP connection is set between two "ports" by an initial synchronization exchange. A TCP port is identified by an IP address and a 16-bit port number, i.e., a sub address that identifies an application within the host. The pair of IP addresses and port numbers uniquely identifies the connection.

The stream of octets is fractioned into TCP packets. Each packet carries a sequence number—the number of the first byte of the packet in the stream. That number is used to "reorder" the received packets. Regular acknowledgments inform the sender of the correct reception of the packets. Packets are protected by a timer. If a packet is not acknowledged after a time-out period, it will be repeated, thus correcting the error. The acknowledgments can be "piggybacked" in the data packets in the case of symmetric connections. They carry a "credit" indication, telling the partner how many bytes it can send without overflowing the recipient's buffers.

TCP is an evolving protocol. It was first standardized in 1978, and again in 1979 and 1981 [29, 30, 31], but major improvements on the timer management and congestion control were introduced by Van Jacobson in 1988 [25]. In the recent version of TCP, the value of the retransmission timers is determined by a statistical processing of acknowledgment delay, i.e., an estimation of the delay's average and standard deviation. This enables efficient retransmission over a large range of network conditions. The "slow start" algorithm helps avoid network congestion by always starting transmission at a low data rate which is then gradually increased and which will be rapidly decreased if a problem is detected. A new set of evolutions was proposed in 1992 [32] for adapting TCP to very high transmission rates, removing any structural limitations and allowing transfer at Terabits/s if indeed the hosts can process packets at that speed.

Most of the "standard" Internet applications are built on top of TCP. This is the case with telnet, FTP, or SMTP; this is also the case with new "multimedia document" applications such as "gopher" or "www." We will see that TCP is also used by the "Border Gateway Protocol" (BGP).

3.6.2 UDP

The User Datagram Protocol is an alternative to TCP for applications that prefer to use the datagram service directly. UDP allows applications to post packets to UDP "ports" identified by an IP address and a 16-bit port number. These applications will have to provide their own mechanisms for error correction and congestion control.

There are generally three reasons that make certain applications prefer to use UDP. Some client-server applications, like the DNS, consist of very simple exchanges: one query followed by one reply. Managing connections would be a waste, since the connection would have to be torn down immediately after a single packet exchange. Other applications are designed to run with extremely few resources. The classic example is the "Trivial File Transfer Protocol" [33] which is designed for use during "boot strap." Programming a simple loop of "sending a request," "await a response," requires less code than a full-scale file transfer over TCP.

Management applications like SNMP use UDP for another reason. They want to have complete control of their operation and want to make management decisions in case of transmission errors. They may wish, for example, to switch to another server, adopt a different transmission strategy, or concentrate on the high-priority tasks. This is also the case of many routing protocols—should a timer occur, it makes more sense to build a new message that reflects the new routing conditions than simply to let TCP retransmit the same data again and again.

3.6.3 DNS

The "domain name service" is the Internet name server, a very large distributed database. All Internet systems, routers, or hosts have a "domain name," e.g., "ds.internic.net." These names are used for retrieving the host addresses and for building mail addresses. The DNS also allows "reverse lookups," i.e., retrieving the domain name corresponding to an IP address.

The domain names have a hierarchical structure. The "top-level" domains correspond to classes of users (e.g., ".edu" or ".com") or to countries (e.g., ".us" or ".fr"). These top-level domains register "subdomains" (e.g., "isoc.org" or "inria.fr"). They check that the name is unique and keep track of the name server for that subdomain—the hosts that manage the corresponding part of the database. The hierarchical subdivision can be pursued recursively, for example, to name units of organizations or hosts. The structure guarantees that all databases can be accessed—the upper layer of the hierarchy can tell their location. The DNS protocol includes optimizations for speeding up the retrieval or increasing the resilience—a server's data may be copied in a "secondary server"; the responses to the most frequently asked questions may be kept in caches.

The most frequently used service is probably the "name to address" conversion. Directly listing host addresses in the user interfaces is impractical; a textual name is easier to remember than a numerical address. Applications should normally see names only for two other reasons: it provides isolation against changes of addresses, and it allows applications to pick "the best address" at any time. If a host has several network interfaces, it will have several addresses. The DNS will return all of them, and the transport interface should be allowed to pick the best one.

DNS names are also used in Internet "mail" addresses. Sending a message to "huitema@sophia.inria.fr" is normally accomplished by setting up a TCP connection to the SMTP server on the host "sophia.inria.fr" and requesting that program to deliver a message to the user "huitema." There are, however, many cases where the right-hand side of the address does not correspond to a host or when that host is not directly accessible. The DNS can thus return "mail relay" information, listing alternate hosts that can relay the message toward the named domain.

The DNS reverse look-up service returns a DNS name as a function of an IP address. It uses a special naming hierarchy. If a host receives an IP packet, it can identify the sending host by its IP source address (e.g., "138.96.24.84"). It will derive a conventional domain name from that address (e.g., "84.24.96.138.in-addr.arpa") and by querying the DNS retrieve the domain name of the host ("mitsou.inria.fr"). However, this service will work only if the match has been explicitly registered in the database of the server that manages the appropriate fraction of the "in-addr.arpa" domain.

Note that DNS names play absolutely no role in the routing of IP packets. Two hosts may have similar names, yet belong to different networks. To quote an example from my own organization, both hosts "merlot.inria.fr" and "margaux.inria.fr" belong to INRIA. Yet one of them is located in Rocquencourt near Paris and the other in Sophia-Antipolis near Nice, a distance of 700 kilometers (km). Their IP addresses are not correlated, and they are indeed not reached by the same route. Similar examples abound. Organizations located in a given country are normally named within that country's domain but may be served by any of the country's Internet providers. The routes toward them will not be correlated since there are as many "entry points" in a country as network providers.

3.6.4 SNMP

The "Simple Network Management Protocol" is an evolution of the "Simple Gateway Monitoring Protocol" [34]. The first version of SNMP was defined in 1988, was updated in 1989, and became an Internet standard in 1990 [35].

SNMP enables network managers to remotely monitor and control the evolution of network objects, e.g., routers or transmission equipment. The state of each object is represented by a number of variables and tables; the structure of these data is defined by a "management information base" (MIB). Monitoring is performed by reading these variables through SNMP commands; control is performed by "setting" some essential parameters to a new value. There are MIBs defined for a very large number of "managed objects," notably the generic MIB which describes an IP router [36] and specific MIBs which describe the variables and tables of each routing protocol.

SNMP is a very simple protocol, based on the client-server model and implemented over UDP. It has been designed to allow implementation in low-cost systems with little memory and computing resources. This was demonstrated by the implementation of a "toaster" controller on an 8-bit Z.80 microsystem. The simplicity of SNMP made it possible to require its support by all Internet systems, which in turn greatly facilitates the management of the Internet.

A new version of SNMP was defined by the IETF in 1993 [37] . The most important evolution of version 2 is the incorporation of more efficient security mechanisms based on state-of-the-art cryptographic technics. It also includes a couple of simplifications and an MIB description format that can be compiled easily [38].

3.7 Interconnecting Local Networks

In order to use the Internet, a host must implement IP and ICMP. It will send its datagrams to a router and will rely on that router for forwarding them. The routers must maintain routing tables that indicate the best path to each destination.

The connectivity of the Internet depends on the consistency and the regular updating of all the routing tables in all the Internet routers. This is the role of the routing protocols which we will detail in the next chapters.

References

1. S. E. Deering, "Host Extensions for IP Multicasting," RFC-1112, May 1988.

2. J. Reynolds and J. Postel, "Assigned Numbers," RFC-1700, October 1994.

3. D. Cohen, "On Holy Wars and a Plea for Peace," IEN-137, April 1, 1980.

4. J. Postel, "Internet Control Message Protocol," RFC-792, September 1, 1981.

5. S. Deering, "ICMP Router Discovery Messages," RFC-1256, September 5, 1991.

6. G. Malkin, "Traceroute Using an IP Option," RFC-1393, January 11, 1993.

7. D. Mills, "DCNET Internet Clock Service," COMSAT Laboratories, RFC-778, April 1981.

8. D. Mills, "Network Time Protocol NTP," RFC-958, September 1, 1985.

9. D. Mills, "Network Time Protocol Version 1 Specification and Implementation," RFC-1059, July 1, 1988.

10. D. Mills, "Network Time Protocol Version 2 Specification and Implementation," RFC-1119, September 1, 1989.

11. D. Mills, "Network Time Protocol (v3)," RFC-1305, April 9, 1992.

12. D. Mills, "Algorithms for Synchronizing Network Clocks," RFC-956, September 1, 1985.

13. D. Mills, "Experiments in Network Clock Synchronization," RFC-957, September 1, 1985.

14. D. Mills, "Measured Performance of the Network Time Protocol in the Internet System," RFC-1128, October 1, 1989.

15. D. Mills, "Simple Network Time Protocol (SNTP)," RFC-1361, August 10, 1992.

16. D. Plummer, "Ethernet Address Resolution Protocol: Or Converting Network Protocol Addresses to 48-bit Ethernet Address for Transmission on Ethernet Hardware," RFC-826, November 1, 1982.

17. D. Provan, "Transmitting IP Traffic Over ARCNET Networks," RFC-1201, February 1, 1991.

18. J. Renwirk and A. Nicholson, "IP and ARP on HIPPI," RFC-1374, November 11, 1992.

19. D. Katz, "Transmission of IP and ARP Over FDDI Networks," RFC-1390, January 5, 1993.

20. J. Lawrence and D. Piscitello, "The Transmission of IP Datagrams Over the SMDS Service," RFC-1209, March 6, 1991.

21. J. Korb, "Standard for the Transmission of IP Datagrams Over Public Data Networks," RFC-877, September 1, 1983.

22. A. Malis, D. Robinson, and R. Ullmann, "Multiprotocol Interconnect on X.25 and ISDN in the Packet Mode," RFC-1356, August 6, 1992.

23. T. Bradley, C. Brown, and A. Malis, "Multiprotocol Interconnect over Frame Relay," RFC-1490, July 26, 1993.

24. M. Laubach, "Classical IP and ARP over ATM," RFC-1577, January 20, 1994.

25. R. Braden, "Requirements for Internet Hosts—Communication Layers," RFC-1122, October 1, 1989.

26. R. Finlayson, T. Mann, J. Mogul, and M. Theimer, "Reverse Address Resolution Protocol," RFC-903, June 1, 1984.

27. B. Croft and J. Gilmore, "Bootstrap Protocol (BOOTP)," Stanford and SUN Microsystems, RFC-951, September 1985.

28. R. Droms, "Dynamic Host Configuration Protocol," RFC-1541, October 27, 1993.

29. J. Postel, "Specification of Internetwork Transmission Control Protocol, TCP Version 4," IEN-55, September 1978.

30. J. Postel, "Transmission Control Protocol," IEN-112, August 1979.

31. J. Postel, "Transmission Control Protocol," RFC-793, September 1, 1981.

32. D. Borman, R. Braden, and V. Jacobsen, "TCP Extensions for High Performance," RFC-1323, May 13, 1992.

33. K. Sollins, "The TFTP Protocol (Revision 2)," RFC-1350, July 10, 1992.

34. J. Case, J. Davin, M. Fedor, and M. Schoffstall, "Simple Gateway Monitoring Protocol," RFC-1028, November 1, 1987.

35. M. Schoffstall, M. Fedor, J. Davin, and J. Case, "A Simple Network Management Protocol (SNMP)," RFC-1157, May 10, 1990.

36. K. McCloghrie and M. T. Rose (editors), "Management Information Base for Network Management of TCP/IP-based Internets: MIB-II," RFC-1213, March 1991.

37. J. Case, K. McCloghrie, M. Rose, and S. Waldbusser, "Introduction to Version 2 of the Internet-standard Network Management Framework," RFC-1441, May 3, 1993.

38. Marshall T. Rose, *The Simple Book*, 2d ed. Prentice Hall Series in Innovative Technology, April 1993.

39. R. Droms, "Dynamic Host Configuration Protocol, " RFC-2131, March 1997.

40. S. Alexander, R. Droms, "DHCP Options and BOOTP Vendor Extensions," RFC-2132, March 1997.

41. K. McCloghrie, D. Perkins, J. Schoenwaelder, "Structure of Management Information Version 2 (SMIv2)," RFC-2578, April 1999.

From IPv4 to IPv6

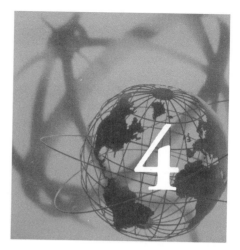

The choice of 32-bit addresses may have been a good decision in 1978, but by 1991 stresses were becoming apparent. According to the trends that were observed then, all class B network numbers would be allocated by 1994, the routing tables would explode soon, and all IPv4 addresses could well be allocated by 2002. The IAB sponsored a working group on the issue, whose main result was to initiate the "classless interdomain routing" effort (CIDR) that we will discuss in the third part of this book. But CIDR was only expected to provide temporary relief, and it was felt that we needed a replacement for the Internet protocol itself. The process was, for all its duration, tumultuous and controversial. The IAB initially proposed to build this new protocol out of CLNP, the Connection-Less Network Protocol defined by the ISO as part of the Open System Interconnection architecture, but this triggered a revolt by the rank and file of the IETF.

The cancellation of the IAB decision opened a period of competition. Several teams tried to develop their own solutions to the crisis and proposed their own versions of a new Internet Protocol. The IESG organized these groups in a specific area, managed by two co-directors, Scott Bradner and Alison Mankin, trying to set up a process that would converge on the best choice in a manner as fair and open as possible. In July 1994, the directorate selected the "Simple Internet Protocol Plus" proposal, whose main author was Steve Deering, as the basis for the new IP. The proposal then went through a cycle of successive refinements, leading to the specification of the "Internet Protocol version 6" which is now a stable "draft standard." The main feature of IPv6 is the new address size, 128 bits instead of 32, but IPv6 also figures a simpler header format and a number of revisions in the basic services.

4.1 IPv6 Address Architecture

Since IPv6 is based on the same architecture principle as the classic Internet protocol, IPv4, one could very well expect the IPv6 addresses to be larger versions of the IPv4 addresses, and one would be basically right. Like IPv4 addresses, IPv6 addresses identify an interface connected to a subnetwork, not a station. As in IPv4, a station that is *multihomed* will have as many addresses as interfaces. In fact, one big difference from IPv4 is that IPv6 routinely allows each interface to be identified by several addresses, in order to facilitate routing or management.

The IPv6 addresses belong to one of three categories:

☞ Unicast

☞ Multicast

☞ Anycast

Unicast is a new name for what we used to call point-to-point addresses. These addresses identify exactly one interface. More precisely, they identify exactly one interface within their scope of validity. A packet sent to an unicast address will normally be delivered to that interface.

A multicast address identifies a group of stations, or more precisely a group of interfaces. A packet sent to a multicast address will normally be delivered to all the members of the group.

An anycast address also identifies a group of stations. The difference between multicast and anycast is in the transmission process. Instead of being delivered to all members of the group, packets sent to a unicast address are normally delivered to only one point—the nearest member of the group. This facility did not exist in IPv4, although some researchers, notably Craig Partridge, conducted limited scope experiments and demonstrated its feasibility.

4.1.1 Notation of IPv6 Addresses

An IPv6 address is composed of 128 bits. The designers of the protocol chose to write these 128 bits as eight 16-bit integers separated by colons. Each integer is represented by four hexadecimal digits, as in:

FEDC:BA98:7654:3210:FEDC:BA98:7654:3210

Hexadecimal notation has the advantage of being relatively compact and straightforward. It is, however, a bit difficult to manipulate. Some see this lack of user friendliness as a definitive advantage. Users, they say, should manipulate names, not addresses. But system managers do have to manipulate these addresses. They will have to type them into directory files or administrative databases. One way to make their lives a little bit easier is to allow some abbreviations. Let's start by observing that, at least in the initial stage, we will not be using all 128 bits. There very likely will be many zeros, as in

1080:0000:0000:0000:0008:0800:200C:417A

A first improvement is the authorization to skip leading zeros in each hexadecimal component, that is, writing 0 instead of 0000, 8 instead of 0008, 800 instead of 0800. Another simplification is the double-colon convention. Inside an address, a set of consecutive null 16-bit numbers can be replaced by two colons. For example, we can replace three consecutive null numbers in the previous example and obtain the short form:

1080::8:800:200C:417A

Expanding the abbreviation is quite simple. Align whatever is at the left of the double colon to the left of the address: these are the leading 16-bit words. Then align whatever is at the right of the colons to the right of the address and fill up with zeros. The following are valid short forms and their extended notations:

FEDC:BA98::7654:3210, FEDC:BA98:0:0:0:0:7654:3210

FEDC:BA98:7654:3210::, FEDC:BA98:7654:3210:0:0:0:0

::FEDC:BA98:7654:3210, 0:0:0:0:FEDC:BA98:7654:3210

The double-colon convention can only be used once inside an address. For example, the address 0:0:0:BA98:7654:0:0:0 could be abbreviated as ::BA98:7654:0:0:0 or 0:0:0:BA98:7654::, but certainly not as ::BA98:7654::, which would be ambiguous.

Some IPv6 addresses are obtained by prepending 96 zero bits to an IPv4 address. To reduce the risk of erroneous transposition between the dot-decimal notation of IPv4 and the colon-decimal notation of IPv6, the specification introduces a specific format for these addresses. Instead of writing

0:0:0:0:0:0:A00:1

one can leave the last 32 bits in dot decimal form, as in

::10.0.0.1

The specification also introduces a notation for prefixes, i.e., the high-order bits of the addresses used by routing protocols. This notation is derived from IPv4, i.e., a regular IPv6 address followed by a slash and a number of bits. For example, the notation

FEDC:BA98:7600::/40

describes a 40-bit-long prefix, whose binary value is:

1111111011011100101110101001100001110110

Prefixes, like addresses, may be represented with the compressed notation. We have, however, to be careful, because prefixes may well include two ranges of zeroes. Suppose, for example, that we start from the IPv6 address

FEDC:BA98:0000:0076:0000:1234:5678:9ABC

and that we want to represent the 64-bit prefix of the network to which the interface belongs. We could think of (at least) four representations:

FEDC:BA98:0000:0076:0000:1234:5678:9ABC/64

FEDC:BA98::76:0:1234:5678:9ABC/64

FEDC:BA98:0:76::1234:5678:9ABC/64

FEDC:BA98:0:76::/64

The last one is obviously preferred, because it does not include any information that does not belong to the prefix. The other three, albeit correct, should only be used when both the host address and the prefix information have to be presented. The one mistake that should be avoided is the following:

FEDC:BA98::0076/64

It looks almost the same, but it expands to

FEDC:BA98:0000:0000

which is probably not what was expected....

4.1.2 Unicast Addresses, Prefixes and Subnets

IPv6 addresses follow the general structure of post-CIDR IPv4 addresses: host interfaces belong to subnets, and the addresses are composed of a subnet prefix and a host identifier. The subnet prefix itself is composed of a network identifier followed by a subnet identifier. In fact, the whole structure allows for an arbitrary number of components, of arbitrary sizes: small networks can be "aggregated" in larger networks, which can in turn be aggregated in even larger provider networks, so that at the highest level of the hierarchy the whole of the routing tables can be summarized by a few wide prefixes. In theory, the host, subnet, and network identifiers were supposed to be of variable length. In practice, fixed lengths were chosen for some of these fields.

The first IPv6 addresses will be allocated according to what was known as a provider-based plan, but which is now described as an aggregatable plan. Aggregatable global unicast addresses are composed of the 3-bit prefix 001 followed by four components. In the original IPv6 addressing architecture, all these components had a variable length, but the current trend is to insist on fixed length, essentially because this makes renumbering easier: replacing a 16-bit value by another 16-bit value is much less problematic than replacing it by a 15-bit value, let alone a 17-bit value.

Length (bits)	3	13	8	24	16	64
Address Part	001	TLA	reserved	NLA	SLA	Interface-ID

The second component of these addresses is the Top Level Aggregator (TLA). A TLA is assigned to a "first-level" entity in the routing hierarchy; for example, a large provider or maybe an "exchange point" that is used to join a set of secondary providers. The IANA is expected to allocate ranges of TLA to the various continental registries, which might further delegate the allocation of sub-ranges to national or regional registries, such as, for example, the French NIC managed by INRIA for French networks. In the core of the Internet, in the networks that compose the so-called default-free zone, the routing tables will need to have one entry per TLA, and are not expected to contain any more information, except indeed for the routing inside the TLA. The reserved size, 13 bits, is thought to be sufficient, since there are certainly fewer than 8,192 first-level providers or exchange points worldwide. However, in order to avoid a "gold rush" it was decided to also reserve the next 8 bits for possible extension of the TLA field, should 13 bits prove not to be sufficient.

The third address component identifies the Next Level Aggregator (NLA), which replaces the less generic subscriber identifier in the previous specification. That component is 24 bits long, and it will probably be structured by long-haul providers and exchanges, allocating, for example, the N topmost bits to identify a second-tier provider and the remaining 24-N bits to identify a subscriber to that second-tier provider. In fact, the official terminology cautiously avoids the words "subscriber" and "provider," but rather mentions a next-level aggregator of rank 1 and a Site identifier, which can in turn be further subdivided to allow many levels of hierarchy, as shown in the following examples:

n	24-n bits	16	64 bits
NLA1	Site	SLA*	Interface ID

n	m	24-n-m	16	64 bits
NLA1	NLA2	Site	SLA*	Interface ID

n	m	o	24-n-m-o	16	64 bits
NLA1	NLA2	NLA3	Site	SLA*	Interface ID

The fourth component of the address is the Site-Local Aggregator (SLA). The 16-bit identifier is normally allocated to a link within a site. The site itself is an atom in the addressing hierarchy. When a site is renumbered—for example, after changing provider—the TLA and the NLA components of the address may change, but the SLA and Interface ID will remain constant.

The last component of the address is the interface identifier that is unique to an interface connected to that link. In most cases, the 64-bit identifiers will be based on the IEEE EUI-64 format.

4.1.3 Special Address Formats

In addition to provider-based addresses, we may expect to encounter five more kinds of unicast addresses:

☞ Unspecified
☞ Loopback
☞ IPv4-based
☞ Site local
☞ Link local

The *unspecified address* is composed of 16 null bytes. It could be noted simply as two colons, the shortcut for 0:0:0:0:0:0:0:0. This address can only be used as a source address by a station that has not yet been configured with a regular address. It can also be used in some control messages when the presence of an address is semantically required but no address is available. It shall never be used as a destination address.

The loopback address 0:0:0:0:0:0:0:1 may be used by a node to send an IPv6 datagram to itself. The loopback address and the unspecified address may never be assigned to an interface.

It is possible to construct IPv6 addresses by prepending a null prefix, made of 96 zero bits, to the 32-bit *IPv4 address*. These addresses will typically be noted by combining the double-colon and the dotted decimal notation of IPv4, as in ::10.0.0.1. We should note that the reserved prefix of eight zero bits is common to the unspecified address, the loopback address, and IPv4-derived addresses.

Many organizations use the TCP-IP technology without being actually connected to the Internet, either because they are afraid of the security implications of a direct connection or because they want to set up and try their internal network without waiting to complete the connection procedure. The *site-local* addressing prefix, 1111 1110 11, has been reserved for these organizations. A typical site-local address will consist of this prefix, a set of zeros, the subnet identifier, and the station identifier:

	12 bits	36 bits	16 bits	64 bits
Field	Link local prefix	Reserved	Subnet id	Station-id
Value	1111 1110 11	0	(local choice)	64 bit unique ID

The site-local addresses cannot be routed on the global Internet. Their uniqueness is only guaranteed within a site. They can only be used for exchanges between two stations within a single site.

Stations that are not yet configured with either a provider-based address or a site-local address may use the *link local addresses*. These addresses are composed of the link local prefix, 1111 1110 10, a set of zeros, and a station identifier:

	12 bits	52 bits	64 bits
Field	Link local prefix	Reserved	Station-id
Value	1111 1110 10	0	64 bit unique ID

These addresses are only defined within a link and can only be used by stations connected to the same link or to the same local network. Packets sent to these addresses will never be relayed by a router.

4.1.4 Multicast Addresses

The design of the IPv6 multicast address takes advantage of the experience gained on research networks such as Dartnet since 1988 and also on the MBONE since 1992. Multicast addresses have the following format:

8 bits	4 bits	4 bits	112 bits
11111111	Flags	Scope	Group ID

The first octet of the address is the multicast prefix 11111111. It is followed by 4 bits of flags, 4 bits of scope, and a group identifier. Out of the 4 bits of flags, only the fourth is defined in the IPv6 specifications. The three other bits are reserved and should be initialized to zero:

0	0	0	T

The fourth bit is abbreviated T for Transient. A permanently assigned address is a well-known address, assigned by a global Internet numbering authority. A transient address is one that is not permanently assigned. This is what is typically in use in the MBONE today. When a group decides to conduct a multicasting session, it asks the *session directory* tool to pick an address at random. The unicity of this random address is verified by a collision detection algorithm. Once the session is terminated, the address is released.

The scope is encoded as a 4-bit integer. It is used to limit the scope of the multicast group, for example, to ensure that packets sent into a local videoconference do not leak on the world-wide Internet. The values are defined in the following table:

Scope	Definition
0	reserved
1	node-local
2	link-local
3	unassigned
4	unassigned
5	site-local
6	unassigned
7	unassigned
8	organization-local
9	unassigned
A	unassigned
B	unassigned
C	unassigned
D	unassigned
E	global
F	reserved

The same functionality could only be obtained in IPv4 by careful tuning of the TTL field. The IPv6 specification allows a much more precise definition. However, it obliges routers to enforce scope boundaries. In particular, the site and organization scopes can only be enforced if routers know which link belongs to what site and to what organization.

We should note that the scope indicator does not influence the meaning of a permanently assigned group. Consider, for example, the group identifier 43 (hex), which has been assigned to the *Network Time Protocol* (NTP) servers. We can decline it with five scopes, 1, 2, 5, 8, and E, to obtain five multicast addresses:

☞ FF01::43 represents all NTP servers on the same node as the sender.

☞ FF02::43 represents all NTP servers on the same link as the sender.

☞ FF05::43 represents all NTP servers in the same site as the sender.

☞ FF08::43 represents all NTP servers in the same organization as the sender.

☞ FF0E::43 represents all NTP servers in the Internet.

Unlike NTP, many groups can only be used within some limited scopes. For example, sending a message to "all dynamic host configuration servers on the Internet" would not make much sense.

Group identifiers such as "all NTP servers" are normally allocated by the Internet Assigned Numbers Authority. They are generally hardwired in the application that characterizes the group. All network time management programs, for example, are expected to know that the address of "all NTP servers on the site" is FF05::43. They will declare their membership to this group when the program is started, exactly in the same way that members of a videoconference will join the multicast address that has been dynamically allocated to their group.

The IPv6 specification only defines four permanent group identifiers, which all IPv6 nodes are expected to understand:

☞ The group identifier 0 is reserved. It shall not be used with any scope.

☞ The group identifier 1 defines all the IPv6 nodes' addresses. It can be used with a scope of 1, FF01::1, to identify all nodes on this node, or with a scope of 2, FF02::1, to identify all nodes on this link.

☞ The group identifier 2 defines all the IPv6 routers' addresses. It can be used with a scope of 1, FF01::2, to identify all routers on this node, or with a scope of 2, FF02::2, to identify all routers on this link.

☞ The group identifier 10000 (hex) defines the group of all dynamic host configuration servers (DHCP servers and relays). It should be used with a scope of 2, FF02::1:0, to identify all DHCP servers and relays on this link.

The specification also reserves a range of multicast addresses, from FF02::1:0:0 to FF02::1: FFFF:FFFF, which is used by the IPv6 equivalent of the Address Resolution Protocol.

4.1.5 Anycast

While multicasting has been happily tried by tens of thousands of IPv4 stations on the MBONE, anycasting was still a research project when the IPv6 specs were written. The principle of anycasting, in itself, is very simple. Instead of sending one packet to a specific server, one sends the packet to a generic address that will be recognized by all the servers of a given type, and one trusts the routing system to deliver the packet to the nearest of these servers. One could use anycasting to find out the nearest name server, the nearest file server, or the nearest time server.

Anycast addresses are treated by hosts in exactly the same way as unicast addresses. They should contain a valid prefix, typically the identification of the "subnet," in which the anycast address is valid, and a unique identifier. In the most common formats, the identifier occupies the last 64 bits of the address and is structured in EUI-64 format, using a reserved prefix to avoid collisions with registered identifiers:

Subnet prefix (64 bits)		Unique identifier (64 bits)	
n bits	64-n bits	57 bits	7 bits
Subnet prefix	Subnet pad.	1111110111...111	Anycast Id.

The load is on the routing system, which has to maintain one route for each anycast address that is active in a given subnet.

4.2 The IPv6 Header Format

The new IPv6 header is composed of a 64-bit header, followed by two 128-bit IPv6 addresses for source and destination, for a total length of 40 bytes.

Version	Traffic class	Flow label	
Payload length (16 bits)		Next header type	Hop limit
Source address (128 bits)			
Destination address (128 bits)			

Just looking at this format, we see the prominent changes between v4 and v6:

☞ The header format is much simpler.
☞ There is no header checksum.
☞ There is no segmentation procedure.
☞ The options have disappeared.

4.2.1 A Simpler Header

The experience acquired between 1978 and 1994 allowed the authors of IPv6 to propose a much simpler header for the IPv6 packets. In fact, the first 64 bits of the packet only include 6 parameters:

☞ Version field (4 bits)
☞ Traffic class (8 bits)
☞ Flow label (24 bits)
☞ Length of the payload (16 bits)
☞ Type of the next header (8 bits)
☞ Hop limit (8 bits)

The version field carries the binary value 6, and is used to distinguish IPv6 packets from IPv4, should these packets be carried on the same channels. In fact, whenever possible, IPv4 and IPv6 will be demultiplexed at the media layer. For example, IPv6 packets will be carried over Ethernet with the content type 86DD (hexadecimal) instead of IPv4's 8000.

The traffic class is essentially equivalent to the IPv4 "Type of Service," which is currently under revision as part of the "differentiated services" initiative. We will present this initiative in our chapter on resource reservations.

The flow label is used to distinguish packets which "require the same treatment," i.e., which are sent by a given source to a given destination, with a given set of options. We will also detail the handling of these fields in chapter 14.

The total length of IPv4 is replaced by the *payload length* of IPv6. There is a subtle difference, because the payload length, by definition, is the length of the data carried after the header.
In IPv4, the length value includes the length of the IPv4 header. In IPv6, it excludes it. In IPv6
as well as IPv4, the length field is encoded on 16 bits, which limits the packet size to 64 kilo-
bytes. We will see later that IPv6 has in fact some provision for larger packets, using the "jumbo-
gram" option.

The protocol type field was renamed *next header type* to reflect the new organization of the
IP packets. In IPv4, the IP header is always immediately followed by the transport protocol data,
for example, a UDP or TCP packet. The simpler of the IPv6 packets will have exactly the same
structure, in which case the next header type will be set to the protocol type of UDP (17) or TCP
(6). But we will see in the next section that one can also interleave *extension headers* between the
IP and TCP or UDP payload. The next header type will then be set to the type of the first extension header.

The renaming of the time-to-live (TTL) field to *hop limit* follows a sound design principle:
truth in advertising. In IPv4, the time to live was expressed as a number of seconds, indicating
how long the packet could remain in the network before being destroyed. The notion of time to
live was based on a theoretical analysis of transport control protocols. If packets were allowed to
remain infinitely in the network, old copies could pop out at unexpected times and cause protocol errors. TCP, for example, has the notion that a *connection context* shall remain idle for some
time after the end of the connection, in order to ensure that all packets belonging to the old
instantiation of the context have been purged from the network. This mechanism only works if
the transport protocol machinery knows how long a packet can stay in the network, which is
indeed the purpose of the TTL field. The IPv4 specification mandates that the TTL be decremented by each router from 1 second or the time spent waiting in the router queues if it is larger
than 1 second. But it is very difficult to actually estimate the waiting time of a specific packet.
Since this time is usually counted in milliseconds rather than seconds, most routers simply decrement the TTL by 1 at each relay. This behavior has been made official in IPv6, hence the new
name of the field. It counts a number of hops, not a number of seconds. Transport protocols are
supposed to provide their own protections against the resurgence of old packets, for example, by
using time stamps as specified in RFC1323 or large numbering fields.

4.2.2 Simplifications

The IPv4 header was based on the state of the art of 1975. We should not be surprised to
learn that, about 20 years later, we know better. We could thus proceed with three major simplifications:

☞ Assign a fixed format to all headers.
☞ Remove the header checksum.
☞ Remove the hop-by-hop segmentation procedure.

IPv6 headers do not contain any optional element. This does not mean that we cannot
express options for special-case packets. But we will see in the next section that this is not

achieved with a variable-length *option field* as in IPv4. Instead, *extension headers* are appended after the main header. An obvious consequence is that there is no need in IPv6 for a header length field (IHL).

Removing the header checksum may seem a rather bold move. The main advantage is to diminish the cost of header processing, because there is no need to check and update the checksum at each relay. The obvious risk is that undetected errors may result in misrouted packets. This risk is minimal, however, since most encapsulation procedures include a packet checksum. One finds checksums in the media access control procedures of IEEE-802 networks, in the adaptation layers for ATM circuits, and in the framing procedures of the Point-to-Point Protocol (PPP) for serial links.

IPv4 included a fragmentation procedure so that senders could send large packets without worrying about the capacities of relays. These large packets could be chopped into adequately sized fragments, if needed. The recipients would wait for the arrival of all these segments and reconstitute the packet. But we learned an important lesson from the experience with transport control protocols: the unit of transmission should also be the unit of control. Suppose that we try to transmit large packets over a network that can carry only small segments. The successful transmission of a packet depends on the successful transmission of each segment. If only one is missing, the whole packet should be transmitted again, resulting in a very inefficient use of the network. The rule with IPv6 is that hosts should learn the maximum acceptable segment size through a procedure called *path MTU discovery*. If they try to send larger packets, these packets will simply be rejected by the network. As a consequence, there is no need in IPv6 for the segmentation control fields of IPv4—the packet Identification, the segmentation control Flags, and the Fragment Offset. IPv6 includes, however, an end-to-end segmentation procedure, which will be described in the next section. Also, all IPv6 networks are supposed to be able to carry a minimum packet size of 1280 octets. Hosts that do not want to discover, or remember, the path MTU can simply send small packets.

4.2.3 From Options to a Daisy Chain of Headers

The IPv4 header had room for options, allowing special-case treatment of some packets. The original specification included codes for security options, source routing, and recording or time stamping. Options, however, fell gradually out of use, mostly because of performance effects. The routing code is highly optimized for the most common case, and the packets that deviate from that common case are handled by some "exception" procedure, often implemented with much slower hardware. As a result, options have been all but eliminated from the IPv4 practice.

There are, however, good reasons to require special-case treatment of some packets, for example, if one wants to request a specific route through source routing or if one wants to specify a particular handling of the packet by the receiver. Learning a lesson from the IPv4 experience, IPv6 specifies how these special-case treatments can be obtained through extension headers. In IPv4, the payload—for example, the TCP packet—immediately follows the IP header. But in IPv6, it is possible to insert an arbitrary number of *extension headers* between the IP header and the payload. Each header is identified by a header type and carries the header type of the following header in the chain, or that of the payload in the case of the last extension.

The current IPv6 specification defines six extension headers:

☞ Routing
☞ Fragment
☞ Encrypted security payload
☞ Authentication
☞ Destination options
☞ Hop-by-hop options

4.2.4 Routing Header

The handling of options within IPv6 is best exemplified with the routing header, which plays the same role as the source routing option of IPv4. This header essentially carries a list of intermediate addresses through which the packet shall be relayed—a *source route* that may be either strict or loose.

Next header	Hdr. ext. length	Routing type = 0	Segments left
Reserved			
IPv6 address (1)			
IPv6 address (2)			
...			
IPv6 address (N)			

The routing header is composed of a set of parameters, followed by a list of addresses. The first 32 bits contain four 8-bit integers:

☞ The next header, which identifies the type of header immediately following the routing header in the daisy chain of headers
☞ The length of the extension header, expressed as a number of 64-bit words
☞ The routing type, set to 0 according to the current specification; further values would perhaps later be used to identify alternative header format
☞ The number of addresses or "segments" that are not yet processed

In IPv6, routers will only look at the routing header if they recognize one of their own addresses in the destination field of the main header. Intermediate routers that are not explicitly mentioned in the source route will forward the packet without any additional processing. This should result in better performance.

The station that recognizes one of its own addresses in the destination field examines the routing header. It will first check whether there is a segment left. If there is none, the packet has arrived at the end of the source route. The station skips over the routing header and processes the next header, whose type is indicated in the next header parameter. Otherwise, the station shall proceed with the source routing. The station swaps the destination address and the next element in the address list, then decrements the number of segments left and forwards the packet.

4.2.5 Fragment Header

Contrary to IPv4, IPv6 routers do not fragment oversized packets. Everything happens as if the IPv4 *don't fragment* bit was implicitly set. If a packet is larger than the next hop's MTU, it will be rejected and an ICMP message will be sent back. However, there is a provision in IPv6 to fragment packets before they are sent in the network. These will typically be used by protocols such as UDP, when the application wants to send a message that is too large to fit in a single packet. The UDP payload will be transmitted in a succession of IPv6 packets. In each of these packets, a fragment header will be interposed between the IPv6 header and the actual payload:

First packet	IPv6 header, next header = fragment	Fragment header (initial)	UDP header + payload
Next packet	IPv6 header, next header = fragment	Fragment header	
Final packet	IPv6 header, next header = fragment	Fragment header (final)	

Each fragment will be routed independently. The fragmentation is performed by the initial sender, not by the network. The reassembly is performed at the final destination. The fragment header contains sufficient information to enable the destination to concatenate the fragments.

Next header	Reserved	Fragment offset	Res	M
Identification				

Apart from the next header parameter, which identifies the next header in the daisy chain, the fields in the IPv6 fragment header are almost identical to the fragmentation control parameters of the IPv4 header. The *identification* is equivalent to the packet identification, with the notable difference that it is encoded on 32 bits instead of 16. The *fragment offset* also plays the same role as the offset field of IPv4, but is encoded slightly differently. IPv4 uses the least significant 13 bits of a 16-bit word, while IPv6 encodes the offset in the most significant bits. In both cases, fragmentation is supposed to occur on a 64-bit word boundary. The IPv4 offset must be multiplied by 8 to obtain an octet offset, while in IPv6 it suffices to zero the three least significant bits. In fact, the main difference lies in the flag fields. There is no fragmentation control bit in the IPv6 header because this header is only inserted when the sender has decided to fragment the packet. We will only find a *more fragment* bit, which will be set to 1 for all but the last fragment of a complete packet.

4.2.6 Security Headers

IPv6 provides two types of security headers, the authentication header (AH) and the encrypted security payload (ESP). The AH is used to prove that the packet comes for the specified origin, and that it was not in any way modified during the transit. The AH does not actually hide the payload, which is transmitted "in the clear." The ESP also provides the authentication service, but in addition encrypts the payload so that it cannot be observed in transit.

Examples of IPv6 packets using AH or ESP

The authenticated header has a very simple syntax. It starts by a 64-bit header which comprises the number of the next header in the daisy chain, the length of the header in units of 32 bits, 16 reserved bits which should be left to zero, and the 32-bit Security Parameter Index of the security association. This fixed 64-bit header is followed by the authentication data, encoded as a variable number of 32-bit words. The encrypted security payload starts with a 32-bit Security Parameter Index and continues with encrypted data whose exact syntax depends on the encryption algorithm.

4.2.7 Destination Options Header

There will be two ways to add functionality to IPv6. The first is to define a new extension header type that will be carried transparently throughout the network and will only be examined by the station specified in the destination address. This first extension method has, however, two inconveniences.

☞ It requires the allocation of header-type numbers. There are only 256 such numbers, and they are used for extension headers as well as payload types, such as UDP, TCP, or alternatives. They are a relatively scarce resource that should not be wasted.

☞ It requires that both source and destination understand the new option. If a station does not understand the type of a header, it can only reject the whole packet.

The IPv6 *options header* obviates this inconvenience. It uses a single header type (60) to define a generic *destination options* header. This header may contain as a parameter one or several options identified by option types. Each option is encoded as a variable number of octets.

The problem with this kind of extensible syntax is that some destinations may well fail to recognize some of the newly added options. The consequences of such failures may vary. Some options merely provide additional information on the packet context or express preferences. If they are not recognized, they can be safely ignored. The processing node will merely skip the option data field, whose length is indicated by the option data length octet, and try to process the remaining options in the header. Some options, on the contrary, are critical and cannot be safely ignored. The packet must be discarded. However, when a station discards a packet, the general rule is to send back an ICMP report. This may or may not be what the sender expects. The option codes, in addition to identifying the option, also use two bits to specify the expected behavior when the option is not recognized: just ignore it, silently discard the packet, discard the packet and send an ICMP report.

4.2.8 Hop-by-Hop Options

The destination option header is a regular extension header, which will only be processed when the packet has reached its final destination. This is in conformance with the general IPv6 philosophy of avoiding unnecessary processing by intermediate relays. However, some management functions or debugging functions require that additional information be passed to all routers. This is the purpose of the hop-by-hop options header. It is identified by the header type 0. A null next header value in the IPv6 header implies the presence of the hop-by-hop option header that shall be processed even if the destination address is not one of the local node addresses.

The hop-by-hop options header has exactly the same format as the destination option header, and hop-by-hop options also have the same encoding rules as the destination options. One such option is the *jumbo payload* option, with option type 194. This option is used to send very large packets whose length could not be encoded on 16 bits. When this option is used, the IPv6 length field is set to zero. The processing node shall decode the jumbo payload option to find out the actual packet length, encoded as a 32-bit integer. To facilitate the processing of this length field, the alignment requirement of option 194 is set to 4n + 2 so that the length field itself starts on a 32-bit boundary.

The jumbo payload option shall not be used if the length is less than 65,535 octets. It shall also not be used if the packet carries a fragment header. In fact, the definition of the jumbo payload option is a compromise between the initial design of IPv6 and the networking requirements of supercomputers.

4.2.9 Extension Header Order

A packet may well contain more than one extension header. This should not pose any problem to the receiving nodes, which will simply process the headers in the order in which they are received. The early design documents described this as an "onion-peeling" procedure. Each successive layer would be processed in turn, just like removing each layer of an onion in turn. Indeed, some of the layers have a magic of their own, like the fragment layer or the routing layer, or rather the routing header and fragment header. Fragmented packets must be reassembled before any further processing. It is only after the last fragment has arrived that the node can start unpeeling the next header. The routing header is a different case. If a node is not the last in the list of intermediate relays, it should update the destination field and forward the packet, without even looking into the next header.

The processing order is determined by the order of the headers in the daisy chain. This order is specified by the initial sender. The IPv6 specifications include a recommended order of headers:

1. IPv6
2. Hop-by-hop options
3. Destination options (1)
4. Routing

5. Fragment
6. Authentication
7. Destination options (2)
8. Upper-layer (for example, TCP or UDP)

Each of these headers is indeed optional. There is no need to insert a hop-by-hop header if one does not use hop-by-hop options. One will not use the routing header if one does not want to mandate a specific routing. One will not use any fragmentation header if the packet is smaller than the path's MTU. The recommended order is in fact a ranking of headers; it provides guidelines for implementors. We may observe that the destination option header is listed twice. If we want to specify tunnelling options that will be processed by all intermediate relays, we will place these options before the routing header. If, on the other hand, we want to pass information to the final destination, we will insert the option header immediately before the upper-layer header.

If we want to mandate only one relay in the path, we may replace the routing header by a complete IPv6 packet in order to build up a tunnel. The header type for the encapsulation of IPv6 is 41. This encapsulated payload will have the same recommended ordering as the routing header. The processing of the header will be somewhat faster, because all data that precede the encapsulation are simply removed.

There may be some need (e.g., for debugging purposes) to send a packet that does not include any upper-layer data. In this case, the daisy chain of headers should be ended by a *no next header* type, whose value is 59.

4.3 ICMP v6

The Internet Control Message Protocol (ICMP) was also revised during the definition of IPv6. The revision followed the same guidelines as that of the Internet Protocol itself. The protocol was streamlined. Some functionalities which were present in the IPv4 ICMP but were not used anymore have been removed. Then, the protocol was made more complete by incorporating the multicast control functions of the IPv4 Group Membership protocol, IGMP. (We will present IGMP in the multicast chapter.) Some formats were extended to carry the larger fields of IPv6. As a result, the new ICMP is not compatible with the old one. In order to avoid any confusion, it is identified by a different header type—58 instead of 1.

Type	Length	Checksum
ICMP body		

Generic format of ICMP messages

All ICMP messages share the same format, a 32-bit header followed by a variable-length ICMP body. The header includes the ICMP message type, a code field used to create an additional level of message granularity beyond the type, and a 16-bit checksum that protects both the ICMP message and a "pseudo-header." The pseudo-header includes the IPv6 source and destination addresses and compensates, in a way, for the lack of checksum in the IPv6 header. The ICMP specification only defines six basic ICMP message types:

1	Destination Unreachable
2	Packet Too Big
3	Time Exceeded
4	Parameter Problem
128	Echo Request
129	Echo Reply

Types 1 to 4 define error messages that IPv6 stations send when they cannot process an IPv6 message. Type 128 and 129 are used to implement the IPv6 version of "ping." Additional ICMP message types are defined in the neighbor discovery and autoconfiguration specifications that we will present in the next section and in the multicast listener discovery procedures that we will present in the multicast chapter.

4.4 Address Resolution

To transmit Internet packets on a particular subnet, on a particular media, the Internet stations must determine the subnet address or media address of the target station. When Steve Deering wrote the initial specification of SIP, he assumed that SIP would rely on the same Address Resolution Protocol (ARP) as IPv4. But further work in the SIP, SIPP, and IPv6 working groups led to the development of the neighbor discovery procedure that encompasses the functions of ARP as well as those of router discovery.

A characteristic of IPv6 neighbor discovery is that it is defined in generic terms as part of IPv6 ICMP. This is a major difference from IPv4, in which a different address resolution protocol could be defined for each new media. There is indeed a matter of chicken and egg here. ICMP messages, like any IPv6 messages, can only be transmitted if the host knows the media address of their destination. This is solved by the use of multicast transmission. As long as the media address of the destination remains unknown, the messages are sent to multicast addresses. The media-level multicast address is supposed to be determined by an algorithm that may vary from media to media. For media of the IEEE-802 family such as Ethernet or FDDI, the 48-bit multicast address is obtained by concatenating a fixed 16-bit prefix, 3333 (hexadecimal), and the last 32 bits of the IPv6 multicast address. This prefix has been reserved by Xerox for use with IPv6.

The description of the neighbor discovery procedures will assume that the host maintains four separate caches:

☞ The destinations' cache has an entry for each destination address toward which the host recently sent packets. It associates the IPv6 address of the destination with that of the neighbor toward which the packets were sent.

☞ The neighbors' cache has an entry for the immediately adjacent neighbor to which packets were recently relayed. It associates the IPv6 address of that neighbor with the corresponding media address.

☞ The prefix list includes the prefixes that have been recently learned from router advertisements.

☞ The router list includes the IPv6 addresses of all routers from which advertisements have recently been received.

In the remainder of this section, we will assume that these tables are present when we describe the basic discovery procedures.

4.4.1 Getting Information from Routers

The router list is built from the "router advertisements" received by the host. This is in fact a major difference with the IPv4 practice, where hosts are often expected to either spy onto routing exchanges or be parametrized with the address of the router. In IPv6, routers are expected to regularly transmit router advertisements. If they do not receive any advertisement, the hosts know that they cannot join any router: the subnet to which the interface is attached is not "connected."

Type = 134	Code = 0			Checksum	
Cur. Hop Limit	M	O	Res.	Router Lifetime	
Reachable Time					
Retransmission Timer					
Options...					

Router advertisement message

The router advertisements provide routing information.

☞ The *max hop limit* is an 8-bit unsigned integer. It is programmed by a network manager as a parameter of the router's interface and is passed by routers to hosts as a suggestion of a reasonable value to use when sending IPv6 packets.

☞ The *router lifetime* parameter is a 16-bit integer. It indicates the number of seconds during which the advertising router could be held in the hosts' router lists, to be used as a default router.

☞ The *reachable time* is a 32-bit integer. It indicates the time, in milliseconds, during which any neighbor is expected to remain reachable after it has somehow advertised its media address. It may be set to zero if the router does not want to indicate a specific value.

☞ The *reachable retransmission timer* is a 32-bit integer. It indicates the interval, in milliseconds, between successive solicitations of a neighbor that is not returning solicited neighbor advertisements. Here again, a value of zero means that the router does not want to specify a value.

☞ The *source link layer* option allows routers to advertise their media address so that each host will not need to send a neighbor solicitation message to the router.

☞ The *MTU option* is transmitted by routers that operate on links, such as token rings, that do not have a well-defined MTU. The router advertisement provides an easy vehicle for managers who want to specify a value common to all hosts. This option is encoded on exactly 64 bits (length = 1) and is identified by the option type 5.

4.4.2 The Neighbor Discovery Algorithm

To transmit a packet, the host must first find out the next hop for the destination. The next hop shall be a neighbor directly connected to the same link as the host. The host should then find a valid media address for that neighbor.

In many cases, a packet will already have been sent to the destination, and the neighbor address will be found in the destinations' cache. If this is not the case, the host will check whether one of the cached prefixes matches the destination address. If this is the case, the destination is local; the next hop is the destination itself. In the other cases, the destination is probably remote. The host should then select a router from the table of routers and use it as the next hop.

Once the next hop has been determined, the corresponding entry is added to the destinations' cache, and the neighbors' cache is looked up to find the media address of that neighbor. At this stage, there are four possibilities:

1. If there is no entry for that neighbor in the cache, the host should send a neighbor solicitation message. The neighbor is then added to a new cache line whose status is set to *incomplete*.

2. If there is already an entry for that neighbor, but its status is incomplete, the host should wait for the completion of the procedure to learn the media address and send the packet.

3. If there is a *complete* line in the cache for the neighbor, the media address is known and the packet can be sent immediately.

4. If the neighbor's entry in the cache has not been refreshed for a long time, its status is suspect. The media address can be used, but a neighbor solicitation message should be sent.

Type = 135			Code = 0	Checksum	
R	S	O	Reserved		
Solicited address					
Options...					

Neighbor solicitation message

The *neighbor solicitation* messages are ICMP messages of type 135. The code is set to zero, and the checksum is computed according to ICMP rules. The message contains a target address parameter, set to the address of the solicited neighbor. An option field should contain the media address of the soliciting host encoded as a source link-level address option, as in the router solicitation message.

The IPv6 source address of the solicitation messages is always set to the link local address of the interface, and the hop count is always set to 1. The destination address, however, is not the IPv6 address of the solicited neighbor but a multicast address derived from it, the *solicited node multicast address*. The media address used for sending this ICMP message will be derived from this multicast address.

The solicited node multicast address is formed by concatenating a fixed 96-bit prefix, FF02:0:0:0:1, and the last 32 bits of the node's IPv6 address. All nodes are expected to compute the solicited node multicast addresses corresponding to each of their configured addresses, including the link local address, and to join the corresponding multicast groups.

The solicitation message will be received by all hosts that have at least one address whose last 32 bits match those of the solicited neighbor's address. Each of them will examine the target address parameter. If it matches one of its addresses, the solicited host will reply with a *neighbor advertisement* message. The advertisement is sent back to the solicitor's IPv6 address, using the link layer address specified in the solicitation. The source address should normally be the solicited IPv6 address, but there can be some exceptions, which we will detail in the next section.

Type = 136		Code = 0	Checksum
R	S	O	Reserved
Solicited address			
Options...			

Neighbor advertisement message

The *neighbor advertisement* messages are ICMP messages of type 136. Their target address parameter is the solicited target address. They contain the media address of the target in a *target link layer address* option, whose format is identical to that of the source link layer address option except for the type field. Target address options have the type 2. The second 32-bit word of the ICMP message starts with three 1-bit flags: R, S, and O. The router flag (R) is set to 1 when the solicited node is a router. The solicited flag (S) is set to 1 when the advertisement is sent in response to a solicitation. The override message (O) is set to 1 when the new value should override a previous cache entry.

When the soliciting host receives the advertisement message, it updates the corresponding entry in its neighbor cache. The entry is now complete, the neighbor is reachable, and packets can be transmitted.

IPv6 stations may in some circumstances send unsolicited advertisements. In this case, the destination will be set to the all nodes multicast address and the S bit will be set to 0.

4.4.3 Redirects

The procedure used by hosts to find the next hop is very simple. There will be cases when the hosts will pick the wrong next hop, for example, if there are several routers connected to the link but they send the packet to the wrong one, or if they send the packet to a router although the destination is in fact connected to the same link. Picking the wrong next hop is an error, albeit a benign one. The router that receives the misdirected packet will retransmit it to the correct next hop. The packet will eventually reach its destination, but it will be transmitted twice on the local link.

After redirecting the packet to the correct destination, the router may send a redirect message to the host so that the next message sent to that destination travels only once on the local network.

The *redirect* messages are ICMP messages of type 137. They contain two address parameters. The destination address is that of the offending packet that triggered the redirection. The target address is that of a better next hop for that destination. The message may contain the media address of this next hop, encoded as a *target link layer address* option. It may also contain a copy of the first bytes of the offending packet, encoded as a redirected header option.

Type = 137	Code = 0	Checksum
Reserved		
Target address		
Destination address		
Options...		

Redirect message

When a host receives a redirect message, it should update the destination's entry in its destination cache, replacing the erroneous next hop by the suggested value. If the target link layer address option is present, the host will also update the next hop's entry in the neighbors' cache.

4.4.4 The Case of Nonconnected Networks

The neighbor discovery algorithm relies on the presence of routers, especially as a fallback next hop when the destination is not recognized as local. The hosts should, however, also be capable of operating in routerless environments, such as small offices.

The absence of a router will be easily recognized by the hosts, because they will never receive any router advertisement. The router list and the prefix list will remain empty. In this situation, the hosts should only use their link local addresses as source addresses. It may well occur, however, that some stations on the same link have been configured with other addresses, either manually or by using a configuration server. A typical example would be that of anycast addresses.

In the absence of routers, the hosts will simply consider all addresses to be local. The next hop for any destination will be that destination itself. If it happens to be connected to the same link, the link layer address will be discovered and packets will be exchanged.

4.4.5 Black Hole Detection

IPv6 includes automatic autoconfiguration and router discovery procedures. The reference implementation that we described uses caches to remember the results of next hop computation and redirects as well as the media addresses of neighbors. There is always a risk that these procedures will go afoul and that the station ends up sending packets to a router that is not operational anymore, to a media address that is not connected anymore. The result would be a black hole. Packets will be sent toward a dead end—they will be lost somewhere in an electronic limbo. It is thus very important to check that the information present in the various caches is still valid. This is the role of the *neighbor unreachability detection* procedures defined as part of IPv6 neighbor discovery.

A host can often learn that a destination is reachable without any specific procedure. The most obvious case is when the packets sent on a TCP connection between that host and the destination are regularly acknowledged or, in fact, when any upper-level connection is making progress. In that case, the TCP process or the upper-level process can pass *reachability indications* to the IPv6 process, indicating that the corresponding entries in the destinations' and neighbors' caches are still valid. Some applications are, however, strictly unidirectional. If a host is sending video packets over UDP, it probably does not expect acknowledgments. In that case, the entry in the neighbor cache will age.

When no confirmation has been received for a reachable time interval, by default 30 seconds, the entry in the neighbor cache becomes dubious. The entry can still be used for sending a few packets. A few seconds after transmitting the next packet, the host should actively seek confirmation of the neighbor's reachability by sending a solicitation message. If the neighbor responds with a solicited advertisement, the reachability is confirmed and the entry may remain in the cache for another reachable time interval. Note that only solicited advertisements, explicitly addressed to the solicitor, count. Receiving a multicast message only proves one-way connectivity. It does not prove that the solicited host receives the solicitor's messages.

If the solicitation fails, it can be repeated a few times. If no response arrives in that interval, the neighbor is considered unreachable. Packets bound to that neighbor will be discarded, and an ICMP message will be sent back to indicate unreachability. The corresponding entry is removed from the neighbor's table and a new next hop must be computed for all the destinations that were reached through that neighbor.

If some of the routers in the routers' list are unreachable, the host should not choose them as the next hop for default destination. If all routers are unreachable, the host should try each in turn so that they will all be tested for reachability.

A particular case of unreachability may occur when a station ceases to behave as a router and becomes a simple host, when its routing capabilities are disabled. This station will still respond to solicitations, but the hosts should examine the router flag (R) in the advertisements. If the host believes that the station was the router but receives an advertisement in which the R flag is null, it should remove the corresponding entry from the list of routers. It should also choose a new next hop for all the entries that were previously reached through that router.

4.4.6 Random Delays

The neighbor discovery procedures use a number of timers and repetitions. In many cases, some messages have to be repeated at regular intervals. This is the case for router advertisements and solicitation messages during the duplicate detection procedure or the unreachability detection procedure. To avoid simultaneous transmission of messages by multiple sources and the resulting peaks of traffic and collisions on the wire, the value of these intervals is not fixed, but chosen at random between a minimum and a maximum. Examples of random intervals are:

☞ The interval between successive transmission of router advertisements in order to avoid synchronization between all routers.

☞ Advertisements sent by routers in response to solicitations may be delayed by a small random value in order to avoid simultaneous arrival of multiple advertisements at the soliciting host. If the advertisements are multicast, they must be delayed.

☞ Hosts should wait for a small random delay before sending their initial solicitations. If many hosts are initialized at the same time—after a power failure, for example—the small delay will avoid a solicitation storm.

The random values, or rather the pseudo-random values, are generally provided by a pseudo-random number-generation algorithm. This pseudo-random number generator should indeed be designed to be as random as possible. Obviously, if all stations used the same algorithm and initialized it at the same time with the same values they would all obtain the same sequence of pseudo-random numbers. This would result in undue synchronizations and collisions. A reasonable precaution is to seed it with node-specific numbers, for example, the Ethernet address of the interface or the serial number of the computer.

4.4.7 Protection Against Off-link Messages

The reliance on ICMP messages for neighbor discovery introduces a potential risk. Vile hackers, from a part of the Internet of which you had not heard before, could send forged router advertisements or redirect messages to your machine, playing havoc with local routing and address assignment.

The "off-link" menace is eliminated by a clever choice of the hop-count, suggested by Bob Gilligan. The hop-count of all address configuration and neighbor discovery messages will be set to the maximum value, 255.

This is harmless, because these messages will never be relayed. It is also a very powerful test. As the hop-count is decremented by every relay, only local packets may arrive with a hop-count of 255. By discarding incoming neighbor discovery packets whose hop-count is not set to 255, hosts will effectively protect themselves against off-link.

4.5 Automatic Configuration

Address configuration is an integral part of any IPv6 implementation. It comes both in a stateless mode and in a stateful mode, the latter using an IPv6 version of DHCP. Addresses would be assigned to interfaces for a limited lifetime.

4.5.1 Link Local Addresses

As soon as an interface is initialized, the host can build up a link local address for this interface by concatenating the well-known link local prefix and a unique token—a number that is unique to this host on this link. In most cases, the unique token is a 64-bit EUI-64 identifier, which can be derived from the 48-bit Ethernet address. These identifiers are supposed to be unique worldwide.

Link local addresses can only be used on the local link. This may be adequate in an isolated network, but they will not be sufficient for organizing a large network. In this case, the link local addresses will be used to bootstrap the acquisition of global addresses through either the stateless or stateful procedures. But first, one must check that the address is indeed unique.

4.5.2 Duplicate Detection

The autoconfiguration procedure can only work if a unique token is assigned to each interface. In principle, most interfaces come out with a worldwide unique EUI-64 identifier, which should form perfectly adequate tokens. But errors may occur because some manufacturers of very low-cost devices are known to use unregistered numbers, leading to potential collisions. Then there is always the case of odd networks that do not use IEEE-802 addressing. Resorting to random numbers may cause problems, in particular when the random generators are not well behaved. Because duplicate addresses can cause severe problems, it is important to detect and report these errors as soon as possible.

The detection of duplicate addresses uses the neighbor discovery procedures. Once an address has been configured, the host sends a solicitation message toward that address and waits for one second. If another station has been configured with the same address, it will reply and advertise its link layer address, exposing the collision. At this point, the host will know that its number is not unique and that the corresponding addresses should not be used. It will then either pick a new number, if that is possible, or display an error message and ask for human intervention.

This procedure is not perfect. The absence of a reply may be caused by the absence of a collision, but it may also be due to the loss of the initial solicitation or of the reply itself. Stations are supposed to retry the procedure several times before being reasonably sure of the uniqueness of their token. These trials should be sufficiently spaced to avoid link layer congestion. According to the current specification, the message should be sent only once, after a delay chosen at random between 0 and 3 seconds.

4.5.3 Stateless Autoconfiguration

IPv6 nodes start initializing their behavior by joining the *all-nodes* multicast group. This is done by programming their interfaces to receive all the packets sent to the corresponding multicast address, FF02::1. They will then send a solicitation message to the routers on the link, using the *all-routers* address, FF02::2, as destination and their own link local address as source.

Type = 133	Code = 0	Checksum
Reserved		
Options…		

Neighbor advertisement message

A *router solicitation message* is an ICMP message of type 133. The ICMP code is set to zero and the checksum is computed according to the usual procedure for ICMP messages. The solicitation message may include options, which are encoded in a type-length-value format, using one octet for the type, one octet for the length, and a variable number of octets for the value itself. The only option that is expected in the solicitation message is the link layer address of the source, for example, its Ethernet or token ring address.

Routers will reply to the solicitation by sending back *router advertisements*. Depending on timers and network configuration, the advertisements can be sent either directly to the host or to the all-hosts multicast addresses. Router advertisements contain several parameters. The parameters used by the address configuration procedures are two control bits, noted M and O, and the *prefix information* option. The *managed address configuration* bit is set to 0 when the stations are authorized to perform stateless autoconfiguration. If it is set to 1, the stations should not attempt to build up addresses themselves, but should contact an address configuration server, using a stateful protocol. The *other configuration* flag is set to 1 when the stations can do stateless address configuration, but should contact a configuration server for obtaining other parameters. When the M bit is null, the station will examine the list of prefixes encoded as options.

There may be several prefix information options in a message, each of which encodes a 128-bit address; a prefix length expressed as a number of bits; and a valid and a preferred lifetime, expressed as a number of seconds before the address may be invalidated or deprecated. Two 1-bit flags qualify the prefix. The *on-link* bit, L, is set when the prefix is specific to the local link, when it can be entered in the list of local prefixes used by the neighbor discovery procedures. The *autonomous configuration* bit, A, is set when the prefix may be used for autonomous address configuration. In this case, the station will construct an address by replacing the last bits of the prefix by the interface's unique token, typically by the EUI-64 identifier of the interface.

The station that has sent a solicitation is supposed to wait for a response. To protect itself against transmission errors, it will repeat its solicitation if it does not receive a response after a reasonable delay, for example, after 2 seconds. However, it should not repeat the solicitation more than three times. Failure to receive a response after three solicitations indicates that there is probably no router on the link. The station can only communicate with other stations connected on the same link. It should only use its link local address.

4.5.4 Stateful Configuration

Stateless configuration has many advantages. It is very simple to use and does not require any servers. It has, however, two inconveniences: a relatively inefficient use of the address space and a lack of network access control.

Stateless autoconfiguration is based on unique tokens that tend to be 64 bits long. Using 64 bits of address space for a single Ethernet segment is not very efficient, especially if we consider that the whole Internet today uses 32-bit addresses. We may consider that this addressing inefficiency is a small price to pay for simpler management, that each customer network will have at least 80 bits of address space, and that the remaining 16 bits are more than enough to number all the customer subnetworks. But the managers of very large networks may have a different opinion. They may want to use an internal addressing hierarchy that will require much more than 16 bits. If addresses are assigned by servers, they could be made arbitrarily short, for example, using only 8 bits per segment if less than 256 computers are connected to the segment.

Stateless autoconfiguration may also ease the task of spies and hackers. The whole idea of plug and play is that the legitimate user takes the machine out of the box, plugs it in, and runs. This also means that if hackers manage to carry computers within the premises, they will be able to just plug them in and run as if they were legitimate local users. One may well argue that this is already the case, that it suffices for the hacker to use the address of one of the local machines that happens to be silent at the time of the intrusion. One may further argue that real security has to involve authentication and encryption, that just disabling autoconfiguration is not very useful. But some managers will insist on enforcing administrative controls nevertheless.

The routers' advertisements may specify that the host should use *stateful configuration* by setting up the *managed configuration* bit. If the host receives a message as to where this bit is set, it should solicit the nearest address server. Isolated hosts will not receive any router advertisement. They should also try to contact a local address server.

The stateful configuration protocol is an IPv6 version of the IPv4 Dynamic Host Configuration Protocol (DHCP). This protocol will be upgraded to deliver IPv6 addresses as well as IPv4 addresses. The multicast address FF02::1:0 has been reserved for the group of all DHCP servers. It should be used to discover the local server.

4.5.5 Lifetime of Addresses

For a very long time, Internet users believed that they owned their IPv4 address, their network number. We will show, when we present "Classless Inter-Domain Routing," that this cannot be the case anymore. One should be able to aggregate network numbers, which implies a dependency between addresses and network topology.

Network topology can change in many ways. Customers may change providers, company backbones may be reorganized, or providers may merge or split. If the topology changes with time and if the addresses must somehow reflect the topology, then addresses will have to change from time to time.

Addresses obtained through either stateless or stateful configuration will have a limited lifetime. In the stateful configuration, the lifetime will be indicated by the address server. In the stateless configuration, the lifetime of the address will be deduced from the lifetime of the prefix, as indicated in the routers' advertisement.

An address whose lifetime has expired becomes invalid. It shall not be used anymore as a source address by the local host nor as a destination address by its partners. This can have very harsh consequences on ongoing communications. TCP connections, for example, are established between a pair of Internet addresses. If one address becomes invalid, the TCP connection will be interrupted. The only ways to alleviate this are to change the TCP and to avoid using addresses that will soon become invalid.

The address configuration working group of the IETF had no mandate to change TCP, but it did insert a mechanism that makes it easier to predict that one address will shortly become invalid. IPv6 addresses will have two lifetimes: the valid lifetime and the preferred lifetime. An address whose valid lifetime has expired should not be used at all. An address whose preferred lifetime has expired becomes invalid. It should not be used for starting new connections. When a TCP process starts a connection, it knows the destination address, but can choose any of the local addresses as a source address. It should pick the one that has the longest preferred lifetime or, at a minimum, it should avoid using any address that is already deprecated or that will very soon be deprecated.

Hosts are expected to receive router advertisements continuously. They will examine the prefixes contained in these advertisements. If the prefix is already known, they will use the valid and preferred lifetimes contained in the advertisement to update the one that they stored when the corresponding address was autoconfigured. If they learn a new prefix, if the autonomous configuration flag is set, they will autoconfigure a new address. This way the set of addresses attached to each interface is expected to continuously evolve.

Both valid and preferred lifetimes may be set to infinity, a conventional value encoded as 32 one bits. In this case, the address will never be invalidated or deprecated. This is by definition the case of the link local address, which will remain permanently valid.

4.5.6 Updating the Name Servers

Host configuration requires more than just address configuration. We will see that the neighbor discovery procedures allow hosts to configure key parameters such as the local subnetwork prefixes or the addresses of the local routers. But normal Internet operation also requires that the host learn its name. This name and the host's addresses should be registered in the Domain Name Service (DNS).

A normal complement to dynamic address configuration is dynamic update of the DNS. This procedure is currently being studied in the IETF.

4.6 When Will We Deploy IPv6?

The IETF has been working on the IPv6 specifications since 1994, but the deployment of IPv6 has hardly begun. In a book published in 1997 [1], I wrote that "the successful transition to IPv6 is conditioned by the publication of standards, by the delivery of IPv6 products and by the existence of a management infrastructure." Standards are now ready: the main specification has reached "draft standard" status, and the other specifications are either in "draft" or "proposed" status. Many implementations are already available, for most varieties of personal computer systems, workstations, and routers. These implementations have been shown to interoperate through various tests, conducted in particular by the Inter Operability Laboratory of the University of New Hampshire. An early management infrastructure has been set in place, using test addresses and the "6 Bone." This name is a short notation for IPv6 BackBone; it is implemented as an overlay over the Internet. In short, all the milestones that I mentioned in 1997 have been met. But all these deployments are definitely of an experimental nature. In 1999, there is hardly any real IPv6 usage.

To use popular proverbs, we can say that part of the problem is "chicken and egg," and part is "carrot and stick." The "chicken and egg" part is very obvious. Manufacturers of routers, developers of operating systems, and network service providers will only propose fully supported IPv6 products if there is sufficient customer demand, but customer demand can hardly manifest itself when no such products are available. To break this circle, the "carrot and stick" part becomes necessary. IPv6 provides some advantages over IPv4, in particular a better support for real time and security, while the looming menace of address exhaustion may act as a stick. Deployment of new large networks in places like China or India may be thwarted by the limited availability of IPv4 addresses; connection of "information appliances" to the Internet will require large blocks of addresses. For current users, the main advantage will be the ease of configuration provided by the autoconfiguration procedures.

IPv6 deployment may be postponed indefinitely. It may also start at any time if, for any reason, the chicken and egg circle is broken—for example, if Microsoft decides to provide IPv6 support in a future version of Windows. In that case, the pressure could build very fast, and the whole Internet could transition to IPv6 in a few years.

In the next chapters that present routing protocols, we will systematically address how these protocols are being upgraded to support IPv6.

References

1. C. Huitema, "IPv6, the Next Internet Protocol," 2d ed., Prentice Hall, 1997.

2. S. E. Deering, R. Hinden, "Internet Protocol, Version 6 (IPv6) Specification," RFC-2460, December 1998.

3. R. Hinden and S. Deering, "IP Version 6 Addressing Architecture," RFC-2373, July 1998.

4. R. Hinden, M. O'Dell, and S. Deering, "An IPv6 Aggregatable Global Unicast Address Format," RFC-2374, July 1998.

5. R. Hinden and S. Deering, "IPv6 Multicast Address Assignments," RFC-2375, July 1998.

6. R. Hinden, "Proposed TLA and NLA Assignment Rule," RFC-2450, December 1998.

7. R. Hinden, R. Fink, and J. Postel, "IPv6 Testing Address Allocation," RFC-2471, December 1998.

8. A. Conta and S. Deering, "Internet Control Message Protocol (ICMPv6) for the Internet Protocol Version 6 (IPv6) Specification," RFC-2463, December 1998.

9. S. Kent and R. Atkinson, "Security Architecture for the Internet Protocol," RFC-2401, November 1998.

10. S. Kent and R. Atkinson, "IP Authentication Header," RFC-2402, November 1998.

11. S. Kent and R. Atkinson, "IP Encapsulating Security Payload (ESP)," RFC-2406, November 1998.

12. T. Narten, E. Nordmark, and W. Simpson, "Neighbor Discovery for IP Version 6 (IPv6)," RFC-2461, December 1998.

13. S. Thomson and T. Narten, "IPv6 Stateless Address Autoconfiguration," RFC-2462, December 1998.

14. M. Crawford, "Transmission of IPv6 Packets Over Ethernet Networks," RFC-2464, December 1998.

15. M. Crawford, "Transmission of IPv6 Packets Over FDDI Networks," RFC-2467, December 1998.

16. M. Crawford, T. Narten, and S. Thomas, "Transmission of IPv6 Packets Over Token Ring Networks," RFC-2470, December 1998.

17. D. Haskin and E. Allen, "IP Version 6 over PPP," RFC-2472, December 1998.

18. A. Conta and S. Deering, "Generic Packet Tunnelling in IPv6 Specification," RFC-2473, December 1998.

19. G. Armitage, P. Schulter, M. Jork, and G. Harter, "IPv6 Over Non-Broadcast Multiple Access (NBMA) Networks," RFC-2491, January 1999.

20. G. Armitage, P. Schulter, and M. Jork, "IPv6 over ATM Networks," RFC-2492, January 1999.

Part II
Interior Routing Protocols

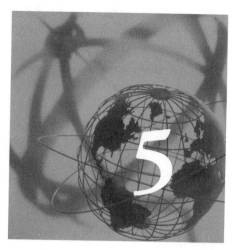

Why Is RIP So Simple?

$\mathbf{T}$he most widely used "interior gateway protocol" in today's Internet is probably "RIP." These initials stand for Routing Information Protocol, but the long form is seldom spelled out—internauts seem to love acronyms and use them as common words.

5.1 Routing Information Protocol

RIP is a very simple protocol of the "distance vector" family. The distance vector protocols are often referred to as "Bellman-Ford" protocols because they are based on a shortest path computation algorithm described by R. E. Bellman [1], and the first description of the distributed algorithm is attributed to Ford and Fulkerson [2]. Distance vector protocols have been used in several packet networks, such as the early Arpanet or Cyclades. These early experiments have been the basis for numerous developments, notably PUP and then the XNS Routing Information Protocol by Xerox—the first occurrence of the acronym RIP. The Internet RIP was initially developed as a component of the Berkeley UNIX networking code and was in fact largely inspired by XNS-RIP.

After presenting the distance vector algorithm and the particular design choices of the first and second versions of RIP, we will review a number of improvements which have been suggested to this algorithm.

5.2 An Introduction to Distance Vector Protocols

As we said, RIP is a protocol of the distance vector family. In order to explain RIP, let's forget for a moment the Internet and its complexity and consider a network of five nodes and six links.

This is an example network: we don't differentiate between hosts and routers, subnets and links, or packet switches and terminals. The nodes in our test network are capable of relaying packets, and the purpose of the routing exchanges is to compute routing tables that indicate to each of these nodes how to reach a given peer. Each node is identified by its address, which we represent as A, B, C, D, or E, and the routing table has one entry for each of these addresses. For simplicity's sake, we will assume that the links are symmetric. We will use this simple example to present the behavior of the distance vector protocols.

5.2.1 Cold Start

Suppose now that we initialize the network by powering up all nodes simultaneously, doing what specialists call a "cold start." We will require minimum permanent knowledge in each of the nodes, merely to remember their own addresses and to be able to identify the links to which they are attached. This is characterized as "local knowledge": the nodes know their own local conditions, but ignore the global network topology. They don't know how many other nodes there are; they don't even know who is at the other end of their local links. In this initial condition, the routing tables are skeletal. They contain one single entry, for the node itself. For example, the table of A has the value:

From A to	Link	Cost
A	local	0

Node A abstracts this table in a distance vector that has exactly one component:

A = 0

It will "broadcast" this distance vector to all its neighbors or, more precisely, on all the local links. As a result, both B and D will receive the information and will be able to enlarge their knowledge. Take the example of B. Before receiving the message from A, its routing table had only one entry.

From B to	Link	Cost
B	local	0

Node B receives on link number 1 the distance vector A = 0. Upon reception of this message, it updates all the distances by adding to them the cost of the local link, which we will assume to be 1, and transforms the message into A = 1. It will then compare the information in the distance vector to its local routing table entries, observe that A is still unknown, and thus add a new entry to the table.

From B to	Link	Cost
B	local	0
A	1	1

It can now prepare its own distance vector and send it on the local links: i.e., 1, 4, and 5:

```
B = 0, A = 1
```

During this period, D will also have received the initial message from A and have updated its routing tables to:

From D to	Link	Cost
D A	local 3	0 1

It will also have to transmit its own distance vector on links 3 and 6.

```
D = 0, A = 1
```

The message from B will be received by A, C, and E; the one from D will be received by A and E. We will suppose, for the clarity of the exposition, that the message from B is received first.

On receiving the message on link 1, A will update the distances to B = 1, A = 2. It will observe that the distance A = 2 is larger than the local entry and will thus insert the information only on node B. Then, when receiving the message from link 3, it will insert the information on node D. The new table will be:

From A to	Link	Cost
A B D	local 1 3	0 1 1

Node C will receive the distance vector B = 0, A = 1 on link 2, and will update its own routing table to:

From C to	Link	Cost
C B A	local 2 2	0 1 2

Node E will also receive the distance vector B = 0, A = 1 on link 4, and will update its own routing table to:

From E to	Link	Cost
E B A	local 4 4	0 1 2

It will then receive the distance vector D = 0, A = 1 on link 6, update it to D = 1, A = 2, and will notice that the entry D should be inserted, but that the distance to A through link 6 is exactly equal to the distance to A through link 4. We will assume that in this case it will refrain from modifying the table entry. Therefore the new value will be:

From E to	Link	Cost
E	local	0
B	4	1
A	4	2
D	6	1

Now that A, C, and E have computed new routing tables, they will summarize their information in their own distance vectors which they will send on their local links.

```
From A: A = 0, B = 1, D = 1 on links 1 and 3
From C: C = 0, B = 1, A = 2 on links 2 and 5
From E: E = 0, B = 1, A = 2, D = 1 on links 4, 5, and 6
```

This will trigger an update of the routing tables from B, D, and E to:

From B to	Link	Cost
B	local	0
A	1	1
D	1	2
C	2	1
E	4	1

From D to	Link	Cost
D	local	0
A	3	1
B	3	2
E	6	1

From E to	Link	Cost
E	local	0
B	4	1
A	4	2
D	6	1
C	5	1

B, D, and E can now prepare their own distance vectors.

```
From B: B = 0, A = 1, D = 2, C = 1, E = 1 on links 1, 3, and 4
From D: D = 0, A = 1, B = 2, E = 1 on links 3 and 6
From E: E = 0, B = 1, A = 2, D = 1, C = 1 on links 4, 5, and 6
```

These will be received by A, C, and D, and will result in up-to-date tables.

From A to	Link	Cost
A	local	0
B	1	1
D	3	1
C	1	2
E	1	2

From C to	Link	Cost
C	local	0
B	2	1
A	2	2
E	5	1
D	5	2

From D to	Link	Cost
D	local	0
A	3	1
B	3	2
E	6	1
C	6	2

At this stage, the algorithm has converged. A, C, and D will prepare their new distance vectors and send them on the local links, but these messages will not trigger any updates in the routing tables of B, D, and E. We can say that, through distributed computations, the nodes have *discovered the topology of the network.*

5.2.2 What If a Link Breaks?

We have seen in the preceding section how one could use distance vectors to compute routing tables. These tables have been computed and the different nodes are happily exchanging packets, when suddenly link number 1 "breaks." This can, and does, happen quite often in real-life networks for reasons ranging from power failures to fires, not to exclude the attraction of backhoes for telecommunication lines or the tendency of some operators just to unplug this link because they don't remember anybody using it. The topology is now:

```
(A)     xxxxx   (B)  — 2 —  (C)
 |               |          /
 3               4         /
 |               |        /
(D)  — 6 —  (E)  — 5 —
```

Let's now suppose that the two nodes A and B, which are located at the ends of link 1, discover this failure, for example, by monitoring the transmission equipment. They should immediately update their routing table by noting that link 1 now has an "infinite" cost, and that all nodes previously reached through link 1 are now located at an infinite distance. The new tables will look like:

From A to	Link	Cost
A	local	0
B	1	inf
D	3	1
C	1	inf
E	1	inf

From B to	Link	Cost
B	local	0
A	1	inf
D	1	inf
C	2	1
E	4	1

Nodes A and B will prepare and send their new distance vectors.

```
From A: A = 0, B = inf, D = 1, C = inf, E = inf on link 3
From B: B = 0, A = inf, D = inf, C = 1, E = 1 on links 2 and 4
```

The message sent by A will be received by D, which will update the distances to take into account the cost of link number 3 to

```
A = 1, B = inf, D = 2, C = inf, E = inf
```

The elements of the distance vector will be compared to the entries in its routing table. D will notice that all distances are larger than or equal to the recorded distances, but that link 3, on which the message was received, is exactly the one used for reaching B; thus, the entry for B should be updated to reflect the new value. The new table will look like:

From D to	Link	Cost
D	local	0
A	3	1
B	3	inf
E	6	1
C	6	2

Similarly, C and E will now update their routing tables to:

From C to	Link	Cost
C	local	0
B	2	1
A	2	inf
E	5	1
D	5	2

From E to	Link	Cost
E	local	0
B	4	1
A	4	inf
D	6	1
C	5	1

These three nodes will now prepare and send their new distance vectors.

```
From D: D = 0, A = 1, B = inf, E = 1, C = 2 on links 3 and 6
From C: C = 0, B = 1, A = inf, E = 1, D = 2 on links 2 and 5
From E: E = 0, B = 1, A = inf, D = 1, C = 1 on links 4, 5, and 6
```

These messages will trigger an update of the routing tables of A, B, D, and E to:

From A to	Link	Cost
A	local	0
B	1	inf
D	3	1
C	3	3
E	3	2

From B to	Link	Cost
B	local	0
A	1	inf
D	4	2
C	2	1
E	4	1

From D to	Link	Cost
D	local	0
A	3	1
B	6	2
E	6	1
C	6	2

From E to	Link	Cost
E	local	0
B	4	1
A	6	2
D	6	1
C	5	1

After these updates, A, B, D, and E will send their new distance vectors.

```
From A: A = 0, B = inf, D = 1, C = 3, E = 2 on link 3
From B: B = 0, A = inf, D = 2, C = 1, D = 1 on links 2 and 4
From D: D = 0, A = 1, B = 2, E = 1, C = 2 on links 3 and 6
From E: E = 0, B = 1, A = 2, D = 1, C = 1 on links 4, 5, and 6
```

This will lead to the update of the routing tables of A, B, and C.

From A to	Link	Cost
A	local	0
B	3	3
D	3	1
C	3	3
E	3	2

From B to	Link	Cost
B	local	0
A	4	3
D	4	2
C	2	1
E	4	1

From C to	Link	Cost
C	local	0
B	2	1
A	5	3
E	5	1
D	5	2

A, B, and C will prepare and send their new distance vectors, but these will not trigger any update in the routing tables. The new routes have been computed, and the global connectivity has been restored.

5.2.3 The Bouncing Effect

In the preceding example, we assumed that all links had a cost of 1. This is not necessarily the case: some links are slower or perhaps more expensive than others. Let's assume that link 5 has a cost of 10, while all others have a cost of 1.

We shall concentrate on the routes from the various network nodes to node C. In a stable condition, after a successful cold start, we would have the following routes:

From	Link	Cost
A to C	1	2
B to C	2	1
C to C	local	0
D to C	3	3
E to C	4	2

Suppose now that link number 2 breaks. This failure is immediately noticed by B, which updates the "distance to B" to infinity. For a short period, the entries toward C in the table look like:

From	Link	Cost
A to C	1	2
B to C	2	inf
C to C	local	0
D to C	3	3
E to C	4	2

We shall suppose that, just before B has had the time to send its distance vector to its neighbors, A sends its own distance vector to B and D. Most implementations of the distance vector protocols mention that the messages should be repeated at regular intervals in order to cope with network losses, so this spurious transmission may very well happen. The message will have no effect on D, as the distance corresponds to what is already in the table. But B will add the cost 1 to the distance 2 advertised by A for C and notice that the cost 3 is lower than the infinite cost present in the tables. It will update its own table to indicate that C is now reached through link 1 with a cost of 3 and it will advertise this new distance to its neighbors A and E. As the advertisement comes over links 1 and 4 that A and E use respectively to reach C, they will update their routing tables. The situation is now:

From	Link	Cost
A to C	1	4
B to C	1	3
C to C	local	0
D to C	3	3
E to C	4	4

Note that the routing tables now include a loop: packets bound to C will reach B and then bounce back and forth between A and B until their "time to live" expires. This phenomenon is called the "bouncing effect." It will cease only after the network converges on a new, coherent version of the routing table.

If, at this moment, C advertises its distance vector on link 5, the node E will add the cost 10 to the incoming metric of 0, observe that this total cost is higher than the current content of the tables, and ignore the message. Now, if A and E broadcast their new distance vector, it will trigger an update at node B and D, which routes towards A and E. The new value is:

From	Link	Cost
A to C	1	4
B to C	1	5
C to C	local	0
D to C	3	5
E to C	4	4

After B transmits its own distance vector, the cost of entry for C at node A will increase to 6. A will then transmit this new cost to both D and B, resulting in:

From	Link	Cost
A to C	1	6
B to C	1	7
C to C	local	0
D to C	3	7
E to C	4	6

At this stage, the messages sent by C are still ignored by E, because the cost of entry for C at E is still lower than 10. In fact, at each round of exchange, the distance to node C will be incremented by 2 in each of the nodes A, B, D, and E. After the next round, we will get:

From	Link	Cost
A to C	1	8
B to C	1	9
C to C	local	0
D to C	3	9
E to C	4	8

The next message from B will trigger an update to 10 of the cost at A, which will transmit the new value to B and D, which will both update their cost to 11. B will transmit the value 11 to A and E, which yields:

From	Link	Cost
A to C	1	12
B to C	1	11
C to C	local	0
D to C	3	11
E to C	4	12

Now, if E receives an advertisement from C, it will take it into account and, shortly after the table entries, converge to the new value.

From	Link	Cost
A to C	1	12
B to C	4	11
C to C	local	0
D to C	6	11
E to C	5	10

Finally, the computation is complete. But it has taken a number of steps, essentially because the network has to increase the various distances gradually. As one "round" of messages increases the cost of 2 units, we needed five exchanges to increase them by the value of 10, which is necessary to reach the next step. Note that this is a random process, as the outcome may vary according to the order of transmission of their messages by the various sites. Note also that the intermediate states are very painful—as loops do occur, packets will accumulate and very likely "congest" the corresponding links. Then, the congestion may trigger the loss of packets, including the loss of routing messages. This will further delay the convergence to stable state.

5.2.4 Counting to Infinity

Consider again the example of section 5.2.2. We have seen how new routes were computed after the failure of link number 1. Let's now suppose that the link number 6 also breaks, giving the following topology:

Note that this link failure isolates nodes A and D from the nodes B, C, and E. Let's abandon B, C, and E to their fates and look at what happens between A and D. D has noticed the link failure and has updated its routing tables accordingly.

From D to	Link	Cost
D	local	0
A	3	1
B	6	inf
E	6	inf
C	6	inf

If D has the opportunity to transmit its new distance vector immediately, A will immediately update its table and notice that all nodes, except D, are now unreachable: the algorithm will have converged. But if A first has a chance to transmit its last distance vector:

```
From A:  A = 0,  B = 3,  D = 3,  C = 3,  E = 3
```

then the table at D will be updated to:

From D to	Link	Cost
D	local	0
A	3	1
B	3	4
E	3	4
C	3	4

We have now installed a loop, as in the previous example. But, as B, C, and E are effectively isolated, there is no chance to converge naturally to a stable state. At each exchange, the distances to B, C, and E will just increase 2 units. This process is called "counting to infinity" and can be stopped only by a convention on the representation of infinity as some very large distance: i.e., larger than the length of the worst possible path in the network. When the distance has reached this value, the entry in the routing table is considered infinitely remote and thus unreachable.

As in the previous case, we can see that the intermediate state of the network during the count to infinity is very messy: packets will loop, links will be congested, and routing packets themselves can be lost due to congestion. But one can prove that, in the absence of further changes in the topology, the network will slowly converge to the new state.

5.2.5 Split Horizon

The bouncing effect and the long time taken for counting to infinity are very undesirable features of the distance vector protocols. Several techniques have been investigated to try to minimize this effect, among which "split horizon" and "triggered updates" are implemented in RIP.

Split horizon is based on a very simple precaution: if node A is routing packets bound to destination X through node B, it makes no sense for B to try to reach X through A. Thus, it makes no sense for A to announce to B that X is only a short distance from A. The change from the original version of distance vector protocol is minimal: instead of broadcasting the same distance vector on all outgoing links, the nodes will send different versions of this message, to take into account the fact that some destinations are actually routed through the said outgoing link.

Split horizon comes in two variations. In the simple form, the nodes simply omit from their messages any information about destinations routed on the link. This strategy relies either on routes never being announced or on old announcements fading away through a time-out mechanism. The form known as "split horizon with poisonous reverse" is more aggressive: the nodes will include all destinations in the distance vector message, but will set the corresponding distance to infinity if the destination is routed on the link. This will immediately kill two-hop loops. It is very easy to show that this technique would have immediately eliminated the count to infinity in the example network examined in section 5.2.4.

Split horizon, however, does not protect against all forms of loops. Consider the subset B, C, E of the previous example.

Just after the failure of the link between E and D, the routing tables in B, C, and E include the following entries:

From	Link	Cost
B to D	4	2
C to D	5	2
E to D	6	inf

E has noticed the failure of the link and sends an advertisement message on links 4 and 5, mentioning that the distance to D is now infinite. Suppose that this message reaches B, but that, due to a transmission error, it does not arrive at C. The routing table entries are now:

From	Link	Cost
B to D	4	inf
C to D	5	2
E to D	6	inf

Suppose now that the time has come for C to send its own distance vectors. It uses poisonous reverses, so it will advertise an infinite distance to E on link 5 and a distance of 2 on link 2. As a result, B will update its own routing tables and advertise an infinite distance on link 2 and a distance of 3 on link 4. The routing table entries have now been changed to:

From	Link	Cost
B to D	2	3
C to D	5	2
E to D	4	4

We observe a three-hop loop between C, B, and E. It is easy to show that further exchanges of messages will result in gradual increases of the distances without changing the routing. We are back to the counting-to-infinity example.

5.2.6 Triggered Updates

During all of the previous presentation, we have clearly avoided dealing with one particular issue: when to send the distance vectors to one's neighbors. This decision is, in fact, an arbitration among a set of constraints: timeliness of information, necessity to wait for a complete set of updates before making decisions, resistance to packet losses, monitoring of the neighbors, and so on.

Several implementations of distance vector protocols, and RIP is no exception, rely on the regular sending of distance vector packets by the nodes both for monitoring the neighbors and for correcting packet losses. A "timer" is associated with each entry in the routing table. If the information is not "refreshed" by the reception of a new packet before the expiration of this timer, one assumes that the neighbor in charge of the route has probably failed, and one marks the distance to the destination as infinite. This timer has to be chosen so that it is much longer than the period of transmission of the information. It would be irresponsible to mark a route as unavailable just because one packet was lost. RIP, for example, suggests that this timer should be set to six times the transmission interval, so that the route remains operational if at least one packet out of six is received. Indeed, one has also to take into consideration the network load induced by the repetition of the advertisements: the period cannot be too short.

A long period between emissions, however, has one annoying consequence: if a change in the network condition occurs just after an emission, one will have to wait until the end of the period for signalling this change to the neighbors. The procedure, known as "triggered updates," is an attempt to increase the responsiveness of the protocol by requesting nodes to send messages as soon as they notice a change in their routing tables without having to wait for the end of the period. This procedure certainly speeds up the convergence; in the RIP documentation [3], it is even claimed that, by sending triggered updates fast enough, one will immediately propagate the "right" information and thus avoid most of the intermediate routing loops. It is very clear that the bouncing effect and count to infinity that we analyzed in sections 5.2.3, 2.4, and 2.5 are caused by spurious messages from routers that merely repeat the state of their tables "before the change." But there are many reasons, e.g., spurious packet losses, why, even in the presence of split horizon with poisonous reverse and triggered updates, we will still see some loops forming that will have to be resolved by counting to infinity. Even in the last case, though, triggered updates have an advantage: it takes a much shorter time to count to infinity if packets are sent immediately than if they are spaced apart by a long period.

5.2.7 Some Mathematics

Routing protocols try to compute network routes that follow the shortest path to a destination. Computing shortest paths in graphs is a well-known mathematical problem, with applications far beyond computer networking. The distance vector protocols are based on the

Bellman-Ford algorithm, which is a distributed version of a very simple shortest-path algorithm. We will first describe the centralized version.

☞ Let N be the number of nodes, M the number of links.

☞ Let L be a table of links of size M, where L[l].m is the metric of the link, L[l].s the source of the link, and L[l].d the destination.

☞ Let D be a matrix of size [N,N], where D[i,j] is the distance from i to j.

☞ Let H be a matrix of size [N,N], where H[i,j] is the link on which i routes the packets bound to j.

To run the algorithm:

1. Initialize all D[i,j] to 0 if i = j, to infinity otherwise. Initialize all H[i, j] to −1.
2. For all links l, for all destinations k: set i = L[l].s, j = L[l].d, compute d = L[l].m + D[j,k].
3. If d is lower than D[i,k], update D[i,k] = d; H[i,k] = l.
4. If at least one D[i,k] was updated, repeat step 2. Otherwise, the computation is complete.

It is easy to show that the algorithm does converge in a number of steps which is equal to or lower than N, so that the global complexity is, at most, $0(M.N^{**}2)$.

In this centralized version, we compute all routing tables in parallel for the whole network. In the distributed version, each node is only concerned with one fraction of the data: the links that start from the node, the columns D[i,*] and H[i,*] of the distance and route matrices. The column D[i,*] is, in fact, the distance vector, which is passed to each neighbor after an update.

5.3 RIP, Version 1

RIP was initially designed as a component of the networking code for the BSD release of UNIX, incorporated in a program called "routed," for "route management daemon." It is, in its first version, an extremely simple protocol requiring minimal configuration, which can be understood and programmed with very little effort. It was then used in many different products and was documented in the RFC-1058 in June of 1988 by Charles Hedrick. RFC-1058 also suggested several improvements to the initial implementation, like the implementation of split horizon and triggered updates.

5.3.1 RIP, a Distance Vector Protocol

RIP is one distance vector protocol among many. These protocols differ from each other in many respects: for example, by their type of metric, the structure of the addresses, the range of links they support. RIP was designed as an "internal gateway protocol" (IGP) for exchanging information within an "autonomous system" (AS), a network of relatively limited size. We will see later how another category of protocols, the "exterior gateways protocols" (EGP), is used to glue together the autonomous systems that compose the Internet.

The addresses present in the RIP tables are 32-bit Internet addresses. An entry in the routing tables can represent a host, a network, or a subnet. There is no "address type" specification in the RIP packets; the routers have to analyze the address to understand what is being passed. They first separate the network part from the "subnet + host" part as a function of the address class: i.e., A, B, or C. If the "subnet + host" part is null, the entry represents a network; if it is not null, it represents either a subnet or a host. In order to discriminate between these two possibilities, one has to know the particular subnet mask that is used within a given network: if the host part is null, this is a subnet address; it is a host address otherwise. RFC-1058 does not assume that the subnet mask is available outside of the network itself. The subnet entries are not supposed to be propagated outside of their network, and all of them should be replaced by a single entry for the network itself. Note that the support of host routes is optional: the routers that do not want to maintain inflated tables are allowed to drop the host entries. The address 0.0.0.0 is singled out for representing a default route, e.g., toward networks outside the autonomous system.

By default, RIP uses a very simple metric: the distance is the number of links that have to be used to reach the destination—the "hop count." This distance is expressed as an integer varying between 1 and 15; the value 16 denotes the infinity. There is some half-hearted text in RFC-1058 about using more complex metrics to express preference for some links, but this would be hard to implement given the small value chosen for infinity. On the other hand, choosing a larger value would increase the duration of incoherent states when counting to infinity is performed and would thus be dangerous.

RIP supports both point-to-point links and broadcast networks, e.g., Ethernets. RIP packets are carried over UDP and IP. The RIP processes use the UDP port 520 both for emission and for reception. Using a specific port, with a number less than 1024, was in line with the system protections of BSD-UNIX, as only privileged process launched by the root operator could use this port. Packets normally are sent as broadcast; they will be received by all routers connected to a broadcast network (e.g., Ethernet).

Packets normally are sent every 30 seconds, or faster in the case of triggered updates. If a route is not refreshed within 180 seconds, the distance is set to infinity and the entry will later be removed from the routing tables. In order to avoid "tempests of updates," successive triggered updates are spaced by a random timer, varying between 1 and 5 seconds.

5.3.2 Message Format

The RIP messages start with a 32-bit command + version identifier, followed by a set of address + metric pairs, or "route entries." Each route entry is encoded over 20 bytes or five long words.

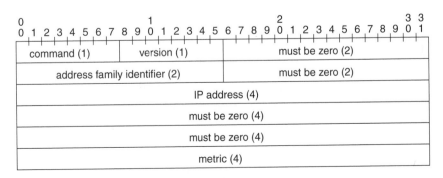

All fields are expressed as 32-bit integers and are transmitted in "network order"—most significant byte first. Several values of the "command" field had been defined in the initial implementations, but implementors of RIP are supposed to consider only two of them—a request code of value 1 and a response code of value 2. The version field is set to 1.

The explanation for the rather inefficient encoding of the addresses and metrics is very simple, if one remembers the origin of the protocol in the UNIX-BSD networking code, where addresses are expressed using the "socket address" structure composed of a 16-bit "address family identifier" followed by up to 14 bytes of data. Encoding the metric on 32 bits, although it only varies between 0 and 16, was a natural consequence mandated by the requirement to align the address-distance pair on a long-word boundary. The initial ambition of the programmers was to accommodate a large set of address families for use in the XNS or X.25 networks. However, in practice, RIP has not been used to support protocols other than IP. In theory, the address family identifier could take several values; in practice, RIP implementations always use the value 2 reserved for IP and ignore entries for other values.

5.3.3 Processing of RIP

As seen above, the RIP protocol includes a request and a response command. The normal operation of the RIP protocol is through the broadcasting of responses, either at regular 30-second intervals or triggered by routing table updates.

The RIP process, upon reception of a response message, will update its routing table. Each entry in the routing table contains at least

- ☞ The address of the destination
- ☞ The metric associated with that destination
- ☞ The address of the "next router"
- ☞ A "recently updated" flag
- ☞ Several timers

When processing the incoming response, the router will examine the entries one by one. It will do a set of validation checks to see, for example, that the address is a valid class A, B, or C address; that the network number is not 127 (loop-back) or 0 (except in the case of the default address 0.0.0.0); that the host part is not a "broadcast" address; and that the metric is not larger than infinity. Incorrect entries are ignored and RFC-1058 advises that they should in fact be reported as errors. If it was not equal to infinity, the incoming metric is increased by 1 in order to account for the last hop. Then, the routing table is searched for an entry corresponding to the destination, and the generic "distance vector" processing is performed:

- ☞ If the entry is not present and if its metric in the received message is not infinite, add it, initializing the metric to the received value and the next router to the sender of the message before starting a timer for that entry.
- ☞ If the entry is present with a larger metric, update the metric and next router fields and restart the timer for the entry.

☞ If the entry is present and the next router is the sender of the response message, update the metric if it differs from the stored value, and, in any case, restart the timer.

☞ In all other cases, the received entry is ignored.

If the metric or the next router changed, the entry should be marked as "updated." Note that RFC-1058 details an optional timer-related heuristic about "equal metrics," derived from the BSD implementation: if information is received for a destination that is "timing out," then the next router field is updated even if metrics are equals, not only if the received metric is lower.

A response will be sent at the regular 30-second interval, or it can be "triggered" by an update to the routing tables. In fact, triggered updates can cause excessive network loads, and RFC-1058 specifies a set of precautions to limit their rate. The response should not be sent immediately upon reception of the update but, rather, after a small random interval, between 1 and 5 seconds. This allows for related updates to arrive from other neighbors and be summarized in the next message; it also has the effect of limiting somewhat the network load. Then, the system administrator may limit the rate at which triggered updates can be sent on some links.

A separate response message is prepared for all connected interfaces. The information may vary due to split horizon processing and also to subnet summarization. The message will normally report the address and metric pairs for all entries in the routing table. However, when the message is sent as a triggered update, it does not have to include all entries in the routing tables, but only those that have been updated since the last transmission. The maximum message size chosen is 512 bytes, which allows for up to 25 entries per message. If there are more than 25 entries to report, RIP will send multiple packets. The source address for the message should always be the IP address associated with the interface on which the message is sent. The "incoming interface" information is not normally available at the UDP interface in the BSD implementations.

Entries corresponding to subnets should be reported only if the interface belongs to the same network as the subnet. For other interfaces, all subnet entries should be summarized in one network entry. Entries with infinite metrics need only be reported if they have been updated recently—there is no danger in letting them fade away from the neighbor's tables after a time out, and it is always interesting to reduce the network load. The same applies to entries that have an infinite metric due to split horizon processing—they can be omitted if the "next router" has not been updated recently.

As mentioned above, RIP processes can also receive requests. A request is normally sent when a router is starting operation in order to get from its neighbors an initial value of the routing tables. There are, in fact, two forms of requests, asking either for a full listing of the routing tables or for only specific routes.

One asks for a full listing of the routing tables by specifying only one address + metric pair in the request for the default address 0.0.0.0. and a metric of infinity. In that case, the router will reply by a normal response, similar to those issued periodically in the normal operation of the protocol, including split horizon processing.

Any other form of request requires the listing of only the specified entries. The response will be sent point to point to the requesting host and will contain an exact copy of the distance information in the routing tables, without performing split horizon processing. This form of request was not meant for normal operation, but rather for debugging purposes.

5.3.4 Silent Nodes

The modern Internet architecture clearly separates the hosts that use the Internet from the routers that engage in routing. Hosts usually have only one interface, although multihomed hosts may have several for redundancy or load sharing. In any case, hosts don't do routing and never relay IP packets; this is the job of routers. As a consequence, routing protocols like RIP are the business of routers, and hosts should not even know their existence.

But RIP is not a modern protocol. The routed program was engineered more than 10 years ago, at a time when the distinction between hosts and routers was somewhat blurred. And the programmers, having observed that the RIP packets would be broadcast every 30 seconds on the local networks, thought that it would be a good idea for hosts to just listen to this information and to maintain their own routing table. This way, multihomed hosts could decide which interface to use for what direction; even simple hosts could decide which router to select as a relay for a given destination when several routers were connected to the local network. Such hosts will perhaps send an occasional request, but will normally never send responses. They are described in RFC-1058 as "silent hosts."

This strategy worked—as long as all routers used RIP-1. Nowadays, there are good chances that they will use another protocol, such as RIP version 2, OSPF, or IGRP—and the host that would rely on that strategy would be left with a somewhat incomplete routing table! There is thus a wide consensus in the Internet against this mode of operation. The normal behavior of a host is to send packets to remote destinations to a default router, which will perhaps in some cases relay the packet to another router on the same local network and notify the address of this preferred router through an ICMP redirect message.

5.3.5 Configuration and Interfaces

Running RIP on a router always supposes some configuration of the protocol. In the simplest version, the RIP process must learn the list of local interfaces, the associated addresses, and the subnet masks. In the absence of other information, RIP will use a default metric of 1 for each interface and will initialize the routing tables with one entry for each of the local subnets, with a distance of 1 (hosts on these subnets are one hop away from the local router). The process will send a request to its neighbors, in order to complete the local tables and start operation.

There are however many reasons why the administrator will not want to broadcast RIP messages on all the local interfaces. For example, there may well be only this router on one of the subnets, and sending regular broadcasts would just be a waste of resources. There may indeed be other reasons, such as the need to operate some interfaces with fixed routing or with a protocol other than RIP. The administrator may need to validate, or invalidate, interfaces. Then, one has to consider the case of "nonbroadcast" interfaces. There will be no way to discover just the neighbors; one will have to send them point-to-point messages, and the administrator will have to provide the list of their addresses. This point-to-point operation will also be needed if several "logical" networks share a single subnet. In some cases, the administrator may also want to play with the interface's metrics to privilege one or another route.

There are also many reasons why the administrator will want to fix some routing table entries, such as to document destinations that are accessible through fixed routing. These destinations will have to be inserted "permanently" in the local routing tables. Then, one may also want to specifically disallow some destinations to which one does not want to communicate. Information about these destinations should be "filtered out" of the incoming responses.

The RIP process will have to pass the routing information that it computes to the IP routing process; it also will have to access local information about the status of interfaces. Indeed, in the absence of such information, the monitoring of RIP messages will result in timing out a failing interface after 180 seconds. But this is fairly slow and also imprecise. The fact that one receives messages from a neighbor does not always mean that this neighbor receives information about us.

5.4 RIP, Version 2

Doing a second version of RIP was felt to be necessary by some, but it was thought an utterly bad idea by some others who essentially thought that distance vector routing should be abandoned and replaced by modern protocols such as OSPF or IS-IS, not upgraded. RIP-2 is defined by Gary Malkin in RFC-1388 [4], which contains a very unusual "justification" section that I can't help quoting in full:

> With the advent of OSPF and IS-IS, there are those who believe that RIP is obsolete. While it is true that the newer IGP routing protocols are far superior to RIP, RIP does have some advantages. Primarily, in a small network, RIP has very little overhead in terms of bandwidth used and configuration and management time. RIP is also very easy to implement, especially in relation to the newer IGPs.
>
> Additionally, there are many, many more RIP implementations in the field than OSPF and IS-IS combined. It is likely to remain that way for some years yet.
>
> Given that RIP will be useful in many environments for some period of time, it is reasonable to increase RIP's usefulness. This is especially true since the gain is far greater than the expense of the change.

In short, this is an apology for daring to work on such a lower form of technology. RIP-2 tries to define a set of useful improvements to RIP, such as subnet routing and support for CIDR and authentication or multicast transmission. It is a compatible upgrade, and a transition strategy is defined. RFC-1388 is completed by RFC-1387 [5], an analysis of the protocol, and by RFC-1389 [6], the definition of the RIP-2 MIB.

5.4.1 Formats and Compatibility

The RIP-1 format contains a number of "must be zero" fields. These fields provide room for improvement and are redefined in RIP-2. RIP-2 messages, like RIP-1 messages, are composed of a 32-bit "command" header followed by a set of 20-byte "route entries." The command header contains the same command and version fields defined for RIP-1.

```
 0                   1                   2                   3 3
 0 1 2 3 4 5 6 7 8 9 0 1 2 3 4 5 6 7 8 9 0 1 2 3 4 5 6 7 8 9 0 1
+-+-+-+-+-+-+-+-+-+-+-+-+-+-+-+-+-+-+-+-+-+-+-+-+-+-+-+-+-+-+-+-+
|        Address Family Identifier (2)    |      Route Tag (2)   |
+-----------------------------------------+----------------------+
|                          IP Address (4)                        |
+----------------------------------------------------------------+
|                        Subnet Mask (4)                         |
+----------------------------------------------------------------+
|                          Next Hop (4)                          |
+----------------------------------------------------------------+
|                           Metric (4)                           |
+----------------------------------------------------------------+
```

The main difference between RIP-2 and RIP-1 is the format of the route entries. RIP-2 route entries keep from RFC-1058 the definition of the "address family identifier" (AFI), "IP address," and "metric fields," with the addition of one new AFI for carrying "authentication data." It defines then a number of new fields.

☞ The next hop field is used to eliminate "double hops" over the same subnet,

☞ The subnet mask enables better subnet routing.

☞ The route tag is used to flag "external routes" and is for use in conjunction with EGP or BGP.

RIP-2 packets are sent with a version number set to 2. This, together with the extensions provisions of RIP-1, enables some degree of interworking with the old specification—when receiving a packet with a version number larger than 1, RIP-1 routers just ignore any entry where a "must be zero" field has a nonzero value. They will thus correctly process all entries that do not use the RIP-2 extensions, such as simple network entries without subnet indications.

We should note that the draft version of RIP-2 encoded a "routing domain" identifier in the last 16 bits of the command header, which could be set to an "autonomous system identifier" (see chapter 8 for a definition of autonomous systems). Routers could check this identifier and reject accidentally received broadcast messages that were not meant for their routing domain. However, this feature was not widely used, and was somewhat redundant because the authentication procedures also guarantee that accidentally received messages will be ignored. The routing domain field is not defined in the final standard (RFC-2453).We will detail in the remainder of this section the handling of authentication, subnet routing, and "wire sharing," as well as the operation in "multicast" mode. The interface between EGP or BGP and RIP will be detailed in chapters 8 and 9.

5.4.2 Routing per Subnet

RIP-1 supported subnet entries only within the subnetted network. Outside of this network, the subnet mask was not supposed to be known, and there was no way to distinguish between a subnet and a host entry. This enforces strict hierarchical routing: outsiders would pass packets to the nearest router within the network, regardless of the subnet to which the destination belonged. A consequence of strict hierarchical routing is a requirement for connectivity. Any router in the network is supposed to know how to access any of the subnets. If the network happens to be partitioned between nonconnected subnets, some packets will be lost. The following figure gives an example of such a situation. The routers A and E both summarize the subnet information and signal a route to the network 10.0.0.0. A packet bound to 10.2.0.1 can thus be passed to either B or F. Suppose we send it to B, which will send it to A. Since the link between C and D is down, A will have no solution but to mention that the destination is "unreachable."

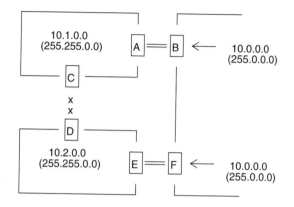

RIP-2 allows routing on the subnet outside of the network by passing mask information in parallel with the address. In fact, this also allows several useful complements to subnet routing, such as support of variable length masks within the same network or aggregation of several class C addresses within one address group as in CIDR.

We have seen in the format section that the mask is passed in one of the "must be zero" fields of the version 1 packets. As a consequence, the subnet entries will be ignored by RIP-1 processes.

5.4.3 Authentication

RIP-1 is not a secure protocol. Any host sending packets from UDP port 520 would be considered a router by its neighbors, which will believe its advertisement. Indeed, only a privileged user could obtain the right to emit from port 520 on a BSD UNIX system, and that would perhaps be a protection in a homogeneous environment. But the world has changed. Minicomputers have been replaced by PCs and workstations; one does not have to be a "system guru" any longer to obtain "super-user" status on these machines. Indeed, careful administrators could resort to manual configuration of a "list of authorized neighbors." But that will not be a protection against malicious users. In the absence of any serious authentication procedure, faking a router's identity does not require an exceptional brain capacity.

The designers of "routed" could have learned from history. A very famous crash was caused in the early Arpanet by a misfunctioning router that kept advertising bogus distance vectors, where the metric was set to 0 for all destinations. Its neighbors duly updated their routing tables, and very quickly all the traffic converged to that single node, leading to massive congestion. Deploying buggy software is always a bad idea, but malicious hackers could very easily emulate the same incident!

RIP-2 does include an authentication procedure. It specifies that the first entry in a packet can be replaced by an "authentication segment."

The packet will thus contain an initial 32-bit "command" specification, followed by an authentication segment, and then up to 24 destination-metric pairs. The authentication entry is characterized by an "address family identifier" of 0xFFFF; it carries an "authentication type" that identifies the type of authentication algorithm in use and 16 bytes of authentication data. One will note that the format of the authentication option has been chosen to maximize compatibility. RIP-1 routers will simply observe that the address family identifier is not set to 2, skip the entry, and proceed with the 24 remaining entries.

Upon reception of a packet, the routers will first check that the authentication field is present, and that it proves the origin of the packet. If RIP-2 is running in secure mode, it should be possible for an administrator to mandate authentication of all packets and to request that the RIP processes ignore any unauthenticated message.

The RIP-2 standard itself (RFC-2453) only defines a "simple password" procedure. In this procedure, the type is set to 2 and the data contain the password, left aligned and right padded with binary zeros. This is hardly a secure procedure. Malicious users still will not have to use their brains much to listen to RIP packets on an Ethernet wire, copy the password, and replay their attack. A much stronger procedure is defined in RFC-2082, which explains how the password can be encrypted with MD5 to avoid clear-text transmission of secrets over the wire, guarantee the integrity of messages, provide protection against "replay" attacks, and enable safe distribution of secret keys. RFC-2082 redefines the RIP packet format to contain a security header and a security trailer:

Command (unchanged)
Security header: AFI = 0xFFFF, Autype = 3
Route entries
Security trailer: AFI = 0xFFFF, Autype = 1

The security header is encoded as a standard 20-byte route entry. It contains various security elements, but does not contain the authentication data, whose length depends on the authentication algorithm:

0xFFFF	Autype = 3	
RIP-2 Packet Length	Key ID	Auth Data Len
Sequence Number (non-decreasing)		
must be zero		
must be zero		

☞ The authentication type 3 defines the "Keyed Message Digest" procedure specified in RFC-2082 [12].

☞ The RIP packet length indicates the "standard" portion of the RIP packet, including the command, the security header, and the route entries, but excluding the security trailer.

☞ The Key-ID indicates which key is used for protecting this message.

☞ The Authentication data length indicates the length of the authentication data in the security trailer.

☞ The sequence number is a 32-bit integer, used to fend off replay attacks. A router will reject all messages whose sequence number is not larger than that of the last valid message received for the specified Key-ID.

The security trailer encodes the authentication data. It is encoded on a variable number of 32-bit words:

0xFFFF	Autype = 1
Authentication data (16 bytes when the MD5 algorithm is used.)	

In order to use the keyed authentication procedure, routers must first be programmed with a "secret key" and agree on an authentication algorithm. This can be accomplished either through "manual" configuration, or by using a key exchange procedure. The combination of the key and the algorithm constitute a context, which is identified by the Key-ID.

The authentication data is computed before sending the message, by combining the secret and the data according to the agreed-upon algorithm. RFC-2082 specifies one such algorithm, MD5, but it is very clear that other algorithms may have to be used in the future: for example, if MD5 is one day "crypto-analyzed" or, in plain English, broken.

To use MD5, the sending entity first composes all the fields of the message, including the first 32 bits of the trailer, but without including the authentication data. The authentication header is initialized, providing the Key-Id, the length of the authentication data, and the message length. Then, the sending station prepares a pseudo-message by initializing the authentication data to the value of the key, or MD5 secret, and by appending to the message a variable number of pad bytes, as defined in RFC-1321, and a 64-bit word that expresses the actual length of the message. The sending station will then compute the MD5 "hash" of this pseudo-message. The resulting 16 bytes constitute the authentication data. They are copied into the message to, overwriting the secret key. The transmitted message will not include the pad bytes or the length indication.

Initial message	Pseudo-message	Transmitted message
Command	Command	Command
Authentication header	Authentication header	Authentication header
Route entries	Route entries	Route entries
First 32 bits of trailer	First 32 bits of trailer	First 32 bits of trailer
	Authentication data: MD5 secret	Authentication data: result of MD5 hash
	Pad bytes (per RFC-1321)	
	32 MSB of length	
	32 LSB of length	

The receiving station will perform the reverse process. It will constitute a pseudo-message using the secret that corresponds to the Key-ID, and the length of the received message. It will then compare the MD5 hash of the pseudo-message to the received authentication data. If the two values match, the data are authentic. If they don't, the message will be rejected.

5.4.4 Next Hop

There are several cases where two different autonomous systems share the same "wire," in particular when this wire (for example, an Ethernet cable or an FDDI ring) is used as a backbone for connecting several different networks. There is one pitfall induced by carrying several networks on the same wire. The router A from domain X sending a packet to destination F within domain Y will naturally send the packet to D, i.e., the router of domain Y that is the nominal interface to the domain X. D will know from the domain-Y specific routing tables that the best route to F goes through router E, and it will relay the packet. Now, we observe that the packet travels two times on the same Ethernet: from A to D, then from D to E. This is clearly suboptimal.

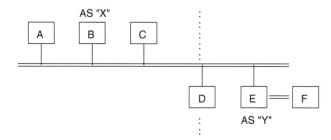

RIP-2 solves this problem by introducing a "next-hop" concept. The router D knows that the packets to F go through destination E. So, when it advertises destination F in the domain X, it will send not only the address-metric pair but also a next-hop indication, telling routers like A that "the distance to F is f, but the best relay is not me, D, sending this message, but rather E." Thus, routers like A will be able to direct packets bound to F through E, without an extra hop through D.

The next-hop value is set to the null address 0.0.0.0, when packets bound to the specified destination should be directly forwarded to the router that originates the advertisement. It will be set to the address of a preferred router when this is not the case.

5.4.5 Multicasting

RIP-1 uses a broadcast address to send routing advertisements to "all packets on a wire." As a result, these packets are received not only by routers but also by all hosts on the wire. There is no practical way to program an Ethernet or token ring interface to "filter all broadcast packets"— the host would then be missing important information. In order to enable this filtering, one must use a MAC layer multicast address, to which only routers will listen.

Indeed, RIP-2 does not exactly define a MAC address. This would be "subnet technology-specific." RIP-2 achieves the same result by defining an IP class D address to be used for periodic multicasts. The IP multicast address is 224.0.0.9. We will detail the multicast routing in chapter 12; let's just note here that no particular multicast networking is needed for RIP-2, as packets are simply multicast on the local network and are not forwarded. The group management protocol, IGMP, is not needed.

Operation in multicast mode certainly affects the compatibility with RIP-1, as the RIP-1 nodes will probably not receive the multicast packets. For this reason, RFC-1388 details three modes of operation.

1. Send RIP-1 packets in broadcast mode.
2. Send RIP-2 packets in broadcast mode.
3. Send RIP-2 packets in multicast mode.

The first mode ensures full compatibility but no advantage. It can be understood as a "deployment" mode, in which the capacity is installed but not used until a sufficient proportion of the routers has been upgraded. The second mode corresponds to the transition and is used as long as some routers in the autonomous system remain "RIP-1 only." These remaining routers will see the RIP-2 packets, and occasionally reject parts of them, e.g., the authentication entries or the subnet information. The third mode corresponds to the final stage, when all routers have been upgraded to RIP-2.

5.5 Using RIPng for IPv6

As IPv6 has essentially the same routing requirements as IPv4, RIP can be used for IPv6 in much the same way that it is used for IPv4. The adapted protocol, called RIPng, is extremely similar to RIPv4. It uses the same algorithms, the same timers, the same logic. In fact, it is almost possible to use the same code, except for two important differences:

☞ the use of IPv6 security instead of RIPv2 authentication entries, and
☞ the adapt the packet formats in order to carry the longer IPv6 addresses.

We will detail these changes in the next subsections.

5.5.1 Using IPv6 Security for RIPng

The IPv6 security services are superior to the provisions of RIPv2. The authentication header protects both the data and the IP addresses, which are not protected by the RIP authentication system. The encryption service could be used to protect the RIPng packets from casual listeners.

As a consequence, the working group decided to not include any authentication mechanism in RIPng. This has two consequences. First, the dubious "simple password" procedure is effectively deprecated. Second, the protocol becomes simpler. There is no more need to distinguish between authentication entries and route entries, which means that one can get rid of the "address family identifier," a leftover of the initial Berkeley Unix implementation.

5.5.2 Changes in Format

The basic format of the RIPng packet is the same as the format of the RIPv2 packet: a 32-bit command header followed by a set of 20-byte route entries. The parameters of the command header are the same as the RIPv2 parameters: a command code, whose values are the same as for RIPv2, and a version number,

command (1)	version (1)	must be zero (2)
Routing entry 1 (20 bytes)		
…		
Routing entry N (20 bytes)		

The routing entry format, however, has been thoroughly revised to accommodate the 16 octets of IPv6 addresses:

IPv6 address (16 bytes)		
route tag (2)	prefix len (1)	metric (1)

The combination of the IPv6 address and the prefix length identifies the route that is advertised. The route tag plays the same role as in RIPv2 entries: it typically identifies the autonomous system through which the packets will be routed. The metric is encoded on a single byte, which is not a problem since authorized values, as in RIPv2, can only vary between 0 and 16.

When we do a field-by-field comparison of the RIPv2 and RIPng routing entries, we observe that the RIPng entries do not include the Address Family Identifier, subnet mask, and Next Hop fields. The AFI is in fact not necessary, since RIPng packets only carry one type of route entries, and the subnet mask is superceded by the prefix length field. However, there is still a need in some IPv6 networks to use the "next hop" information. Carrying an additional 16-byte next hop address in each message would be too much overhead, so the RIPng working group decided to encode the next hop information in a separate route entry:

Next hop IPv6 address (16 bytes)	
must be zero (3)	metric = 0xFF

The next-hop entries are distinguished by the special value of the metric field, which is set to 0xFF, or 255, a value that is outside the valid range of metrics values.

The next hop information is presented before the routing entries that it qualifies. In the following example, we see a packet containing 5 routing entries and two next hop indications:

Command
Routing entry (1)
Routing entry (2)
Next Hop (a)
Routing entry (3)
Routing entry (4)
Next Hop (b)
Routing entry (5)

The first two entries, in our example, are not preceded by any next-hop indications: the corresponding packets should be routed through the advertising router. The routing entries 3 and 4 are preceded by a next hop indication: the packets bound to destinations 3 and 4 should be routed through the router "a." The routing entry 5 is qualified by the next hop indication "b," which indicates the route of the corresponding packets.

5.6 Further Improvements

Many authors have proposed improvements to the RIP protocol and, more generally, to the distance vector technology. In this section, we will present proposals for breaking unwanted synchronizations, for reducing network load through acknowledgments, for a better loop control or for more precise metrics. The descriptions of IGRP and EIGRP, in chapter 7, also list other improvements to the distance vector protocols, such as "composite metrics," "path holddown," "route poisoning," or the "diffusing update algorithm."

5.6.1 Breaking Synchronizations

In a communication at the 1993 SIGCOMM conference [7], Van Jacobson and Sally Floyd reported their finding about synchronization patterns in the Internet. Study of voice session statistics, and also systematic probes conducted with the "ping" program, evidenced periodic peaks in either delays or loss rates. Every 30 seconds, the network would exhibit very long delays or high packet loss rates. Everything happened as if periodic congestion appeared at these regular intervals. Analyzing further, Van discovered that what was happening was, in fact, the synchronization of all RIP routers: all routers in one autonomous system were sending their routing updates at about the same time, every 30 seconds. This caused a periodic surge in traffic, likely to increase the routing delays. It would also monopolize the router's processor for short intervals during which the IP packets carrying special options would not be processed. In one implementation, the routers would even refuse to forward any packet as long as the routing was not updated, for fear of using an incorrect route. This particular behavior has since been corrected, since there is just no way for a router to guarantee that a table is "up to date" and since introducing delays is almost always a very bad idea. But it is also important to eliminate the synchronization itself.

The problem was, in fact, foreseen during the design of RIP, and RFC-1058 included some recommendation for avoiding synchronization. The cure advocated by RIP was essentially to rely on the routers being initialized at random times and to send the update message at very precise 30-second intervals. As the first messages were sent at random intervals, precisely repeating the same pattern at very regular intervals should maintain the desynchronization. For routers that could not maintain an accurate periodicity, RFC-1058 recommended to offset the timer by addition of a small random time. However, it gave no indication on the amount of random time which was desired. As the stated objective was to avoid collisions on broadcast networks, the interval chosen was generally very small, e.g., a certain number of packet transmission intervals.

In the network that was analyzed, the synchronization was in fact caused by a specific implementation choice. After the periodic timer expires, the router will start formatting its update packets. But it could during this phase receive update packets from other routers, which it will have to process immediately. It is only after finishing both emission and reception processing that it will restart the 30-second timer. As a result, the effective period will be equal to 30 seconds plus the processing time for emission and reception. The reception processing increases when several routers are synchronized, as each of them receives more packets. As a consequence, a cluster of synchronized routers will exhibit a larger period than an isolated nonsynchronized router. After a few iterations, a collision will occur and the isolated router will "fall in sync" with the cluster, enlarging it and enlarging at the same time its attractiveness. Pretty soon, all routers in the network will be synchronized.

The only way for an individual router to break away from the cluster is to use a different period. However, the random variations that were present in RIP implementations were too short to achieve this result. Van Jacobson and Sally Floyd computed that the randomization, to be efficient, should be much larger than the total update processing time, which was typically asserted as a few one hundred milliseconds per update for a single router, and proportionally more in the case of many synchronized routers. Using only a small random variable is sufficient only if there are few routers in the network; otherwise, if a cluster of sufficient size occurs, the randomization will not be sufficient to break away from it, and the whole set of routers will eventually synchronize itself. It is indeed only a matter of time for such clusters to occur.

The correction suggested is to include a very large random portion in the update interval—e.g., to set the timer at a random value between 15 and 45 seconds [7]. This will, on average, produce the same update rate as the fixed 30-second delays, but it will avoid the synchronization effect or break existing synchronizations for most practical network sizes.

One should note that RIP is not the only routing protocol to exhibit this synchronization characteristic—the problem is in fact quite generic. One could even think that synchronization is just a fact of life that can appear in any large, complex, system, from clocks hung on the same wall to groups of butterflies. Synchronization effects have also been reported between TCP-IP connections through the congestion control mechanisms or between backup procedures launched at the same time on different machines. The conclusion hammered out by Van Jacobson is that if one really wants to achieve randomization in a large system, one has to engineer for it and include explicit random variables; hoping that external events will naturally induce desynchronization is almost never a safe bet!

5.6.2 Acknowledged Updates

Broadcasting an update to all neighbors every 30 seconds is a very natural thing to do on an Ethernet cable or an FDDI ring. It is much less desirable on switched networks, e.g., X.25 or ISDN, where "silence is golden." On these networks, one has to establish a circuit (ISDN) or a virtual circuit (X.25) before transmitting a packet. The very fact of establishing a circuit bears a fixed cost—one unit of charging. ISDN circuits are typically charged proportionally to the duration of the calls; X.25 charging generally combines circuit duration and volume of traffic. The textbook solution for transmitting IP over such networks is to set up a circuit when an IP packet is queued to the destination and to close it if no traffic is observed for some period. This silence detection timer should be reasonably longer than the time needed to establish a circuit and is typically set to a few seconds. Sending a routing update every 30 seconds will, indeed, result in resetting the circuit that often.

Another characteristic of these networks is their low capacity—64 kilobits/second (kbps) for an ISDN B channel, or 9,600 bps for a typical X.25 virtual circuit. Pragmatic constraints restrict the amount of queuing authorized to a few packets—say, one or two seconds' worth of transmission. Implementors fear that by allowing more queuing they would also allow very long transmission delays and that they should just drop incoming packets if the queue is full. This design choice is quite frequent, although we will see in chapter 14 that more efficient solutions could in fact be preferred. One or two seconds of transmission, on a 9,600-bps link, is equivalent to 2 to 4 RIP packets of 512 octets, each carrying 25 entries. Suppose now that an update includes 200 entries, or 8 packets. If the RIP process sends 8 packets in short succession, a queue will build up before the X.25 virtual circuit. If the queue is limited to 4 packets, then the last 4 packets of the update will be dropped. They may even be dropped repeatedly, every 30 seconds; the last 100 entries will never be announced to the other end of the virtual circuit, with obviously negative effects on the overall routing.

In a contribution to the RIP working group, Gerry Meyer analyzed this problem and suggested a solution based on acknowledged transmissions of updates [8]. For each packet composing a routing update, the sending router should expect an acknowledgment, and should attempt retransmission if this acknowledgment does not arrive within a time-out. This secure procedure should be completed by a pacing of the transmissions compatible with the available data rate. Meyer suggested including it in RIP by defining three new commands.

☞ A new type of response, called "triggered response"
☞ A "triggered acknowledgment"
☞ A new type of request, called a "triggered request"

A triggered response is similar to a normal response, but it also contains a packet number that should be repeated in the triggered acknowledgment. A triggered request is identical to a normal request, but should be responded to by a triggered response. It could be used in an initial exchange between the router and its neighbors to discover whether they support the "acknowledged transmission" option.

The goal of this procedure is to get rid of the periodic updates by transmitting only triggered updates upon changes in the local routing tables. In order to achieve this objective, however, one has to modify the classic RIP processing in two ways: one should not use the periodic updates as an indication of the link state, and one must keep the neighbor's distance information even when the neighbor is not the best route to the destination.

The first condition is easy to understand: if one does not transmit periodic messages, one should use another source of information to detect that the link is up. Gerry Meyer described the alternative as "presumption of reachability." One considers that the neighbor is reachable unless otherwise informed. Remember that in the normal case, when the link is silent, we don't even try to set up a circuit. The actual link status will be tested only when packets have to be transmitted; if at that stage we fail to establish the circuit, then the interface will be declared down, and it will be the task of a circuit manager to periodically test its status and inform the RIP process.

The second condition is not much more subtle: in classic RIP implementations, one needs to keep in the routing table only the best router for a given destination and the corresponding distance. If one receives a triggered update from another router announcing a larger distance, the triggered update would be acknowledged and immediately discarded. Now, if the link to the former best router fails, this information will not be available and will not necessarily be retransmitted. In order to really support the acknowledged updates mechanism, routers should never discard any routing information. They should keep for each destination the list of distance information received from each of their neighbors, together with a timer indication. Information received through classic updates should time out after 180 seconds, while indications received through acknowledged updates should never time out. If one link changes status—e.g., becomes unavailable—one will immediately pick the "next best" neighbor, without waiting for periodic or triggered updates.

One should point out that the idea of keeping several neighbors' information is beneficial, even in the absence of acknowledged updates. An implementation of RIP can very well keep in memory the distance information from all of its neighbors for faster reactions. If this is requiring too many resources, one could at least keep track of both the best route and the second best in order to avoid suffering from a complete lack of available routes for the destination in case of single link failure.

Gerry Meyer and Steve Sherry later published an updated proposal [16] that improves on the solution presented in RFC-1582. The new solution allows for partial updates, reducing the volume of traffic, and also for immediate consideration of some updates, speeding up the convergence of the routing process.

5.6.3 Support of Multiple Metrics

RIP uses a very simple metric—the number of hops in a path. This metric is not the only one possible, and it is certainly not the best one, as it does not differentiate between an expensive and slow X.25 virtual circuit and a fast and free FDDI ring. A consequence is that it is not very advisable to use RIP in a network mixing several links of very different characteristics.

The distance vector technology certainly does not impose the usage of this simplistic metric. As far back as 1975, before IP was even invented, the Cyclades routing protocol was being updated to cope with different types of link [9]—instead of incrementing the metric by 1 for each hop, they increased it by the average time needed to transmit a packet, i.e., the division of the average packet length by the data rate of the link. This worked very well and the algorithm always selected the fastest path to the destination, but we must observe that the range of link data rates in the Cyclades network was relatively narrow—between 4,800 and 48,000 bps. If we were to use the same metric with IP, we would suppose a nominal packet length of 512 octets and derive the following costs for a typical mix of links:

Link speed	Metric (ms)
9,600 bps	426,667
64 kbps	64,000
1.5 Mbps	2,730
10 Mbps	410
100 Mbps	41

We can immediately see that, although we will generally converge very fast toward the best path, we will have a practical problem in choosing a value for infinity. We will have to choose an infinity of about 7 seconds if we want to allow up to 16 hops on 9,600-bps link, or maybe 1 second if we want to allow only two 9,600-bps hops. But if we do this, we can trigger a very long time for counting to infinity if the loop involves only high-speed links, as 1 second allows for 366 hops at 1.5 megabits/second (Mbps), 2,439 at 10 Mbps or 24,390 at 100 Mbps. In short, we would observe an efficient network as long as triggered updates and split horizon are sufficient for convergency, but this network would come to a stop for a long period upon random incidents.

A practical solution to this problem was proposed in a contribution to the SIP working group, which was trying to devise a version of RIP for the experimental SIP protocol. The metric has two components: the hop count of the path (similar to RIP) and the throughput of the path, measured as 10 times the decimal logarithm of the maximum data rate, expressed in kbps. When adding a segment to an existing path, the hop count is incremented by 1 and the throughput is set to the minimum of the path value and the segment value. In order to discriminate against long paths, the throughput indicator is then decremented by 1: -0.1 is the decimal logarithm of 0.8, subtracting 1 is equivalent to a reduction of 20%. Any path that has a hop count equal to or larger than 32 is discarded as infinite. The selected path is the one with the largest throughput indicator; if two paths have the same throughput, the one with the smallest hop count is selected.

Another solution is to rely on "path holddown" instead of counting to infinity; we will see how IGRP uses this solution. We will also see in the next chapter that link state protocols like OSPF allow a much more precise handling of metrics.

5.6.4 Loop Resolution

RIP-2 is already an enhancement to RIP-1, introducing some level of authentication and a capability to route on subnet prefixes or classless addresses. Breaking the randomization, reducing the number of messages, or using more efficient metrics would be straightforward enhancements to RIP-2. But they would not solve one major problem: the need to count to infinity when some complex loops have to be broken. According to RFC-1058, successive triggered updates must be spaced by a random delay, between 1 and 5 seconds. In a three-party loop, each round of updates increases the metric by a factor of 3; up to five rounds will be necessary to count to the infinite value, 16. These five rounds will last 15 to 75 seconds, during which packets will keep circling the loop, with all sorts of negative implications—such as local congestions due to the accumulation of looping packets. In fact, the local congestion may cause the loss of a triggered update, which will only be corrected by the next periodic emission, increasing again the lifetime of the loop. This risk alone explains why many routing specialists are extremely hostile to distance vector protocols in general, including RIP.

In fact, distance vector protocols can be improved by the "source-tracing" algorithm. This algorithm has been presented simultaneously by two teams during the 1989 SIGCOMM [10, 11]. The idea is to increase the information content of the routing tables and of the routing updates, adding a first-hop indication to the destination and metric pairs. The first-hop field is set to a conventional value of 0 when the entry is local and is relayed when the update is propagated; if a value of 0 is received, it is replaced by the address of the local router.

One can use this information to check recursively that the route to a destination is loopless. The condition is verified if the route to the first hop is loopless and if the first hop is not the local router—except, indeed, if the route has exactly one hop. If a loop involving the local router does exist, then the router will necessarily be either the first hop to the destination, the first hop to that first hop, or an intermediate first hop. Both papers included a demonstration that, in the absence of message losses, the loops will be detected immediately.

Although this algorithm looks very attractive, it cannot be implemented easily as an extension to RIP. One would indeed have to modify the format of RIP-2 packets. There is no room left for another address field, but this could easily be accommodated. One would also have to accommodate three specificities of RIP: the usage of interface addresses, the absence of router entries in the tables, and the practice of subnet aggregation.

RIP uses interface addresses as sources of the routing updates. When receiving a message where the first-hop field is empty, one should replace this field by the address of the router. But which address? One can envision picking the address of the incoming interface, which would thus be constant for all advertisements; the address of the outgoing interface, which would thus be different for each advertisement; or one selected address, independent of the incoming interface. In fact, this problem can easily be solved by taking a look at the proposed algorithm. In Cheng et al., the source tracing is presented primarily as a sophisticated form of split horizon [10]. The algorithm is executed when one wants to announce a route toward destination D to neighbor N:

1. Let H be the address of the first host toward D.
2. If H is one of the local addresses, the route is sane. Exit.
3. If H is the address of the router N, a loop is detected. Set the metric to infinity. Exit.
4. Replace D by H, continue at step 1.

But this is not very practical in the RIP environment, as the router is broadcasting the updates to "all neighbors on a wire." We may want to perform the algorithm upon reception of a new metric for destination D from router R. The updated algorithm is then:

1. Let H be the first hop toward D.
2. If H is equal to R, the route is sane. Exit.
3. If H is one of the local addresses, a loop is detected. Set the metric to infinity. Exit.
4. Replace D by H, continue at step 1.

The algorithm works fine if empty first-hop indications are replaced by the outgoing interface address, which will also be the source address for the update.

Then, one should note that the algorithm supposes that one can always compute the route to the first hop, i.e., that there is one entry in the routing tables for each router in the network. But this is not true in RIP: there is one entry per subnet, and inserting one entry per router would cause some extra overhead. The algorithm should thus be modified to:

1. Let H be the first hop toward D.
2. If H is equal to R, the route is sane.

3. If H is one of the local addresses, a loop is detected. Set the metric to infinity.

4. Find the route entry that best matches H. Replace H by the first hop for this entry. Continue at step 2.

The algorithm will converge if there is always one route for all first hops. If first hops are interface addresses, then the routers should at least advertise a route to the subnet to which the interface belongs. If for some reason they cannot do so, then they will have to advertise a host route for the interface.

Then, we have to consider the "aggregation" problem—for example, when several subnet entries are replaced by one network entry. Various subnets may well have different first hops; in fact, they may well have different metrics. The aggregation of routes aims at hiding the internal structure of the subnet. It is thus also logical to hide the first-hop information, to consider that the network is local, and to advertise an empty first hop.

In fact, few people are convinced that the "source-tracing" algorithm is really needed. It can be described simply, but it increases sizably the processing of entries. In short, it is contrary to the general simple-to-implement philosophy of RIP.

5.7 The Cost of Simplicity

RIP is simple, and that is the reason it is used. It can be implemented in a few hours, without having to investigate sophisticated algorithms. There are only two messages in the protocol and only one table. The risks of a big mistake are scarce, and the general result will be quite acceptable if the network topology is relatively simple and if link failures are rare.

But for large and complex networks RIP is probably wholly inadequate. It does compute new routes after any change in network topology, but in some cases it does so very slowly, by counting to infinity. During the time it takes to perform the computation, the network is left in a transient state where loops may occur and cause temporary congestion. In any case, RIP cannot be used in networks in which routes may use more than 15 hops, because a metric of 16 indicates infinity. Most specialists prefer to use more elaborate protocols, of the link state family.

References

1. R. E. Bellman, "Dynamic Programming," Princeton University Press, Princeton, N.J., 1957.

2. L. R. Ford, Jr., and D. R. Fulkerson, "Flows in Networks," Princeton University Press, Princeton, NJ, 1962.

3. C. Hedrick, "Routing Information Protocol," RFC-1058, June 1988.

4. G. Malkin, "RIP Version 2," RFC-2453, November 1998.

5. G. Malkin, "RIP Version 2 Protocol Analysis," RFC-1721, November 1994.

6. G. Malkin and F. Baker, "RIP Version 2 MIB Extension," RFC-1389, January 1993.

7. S. Floyd and V. Jacobson, "The Synchronisation of Periodic Routing Messages," *ACM SIGCOMM '93 Symposium*, September 1993.

8. G. M. Meyer, "Extensions to RIP to Support Demand Circuits," RFC-1582, February 1994.

9. L. Pouzin et al., "The Cyclades Computer Network," North-Holland, 1982.

10. C. Cheng, R. Riley, S. Kumar, and J. J. Garcia-Luna-Aceves, "A Loop-free Extended Bellman-Ford Routing Protocol Without Bouncing Effect," *ACM SIGCOMM '89 Symposium*, September 1989.

11. B. Rajagopalan and M. Faiman, "A New Responsive Distributed Shortest-Path Routing Algorithm," *ACM SIG-COMM '89 Symposium*, September 1989.

12. F. Baker and R. Atkinson, "RIP-2 MD5 Authentication," RFC-2082, January 1997.

13. G. Malkin and R. Minnear, "RIPng for IPv6," RFC-2080, Ipsilon, January 1997.

14. G. Malkin, "RIP Version 2 Applicability Statement," RFC-2081, November 1998.

15. G. Malkin, "RIPng Protocol Applicability Statement," RFC-2081, November 1998.

16. G. Meyer and S. Sherry, "Triggered Extensions to RIP to Support Demand Circuits," January 1997.

Why Is OSPF So Complex?

6

$\mathbf{R}$IP is both limited and simple. OSPF, on the other hand, is both very powerful and somewhat complex.

6.1 Open Shortest Path First

The very early packet networks, such as Arpanet or Cyclades, used distance vector protocols, similar to RIP. In fact, the question at the time was whether one should use distributed routing at all. Several commercial designs relied on a management center that would compute the routing tables centrally and download them into the network nodes. One of the arguments for this "central command" was the relative immaturity of the distributed protocols. We saw in the previous chapter that distance vector protocols do, indeed, exhibit some undesirable characteristics.

The link state technology was developed for use in the Arpanet to overcome these critics [1, 2]. Instead of exchanging distances to destinations, the nodes will all maintain a "map" of the network that will be updated quickly after any change in the topology. These maps can be used to compute more accurate routes than can be computed with the distance vector protocols. In fact, the routes will be as precise as if they had been computed centrally, although the computation will still be distributed. The early work on the Arpanet has led to several protocol designs that use the link state technology, e.g., the IS-IS protocol for the OSI network layer. OSPF is the link state protocol developed by the IETF for use in the Internet. It is now the protocol recommended by the IAB as a replacement for RIP.

In this chapter, we will first present the link state technology and the reason why this technology is generally deemed superior to the distance vector family. Then, we will present the design of OSPF, its link state database and its components, before trying to answer the key question: how could the IETF come out with such an incredibly complex design described in about 100 pages of thinly written text, when less than 20 pages are needed to describe RIP?

6.2 What Is a Link State Routing Protocol?

Link state protocols are based on the "distributed map" concept: all nodes have a copy of the network map, which is regularly updated. In this section, we will examine how the map is in fact represented by a database, how updates are "flooded" to the network nodes, why the map updates must be secured, how networks can split and then rejoin, and why some protocol of the link state family came to be called "shortest path first" (SPF).

6.2.1 The Link State Database

The principle of link state routing is very simple. Instead of trying to compute "best routes" in a distributed fashion, all the nodes will maintain a complete copy of the network map and perform a complete computation of the best routes from this local map. The network map is held in a database, where each record represents one link in the network. For example, the network:

```
(A)   — 1 —  (B)   — 2 —  (C)
 |            |          /
 3            4         /
 |            |        /
(D)   — 6 —  (E)   — 5 /
```

will be represented by the database:

From	To	Link	Distance
A	B	1	1
A	D	3	1
B	A	1	1
B	C	2	1
B	E	4	1
C	B	2	1
C	E	5	1
D	A	3	1
D	E	6	1
E	B	4	1
E	C	5	1
E	D	6	1

Each record has been inserted by one station that is responsible for it. It contains an interface identifier, the link number in our case, and information describing the state of the link: the destination and the distance or "metric." With the information, each node can easily compute the shortest path from itself to all other nodes. With modern computers, it takes only a short time to compute these routes, typically a fraction of a second if the network is not too large. As all nodes have the same database and execute the same route-generation algorithm, the routes are coherent and loops cannot occur. For example, if we send a packet from A to C in our network, we will rely upon computations by A and B.

```
(A) >> ⁻1 —  (B) >> ⁻2 —  (C)
 |            |          /
 3            4         /
 |            |        /
(D) >> ⁻6 —  (E) >> ⁻5 /
```

A has computed from the database that the shortest route to C is through B, so it sends the packet on link number 1. B will then send the packet on link number 2.

6.2.2 The Flooding Protocol

The purpose of a routing protocol is to adapt the routes to the changing conditions of the network. This can be done only if the database is updated after each change of link state.

```
(A)     xxxxx     (B)   — 2 —   (C)
 |                 |              /
 3                 4            /
 |                 |          /
(D)   — 6 —       (E)   — 5 /
```

The change of status of link number 1 is detected by the nodes A and B, which will have to update the corresponding records in the database and transmit them to all the other nodes. The protocol used for this transmission should be both very fast and very reliable. This is generally achieved by a flooding protocol. Just after detecting that link 1 has come down, A will send to D an update message on link number 3:

```
From A, to B, link 1, distance = infinite
```

D will immediately relay this message to E on link number 6, which will in turn relay it to B on link 4, and to C on link 5.

In fact, the message needs to be a little more complex than what we just explained. If we did not take sufficient precautions, it would be possible for an old message to come back and pollute the database. Thus, each message contains either a time stamp or a message number, which enables the receiving node to distinguish old and new information. The flooding algorithm can thus be expressed very simply as follows:

1. Receive the message. Look for the record in the database.
2. If the record is not yet present, add it to the database. Broadcast the message.
3. Else if the number in the database is lower than the number in the message, replace the record by the new value. Broadcast the message.
4. Else if the number in the database is higher, transmit the database value in a new message through the incoming interface.
5. Else if both numbers are equal, do nothing.

In this algorithm, the broadcast operation will cause the transmission of the message on all interfaces except the incoming one. If we assume that the initial number associated with the database record was 1, the message sent by A will thus be

```
From A, to B, link 1, distance = infinite, number = 2
```

D will update its database information and broadcast the message to E. E will also update its database and transmit the message to B and C, which will also update their records and attempt to transmit the information to C and B, respectively. When they receive the second message, C and B will notice that the number is equal to the one in the base, so they will not retransmit it any further—the flooding stops here. During the same period, B will have transmitted its new status of link 1 to C and E.

```
From B, to A, link 1, distance = infinite, number = 2
```

The flooding protocol will carry this update to D and then to A, after which the new routes will be computed.

From	To	Link	Distance	Number
A	B	1	inf	2
A	D	3	1	1
B	A	1	inf	2
B	C	2	1	1
B	E	4	1	1
C	B	2	1	1
C	E	5	1	1
D	A	3	1	1
D	E	6	1	1
E	B	4	1	1
E	C	5	1	1
E	D	6	1	1

— The database after flooding —

Note that the comparison of sequence numbers is not completely obvious. Since the objective is to keep the network operational for a very long time, the sequence numbers could potentially become extremely large, exceeding the number of bits reserved for their encoding in the packets or in the database records. The protocols generally use a "modulo N" numbering—e.g., where the number that follows 4,294,967,295 (2 to the power 32, minus 1) is 0, not 4,294,967,296. Such a number space is circular; one needs an explicit convention to define when X is larger than Y.

The sequence numbers are normally incremented slowly, e.g., after a link transition or after a rather long timer. Thus, if one needs to add only a small increment to X to obtain Y, then it is realistic to guess that Y was sent later than X, and vice versa. Indeed, one has to define what "a small increment" is; one also has to define the comparison very precisely, so that all routers retain the same version of a given record. The convention used by OSPF was suggested by Radia Perlman in 1983 [3], and is referred to as the "lollipop" sequence space. We will present it later, when we analyze the details of the OSPF protocol. In fact, we may note that if one uses 32-bit sequence numbers, many decades may pass before wraparound.

6.2.3 Bringing Up Adjacencies

In the analysis of distance vector protocols, we considered the case of a second link failure that led to a particular network configuration.

This has interesting consequences in the link state case. The failure of link number 6 will be detected by D and E, but each of them will be able to distribute the new information only to their "connected" neighbors. After executing the flooding, we will thus have two versions of the database: the network will be split between two nonconnected parts. A and D on one side and B, C, and E on the other side will see somewhat different values.

From	To	Link	Distance	Number
A	B	1	inf	2
A	D	3	1	1
B	A	1	inf	2
B	C	2	1	1
B	E	4	1	1
C	B	2	1	1
C	E	5	1	1
D	A	3	1	1
D	E	6	inf	2
E	B	4	1	1
E	C	5	1	1
E	D	6	1	1

The database seen by A and D

From	To	Link	Distance	Number
A	B	1	inf	2
A	D	3	1	1
B	A	1	inf	2
B	C	2	1	1
B	E	4	1	1
C	B	2	1	1
C	E	5	1	1
D	A	3	1	1
D	E	6	1	1
E	B	4	1	1
E	C	5	1	1
E	D	6	inf	2

The database seen by B,C, and E

This is not very important—since any route from A and D to B, C, or E would have to go through a link of "infinite" metric, A and D will notice that B, C, and E are unreachable, while B, D, and E will also notice that A and D are unreachable. In fact, they will be able to compute this new routing status immediately after receiving the new link state without any risk of engaging themselves in the dreadful count-to-infinity procedure. If the two parts remain isolated for a long period, the two versions of the database may well evolve independently—for example, link 2 may well become disconnected. The data base for B, C, and E will change to:

From	To	Link	Distance	Number
A	B	1	inf	2
A	D	3	1	1
B	A	1	inf	2
B	C	2	inf	2
B	E	4	1	1
C	B	2	inf	2
C	E	5	1	1
D	A	3	1	1
D	E	6	1	1
E	B	4	1	1
E	C	5	1	1
E	D	6	inf	2

while the database in A and D will remain unchanged. Again, this is not very important: B, C, and E will compute correct routes for exchanging packets between themselves, while A and D will remain disconnected.

But let's now consider what happens when one of the two links is reset, thus reconnecting the two parties. Merely distributing the new link information would not be sufficient. Suppose that the link number 1 now becomes operational. The records describing it will be corrected in both halves of the network, but the records describing links number 2 and 6 will still be incoherent. Establishing connectivity between two nodes requires more than just sending one database record. One must also guarantee that the two parties end up with "aligned" databases. This process is called "bringing up adjacencies" in OSPF.

The alignment of the two databases is eased by the existence of link identifiers and "version numbers." The two parties must synchronize their databases and keep only the most up-to-date version of each record, i.e., for each link, the record with the "largest" number. Implementing a naive "merge" by exchanging complete copies would be quite inefficient. It may well be the case that most records are similar in the two copies, so there is no need to send them. OSPF solves this problem by defining "database description" packets, which contain only the link identifiers and the corresponding version numbers. During the first phase of the synchronization procedure, both routers will send a complete description of their databases' records in a sequence of description packets. Upon reception of these packets, they will compare the sequence numbers with those present in their own base and build a list of "interesting records," such as when the remote number is larger than the local number or when the link identifier is not present in the local database. In the second phase of the synchronization procedure, each router will poll its neighbor for a full copy of these interesting records through "link state request" packets.

As a consequence of the synchronization, several records will be updated. These updated records will have to be transmitted to the other neighbors, using the normal flooding procedure.

6.2.4 Securing the Map Updates

The whole idea of the link state routing protocols is to maintain a synchronized copy of the link state database in all the nodes of the network. It is essential that all copies be identical, because otherwise the coherency of the routing could not be guaranteed. Indeed, there will be transition intervals during which some nodes will be more up to date than others, such as just after a link failure. But the flooding procedure will quickly propagate the update to all the network nodes.

In 1983, Radia Perlman demonstrated the need to actively protect the distributed routing database against accidental corruption [3]. Examples of accidents can be failures in the flooding or synchronization procedures, maintenance of stale records in the database, memory errors, or even voluntary introduction of misleading information by mischievous agents. Using the experience of the "new" Arpanet algorithm [1,2] and Radia's work, OSPF includes a number of protections against these dangers:

☞ The flooding procedure includes hop-by-hop acknowledgments.
☞ The database description packets are transmitted in a secure fashion.
☞ Each link state record is protected by a timer and is removed from the database if a refreshing packet does not arrive in due time.
☞ All records are protected by a checksum.
☞ The messages can be authenticated, e.g., by passwords.

A particular problem arises when a network node is brought up shortly after a failure. This node will attempt to flood the network with an initial version of its own link state records, starting with the initial sequence number. If the downtime has been short enough, old versions of the node's records will still be present in the database; their number will appear newer and the node will receive a copy of these old records. In order to accelerate convergency, the node should use the received number, increment it, and immediately retransmit its records with this new number.

6.2.5 Why Is It Called "Shortest Path First"?

We have seen in the previous chapter that distance vector protocols are based on the Bellman-Ford algorithm for shortest path computation. This algorithm is very easy to explain, but is not the most efficient. E. W. Dijkstra proposed a faster algorithm that he called "shortest path first" [4]. The SPF algorithm computes the shortest path between one source node and the other nodes in the network. It separates the nodes into two sets: the set of evaluated nodes, E, for which the shortest paths are known, and the set of remaining nodes, R. It also maintains an ordered list of paths, O. The algorithm works as follows:

1. Initialize the set E to contain only the source node S and R to contain all other nodes. Initialize the list of paths O to contain the one segment paths starting from S. Each of these paths has a cost equal to the corresponding link's metric. Sort list O by increasing metrics.
2. If list O is empty, or if the first path in O has an infinite metric, mark all nodes left in R as unreachable. The algorithm has terminated.
3. First examine P, the shortest path in list O (this is where the name comes from). Remove P from O. Let V be the last node in P. If V is already in set E, continue at step 2. Otherwise, P is the shortest path to V. Move V from R to E.
4. Build a set of new candidate paths by concatenating P and each of the links starting from V. The cost of these paths is the sum of the cost of P and the metric of the link appended to P. Insert the new links in the ordered list O, each at the rank corresponding to its cost. Continue at step 2.

We can easily show that the total number of paths that will be considered is equal to the number of links in the network. The algorithm is equivalent to a sort of these paths. If we implement the insertion operation adequately, the algorithm will thus scale as $0(M.\log M)$, where M is the number of links.

In fact, there is no absolute necessity to implement Dijkstra's SPF algorithm in order to run a link state protocol. The only mandatory requirement is that all nodes should use exactly the same metrics so that they find the same shortest path whatever the algorithm. But it is generally a good idea to implement a more efficient algorithm. SPF converges in $0(M.\log M)$ iterations, while Bellman-Ford converges in $0(N.M)$ where N is the number of nodes, generally of the same order of magnitude as the number of links. For large networks with many links, this can make a sizable difference!

This explains the name of the OSPF protocol—"open shortest path first"—because nodes are expected to run the SPF algorithm and because the specification was developed in an open fashion by the IETF.

6.3 Why Is a Link State Protocol Better?

We said in the previous chapter that most network specialists favor link state protocols over the distance vector variety. There are several good reasons for this, including

☞ fast, loopless convergency;

☞ support of precise metrics and, if needed, multiple metrics;

☞ support of multiple paths to a destination; and

☞ separate representation of external routes.

Let's analyze these reasons.

6.3.1 Fast, Loopless Convergence

As mentioned before, distance vector protocols execute a distributed computation using the Bellman-Ford algorithm. The number of steps required by this algorithm is proportional to the number of nodes in the network; in the worst case scenario, it is equal to the number of hops in the longest path. The link state scenario, on the contrary, consists of two phases.

1. a rapid transmission of the new information through the flooding protocol
2. a local computation

Indeed, one could argue that the "triggered updates" mechanism does not, in practice, require many more messages than the flooding protocol. But this is true only in the relatively favorable case where one update is enough to correct the routing tables. Many distance vector protocols require that successive updates be spaced by a "decent" interval—between 1 and 5 seconds for RIP. This interval itself is much larger than the time needed to compute the routing table—about 200 milliseconds (ms) for a 200-node network on a typical router. Also, one should observe that a link failure generally affects several destinations. In a distance vector protocol, the size of the messages will be proportional to the number of destinations; if the number is large enough, one will have to split the distance vector into several packets.

Even more important is the "loopless" property. Immediately after the flooding and the computation, all routes in the network are sane—no intermediate loops, no counting to infinity. Given the disruptive consequences of routing loops, this property alone is enough to make OSPF preferable to RIP.

6.3.2 Support of Multiple Metrics

We saw in the previous chapter that it is difficult with a distance vector protocol to support fine-grained metrics. If the cost of links varies too much—if the cost of the "best" links becomes orders of magnitudes cheaper than that of the "slowest" links—then there is a risk to wait a very long time, when counting to infinity becomes necessary. This risk does not exist with the link state algorithm. As the shortest-path computation is executed with a full knowledge of the topology, one can use arbitrarily precise metrics without slowing the convergence.

In fact, the precision of the computation makes it possible to support several metrics in parallel. This approach was outlined by Radia Perlman [5] and is based on the various requirements of network applications. Defining a "best route" is very arbitrary, and we already mentioned four definitions during the analysis of IP:

☞ the largest throughput
☞ the lowest delay
☞ the lowest cost
☞ the best reliability, defined as the lowest packet loss probability

Indeed, different media have different characteristics. A typical example is the satellite link that is generally less expensive than a terrestrial link of equivalent throughput, but that suffers from a larger delay. Handling different metrics with a link state algorithm requires

☞ documenting several metrics for each link,
☞ computing different routing tables for each metric, and
☞ presenting the selected metric in the packets.

Let's consider for example that we document for each link its throughput, its transmission delay, a cost per bit, and a reliability indicator. Then, one can compute these values for any given path. The throughput is that of the narrowest link in the path; the delay and the cost are the sum of the links' delays and costs; the reliability is a combination of the links' reliabilities. Indeed, this will lead to different shortest paths according to different metrics. Consider the following network:

where (1) is a T1 satellite link, (2) and (3) T1 terrestrial links, (4) and (5) are 64-kbps terrestrial links. The satellite link has a long delay (275 ms), while the terrestrial links have a delay of 10 ms. Now, consider two paths.

☞ D, C, A, B has a throughput of 1.5 Mbps (T1) and a delay of 295 ms.
☞ D, E, B has a throughput of 64 kbps and a delay of 20 ms.

The first path will be preferred if one considers a "throughput" metric, the second one with a "delay" metric.

If one starts using multiple metrics in a network, one must be very sure to make consistent decisions in all the nodes. Suppose that in our example network the node D receives a packet bound to B and routes it according to best throughput, i.e., through C. Now suppose that C receives the same packet and decides to route it according to "best delay"—back to D! By making incoherent decisions, these two nodes have installed a routing loop. There is indeed one obvious solution: have a clear indication in each packet of the metric that should be used for routing.

OSPF version 2 supports this type of extension.

6.3.3 Multiple Paths

It is often the case, in complex networks, that several "almost equivalent" routes exist toward a destination. For example, in

we can observe that the paths from A to E through B and through D have the same length; this is also true for the paths from D to B through A and through E. In the RIP analysis, we chose one of these two paths at random, because there was only one next-hop entry in the routing table. This simple decision has a major drawback: instead of using all the available capacity, one uses only half of it.

Mathematical analysis has proven that splitting the traffic over the two paths is more efficient, provides shorter delays overall [6, 7]. Indeed, this will lead to the out-of-order delivery of some packets as the queues in the intermediate nodes may well have different sizes. But if all the packets accumulated on a single path, the overall size of the queues would be larger. The mathematical analysis has proven that the average delay will be lower in the split-traffic case, which is very intuitive, because the available throughput is larger. It has also proven that the variations of the delay will be lower, which is less intuitive but is due to the reduction in the correlation between packet arrivals on any single path. In short, spreading the traffic over all the available paths is a good idea and should be implemented. Spreading the traffic also cures a less obvious inconvenience of simple routing: if one chooses a single route and it becomes unavailable, all of a sudden the traffic will be rerouted through the alternate path, possibly leading to congestion of this path. This phenomenon was observed in the early Arpanet, whose topology included two main clouds on the East and West coasts of the United States, linked by two paths through the South and the North of the country. Minor changes in topology could cause major swaps of routes and network instability. On the contrary, if the traffic is spread over several paths, only a fraction of it will have to be rerouted after a link failure, and the overall pattern will be much smoother.

A simple improvement to the shortest path computation can provide us with a list of shortest distance paths to any given destination in the network. We showed in section 6.2.5 that the SPF algorithm progressively builds a set E of nodes whose distance to the origin S is known. Nodes are introduced in E in the order of their distance to S. In step 3, we reject the paths that lead to a node already in the set E, because such paths cannot possibly be shorter than the path that we already found. However, they can be of equal length. Thus, a simple modification of the SPF algorithm allows us to detect all the "equal length" paths:

1. Initialize the set E, the list O, as in the standard SPF algorithm.
2. If O is empty, the algorithm as terminated.
3. First examine P, the shortest path in the list O. Remove P from O. Let V be the last node in P. If V is already in the set E, check continue at step 4. Otherwise, P is the shortest path to V. Move V from R to E. Continue at step 5.

4. If the metric of path P between S and V is equal to the previously computed distance between S and V, we have found an "equal cost path" to V. If it is larger, we should ignore P. In all cases, continue at step 2.

5. Build the new set of candidate paths, add them to O, as in step 4 of the standard algorithm. Continue at step 2.

We should note that this algorithm will not, in fact, find all the paths from the source S to the network destination. What we obtain here for each destination is a list of "previous hops," the last node W on a path P before its target V. To reach a destination P, we have to reach one of the selected previous hops $W_1 \dots W_n$. When these hops are not adjacent to the source S, we have to proceed recursively, until we identify a list of direct neighbors $U_1 \dots U_n$. At this point, the source can arbitrarily decide to split the traffic bound to P between the shortest paths to these neighbors: all packets will follow equal cost paths. This procedure is used in OSPF, where it is called "equal cost multi-path." The OSPF specification is that traffic should be split equally between all the equal cost paths.

Splitting the traffic between several paths may however have detrimental effects, especially in the case of TCP connections. The various paths may have equivalent metrics, but the packets routed on separate paths will encounter different queuing conditions, will suffer from different delays, and may arrive in disorder. Many TCP implementations will react to disorder by triggering retransmissions, which will slow the overall performance. The classic remedy to this problem is to split the traffic between the paths in such a way that a given TCP connection is always routed on a single path. Many routers will compute a hash code, H, from the packet source and destination addresses and port numbers. They will then split the traffic based on the hash code values. They can, for example, send all traffic whose hash code is lower than or equal to H_1 on the first path, and all traffic whose hash code is greater than H_1 on the the second path. If there are more than two paths, routers can use a set of values, H_1, H_2, and so on, to split the traffic between the various paths.

Equal cost multi-path is an improvement over single path routing, but it is by no means a final solution to the traffic optimization problem, i.e., how to best balance the load between the various paths. This is an old problem, for which solutions have been proposed since the mid 1970s. A typical approach is to augment the information in the routing database with indication on the load of the various links, and then to combine that load indication into the metric used to compute the shortest paths. The idea is to create a feedback loop that works as follows:

☞ Routers receive new link state records that indicate the load of the paths, and compute the new shortest paths.

☞ The traffic is sent toward the new paths, changing the load of these paths.

☞ The routers measure the new loads and flood a new link state record.

The problem is that any feedback loop oscillates between two extremes. If the loop is too slow, we will not observe much improvement over shortest path routing. If, on the contrary, the loop is too fast, if the new load is measured and flooded very rapidly, we will observe wide oscillations, as traffic is abruptly rerouted from a loaded path to a previously empty path. A first solution to this problem is to take into account both the path length and the path load, and to only use the load indication as a way to split the traffic between the selected paths, so that only some traffic is rerouted from one path to another.

In fact, if we look at the problem from a high level, we find that we are facing a classic flow maximization problem: how to best split the network traffic on a set of possible paths P, where "best" is defined by some cost function. Flow maximization is a difficult problem. Add to this the fact that we really want a distributed solution, where routers make independent decisions that, when combined, are supposed to converge toward the optimum solution; and that we want a feedback-loop solution, where the split of traffic over different routes is recomputed as the traffic conditions evolve.

The exact solution is NP complete: it requires that a central system examines all the possible paths in the network. In practice, one can obtain a good approximation of the solution by only retaining some of the network paths—typically 4 to 6 between each source-destination pair. The problem can then be solved by linear programming:

1. Assign levels of traffic to each of the paths.
2. Sum the contributions of each of the paths to the load of each link.
3. Compute a cost function based on the routed traffic and the cost of the links.
4. Iterate until we have found an optimal point.

Such algorithms can be distributed. The classic solution is to assign a "price" to each of the links. The price reflects the first derivative of the link's cost function, for the submitted traffic. The various nodes use the price as a guide for their assignment of traffic to the different paths. Convergence is obtained when the price of all saturated links in the network is equal. This kind of work, however, is still very much a research issue. Adding information to a link state record is easy; one can think, for example, that the packet loss rate observed on a link is a good approximation of the link's cost. Finding the right period for computing and flooding such information is more difficult, although conservative values ranging from 15 seconds to 2 minutes have been showed to provide good results. More difficult is the selection of "four to six candidate paths." Let's take a counter example, the one of our test network:

```
(A)   —1—   (B)   —2—   (C)
 |                 |           /
 3                 4          /
 |                 |         /
(D)   —6—   (E)   —5—
```

The path from E to C through B is only twice as long as the direct path through link number 5, and it might appear reasonable to send two-thirds of the traffic from E to C through link 5 and one-third through link 4. But B could apply the same logic and also send one-third of its traffic to C through link number 4. A kind of "partial loop" will have been formed, and link 4 will be overloaded very quickly. The network nodes can avoid this pitfall by applying a very simple rule: a packet bound to a node X can be relayed through a node Y only if Y is nearer to the destination than the local node. One can easily demonstrate that this simple ordering function breaks the partial loops demonstrated in our example.

However, in order to estimate the price of the path, one must sum the price of the links in the paths. This requires knowledge of the routing decisions performed by all of the routers in this path, following the general link state routing mantra that "all routers must execute the exact same algorithm." In practice, traffic optimization is still very much a research issue. We will present in section 6.8.3 the "Optimized Multi Path" proposal to implement load sharing in OSPF.

6.3.4 External Routes

In our simple examples, we have considered the internal-routes problem, i.e., how to compute the best path between two nodes within an "autonomous system." But the Internet connectivity extends well beyond this limited scope. The network is generally connected through one or several "external gateways" to one or several "transit networks," reaching millions of hosts worldwide.

When there is only one gateway to the external world, the matter is simple. One needs only to advertise a "default route" to that gateway; distance vectors and link state algorithms can both support this. But when one must choose between several gateways, between several service providers, the default-route solution is very crude. It leads to picking the nearest external gateway, even if another provider would have more efficiently carried the data to its destination. The alternative is to compute specific routes for all destinations, or at least for the most frequently used destinations. This is done differently for the distance vector and link state technologies. In one case, one will add one entry per destination in the distance vector, in the other case one will enter into the database what OSPF calls "gateway link state records." This leads to better performance for the link state algorithm due to more precise metrics and easier computations.

When a gateway starts announcing reachability to an external destination, it can initiate the distance to some value reflecting the cost of the external route. But we have seen that the maximum value of the distance vector metrics had to be kept lower than the conventional infinity; the link state technology will not have these limitations, and the gateway will be able to announce a metric that reflects more precisely the actual distance.

When the number of external entries increases, the size of the link state database or the size of the distance vectors increases linearly. But the cost of the computation of the routes increases as $0(N.\log N)$ for the SPF algorithm used by link state routers, as $0(N**2)$ for the Bellman-Ford algorithm used by distance vector routers. There were about 20,000 routes in the Internet in June of 1994, which does not bode well for the efficiency of fine-grain routing with distance vector protocols!

6.4 The Design of OSPF

OSPF is a link state protocol, and its design follows the general theory of such protocols. There is a distributed database, a flooding procedure, a definition of adjacency, and special records for external routes. OSPF, however, handles more than the simple point-to-point links that we used in our previous examples. Modern IP networks are built from simple point-to-point links, but they also include Ethernets, token rings, and FDDI rings. They are sometimes built on top of virtual circuits networks, notably X.25 and ATM. They may also be very large, much larger than the 5-node example that we used! OSPF has been designed with special support for

☞ separating hosts and routers;

☞ broadcast networks, such as Ethernet or FDDI;

☞ nonbroadcast networks, such as X.25 or ATM; and

☞ splitting very large networks in areas.

Let's analyze how this is accomplished.

6.4.1 Separating Hosts and Routers

A very frequent pattern in modern networks is that IP hosts are connected to a local net-work—for example, an Ethernet connected to the organization's network by a router. If we applied strictly the link state model, we should describe by a link state record the relation between each host and the router. OSPF allows for a simplification, based on the "subnet" model of IP. Since all hosts on the Ethernet belong to a single IP subnet, it is sufficient to advertise one link between the router and the subnet. In OSPF terminology, this is a special variant of "router link" called a "link to a stub network." The link to a neighbor is identified by the IP address of the neighbor; the link to a stub network is identified by its network or subnet number.

6.4.2 Broadcast Networks

Local networks using Ethernet or token-ring technologies offer two characteristic services:

☞ full connectivity—any station can send a packet to any other station; and

☞ broadcast capability—a station can send a packet that will reach all other stations (broad-cast) or all stations within a group (multicast).

Ethernet and token rings are indeed not the only technologies that offer these two services; FDDI and packet radio come to mind as immediate examples. OSPF does not in fact include a special provision for Ethernet but, rather, a generic support of broadcast networks.

The problem we need to solve is the "N squared" problem. Given N routers on a local net, one can establish as many adjacencies as there are pairs of routers: $N.(N-1)/2$. Each router will then advertise N-1 links to the other routers, plus one stub-network link for the hosts on the net-work, a total of N square.

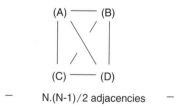

— $N.(N-1)/2$ adjacencies   —

OSPF tries to reduce this to only N adjacencies by designating one of the routers as "more equal" than the others. The other routers will establish adjacencies only with this designated router.

—   Adjacencies with designated router (A)   —

The first step is to elect the designated router. This election is incorporated in the "Hello" protocol—the protocol by which an OSPF router discovers its peers on a given link. After this election, the other routers will bring up adjacencies with the designated router, or synchronize their databases. One can easily demonstrate that, if all routers' databases are synchronized with the designated router's database, then all are synchronized together, and there is no need to engage in N.(N-1)/2 negotiations.

The presence of a designated router will also be used to reduce the number of link state records in the database. The broadcast network will be represented by a set of links between the routers and a "virtual node," as in:

—   Links to a virtual node   —

There really is not an actual router in the middle of the network. This is an abstract construct, used for simplifying the description. The database will include two links per router, from and to the virtual node, i.e., the broadcast network itself. The link from a router to the network is normally advertised by this router, while the designated router is in charge of advertising the links starting from this virtual node; it will use the IP address of its own interface to the broadcast network for identifying these links, called "network links" in the OSPF terminology. There is a potential problem when computing the distance between two nodes on this network: this distance is the sum of the metric of two links—from the source node to the network, and from the network to the destination node. But this second part is very artificial—one would not include it when computing the distance to a host on the network. OSPF solves this problem by requiring the network links to have a null metric.

The presence of a designated router is also used to simplify the flooding procedure. When a router must send a link state advertisement, it transmits it to the designated router only, using the "all-designated-routers" multicast address (224.0.0.6). If this is a new advertisement, the designated router will flood the link state on all its interfaces and will also resend it on the network, using the "all-OSPF-routers" multicast address (224.0.0.5).

The special role played by the designated router can be a liability. If this router fails, the network links will not be advertised further, and all the routers will appear disconnected from each other, although the network is in fact still operational. It is urgent in this case to elect a new

designated router as soon as possible. OSPF speeds up this process by electing a "backup designated router" at the same time as the designated router.

All routers are required to maintain adjacencies with both the designated router and the
backup. The database synchronization procedure which is required when bringing up an adjacency can be quite long, so it is useful to know that the backup is already synchronized. The
backup designated router listens to the all-designated-routers multicast address together with the
designated router, but remains "as silent as possible." It does not retransmit the advertisements on
the broadcast network. It leaves the handling of acknowledgments and repetitions to the designated router. It does not transmit network links advertisements either; this is the role of the designated router.

The failure of the designated router, when it occurs, will be detected by the Hello protocol.
The backup will immediately become designated and a new backup will be elected. All routers
will start building an adjacency with this new backup.

6.4.3 Nonbroadcast Networks

Some IP networks use virtual circuit networks to link their routers. Running IP over X.25
was quite popular in the 1980s in Europe, and it has been used in some major IP networks, such
as MILNET, IXI, JANET or EUROPANET. X.25 networks may not be so popular in the 1990s,
but new technologies such as "frame relay" or "ATM" provide very similar services, although at a
higher or much higher speed. These networks are different from the broadcast networks in one
aspect: they provide full connectivity between their members, but they do not provide a broadcasting or multicasting service. For this reason, they are called nonbroadcast networks in the
OSPF documentation.

There are two ways to use such networks. One can use static configurations of a set of virtual
circuits, which will be used as many point-to-point links. This is simple to design but hard to manage. Each virtual circuit is treated as an independent subnet, and a different address is attached to
the end of each of these circuits. If we want full connectivity, we will have to install N.(N-1)/2 circuits. Routing information is flooded on all circuits, which may be costly on "pay-per-volume"
public networks such as X.25 or ATM. In fact, we are experiencing here the classical N squared
effect of managing global connectivity as a set of point-to-point links. Reducing this complexity by
reducing the number of virtual circuits in the configuration is not desirable either as packets will
have to crisscross the public network, which again increases the pay-per-volume charges.

OSPF applies the same management to nonbroadcast and broadcast networks. The routers
will elect a designated router and a backup, and the routing information will be exchanged only
with these two routers. Having a designated router does not change the routing itself. Virtual circuits will be established between any pair of routers; IP packets will be transmitted directly on
these virtual circuits. But these circuits will be established only "on demand." The only circuits
that will be used quasi-permanently by the routing updates are those linking the "ordinary" routers to the designated router and to the backup.

The main difference between broadcast and nonbroadcast networks derives from the
absence of any multicast facility in a nonbroadcast network. All advertisement packets will have

to be sent point to point. The Hello packets that are used by the election process will carry a list of all the routers on the nonbroadcast network. When the designated router broadcasts an advertisement, it does so by sending a separate copy of the packet to each router. When a router floods an advertisement, it does so by sending one copy to the designated router and another to the backup router.

6.4.4 Multiple Areas

The size of the link state database, the duration of the route computation, and the volume of the messages increase when the size of the network increases. If the network is very large, all these factors become excessive. The memory required is too large, the computation takes too long, and the transmission overhead is unbearable. The classical answer to this problem is "hierarchical routing"—i.e., to split the network into a set of independent parts connected by a "backbone." In OSPF, these independent parts are called "areas," and the "upper" part is called the "backbone area."

Each area behaves like an independent network: the database includes only the state of the area's links. The flooding protocol stops at the boundaries of the area; the routers compute only routes within the area. The cost of the routing protocol is thus proportional to the size of the area, not to the size of the network.

In order to "glue" the network together, some routers belong to several areas—typically to one lower-level area and to the backbone area. These routers are called "area-border routers": there must be at least one area-border router in each area, connecting the area to the backbone. They maintain several link state databases—one for each area to which they belong. Each area includes a set of IP subnets. In order to signal their "reachability," the area-border routers emit special link state records, similar to the external links used by the external gateways to signal accesses to external networks. The external links originate from the border routers and describe outward routes; the "summary links" originate from the area-border routers and describe inward routes. Let's consider an example network:

```
            BB0  —  (b1)  —  BB1
             |              |
            (b2)           (b6)
             |              |
A1  —  (a2)  —  AB2        BC1  —  (c1)  —  C2
 |            |              |            |
(a1)         (b3)          (b5)          (c2)
 |            |              |            |
A3  —  (a3)  —  AB4  —  (b4)  —  BC3  —  (c3)  —  C4
```

This network contains two areas and a backbone area. The routers A1, AB2, A3, and AB4 belong to the area A, with the links a1, a2, and a3; the routers BC1, C2, BC3, and C4 belong to the area C, with the links c1, c2, and c3. The backbone area includes the border routers BB0 and BB1 from the area-border routers AB2, AB4, BC1, and BC3, and from the links b1, b2, b3, b4, b5, and b6.

The area routers will summarize the information so as to reduce the size of the link state database and the number of advertisements. For example, the database of the area A will contain

☞ the link state records corresponding to links a1, a2, and a3 sent by A1, AB2, A3, and AB4;

☞ summary records emitted by AB2 and AB4 for all the IP networks and subnets that are part of the backbone and of area C; and

☞ external records emitted by BB0 and BB1 and relayed by AB2 and AB4.

The summary records represent the links between an area-border router (AB2 or AB4) and a network in the backbone area or in another area. They have a metric equal to the length of the path between the area-border router and the network. Let's suppose, for example, that the link b1 is an Ethernet cable, identified by the IP subnet number nb1. AB2 will build up a "summary link" for nb1 and will set the metric to the sum of the metric of b1 and b2, while AB4 will also build up a link for nb1 but will use as metric of the summary link the sum of the metrics of b1, b2, and b3. Similarly, consider that the link c3 is an Ethernet cable, identified by the network number nc3. The area-border router BC3 will advertise on the backbone a summary link for this subnet, with a metric equal to the one of b3; while BC1 will advertise as metric the sum of c1, c2, and c3. Using this information, both AB2 and AB4 will compute that the shortest path to nc3 goes through BC3. They will send summary advertisements for nc3 in area A, using as metric the sum of c3 (the metric advertised from BC3) and the metric of the backbone path. AB4 will advertise the metric c3 + b4; AB2 will use c3 + b4 + b3. This is in fact very similar to the computation of the distance vector metrics, but it does not bear the same risks, as the topology does not include any possible loops. We have a strict hierarchy in which areas are connected only through the backbone.

The external link state records advertised by the border routers BB0 and BB1 are copied, unchanged, into the area's A database. In fact, summary links explaining how to reach each border router from AB2 and AB4 will also be added to the area's database, so that the area's routers can compute precise external routes. The external part of the database is identical for all areas.

A classic pitfall of hierarchical routing is the problem of "split networks." In the pure form of hierarchical routing, the backbone routers don't differentiate between destinations located inside a "leaf" area. They would pass any packet bound to any destination inside the area to the nearest area-border router—which can be very harmful if, due to link or router failures, the connectivity cannot be maintained inside the area, as in this example:

```
                    BB0  —  (b1)  —  BB1
                    |                 |
                   (b2)              (b6)
                    |                 |
     A1  —  (a2)  —  AB2              BC1  —  (c1)  —  C2
     x                |               |               |
     x               (b3)            (b5)            (c2)
     x                |               |               |
     A3  —  (a3)  —  AB4  —  (b4)  —  BC3  —  (c3)  —  C4
```

The link a1 is down, and the area A is split in two; it would be incorrect to pass to the router AB4 a packet bound to A1, or to AB2 a packet bound to A3. OSPF solves this problem very simply, since it does not in fact follow a strict hierarchical routing model. The area-border routers will not issue summary link state records for all the networks and subnets within area A, but only for those networks and subnets that they can reach. The area structure simplifies the backbone's database by removing from it the details of the area's configuration, but there is still potentially one entry per individual network within the area. The routing in the backbone is thus as precise as necessary, and the splitting of areas is very naturally cured. RFC-1131 explains this with a "colored map" analogy. We could draw the network map and show the area structure by assigning a color to each area or, more precisely, to all links within an area. In the normal situation we have leaves of different colors attached to the backbone, and there is exactly one leaf for each color. But leaves can be split, in which case we simply have two or more leaves of the same color. Indeed, if a fragment of a leaf is split in a way that completely separates it from the backbone, it loses all connectivity, but there is hardly anything that a routing protocol could do in this situation!

The cure for a split backbone is a bit harder to explain. Suppose that after two link failures our backbone is split in two parts: BB0, BB1, and BC1 on one side; AB2, AB4, and BC3 on the other side. There is no connectivity anymore through backbone links alone, but it could be restored if packets could only transit through area C.

```
              BB0  —  (b1)  —  BB1
               x                |
               x               (b6)
               x                |
A1  —  (a2)  —  AB2            BC1  —  (c1)  —  C2
 |              |               x                |
(a1)          (b3)             x               (c2)
 |              |               x                |
A3  —  (a3)  —  AB4  —  (b4)  —  BC3  —  (c3)  —  C4
```

In order to reestablish the connectivity, BC1 and BC3 must have configured a "virtual link" through area C. They must agree to exchange the backbone's database updates by sending them through area C, and they must announce their connectivity by describing the virtual link in the backbone's database. The metric of the virtual link will be computed from the size of the path linking BC1 and BC2 within the area—the sum of the metrics for links c1, c2, and c3, in our case—so that backbone packets use only the virtual link, if this is really the shortest route. Indeed, when BC1 computes its routes, it will discover that the route to AB4, for example, goes through the virtual link. Since there is no real hardware interface corresponding to this, BC1 should be smart enough to replace the "route through the virtual link to BC3" indication with a more concrete "route through link c1 to C2" instruction.

Virtual links will be used to exchange database updates, so that all of the backbone routers remain synchronized. This exchange will be slightly less efficient than the normal flooding procedure, because the intermediate queuing along the virtual path may induce random relays. The normal link state records will have to be flooded, but the external records will not. They are already flooded in the area's database, so they will be very normally received by all the area-border routers.

6.4.5 Stub Areas

The most numerous records in the link state database are generally the external records, describing all other destinations in the Internet. By June 1999, there were more than 60,000 routes. Due to the CIDR assignment strategy, several of these network numbers could probably be aggregated and replaced by "multinetwork" prefixes, reducing their number by an order of magnitude. But the Internet is still growing; in any case, even if the number of prefixes is not larger than a few thousand, areas are unlikely to include that many links. In fact, one problem is precisely reducing the cost of running OSPF in small areas that include only a handful of routers.

Often, these areas are connected only to the backbone by one single area-border router. There is then no point in detailing the external routes! Version 2 of OSPF introduced the concept of "stub" area—an area in which all external routes are summarized by a "default" route.

A stub area behaves exactly like a normal OSPF area, except for a few restrictions, which all derive from the refusal to enter "external routes" in the area's databases. A stub area may be connected by more than one area-border router to the backbone, but there will be no way to choose the area exit router on a destination-per-destination basis, nor to configure a virtual link over a stub area.

There also will be no way to connect a border router to a stub area. This is logical if we consider that border routers connect the autonomous system to the Internet and should normally be attached to the backbone area. But experience has shown that this is often too restrictive. In a number of cases one would like to "hang" a small network to this area—for example, a small secondary autonomous system coordinated through the RIP protocol. The OSPF working group has been studying this problem and has come out with the concept of "not so stubby area" (NSSA) [8]—an area where all external routes are replaced by a default route … except some!

6.5 The Link State Database

OSPF routers—or, more precisely, OSPF routers in the same area—share a database composed of "link state records." These records represent the network topology and are used to compute the shortest path. There are five link state or "LS" types (router, network, summary for IP network, summary for border router, external) and four types of link state records contents, as both summary links for IP network and summary links for border router have the same format.

In this section, we will present the record header and the various types of record contents.

6.5.1 The Link State Header

There are several types of link state records, but all records share the same "link state advertisement header":

LS age	options	LS type
Link State ID		
Advertising router		
LS sequence number		
LS checksum	length	

The "advertising router" is identified by one of its IP addresses, which is selected as "OSPF identifier" for that router. The "age" is a 16-bit unsigned integer, indicating the time in seconds since the link state record was first advertised. The 8-bit "option" fields describe the capabilities of the advertising router:

Out of these 8 bits, only 2 are defined in OSPF-2: E for "external links" and T for "type of service." The value of the E bit is used by the Hello protocol, which we will analyze later. The T bit is set when the router supports nonzero TOS. A value of zero indicates that only the "type 0" metric is supported and that the router does not support TOS routing.

The link state type is an 8-bit integer, which can take one of five values:

1. router link,
2. network link,
3. summary link (IP network),
4. summary link (to a border router), or
5. external link.

The identification of the link is chosen by the advertising router; it is generally an IP address, but the precise significance of this identifier varies with the type of link. The various protocols, e.g., database exchange or flooding, only make the hypothesis that the combination of advertising router ID, link ID, and link state record type uniquely identifies the record; the sequence number identifies one particular advertisement. The checksum is computed according to the standard IP algorithm and protects the header as well as the content. The length field is the total length of the record, including the 20-byte header.

The link state number is a 32-bit signed integer, taken within the "lollipop sequence space":

The sequence numbers vary between 1–N and N–2, where N is 2 to the power 31 (2,147,483,648). The numbers –N and N–1, which could be encoded in the 32-bit space, are not used. When a router starts advertising a link state, it uses the negative number 1–N; it will regularly increment this number in the subsequent advertisements. When the number reaches N–2, the next value will be 0 (N–1 would be illegal) and the numbers will continue to cycle in the positive segment of the sequence space. This explains the lollipop analogy: the negative part of the sequence space is consumed linearly and is represented by the stick, while the cycle of positive numbers is a round candy. The comparison rules follow the shape of the number space. If at least one of the numbers is negative, one can use direct comparisons; but, if both numbers are positive or null, one must use "cyclic" comparison. Suppose that we want to compare the two positive or null numbers a and b, with a being lower than b. We compute the difference $(b–a)$. If this difference is smaller than a half circle (i.e., smaller than $(N–1)/2$), then we decide that b is "newer" than a; otherwise, we will say that a is newer.

We should note that there is a potential problem with the lollipop scheme. When multiple restarts of a router occur in close succession, such that all updates for the router have negative sequence numbers, it is not possible to distinguish the newer from the older updates, since the newest may have the most negative sequence numbers.

6.5.2 The Router Links

The "router links state record" summarizes all the links that start from the advertising router. The link ID specifies the OSPF's router ID; the content starts with a 32-bit word specifying the number of links and the type of router, followed by a set of link descriptions.

--0---EB	---0----	number of links
Link ID		
Link data		
Type	# TOS	TOS 0 metric
TOS=x	0	TOS x metric
TOS=y	0	TOS y metric
- - -	- - -	- - -
TOS=z	0	TOS z metric

Bits 6 and 7 of the first octet, called E and B, are set if the router is an area-border router (E, external) or a border router (B, border). For each link, one finds a link ID, link data, and a link type. This type can take three values:

1. The link is a point-to-point link to another router. The link ID is then the OSPF identifier of this router, and the link data is the router's interface IP address.
2. The link connects to a transit network. The link ID is the IP address of the designated router's interface, and the link data is the router's interface IP address.
3. The link connects to a stub network. The link ID is the IP network or subnet number, and the link data is the corresponding network or subnet mask.

All advertisements must include the metric of the link for the default TOS (0). They may also include a variable number (# TOS) of TOS metrics. Each of these will include a TOS number (the same value that appears in IP packets) and the corresponding metric.

6.5.3 The Network Links

Network links (link state type = 2) are advertised by designated routers for transit networks (broadcast as well as nonbroadcast). The link state ID is the corresponding IP interface ID.

Network mask
Attached router
- - -
Attached router

The content of the record is the 32-bit network or subnet mask followed by the OSPF identifier of all the attached routers or, more precisely, of all the routers that have built up an adjacency with the designated router. There is no "number-of-routers" field, as this can be deduced from the content's length.

6.5.4 The Summary Links

Summary links for IP networks (link state type = 3) and for border routers (link state type = 4) are advertised by area-border routers. Although these routers may advertise several summary links, they will not pack them in a single advertisement similar to the router links, but will issue one separate advertisement for each destination. The link state ID is the IP network or subnet number (type = 3) or the IP address of the border router (type = 4). The content is a 32-bit mask, followed by a set of metrics.

Network mask		
TOS=0	0	TOS 0 metric
TOS=x	0	TOS x metric
- - -	- - -	- - -
TOS=z	0	TOS z metric

The mask is that of the network or subnet, or the hexadecimal value FFFFFFFF for a border router link. The list of TOS metrics is similar to that of router links and always starts with the value of the TOS metric. There is no "number-of-TOS" field, as this can be deduced from the content's length.

6.5.5 The External Links

External links (link state type = 5) are advertised by border routers. As for summary links, there is exactly one destination advertisement per record. The link state ID is the IP network or subnet number of the destination. The content is a 32-bit mask, followed by a set of metrics.

Network mask		
E,TOS=0	0	TOS 0 metric
External route tag (0)		
E,TOS=x	0	TOS x metric
External route tag (x)		
- - -	- - -	- - -
E,TOS=z	0	TOS z metric
External route tag (z)		

The list of TOS metrics is different from that of the router's links in two ways: the TOS field itself includes an E (external) bit at position 0, and the metric is followed by a 32-bit "external tag."

External routes are acquired by the border routers through "external gateway" protocols such as EGP or BGP. These protocols do not necessarily provide estimations of distances in units comparable to the metrics of OSPF. They are more concerned with policies and configurations. The E bit is set to indicate that the metric for this TOS is "not comparable" to the internal metrics and should be considered "larger than any internal route." When the E bit is 0, the metric can be added to the cost of the internal path to compute the cost of a path to the destination through the border router.

The "external route tag" is a 32-bit field used by border routers to exchange information about the route. It is not examined by OSPF.

6.5.6 The Computation of Routes

The link state database is used to compute the network routes, which must be computed again after any change in the topology. The computation follows closely the generic link state model presented earlier. A graph representing the network is extracted from the various link state records. The internal vertices are the OSPF routers and the transit networks; the peripheral vertices are the stub networks, the summarized networks, and the external destinations. The arcs are the various links; they have various TOS metrics.

The SPF algorithm is used to compute the shortest path and equal paths from the local OSPF router to each destination. From this computation, the router derives the next hop for the destination, i.e., the next router to which the data shall be sent and the link that should be used for reaching this next router. After computing the table, the OSPF process passes the information to the "IP forwarding" process.

The routes are first computed for the "default TOS"—for TOS 0. If the router is capable of TOS routing, it should also compute routes for each of the TOSs. Each TOS is identified by four bits—D, T, O, C—in the IP headers (see section 3.3.2), for which "legal" values are defined [9]. As the IP TOS field is actually 5 bits long, OSPF uses the following encodings:

OSPF encoding	RFC-1349 TOS values	
0	0000	normal service
2	0001	minimize monetary cost
4	0010	maximize reliability
8	0100	maximize throughput
16	1000	minimize delay

For example, if an IP packet carries a TOS field of 0100 (maximize throughput), then it should be routed according to the routes computed for the metric number 8. The OSPF link state advertisement may carry different metrics for different TOSs; OSPF specifies that the different values should always be transmitted in ascending order of the TOS number. Routers, even if they support TOS routing, need not advertise a specific metric for all possible TOS values. If no metric is specified for a nonzero TOS, then the value specified for TOS 0 will be used when computing a route.

Routers that do not support TOS routing advertise this feature by setting a "support-of-TOS" bit to 0 in their link state advertisement. Links through these routers should not be used when computing the route for a nonzero TOS. This may, however, result in some destination becoming unreachable for some TOS. The corresponding packets should be routed according to the TOS 0 routes. This cannot result in looping packets, as all routers have the same database and will make the same decision; routers that do not support TOS will always route according to TOS 0.

Metric values are supposed to be integers—the lowest values corresponding to the best routes. For example, the "bandwidth" metric is set to 100,000,000/interface speed (i.e., the number of seconds needed to transmit 100 million bits over the interface). The value is set to 1 if the link has a throughput larger than 100 Mbps [10]. This value is easy to compute from a "natural" description of the interface and thus can be easily "autoconfigured." This same value is also used as the default metric for the link. The default route corresponds to the route with the highest throughput.

The formulas for setting the "delay," "reliability," or "cost" metrics are not defined in the OSPF documentation. The manager who wants to enable type-of-service routing with these criteria will have to check that all links are configured with consistent metrics. The easiest way is to consider that the default metric is acceptable for most of the links. One simply has to increase the appropriate metrics if the link has too long a delay, is not reliable, or is too expensive.

One should consider that the best delay routes are those that minimize the transmission time of a short packet, e.g., one that is 1,000 bits long. This is usually achieved by using the bandwidth metric, since the most important delays occur in queues: longer queues build up in front of slower links. However, some links, such as satellite links, may have an excessive propagation delay. The bandwidth metric can be interpreted as the number of units of 10 μs necessary to forward a 1,000-bit message; the 275-ms propagation delay of a satellite link should thus result in a value of 27,500 for the metric number 16. It will probably not be necessary to enter any specific information for the nonsatellite links, as the throughput considerations dominate.

One could use the same reasoning to assert "monetary" metrics only for those links that have a "volume-charging" nature, such as X.25 or ISDN connections. Similarly, one will assert "reliability" metrics for the links that are known to be less reliable than usual, like packet radio channels. For these cases OSPF defines a special metric value—the maximum possible value, 65,535. Specifying it for a given TOS indicates that the link should not be used for this type of service. One could set, for example, the cost of a pay-per-volume X.25 circuit to 65,535 for the TOS 2. The packets that are routed according to the "minimal monetary cost" metric are never carried over that circuit.

6.6 The Protocols Within OSPF

OSPF routers communicate through the OSPF protocol. This protocol runs directly on top of IP (protocol type 89) and is in fact composed of three subprotocols: Hello, Exchange, and Flooding. The flooding protocol is used to pass routing updates; it is also used to synchronize the "aging" of database records.

6.6.1 The Common Header

All OSPF packets start with a common header:

Version #	Type	Packet length
Router ID		
Area ID		
Checksum		Autype
Authentication		
Authentication		

Most fields within this common header have obvious meanings:

☞ The version number is set to 2 to indicate the current version of OSPF.

☞ The "type" is the OSPF packet type.

☞ The packet length is the number of bytes in the packet.

☞ The "router ID" is the IP address selected for identifying the router.

☞ The "area ID" is the identification of the area. The value 0 is reserved for the backbone area. It is common practice to chose an IP network number for identifying an area.

☞ The checksum is computed on the whole OSPF packet, excluding the 8-octet authentication field, using the classic IP algorithm.

The "autype" field identifies the authentication algorithm. Three values are defined in the standard itself.

0: No authentication

1: Simple authentication

2: Cryptographic authentication

In the simple authentication case, the authentication field carries an 8-character "password." network administrators can configure a different password for each "network," e.g., for each point-to-point connection or each Ethernet. As we mentioned in the analysis of RIP, this is not a terribly foolproof authentication method. It is, however, a good guarantee against inadvertent mistakes, such as plugging a router on an Ethernet without properly configuring it. It also has the side effect that, if two autonomous systems happen to share the same cable, their routers will remain isolated. Each autonomous system uses a different password.

0	Key ID	Auth. data len
Cryptographic sequence number		

The 64-bit cryptographic authentication header

The cryptographic authentication procedure is very similar to the RIP authentication procedure that we detailed in chapter 5, section 5.4.3. When this procedure is used, the 64-bit authentication field is redefined to contain a key identifier, a length field and a sequence number. The key-id identifies the secret password, or key, used for the authentication procedure, and the authentication algorithm. The standard algorithm is MD5. When that algorithm is used, the sender computes an MD5 checksum over the concatenation of the OSPF packet, secret key, pad, and length fields, producing a 16-byte message digest (see [12]).

The message digest is appended to the OSPF packet. It is considered as a "trailer," not an integral part of the packet: its length is not included in the OSPF packet length. Upon reception, the receiver performs the same computation, based on the secret associated with the key-id, and compares the result to the received digest. If the values match, the packet is authentic. If not, the packet will be rejected.

The cryptographic procedure protects against the reception of forged messages. In addition, the cryptographic sequence number protects against replay attacks: routers will reject messages whose sequence number is not larger than that of the previous message received with the same key-id.

The key-id is used to manage the key associated with the interface. To each key are associated four time constants:

☞ the time at which the router will start accepting messages with this key,
☞ the time at which the router will start sending messages with this key,
☞ the time at which the router will stop sending messages with this key, and
☞ the time at which the router will stop accepting messages with this key,

Several keys can be valid at any given time, which allows for smooth transitions.

6.6.2 The Hello Protocol

The Hello protocol is used for two purposes:

☞ to check that links are operational, and
☞ to elect the designated router and the backup on broadcast and nonbroadcast networks.

The protocol uses only one packet format.

OSPF packet header, type = 1 (hello)		
Network mask		
Hello Interval	Options	Priority
Dead Interval		
Designated router		
Backup designated router		
Neighbor		
- - - -		
Neighbor		

All the fields in this format are 32 bits, except for the hello interval (16 bits), the options field (8 bits), and the priority (8 bits). The network mask is the subnet mask associated with the interface. In the absence of subnetting, it will be set to the hexadecimal value FF000000 for a class-A network, FFFF0000 for class-B, and FFFFFF00 for class-C.

The hello packets are sent by the router every "hello-interval" second. They include the address of the designated router on the link, or 0 if there is no designated router yet, and the address of the backup or 0. They also include a list of all neighbors from which a hello packet has been received in the last "dead-interval" seconds. Both hello and dead intervals are parameters of the links that are set up by the administrator—they play the same role as the 30-second and 180-second timers in RIP.

The options field specifies the optional router capabilities. Out of eight possible bits, two are defined:

The T bit is set when the router is capable of TOS routing. The E bit is set when the router is capable of receiving and sending external routes; it is null when the interface belongs to a stub area.

The link between two routers is declared operational if packets can flow in both directions, and if both routers agree on the state of the E bit. Bidirectional connectivity is easily checked by looking at the "neighbor" list of remote routers. If the local router's ID is not listed in their hello packets, it means that they have not yet received the locally sent hellos. The connection is then declared "one way only" and cannot be used for routing. If the local router is listed within the remote hellos, we have a "two-way" connection. Note that the dead-interval timer is not the only way to notice that the link to a neighbor has come down. One can also use lower-level indications—for example, notice the absence of carrier on a modem link. In this case, the neighbor will be removed from the list without waiting for the end of the interval.

When the link is a point-to-point link or a virtual link, there is no need for any further "link qualification" after establishing a two-way connection. The routers will immediately start "bringing up" the adjacency. On network interfaces, one must first select the designated router and the backup.

The election procedure uses the "priority" field carried in the hello packets. Each router is configured with a priority, varying between 0 and 255. The normal result of the election is to select the router with the largest priority; however, this can be altered by the need to avoid changing the designated router too often. If the highest-priority router comes down, another will be selected; this selection will remain even after the highest-priority router comes up again. Routers with priority zero will never be selected as designated routers.

Immediately after the link comes up, the router will be in a "waiting" state and will remain so for a "waiting interval" equal to the dead interval. During this interval the router will transmit hello packets, but it will not propose itself for the election. It will initialize designated and backup identifications to null values, listen to the incoming hello packets, and initialize the backup and designated router identifications as follows: For each neighbor, the router remembers the neighbor's priority and the state of the relation (one way or two ways); it also remembers whether the neighbor proposes itself as designated or backup router. Only the neighbors that have reached two-way status are considered for designated router's election. The election proceeds as follows:

1. If one or several neighbors proposed themselves as backup designated router, the one with the largest priority is selected as designated router. In case of a tie, the router with the largest ID is selected.
2. If no neighbor proposed itself as backup, the neighbor with the largest priority is selected or, in case of a tie, the one with the largest ID.
3. If one or several neighbors proposed themselves as designated router, the one with the largest priority is selected as designated router. In case of a tie, the router with the largest ID is selected.
4. If no neighbor proposed itself as designated router, the backup is "promoted."

A router cannot propose itself as both designated router and backup. Thus, if we need to execute step 4, we must also reexecute steps 1 and 2 to pick a new backup.

The algorithm is in fact executed permanently, and the designated router and backup are reevaluated after the reception of any hello packet. Steps 1 and 3 assure that, if the routers have agreed on a designated router and a backup, this information will be kept stable. In particular, step 2 is normally not executed before the end of the waiting period, so that an "upcoming" router does not suddenly promote itself to backup or designated status. After the end of the waiting period, the router is assured to know of all other routers in the network and can thus propose itself as backup as a result of step 2.

After any change in the neighbor's configuration, the election process will ensure that convergence is obtained on a new backup and a new designated router. At this point the routers may have to build up adjacencies with this new selected router. In principle, they already have a ready adjacency with the former backup, and they need only to bring it up with the new backup, but there may be cases in which both designated and backup have to be reelected.

On point-to-point links and on broadcast networks, the hello packets are sent to the "all-OSPF-routers" multicast address. On virtual links, they are sent to the IP address of the other end of the link. On nonbroadcast networks, the process is a bit more complex. Since one cannot use a multicast address, all routers have to be preconfigured with a list of all routers on the network. This list mentions the routers' priority, or rather the "possibility to become designated router," i.e., the existence of a nonzero priority or the fact that the router is "eligible." All eligible routers must send individual copies of their hello packets to all other eligible routers; the designated routers and backups must also exchange hello packets with all noneligible routers.

6.6.3 The Exchange Protocol

When two routers have established two-way connectivity on a point-to-point link, they must "synchronize" their data bases; on network links, this occurs between the routers and the designated router or the backup router. The initial synchronization is performed through the "exchange" protocol; the "flooding" protocol will then be used to maintain the two databases in synchronization.

The OSPF exchange protocol is asymmetric; the first step of the protocol is to select a "master" and a "slave." After agreeing on these roles, the two routers will exchange the description of their databases, and each will list the records that will be requested at a later stage. The exchange protocol uses "database description packets."

OSPF packet header, type = 2 (dd)					
Interface MTU	options	0	I	M	MS
DD sequence number					
Link State Age	options	LS type			
Link State ID					
Advertising router					
Link State sequence number					
Link State Checksum	Link state age				
...					

The first 32-bit word following the OSPF packet header is entirely null, except for the "option" octet (similar to the one of hello packets) and for three bits called I(initialize, 29), M(more, 30), and MS(master-slave, 31). The next word is the sequence number of the database description packet. The content of the packet is a set of link state record descriptions—ID, advertising router, sequence number, checksum, and age—without any link state record contents.

The router that wants to start the exchange procedure sends an empty packet, with the initialize, more, and master-slave bits set to 1 and the DD sequence number set to an arbitrary value "not previously seen by the other router"—the time of day is suggested [11]. The other router agrees to play "slave" during the exchange by sending an "acknowledgment" packet—a data description packet carrying the same sequence number, with the I and M bits set to 1 and the MS set to 0 (slave). Indeed, several events could perturb this exchange, e.g., a packet loss or a "collision" if both routers try to initialize the procedure simultaneously. The protection against packet losses is through time-outs: in the absence of acknowledgment, the initial packet is repeated every "retransmit-interval" seconds. The resolution of collision is through a simple tie-breaking algorithm: if a router is waiting for an acknowledgment and receives a request—such as an empty DD packet with the three control bits I, M, and MS set—it will compare the sending address to its own. If the sending address is larger than its own, it will accept the slave role and acknowledge the packet; otherwise, it will just ignore the incoming packet, as its own packet will be acknowledged later by the remote router.

Once the roles have been distributed, the asymmetric exchange begins. The master will send the description of the records in its database in a sequence of DD packets; the I bit will be set to 0, the MS bit set to 1, and the M bit set to 1, except for the last packet. The packets will be sequence numbered and should be sent one at a time. After each packet is sent, the slave will send an acknowledgment—a DD packet with the same sequence number, but with the MS bit set to 0. The acknowledgment packets carry the description of the records in the slave's data base. If the acknowledgment is not received within retransmit-interval seconds, the master repeats its packet; if the slave receives a packet with the same sequence number as the previous one, it should repeat the previous acknowledgment. One can easily demonstrate that the master's repetitions will guarantee that both the master's packets and the slave's are correctly received.

When the master transmits its last description records, it will set the M bit to 0. If the slave still has records to transmit, it will send an acknowledgment with the M bit set to 1. The master will continue sending empty description packets with an M bit set to 0 and accepting acknowledgment, until it eventually receives an acknowledgment with the M bit set to 0. At this point, the exchange is complete.

During the exchange, the master and the slave will process the link state records descriptions that they find in the packets and the acknowledgments. They will first check that there is a record with the same "type," "advertising router," and "link state ID" in their own base, and that this record has a larger or equal sequence number, using the lollipop-comparison algorithm. If either condition is false, they must place the record's description in a list of "records to request." After the exchange is completed, they will request the records through link state request packets.

OSPF packet header, type = 3 (rq)
Link State type
Link State ID
Advertising router
- - -

These packets contain a set of link state record identifiers. Each record is described by three 32-bit words: the record type, the record identifier, and the advertising router identifier. Upon reception of such a request, a router will send a set of link state updates, using exactly the same procedures as for flooding new record values. Each time an update is received, the record identification is removed from the list of records to request.

The list may well be too long to be transmitted in a single request. In this case, the router will send only the beginning of the list in a first request packet. There should be only one outstanding request at any given time; if the requested records have not been updated within a "retransmission interval," then the request is repeated. When all the records requested in the first packet have been updated, the router will send the continuation of the list, and so on until the list is empty. At this stage, the two copies of the database are synchronized.

Many events can go wrong during this database exchange procedure. The routers will monitor the hello packets; the exchange will be abandoned if the two-way connectivity is not maintained. During the exchange, they will check that all the database description packets are consistent—for example, that they don't receive out-of-sequence database description packets or packets with an unexpected value of the I or MS bits. If any such event occurs, they will erase their list of records to be requested and restart the "role negotiation." When receiving link state request packets, the router will check that the requested records are present in the local database. If a request for an unknown record occurs, something has gone wrong and the exchange must be restarted through a new role negotiation.

For the sake of simplicity, we assumed that the exchange and requests were executed entirely in sequence. In fact, the routers can start requesting link state records as soon as they build up the list of records to request, as long as there is only one outstanding request at any given time.

6.6.4 The Flooding Protocol

When a link changes state, the router responsible for that link will issue a new version of the link state. We have seen in a previous section the various types of link state records. Each is identified by the combination of advertising router identification, link state identification, and link state type; each carries a sequence number in the famous lollipop sequence space. These updates can also be sent in response to link state request packets. They are carried in link state updates.

OSPF packet header, type	= 4(upd.)
Number of advertisements	
Link State advertisements	

The OSPF header is followed by an indication of the number of advertisements and then by the link state advertisements themselves.

We have explained the flooding protocol in the presentation of the link state technology. For each advertisement, the sequence number is compared to the value in the local database. If this is a new value, the advertisement is scheduled for transmission on all other interfaces. In any case, the advertisements should be acknowledged to the router that transmitted the update packet. In an attempt to make the flooding procedure reliable, this router will retransmit its updates at regular intervals until reception of the acknowledgment.

The advertisements are normally acknowledged in link state acknowledgment packets.

OSPF packet header, type	= 5(ack.)
Link State advertisements headers	

Each acknowledgment packet may contain a number of advertisement headers, similar to those transmitted in database description packets during the exchange protocol. Since one acknowledgment packet may acknowledge several advertisements, it is normal practice to delay its transmission in order to group many link state acknowledgments in a single packet. This delay must be short in order to avoid needless retransmissions.

On broadcast networks, one can even group in a single packet the acknowledgments of several updates received from various neighbors. These grouped acknowledgments will then be sent to the "all-OSPF-routers" multicast address.

One should, however, not attempt to delay the acknowledgment of duplicate advertisements, i.e., advertisements that are not more recent than the value in the local database. These duplicate advertisements may well be the result of repetitions due to lost acknowledgments. OSPF mandates that duplicate advertisements be acknowledged through point-to-point messages, without delays.

There are in fact two ways of acknowledging an advertisement, and sending explicit acknowledgments is only one of them, although the one used most frequently. When a designated router receives an update, it immediately retransmits it to all routers on the network. This retransmission will be heard by the original router; no further acknowledgment will be needed!

The flooding protocol can be used in parallel with the exchange protocol; if a new version of a link state is received, the router may remove that link state from the list of records to request.

6.6.5 Aging Link State Records

It is useful to remove old or stale information from the link state database, but it is also absolutely mandatory to synchronize the various copies of the database. This implies that the removal of stale records should be strictly synchronized.

OSPF manages this synchronized removal through the "aging" mechanism. The records in the database have an "age." This age is set to 0 when the record is first issued. It is incremented each time the record is forwarded, i.e., on each hop of the flooding procedure. Then, it is incremented by 1 every second. When it reaches "MaxAge" (one hour), the record is regarded as too old and is not considered when computing the routes. In order to enforce synchronization, a router will not remove an old record without telling its neighbors through the flooding protocol.

The neighbors will receive the advertisement for the old record. If they simply applied the flooding algorithm, nothing would happen, since this version of the record is already there, albeit with a different age. In fact, the flooding algorithm must consider record ages when receiving a duplicate advertisement.

1. If the received record has the age MaxAge, then it should always be accepted. As a consequence, the local record will be aged and eventually removed from the local database. The new version, with the updated age, will be flushed to other neighbors.
2. In most other cases, the two ages will differ only by a small value. This is a normal consequence of the flooding procedure. The same record can be received from several neighbors through different paths, with variable queuing delays. In these cases, the local value is kept in the database and the received value is not flooded any further.

3. In very rare cases, the two ages may differ by a large delay, i.e., larger than the "MaxAge-Diff" constant, set to 15 minutes in OSPF. Such a large delay cannot result from queues and retransmissions alone. The most likely explanation is that a router was rebooted, and it reflooded a new value of a link state record, using the previously valid sequence number. In these conditions, the most recent record is kept.

A consequence of flooding the aged records is that some routers could receive aged copies of records that they have already removed from their databases. These advertisements will be ignored.

In order to guarantee that records are not unduly flushed out of the database, the routers must reissue them at regular intervals, at least every half-hour. If nothing has changed, the new record has exactly the same content as the preceding record but bears a new sequence number, and its age is set to 0.

6.7 OSPF for IPv6

The IPv6 version of OSPF is a translation of the IPv4 version, making minimal changes to accommodate the new address format and the change of semantics introduced by the new version, such as the possibility of using several address prefixes on a given link.

These minimal changes guarantee that the IPv6 OSPF software can be easily derived from the IPv4 software. They also ensure that anyone who knows how to configure OSPF for an IPv4 network will rapidly understand how to use the IPv6 version.

OSPF for IPv6 is still being developed. According to the working group charter, the current draft should soon be submitted for publication as a proposed standard.

6.7.1 Protocol Changes

The design of the OSPF-v6 packet header shows several of the changes introduced in the new version:

Version=3	Type	Packet Length	
Router ID			
Area ID			
Checksum		Instance Id	0

The first change is the selection of a new version number, 3. This is necessary because the format is incompatible with OSPF version 2. OSPF for IPv6 runs on top of IPv6, between IPv6-capable nodes. The OSPFv6 messages will normally be sent over IPv6 using the "link local" IPv6 addresses, or using multicast addresses reserved for IPv6. The IPv6 link state database will not be shared with the IPv4 database. IPv4 OSPF and IPv6 OSPF will operate in parallel, following the "ships in the night" model, rather than trying to achieve integrated routing.

The second change is more subtle. In fact, there is no change in the size or in the encoding of the "Router ID" that remains a 32-bit field. But the semantic of the identifier changes somewhat. In OSPF version 2, the routers were typically identified by one of their 32-bit IPv4 addresses. In OSPF for IPv6, the router identifier is independent of the IPv6 addresses. It is simply a plain 32-bit number that has to be provisioned, making sure that each router in the OSPF network has a unique identifier.

The third change is the removal of the authentication procedure. In IPv6, authentication is obtained by inserting the AH between the IPv6 header and the OSPF header—or possibly by encrypting the OSPF packets inside the ESP, if confidentiality is desired.

The last change is the insertion of an "instance number" in the header. This is used when an IPv6 link is shared by several independent OSPF networks. Such configurations typically are encountered at the interconnection points between several networks. In that case, each of the networks is assigned an "instance id."

Apart from these changes, the OSPF procedures for IPv6 are basically the same as those of OSPF version 2.

6.7.2 New Database Formats

The format of the database records needs to be updated to take into account the larger addresses, as well as a few changes in semantics. The LSA header itself shows very little changes to the OSPF version 2:

LS Age	LS Type
Link State ID	
Advertising router	
LS sequence Number	
Checksum	Length

The first difference with OSPF version 2 is the encoding of the Link State Identifier, which becomes a pure identifier, without any relation to addresses or subnet prefixes.

The second difference is the removal of the "options" field that enabled routers to negotiate various capacities. Instead, the LS type is enlarged to 16 bits. In this field, the first three bits specify the type of handling requested for the LSA:

☞ The first bit, called "U," indicates how routers should behave if they don't recognize this type. The value 0 indicates that the LSA shall not be flooded beyond the local link, while the value 1 indicates that the record should be stored in the local database and flooded as if it had been understood.

☞ The second and third bits, called S1 and S2, indicate the scope in which the LSA should be flooded. The scope can be set to the local link (00), to the local OSPF area (01), or to the entire OSPF network (10).

This definition will allow for easier extensions, as it enables the introduction of new LS types without requiring that they be understood by all the routers in the network. Nine LS types are defined in the specification:

LS Type (hexa)	Description	OSPF version 2 equivalent
0x2001	Router-LSA	Router link
0x2002	Network-LSA	Network link
0x2003	Inter-Area-Prefix-LSA	Summary link (IP network)
0x2004	Inter-Area-Router-LSA	Summary link (to a border router)
0x4005	AS-External-LSA	External link
0x2006	Group-membership-LSA	Used for Multicast
0x2007	Type-7-LSA	See section 6.8.3
0x0008	Link-LSA	IPv6 addition
0x2009	Intra-Area-Prefix-LSA	IPv6 addition

The content of many of these LSA is updated to take into account the modified data model of IPv6:

☞ Links are identified by the combination of a Router-ID and a Link-ID, locally assigned to the interface by the router. There is no reference to network addresses. In consequence, the Router-LSA will contain, for each link, the local identifier, the identifier of the remote router, and the identifier of the link on that remote router.

☞ Network LSAs contain the identifiers of the routers connected to the network.

☞ Inter-Area-Prefix-LSAs contain a list of prefixes, encoded as a prefix length in bits and an IPv6 address. To each prefix is associated an 8-bit option field describing whether the prefix can be used for unicast routing and for multicast routing, whether the prefix actually describes a local interface on the router, and whether the prefix should be further advertised outside the area.

☞ Inter-Area-Router-LSAs contain the ID of the remote router.

☞ AS-external-LSAs contain a prefix and optional forwarding address, an optional External Route Tag, and an optional Referenced Link State ID. The optional fields may be used by border routers when they communicate with adjacent networks.

The IPv6-specific Link LSAs are used to advertise the link-local addresses of a router to its neighbors.

6.8 Research and Developments

Work on OSPF continues. In the recent years, we have seen new developments that attempt either to solve problems discovered in the operation of large networks or to use the OSPF database for new purposes. This work is exemplified by proposals to deal with database overflow [13], to increase network security [15], and to use the database for better traffic engineering [16].

6.8.1 Overflow

The very concept that makes the strength of OSPF and other database protocols may also cause one of their major weaknesses. All routers in an area must maintain equal copies of the database and must execute the same route computation algorithm. This can lead to some spectacular failures:

☞ If, for some reason, there is a bug in the algorithm or in its implementation, the condition that triggers the bug will occur simultaneously at all routers, which will all fail in unison.

☞ If the flooding procedure fails to synchronize the copies of the database, the routers will make decisions based on partial and incorrect information, which will cause loops and blackholes.

We can assume that the OSPF codes are now well tested, that bugs have been corrected, and that we should only be concerned with flooding errors. There are two principal causes of failure in the OSPF flooding procedure: limited transmission capacity and limited database storage.

The transmission capacity is limited by the available bandwidth on the links, by the need to acknowledge flooding messages before transmitting new ones, and by the processing capacity of the routers. If the rate of update exceeds the transmission capacity, the database will not converge. For this reason, OSPFv2 includes a rate-limiting procedure, stating that *"two instances of the same LSA may not be originated within the time period MinLSInterval."*

The rate limiting is only effective if the number of records in the database is itself limited. A quick examination shows that the network managers have good control on the number of all but one type of LSA: the number of router, network, and summary links depends only on the network's configuration and can be managed by splitting the network into areas. But the managers of backbone networks, at the core of the Internet, have no control over the number of external links. Each time a new network is announced over the Internet, at least one new external link will be created. We will see in the presentation of BGP and CIDR that this number of networks grows quite fast. On average, 8,000 network announcements are added every year, for a current total of nearly 60,000. Moreover, bugs in the implementations of BGP can cause transient errors where the number of announcements suddenly increases, creating an instant flood of new records. The excessive number of records stresses the routers' memory as well as the transmission capacity. If routers find that they have no memory left to store new records, there will be no way to guarantee that the databases are exactly replicated. In addition, the database problem will compound the transmission problems. When an overflow record is presented by the flooding procedure, the routers will not find any copy in the current database, and will thus attempt to flood the network to all their neighbors, even if they had in fact already received a copy of the record.

In [13], John Moy describes an experimental solution to the "database overflow" problem:

☞ Configure a limiting parameter, "ospfExtLsdbLimit," in each router, making sure that all routers in the domain are configured with the same limit.

☞ Refuse the advertisements that would cause the number of external links in the database to exceed the limit. If such advertisements are received, they are dropped and not acknowledged.

☞ Go in an "overflow" state when the number of external links has reached the limit. When going in this state, the router uses the "premature aging" procedure to flush all the "non-default" external link state advertisements that it originated previously.

☞ Refuse to originate any new external link advertisements when in overflow state.

☞ Leave the overflow state after a configured interval.

This procedure is not part of the OSPF standard. It is proposed as an experiment. There is still a debate on the best way to solve the overflow problem.

6.8.2 Secure Networks and Insecure Routers

The cryptographic authentication procedure presented in section 6.6.1 effectively protects the network of routers against external intrusion. It does not however offer a real protection against routers that would have fallen under the control of hackers or rogue operators. Radia Perlman analyzed this problem in her Ph.D. thesis [14] and proposed a general solution based on public key cryptography. In [15] Sandra Murphy, Madelyn Badger, and Brian Wellington propose to adapt this technology to OSPF.

The key idea of the proposed solution is to let all routers digitally sign the advertisements that they originate. The records will be signed with the router's private key, and the signature can be verified using the router's public key, which can be made available to all other routers in the network. A router that receives an advertisement can thus immediately determine whether the announcement comes from the purported source. This effectively eliminates all attacks in which a rogue router modifies the announcements sent by another router. The solution is implemented by:

☞ Creating a "Router Public Key LSA" that stores each router's public key, certified by a trusted entity.

☞ Creating a "secure" type corresponding to each existing LSA. The secure LSA combines the regular information with a signature.

This proposition remains however at an experimental stage, because public key cryptography is perceived as complex and expensive, and also because the proposition is only a partial solution to the security problem.

The signature does not, by itself, protect against rogue routers that would "invent" local information, such as for example nonexistent external links. These records are signed with the router's private key, which is presumably under the control of the rogue operator. The signature also does not protect against rogue routers that would subtly manipulate the flooding protocol.

To remove rogue routers from the network, one needs either a supervising station or a robust distributed decision algorithm. But we can observe that such algorithms can be implemented even in the absence of public key cryptography. For example, the OSPF cryptographic authentication procedure relies on the distribution of keys. A supervising station that detects the presence of a rogue router could trigger a key change, distributing the new keys to only those routers that are known to be "sane."

6.8.3 Load Sharing on Multiple Paths

As we noted in section 6.3.3, traffic optimization requires load sharing on multiple paths. This requires the addition of information to the link state database in order to describe the links' load and cost. It also requires experimentation with new algorithms.

Because of the experimental nature of the exercise, it would be impractical to update each link state advertisement definition to incorporate new information. Instead, the "opaque" link state record [16] has been proposed as a generic way to insert supplementary information in the database. The opaque record can be flooded to all nodes, even those that don't understand its content.

Link State Advertisement Age		Options	LSA Type
Opaque Type		Opaque ID	
Advertising Router			
Link State Advertisement Sequence Number			
LSA Checksum		LSA Length	
Opaque Content			

Three LSA types have been reserved for the Opaque LSA, corresponding to three different flooding scopes. Type 9 opaque LSAs are not flooded beyond a single link, type 10 opaque LSAs are flooded into an area, and type 11 opaque LSAs are flooded in the whole network.

The 32-bit LSA identifier is decomposed in the case of opaque LSAs into two parts, an opaque type that defines the content of the opaque LSA and an opaque ID, an arbitrary identifier chosen by the advertising router. Opaque types 0 to 127 are global types, defined through the IETF process and registered with the IANA. Opaque types 128 to 255 can be used for experimentation. Opaque types could be used for a wide variety of purpose—for example, to experiment with security or accounting. We will detail here how, in Curtis Villamizar's "Optimized Multi Path" proposal [17], the opaque LSA is used to carry information about the state of the link.

OMP is an improvement over equal cost multipath. Instead of splitting the traffic equally between the various equal cost paths, the routers according to OMP will take into account the path's load to direct more traffic onto the less loaded path. OMP proposes to carry the load information in opaque LSA of LSA type 10, flooded within an area, without modifying the standard LSA formats.

Link State Advertisement Age		Options	LSA Type
Opaque Type		Opaque ID	
Advertising Router			
Link State Advertisement Sequence Number			
LSA Checksum		LSA Length	
Version = 1	Reference Type	Packing Method	BW Scale
Reference to a Type 1-5 LSA (32 or 64 bits)			
In Scaled Link Capacity in kilobits per second			
In Link Loading Fraction		In Link Drop Fraction (packets)	
Out Scaled Link Capacity in kilobits per second			
Out Link Loading Fraction		Out Link Drop Fraction (packet)	

Each opaque "link load" LSA parallels one of the regular link state records of types 1 to 5 advertised by the same router. Two opaque types are used, one for "link load" and another for "path load," depending on whether the link state described an actual link or a summary link for a path leading outside the area. The type of the original LSA is specified in the "reference type" field, and its the original identifier is provided in the "Reference to a Type" field. For each link, three parameters are computed in each direction:

1. The *scaled capacity* is an indication of the link's capacity in kilobits per second. It is encoded as a 32-bit field, which limits the scope to about 4 terabits. When future networks exceed that number, the *bandwidth scale* coefficient is used as a scale factor, multiplying the advertised value by 2 raised to the power of the scale.
2. The *loading fraction* describes the observed load of the link. It is expressed as a 16-bit fixed point number. The "packing method" parameter explains how this loading fraction is computed. The currently defined method simply divides the observed traffic by the link's capacity.
3. The *link drop fraction* describes the packet loss rate on the link, expressed as a 16-bit fixed point number.

OMP will split the traffic according to the available paths. The algorithm starts with an initialization phase, in which the available paths are computed. The load is then gradually adjusted as a function of the loading information received in the Opaque LSA, while the set of paths may evolve as the topology changes. The initial set of paths is computed in three steps:

1. Use the SPF algorithm to compute the shortest paths to the destination from all of the router's immediate neighbors.
2. Compute a set of candidate paths by combining the paths starting from the neighbors with the links between the router and these neighbors.
3. Retain the paths that either have the minimal cost or fall within an acceptable margin of the minimum cost. In order to avoid loops, nonminimal cost paths will be retained only if they do not use a virtual link, and if the immediate neighbor is closer to the destination than the origin router.

Once the initial set of paths has been chosen, an initial load sharing structure is computed between these paths. Traffic will be spread using the hashing technique described in 6.3.3. Routers will monitor the traffic sent over their links and flood new load information when the load varies. The flooding interval will be as long as 20 minutes in situations of low load, but can decrease to 60 or 30 seconds in situations of high, variable load. The state of the load sharing will be reexamined when new loading information is received, or otherwise at intervals that vary from 30 seconds in high load and high variability conditions to 5 minutes in stable conditions. The idea is to slowly converge toward the best sharing. The router will, at every load computation interval, do the following:

1. examine the links used by all the paths and determine which are the "critical links"—i.e., those with the highest load;
2. reduce the share of traffic allocated to the path containing a critical link; and
3. increase the share of traffic allocated to the paths that do not contain a critical link.

The idea is to proceed by slow variations in order to avoid oscillation. The load sharing will also be reexamined when the topology of the network changes. In this case, the new set of paths will be computed and will then be compared to the previous set:

1. If paths have been removed, the corresponding load will be split between the remaining paths.

2. Newly added paths will not receive any load. Their share of traffic will increase gradually, after each load computation interval. This is because new paths are always somewhat suspect: they could well flap in and out of service. Allowing only gradual loading reduces the impact of flapping on the network's service.

3. If all paths have been replaced by new paths, the load will be spread among the new paths.

OMP is still very much an experiment. The proposal [17] contains a detailed list of precise interval and increment values, which obviously have been derived empirically from simulations and trials. However, this is a very promising experiment. Adding automated traffic management would reduce the need for complex traffic engineering procedures, a noticeable simplification for network operators.

6.9 Complexity and Services

By all metrics, OSPF is more complex than RIP. The documentation is five times thicker, the management needs more information, and the implementation needs more code. RIP does everything with just two messages; OSPF needs five different messages and three procedures. Link state updates are acknowledged; distance vectors are simply repeated at regular intervals. There is no such a thing as a lollipop sequence space or the election of a designated router in RIP. OSPF routers need to maintain both a link state database and a routing table; RIP routers need only a routing table.

Why, then, design such a complex procedure? Because routing is important. And because OSPF clearly is more efficient than RIP. We have seen that it computes better routes, but it also requires fewer messages. Take the example of the almost 60,000 external routes that were announced by the backbone border routers in June of 1999. Using RIP, one would have to repeat them every 30 seconds; only 30-minute repetitions are needed with OSPF. As each route requires about 24 octets, this is a sizable overhead!

OSPF is probably not a perfect protocol. But the OSPF working group of the IETF is dynamic and keeps making it better. The "optimized multipath" is one example of this evolution. The multicast support facilities we will see in the multicast chapter are another example. We can certainly expect many more of these evolutions!

References

1. J. M. McQuillan, I. Richer, and E. C. Rosen, "Arpanet Routing Algorithm Improvements," *BBN Technical Report 3803*, April 1978.

2. J. McQuillan et al., "The New Routing Algorithm for the Arpanet," *IEEE Transactions on Communications*, May 1980.

3. Radia Perlman, "Fault-Tolerant Broadcast of Routing Information," *Computer Networks*, December 1983.

4. E. W. Dijkstra, "A Note on Two Problems in Connection with Graphs," *Numerische Mathematic*, Vol. 1, pp. 269–271, 1959.

5. Radia Perlman, "Incorporation of Service Classes into a Network Architecture," *Seventh Data Communication Symposium*, Mexico, October 1981.

6. Alain Jean-Marie and Zhen Liu, "Stochastic Comparison for Queuing Models Via Random Sums and Intervals," *Journal of Advanced Applied Probabilities*, No. 24, pp. 960–985, 1992.

7. Alain Jean-Marie and Levent Gün, "Parallel Queues with Resequencing," *J-ACM*, Vol. 40, No. 5, pp. 1188–1208, November 1993.

8. R. Coltun and V. Fuller, "The OSPF NSSA Option," RFC-1587, March 24, 1994.

9. P. Almquist, "Type of Service in the Internet Protocol Suite," RFC-1349, July 1992.

10. F. Baker and R. Coltun, "OSPF Version 2 Management Information Base," RFC-1850, November 1995.

11. J. Moy, "OSPF Version 2," RFC-2328, April 1998.

12. R. Rivest, "The MD5 Message-Digest Algorithm," RFC-1321, April 1992.

13. J. Moy, "OSPF Database Overflow," RFC-1765, March 1995.

14. R. Perlman, "Network Layer Protocols with Byzantine Robustness," Ph.D. Thesis, Department of Electrical Engineering and Computer Science, MIT, August 1988.

15. S. Murphy, M. Badger, and B. Wellington, "OSPF with Digital Signatures," RFC-2154, June 1997.

16. R. Coltun, "The OSPF Opaque LSA Option," RFC-2370, July 1998.

17. C. Villamizar, "OSPF Optimized Multi Path (OSPF-OMP)," work in progress (Internet draft), February 1999.

Other Routing Protocols

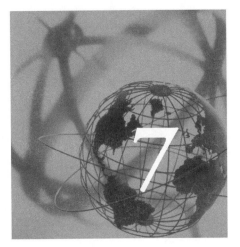

The old rule also applies to networking products: "The one who pays the piper calls the tunes." We have already seen that RIP is much simpler but also less powerful than OSPF. The manager of a simple network will perhaps buy the less expensive routers based on RIP, while the manager of a complex corporate backbone should insist on OSPF. But RIP and OSPF are not the only routing protocols in use in the Internet; there are other choices.

7.1 RIP and OSPF Are Not Alone

Back in the days of the early Arpanet, the routing protocol in use was the "Gateway to Gateway Protocol" (GGP). GGP was a typical distance vector protocol [1, 2], a predecessor of RIP. It was designed at a time when Internet network numbers were all 8 bits long, like the modern class-A format. As there could be only 256 networks in the Internet, the concept of distance vectors could be taken quite literally—the routing update contained a list of 256 distances, where the Nth position in the list corresponded precisely to the distance toward the network number N. GGP was somewhat more complex than RIP. It included a "polling" protocol, similar to the hello subprotocol of OSPF, for testing the connection toward the neighbor gateways. Routing updates were numbered and explicitly acknowledged. The links that were available in the 1970s were simply not reliable enough to avoid an explicit error correction procedure.

The Hello protocol was defined by Dave Mills for the "fuzzball"—an implementation of the Internet protocols on PDP11 minicomputers [3]. A set of up to 256 fuzzballs linked by serial lines, parallel buses, or contention buses can be organized in a "distributed computer network" (DCN). The protocol is characterized by its reliance on synchronized clocks. The metric carried in the distance vector is the delay toward the destination. In fact, the messages carry for each host in the DCN the delay toward that host and sufficient information to estimate the clock offset

161

and compute the delay with the neighboring host. This reliance on clocks and delays as well as the mixing of clock synchronization and route computation is not found anymore in routing protocols; time and routes are maintained by different processes. The design of the "network time protocol" which we mentioned in the IP chapter was certainly influenced by the experience gained on the fuzzball.

Apart from RIP and OSPF, the most used routing protocols in today's Internet are IGRP and, to a certain extent, "dual IS-IS." IGRP is a proprietary protocol defined by one router manufacturer, cisco, which recently produced a new version called "Enhanced IGRP" (EIGRP). Dual IS-IS is the extension for IP of the "Intermediate System to Intermediate System" protocol standardized by ISO for the routing of "Connectionless Network Protocol" (CLNP) packets. We will describe these protocols and try to answer the manager's question: "Which one should we choose?"

7.2 Routers or Intermediate Systems?

It is not quite the purpose of this book to compare the Internet protocols and the Open System Interconnection architecture, OSI, which was developed under the aegis of ISO in the 1980s. The general consensus today is that the objective of OSI—general Internetworking—was quite respectable, but that the means used toward this objective—endless amounts of bureaucracy—brought the project to its knees. The OSI working groups concentrated on producing large amounts of standards and certainly printed a lot of papers; during that time, the Internet was built and a lot of connectivity was achieved. Today, the Internet has many users and the OSI still has some supporters.

The situation was not so in the late 1980s. The Internet was still developing, but many thought that the politically correct future had to be OSI. Using IP was presented as "a transition strategy," and efforts were made to accommodate as much as possible of the OSI work in the Internet, e.g., running X.400 message-handling systems in parallel with Internet mail, or presenting X.500 as the normal solution for Internet "white pages." In many organizations' networks, efforts were made to run the OSI CLNP in parallel with IP.

OSI routers must indeed exchange routing information, and the OSI suite includes a routing protocol called IS-IS. In fact, we should be more precise here. There is no such thing as a "router" in the OSI architecture; there are no hosts either. There are only "systems," open systems indeed. A host is an "end system"; a router is an "intermediate system." There are no routing or networks either; the appellations are "routeing" and "domains." So, the OSI routing protocol is in fact the "Intra-Domain Intermediate System to Intermediate System Routeing Protocol" (IS-IS) [4]. This is a link state routing protocol, similar to OSPF.

When one has decided to run two protocols on the same infrastructure, it is tempting to use only one routing protocol for both. This is even more tempting for protocols of the link state family. The link state database contains two broad types of records: those describing the network's topology and those describing the relation between this topology and the addresses. The description of the topology is very dynamic, but it is also common to all networking protocols. The relation between the addresses and the topology is indeed dependent on the protocol, but it is also quite static. This reasoning is the basis for "dual IS-IS"—an adaptation of IS-IS that allows it to describe both CLNP and IP routes. Using an Internet-designed protocol for this dual purpose would probably not be as politically correct!

7.2.1 ISO, OSI, and Routeing

The IS-IS protocol is part of the OSI routing framework (the "routeing" framework, in fact, but we will stick to the usual vocabulary and use common-language words such as routers, routing, or messages rather than intermediate systems, routeing, or "protocol data units"). The OSI framework is hierarchical, separating routing domains into areas composed of one or many local networks. At first sight, the OSI addresses have only a very weakly specified two-components structure.

The "initial domain part" (IDP) is composed of a 1-octet "address format identifier" (AFI) that determines the format of the "initial domain identifier" (IDI). There are many AFIs defined for many possible formats, such as country identifiers, telephone, or telex numbers. The "domain specific part" (DSP) is composed of digits of octets. Octets are assumed for CLNP. Both IDP and DSP are variable length, for a total of at most 20 octets.

The routing model overlays on that weak specification a four-component structure:

The routing domain part is composed of the AFI, IDI, and possibly the first bytes of the DSP; it identifies the organization. It is followed by a 16-bit "area" identifier. The next 48 bits uniquely identify the host or the router, independently of the area code. A router will use the same identifier for all the areas it belongs to. The 8-bit selector is not used for routing. It plays the same role as the "protocol identifier" within IP. There are different identifiers for the various transport protocols. Note that IS-IS is not identified by a "selector"—this protocol is run directly on top of the "link layer" service, in parallel with CLNP. The "Network Layer Protocol ID" (NLPID) is used to demultiplex various network layer functions; it is carried in the first byte of "network layer" packets.

As in OSPF, all areas are connected through a backbone. More precisely, there is one "level 2" of IS-IS that groups all the backbone routers and is hierarchically superior to "level 1," i.e., the identified areas. An area connects hosts to "level-1 routers" and is identified by one area number; in fact, one can associate several numbers with an area in order to facilitate reorganizations and transitions. At least one of the area's routers belongs to both level 1 and level 2; it connects the area to the backbone and plays the same role as an area-border router in OSPF.

The division of the network into areas is much more rigid than the OSPF equivalent—IS-IS areas are roughly equivalent to OSPF's stub areas. Another difference is the absence of any subnet identification in the OSI routing framework. The address includes the area's and system's identifiers, not the subnet or local network. A consequence is that routers must explicitly keep track of the location of hosts within their area. Hosts declare themselves to the routers connected to the subnet through the "End System to Intermediate System Routeing protocol" (ES-IS). Routers describe these attachments in the IS-IS link state records. This is in fact the only detailed information that level-1 routers maintain. All packets bound to another area or another routing domain are simply passed to the nearest level-2 router. This strict hierarchical model also applies to level-2 routing. Seen from the backbone, all access points to an area are equivalent. Packets bound to an area are always passed to the nearest level-2 router that also belongs to this area.

A consequence of this organization is that areas are expected to remain internally connected. A fracture of a stub area may, in fact, be cured by establishing a "tunnel" through the backbone. If the area has been split into two halves, any of the level-2 routers connected to this area may receive packets bound to the other half of the area. It will transmit them through the backbone by encapsulating them in a packet bound to a router connected to the other half. This tunnelling technique cannot be used for reconnecting a split backbone. One must simply wait for the connectivity to be reestablished.

7.2.2 The IS-IS Protocol

As in OSPF, the IS-IS protocol contains several subprotocols. The Hello protocol is used to discover neighbors and to elect a designated router on broadcast links. The flooding protocol is used to propagate the link state records within the areas or within the backbone.

On a broadcast link, the "IS-IS Hellos" carry the source identification; a "circuit type" that characterizes the router as level 1, level 2, or both; a "priority" code; an identification of the local network; the list of addresses of the areas to which the router belongs; the list of other routers' addresses that the router considers as well connected to the local network. The priority code is configured by the network manager; the router with highest priority is elected the "designated router." If two routers have the same priority, the one with the largest identifier (the 48-bit local network address) is selected. The local network is identified by a 7-byte field composed of the designated router identifier and of a "selector" assigned by this router. This identifier is used by the attached routers in their link state advertisements. The designated router will emit the link state records describing the link from the network to the routers, while the other routers will advertise only a link toward the network. As in OSPF, this designated router election eliminates the "N-squared" effect.

There are in fact four different formats for hello packets. One distinguishes level-1 and level-2 hellos, as well as hellos on broadcast and point-to-point links. A broadcast link may be shared between level-1 and level-2 routers. There will be a different designated router at each level and different adjacencies. There is indeed no designated router on point-to-point links.

The hello packets are repeated at regular intervals and are used to check the link's availability. If both routers agree that they belong to the same area, the link will be reported in a level-1 advertisement. Otherwise, it is reported at level 2.

7.2.3 Flooding, Aging, and Exchanges

IS-IS uses one single procedure for flooding, aging, and exchanges of link state records (LSP). All records have an 8-byte identifier (LSPID), composed of the 48-bit system identifier, a 1-byte pseudo-ID, and a record number (LSP number). The pseudo-ID is normally null, except for designated routers that use it to identify a broadcast network. The records have a limited size; if there is too much information to hold within exactly one record, the routers construct several records identified by successive LSP numbers. Each of these records will be flooded independently. The first record in the sequence must always include a set of key parameters, notably the identification of the areas to which the router belongs. A router's records should be flooded only within the router's areas.

A record in the database is qualified by a sequence number and a "remaining lifetime." The value is characterized by a checksum. The sequence number is a 32-bit integer. It starts from the value 1 and is then incremented regularly; the value 0 is never used. There is no provision for a "lollipop sequence space": direct comparison is always performed. If the router remains operational for a very long time, the sequence number will eventually reach the ceiling. The router will have no solution but to fake a failure; this failure will have to be long enough to trigger a complete purge of the old values from the whole network. Afterward, the router will be capable of using the sequence number 1 again. This event is unlikely, however, as 32 bits allow the encoding of very large numbers—a router could keep sending a new value every second for more than a century before hitting the ceiling.

The flooding procedure has the same goal as that of OSPF, but it is organized somewhat differently. When a router receives a new link state record from one neighbor, it compares the sequence number with the one it has in its own database. If the received sequence number is larger, or if the record was not yet stored in the database, the router stores the received value in the base and marks it for acknowledgment to the sending neighbor and for flooding to all other neighbors. If the received number is lower, the router ignores the received value and notes that it should later send back the stored value to this neighbor. If the sequence numbers match, the checksums are compared. If they match, everything is fine; the record is simply marked for acknowledgment to the sending neighbor. Receiving a link state record with the same sequence number but a different checksum is in fact the indication of an error—this triggers the immediate expiration of the record's lifetime.

Acknowledgment is performed through "sequence number" messages that list a set of record identifications, sequence numbers, checksums, and lifetimes. A router that floods a link state record knows that its neighbors have received it when it receives back a sequence number message carrying the same identifier and sequence number; it will keep flooding the record at regular intervals until it is acknowledged or replaced by a new value. On broadcast links, only the designated router will send the periodic messages, so that all neighbors can check whether their databases are synchronized with the designated router; if a "nondesignated" router determines that the designated router has a record that is out of date, it simply multicasts it on the link.

The sequence number messages are also used for the IS-IS equivalent of the exchange procedure. When a new adjacency is brought up, the routers exchange "complete sequence number" messages. A complete message differs from a partial one in that it carries an explicit range indication, composed of two "system identifications"; the message summarizes all the database records whose system identification is contained within this range. The receiving router can compare this summary with the content of its own database in the same range and note the records that are missing or too old. A router that receives a sequence number message will always mark for flooding the records for which the reported sequence number is lower than that of the local database. If the sequence is complete, it will also mark for flooding the local records that belong to the range but are not mentioned in the message. We may note that two routers will be considered "adjacent" if they have achieved connectivity. This differs from OSPF: in IS-IS, the exchange procedure is in fact integrated in the normal flooding procedure.

If a router receives the identifier of a record that is not present in the local database, it marks it for acknowledgment with sequence number 0. As all sequence numbers are larger than 0, this will trigger the flooding of the record's value by the peer. The router will also mark for acknowledgment all records for which the summarized number is larger than the number present in the database. These acknowledgments will be repeated at regular intervals until an up-to-date value has been received.

As in the case of OSPF, a router that resumes its operation after a short failure may receive a flooding of its own records, i.e., of the records that it flooded just before the failure. It will correct this by flooding again the correct value, using a sequence number larger than the one it received. If no such record exists in the new database after the reinitialization, the router will trigger the immediate aging of the old value.

The remaining lifetime of the database records is decremented every second. When it reaches 0, the record is marked as unusable but remains in the database for "ZeroAgeLife-Time"—60 seconds. The record is also flooded to all neighbors in order to synchronize the aging in the various databases.

7.2.4 Integrated Routing

IS-IS, as defined by ISO, supports only the CLNP protocol. The link state records list the areas to which the router belongs and the distances to the neighboring routers and to locally connected hosts in the case of level-1 records. In fact, for each host or neighbor, four distances are listed according to default, delay, expense, and errors metrics. The default metric normally describes the link's throughput, the delay metric its propagation delay, the expense metric its financial cost, and the error metric its error rate. Path values are computed by adding the different costs.

Ross Callon observes that the only information missing at this level to enable IP routing is a list of identifiers for the connected subnets [5]. IS-IS uses a flexible encoding of parameters within link state records. Each parameter is identified by 1 octet of type (T), followed by 1 octet of length (L) and "L" octets of value; the specification mandates that routers ignore, but retransmit, those parameters for which they have ignored the type. In order to accommodate IP, one needs only to register a new parameter type for connected subnets. This new parameter will be identified by a type or code (128). It will contain a set of 12-octet fields that describe the various subnets.

No. of Octets

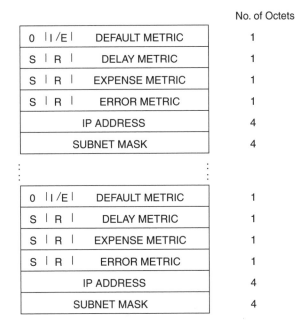

0 |I /E| DEFAULT METRIC	1
S | R | DELAY METRIC	1
S | R | EXPENSE METRIC	1
S | R | ERROR METRIC	1
IP ADDRESS	4
SUBNET MASK	4

0 |I /E| DEFAULT METRIC	1
S | R | DELAY METRIC	1
S | R | EXPENSE METRIC	1
S | R | ERROR METRIC	1
IP ADDRESS	4
SUBNET MASK	4

The parameter may include several subnets, each of which is identified by an IP address and a variable length subnet mask. Four metrics are listed for each subnet. The bit I/E in the default metric is set to 1 for external metrics, larger than any internal distances. The bit S in the other metrics is set to 1 if the metric is not supported. We note that only 6 bits are available to encode the metric's value—this is much less than either OSPF or IGRP. In fact, these short fields are a limitation of IS-IS. Metrics have to be encoded on a scale varying between 1 and 31, which does not allow much precision. Just suppose that your network includes 45-Mbps and 64-kbps links: one is 700 times faster than the other, yet the scale has only 31 positions.

Additional extensions to IS-IS allow building up system identifiers from IP addresses and define the relation between IP type of service and the IS-IS metrics.

7.2.5 IS – IS = 0

Dual-stack IS-IS was proposed for standardization to the IETF at a time when the definition of OSPF was already well in progress. As a result, we observed an emulation between the two teams and some rather nasty behaviors. In fact, a number of members in the OSPF working group feared that IS-IS would be preferred for "political" reasons, as part of a grand plan to convert the Internet to OSI correctness, even if that meant a complete disruption of the service. The attempts by the IAB and IESG to maintain a fair balance between the dual IS-IS and OSPF working groups were judged as symptomatic of that trend, as this policy overestimated the state of development of IS-IS and artificially placed the two efforts on the same standing. This led to a number of grass roots demonstrations, which peaked with the distribution of a famous adorned tee shirt.

It reads "IS minus IS equals zero" and is certainly some form of overreaction. There are, however, some very real differences.

The encapsulation of IS-IS in local networks follows the CLNP model. It is possible to run IS-IS on an IP-only network, but, even if one does not want to forward CLNP datagrams, one will have to install in the routers the low-level code that demultiplexes CLNP and IS-IS packets. The "area" model of IS-IS is designed for CLNP where the rigidity and connectivity requirements are somewhat compensated by the possibility to perform automatic address assignment; when one uses IS-IS for IP, the rigidity remains, but the advantages disappear. IS-IS suffers from at least two other problems: a tiny metric and a limit to what a router can advertise. Having only 6 bits to express a link's metric is not really a good idea. It may make some messages shorter, but it certainly diminishes the routing's precision. Then, using the 8-bit link state record number to identify the link state record will limit to 256 the number of records that a given router can advertise. As the size of each record is limited to the maximum packet size supported by the network, this can prove to be a severe constraint. We need 12 bytes per IP destination, and we have heard of tables containing as many as 20,000 destinations. One could probably find a "kludge"— e.g., allocation of several identifiers to the same router—but the result is not very elegant. There are also a number of tiny details that make OSPF better suited to the needs of IP networks, such as the support of a backup designated router (which is however compensated by a faster designated router election) and the possibility to coexist with RIP through "not-so-stubby areas." More important still is that OSPF is "change controlled" by the IETF. It is an evolving protocol that changes in response to user needs. Recent history has shown that the evolution of OSI protocols was much slower and that it responded to many other forces besides user needs.

In fact, the very idea of "dual routing" is not so seductive at it might appear. The fact is that corporate backbones often carry multiple protocols. But the reason they do so is because they expect different services from these different protocols, and it is very often the case that these different services require slightly different routing algorithms. Trying to accommodate them all in one single model means that one will have to find some form of "largest common denominator," i.e., a compromise. There is no real evidence that integrated routing leads to a more efficient network management than the opposite technique known as "ships in the night" where each protocol is routed with its own tools, in the same way that ships in the night pursue their courses without relying on each other.

7.2.6 Further Work on IS-IS

The IETF may have at some point chosen OSPF over IS-IS, but IS-IS retains a solid core of users, especially on large backbone networks. Proponents of IS-IS generally cite various advantages, such as a more robust flooding protocol, a better handling of large areas, and—last but not least—better quality implementations on some routers. The IS-IS working group of the IETF is developing a set of improvements to IS-IS.

A major improvement is the possibility of transporting IS-IS directly over IP, without using any CLNP encapsulation. This is especially desirable now that CLNP has all but disappeared from the networking scene.

Another improvement is the inclusion of security mechanisms similar to the MD5-based security mechanisms of RIP and OSPF. The generic Type-Length-Value encoding used by IS-IS facilitates the development of this function. There was already a variable length authentication field in IS-IS, where the first value octet was encoding the authentication type. In addition to the originally defined "clear text password" authentication, the working group proposes to define an authentication type for MD5-based authentication. The 16 remaining value octets would encode the hash code.

The group is also working to remove some of the marginal problems of IS-IS. It is reworking the encoding of the reachability information to be more compact and provide better control on the metric of paths that are distributed through several areas. It is addressing practical issues such as the limitation of the difficulties in the original version of IS-IS to maintain more than 255 adjacencies for a given node. Finally, we may observe that many of the improvements to OSPF can be developed in parallel for IS-IS. For example, we described in section 6.8.3 of the OSPF chapter the work of Curtis Villamizar on Optimized Multi Path. But this work is not specific to OSPF, and similar improvements are developed for IS-IS by Curtis Villamizar and Tony Li.

In addition, we should note that, because of its multiprotocol design, IS-IS can support IPv6 without any other modification than the definition of an address family code for v6.

7.3 IGRP

The growth of the Internet gave birth to a whole new industry—the provision of network routers; cisco (they insist on the lowercase spelling of their company name) is one of the few companies that sell these new products, and it has a very large share of the market.

When the company was founded several years ago, the IP routing protocol of choice was RIP. But RIP is a routing protocol plagued with severe limitations, which posed a cruel alternative to router providers: either wait for the IETF to define a new standard or implement a proprietary solution. IGRP was cisco's response to this alternative—a proprietary protocol that cures some of RIP's defects and could be marketed before the IETF finished its work on OSPF.

IGRP is a routing protocol of the distance vector family. Like RIP, it relies on the periodic multicasting of routing updates by a router to all its neighbors. One minor difference with RIP is that it operates at a lower frequency—IGRP updates are sent by default every 90 seconds, instead of 30 seconds in the case of RIP. There are, however, some important differences, such as composite metrics, conservative protection against loops, multipath routing, and handling of default routes [6]. Some of the improvements have been patented by cisco.

7.3.1 Composite Metrics

The IGRP routing updates include for each entry a set of four metrics: delay (D), bandwidth (B), reliability (R), and load (L). It also includes two variables that play no role in the computation of paths—a count of the hops in the route (H) and a computation of the path MTU, i.e., the maximum message length in octets that is acceptable to all links on the path.

The delay is expressed in units of 10 microseconds. It represents the sum of the transmission delays of all the links on the path between the router and the destination. It is encoded on 24 bits in the update message; the maximum value (all bits set to 1) is used to indicate an unreachable destination.

The bandwidth is one of the narrowest links on the path toward the destination. It is expressed on an inverse scale, as the division of 10 million by the data rate of the link expressed in kbps: this can be understood as the number of seconds necessary to transfer 10 billion bits on the link or as the number of 10-ms time units necessary to transfer a 10,000-bit message. The 24-bit encoding allows the data rates to vary between 1,200 bps and 10 gigabits/second (Gbps).

Delay and bandwidth are static characteristics of the links that can be either deduced from the type of link (e.g., Ethernet, FDDI) or entered by the router's manager. Reliability and occupation are dynamic characteristics that are obtained by the routers through link monitoring. The reliability is an expression of the error rate on the path—it encodes the probability that a packet sent on this path will arrive at the destination. It is expressed on 1 octet—255 means 100%. The "occupation" is the load of the narrowest link in the path. It is also encoded on 1 octet, with the same convention.

In order to compare two paths leading to the same destination, IGRP uses a "composite" metric, which can be understood as an expression of the global transmission delay. The actual formula combines all four parameters, D, B, R, and L. We will explain step by step the recipe used for composing the metric.

The transmission delay of a packet is the sum of the path's delay and the packet transmission time, which is equal to the division of the packet length by the data rate. If we suppose a 10,000-bit packet, this is the sum of the delay and bandwidth metrics.

$$T = B + D$$

For other packet lengths, we will have to multiply the bandwidth metric by the packet length (P).

$$T = \frac{P \times B}{10,000 + D}$$

But we should also consider the load of the link. If a link is very loaded, only a fraction of the bandwidth is available. The formula becomes:

$$T = P \times \frac{B \times \left(\dfrac{256}{256 - L}\right)}{10,000 + D}$$

i.e.:

$$T = P \times B \times \frac{256}{10,000 \times (256 - L)} + D$$

This formula does not yet take into account the link's reliability. If the link is very error-prone, the packet will have to be repeated several times, the average number of repetitions being the inverse of the link's reliability. This yields the final expression of the metric.

$$T = \left(P \times B \times \frac{256}{10,000 \times (256 - L)} + D \right) \times \frac{255}{R}$$

This kind of formulation calls for several remarks, however. First, experience has shown that the link's load should be handled with care, taking into account that short-term variations can lead to network instability (see chapter 14). A first precaution is to measure the link's load on a long interval, say several minutes. This is why IGRP uses periodic updates; it will also not consider that a load changes "significantly" if it worsens less than 10%. Another precaution is to take the load only partially into account—to consider that the transmission time is an intermediate value between the ones of the "loaded" and "unloaded" condition. Secondly, the formula takes into account only the effect of the reliability on the average transmission delay; transmission errors also affect the delay's variance. Then, as we are trying only to compare several paths, there is no need to insist on a particular unit for the metric. In the implementation of IGRP by cisco, the composite metric is computed as:

$$M = \left(\frac{K1 \times B + K2 \times B}{(256 - L)} + K3 \times D \right) \times \frac{K5}{R + K4}$$

The coefficients K1 to K5 allow the network manager to balance the various factors; by convention, setting K5 to 0 implies that the reliability is not taken into account. The default version has K1 = K3 = 1, K2 = K4 = K5 = 0; it corresponds to the first step in our discussion, i.e., the transmission delay for a 10,000-bit packet.

Although IGRP is, like RIP, a distance vector protocol, the fact that it carries precise metrics allows each router to parametrize its route selection process as a function of the local preferences. This is easily achieved by tuning the coefficients of the "composite metric" equation—for example, increasing the weight of the bandwidth parameter if one prefers the "largest throughput" routes, or the weight of the delay parameter if one prefers the "shortest" routes.

7.3.2 Handling of Default Routes

RIP and OSPF follow the convention that the routing table entry for the null address 0.0.0.0 describes the default route. This is a useful convention that can reduce the size of the routing tables for networks that have only a limited number of exit points toward the global Internet. In practice, the default route is configured by a management operation on the network's routers that are connected to "the outside world," instructing them to advertise the default route with some fixed metric; this metric is used to set up preferences between the possible exit points.

But this convention of using 0.0.0.0 has one inconvenience: the metric of the default route is not directly related to a distance. IGRP uses a different concept. Some real network numbers are marked as "candidates for being a default." These numbers are typically the addresses of transit networks, such as the NSFnet, located in the "core" of the Internet. The path toward that network will be naturally updated as part of the routing process, which allows for a natural selection of the default route.

7.3.3 Loop Detection

We mentioned in the analysis of RIP that there is a theoretical difficulty in handling complex metrics with a distance vector protocol; because ultimately we have to rely on counting to infinity for loop detection, which can take a very long time with a fine-grained metric.

IGRP does indeed incorporate the split horizon and triggered update techniques that we described for RIP, but it does not use "poisonous reverse." The first versions of IGRP completed these with a protective measure known as "path holddown"; the last versions replace path holddown by "route poisoning."

In the presence of triggered updates, the construction of loops is normally due to transmission errors or to update propagation delays—a router that has detected a path failure receives a message from another router that has not yet received the update and reinjects this stale information into the network. On the other hand, if the triggered update was received properly, the computation would be correct. Path holddown attempts to reduce the risk of loop buildup by imposing a quarantine period after the detection of a link failure. During that period the destination is "on hold" and no update is accepted. The quarantine should be long enough to allow several repetitions of the update message and to "guarantee" that the information will reach all the other routers in the network. Once the quarantine is finished, the normal path selection will resume.

In practice, to be long enough, a quarantine should include two update periods, or last at least 180 seconds. This is quite secure but has the side effect that the destination is guaranteed to remain unreachable for 3 minutes, even if a slower alternate path exists. The latest versions of IGRP use route poisoning as an alternative to holddowns. Route poisoning is based on the observation that, when a loop is building up, the hop count of the path increases; in fact it increases by the loop perimeter at each iteration. An update that increases the hop count announced by a neighbor is thus suspect—it may well be caused by the setup of a loop. It may indeed also be caused by some other perfectly legitimate change in the topology, such as the selection of a longer alternate path between the neighbor and the destination. But IGRP decided to be conservative there and to simply treat every path for which the hop count increases as "unusable." The path will be used again only if a following update confirms the new hop count. This should happen at most 90 seconds later—much sooner than the end of the quarantine.

7.3.4 Multipath Routing

We have noted in the previous chapter that the support of "equal length multipath" was an advantage of OSPF over RIP. However, multipath routing is not limited to link state protocols. Let's look back at the test network we used for the description of RIP.

The router A receives distance vectors from B and D. In the RIP example, the distances advertised by B and D for E were both equal to 1 hop, and the choice of the route through B or D was pretty much taken at random. This was a consequence of the implementation: the routing tables had space for only one next hop. But this is not a requirement of the protocol itself.

The implementation of IGRP keeps a list of possible paths in memory, rather than just one path per destination. Each path is identified by a neighbor node and also by the interface used to reach that neighbor. There may well be multiple links between two routers, for example, in order to increase the network's resilience. This has two advantages: the routers can immediately switch to the "next best" path if the preferred path becomes unavailable. They can also do "load splitting," i.e., spread the traffic over all the "almost-equal-cost" paths.

In the first versions of IGRP, a "variance" coefficient V was used to quantify this notion of "almost equality." A "second-best" path is eligible if its metric M2 is not larger than V times the metric M1 of the best path. But this formula is difficult to apply in practice. We have seen in the OSPF chapter that it is easy to build up partial loops through ill-tuned multipath routing. We should select a secondary path only if the next router on that path is nearer to the destination than the local router. In the latest versions of IGRP, the variance V is always set to 1, thus limiting the selection to "equal length" multipaths.

7.4 Enhanced IGRP

The initial version of IGRP was produced in 1988. This protocol followed a simple design, trying to correct most of RIP's known weak points. However, IGRP is not perfect. The most obvious deficiency concerns the loop detection. Holddowns or route-poisoning techniques prevent loops by imposing only temporary unreachabilities—which may, in fact, last for quite a long time. Then, one can observe that IGRP does not support variable-length subnets or supernets. In this respect, it has the same restrictions as RIP-1. And one can also observe that the periodic repetition of routing updates every 90 seconds induces the same synchronization effects that we described for RIP.

An obvious answer would have been to just discontinue the IGRP effort and switch to OSPF. However, cisco did not do that. It did implement OSPF, but it pursued its work on distance vector routing protocols. Some of cisco's engineers believe strongly that the distance vector technology is in fact superior to the link state technology, that it gives more flexibility with less complexity. We will see that they have some valid arguments. The enhanced IGRP, which is referred to as EIGRP, incorporates a sophisticated extension of the distance vector protocol designed by J. J. Garcia-Luna-Aceves, as well as many miscellaneous improvements [7].

7.4.1 The Distance Vector School

Routing protocols are first categorized by the algorithm that they incorporate, i.e., distance vector or link state. Most routing experts convinced themselves that the link state protocols are "better." The "distributed computation" performed by distance vector protocols is, by nature, subject to undesirable transient states. It takes several iterations of message exchanges before the network converges to a new state. The split horizon and poisoned reverse methods incorporated by RIP are not sufficient to prevent the formation of loops; the holddowns or route-poisoning techniques used by IGRP prevent loops by imposing temporary unreachabilities.

But there is a strong minority of experts that doesn't accept this conclusion. These experts' main argument is that a distance vector protocol is simpler, that implementing it requires less memory, that the operation requires fewer messages. The "simplicity" argument is entirely correct—we saw that the OSPF documentation was five times larger than that for RIP, and the text of the IS-IS standard is even worse. This simplicity has one main advantage: since less code is required and the algorithm is simple, the chances that the program hides a fatal bug are much lower. But simplicity alone is not an entirely convincing argument. There are a number of competent programmers employed by router manufacturers. OSPF or IS-IS solutions are available and have been properly debugged.

It is often asserted that distance vector protocols require less memory than link state protocols. This is certainly true if one considers a simple implementation of RIP, which would store exactly one route per destination, and an implementation of OSPF, where one must also store a link state database. But the comparison is not so clear-cut in the case of sophisticated distance vector implementations. The memory required by simple distance vectors scales linearly with the number of destinations. The one requested by link state protocols is the sum of two components, one proportional to the number of links in the network and the other to the number of destinations. The latter term is the dominant factor today, with more than 60,000 networks connected to the Internet and as many entries. This means that the relative cost of maintaining extra entries for network links is not so high. One should also observe that sophisticated distance vector protocols such as EIGRP maintain multiple information for each destination—as many as possible alternate paths. The memory requirement will in fact depend on the implementation style as much as on the protocol.

The bandwidth argument is not very convincing either. In fact, RIP, a distance vector protocol, requires more bandwidth than OSPF because it needs to refresh the routing information periodically for all destinations, which means that the entire tables have to be transmitted. Link state protocols require less transmission because they flood the link state information only when it changes or after a very long delay. We have to resort to "incremental updates" to diminish the bandwidth requirement of distance vector protocols, i.e., assume that all updates are acknowledged and that each router keeps in memory the destinations and distances advertised by all its neighbors—which means that we lose the supposed "memory" advantage.

In fact, the tenants of distance vector protocols insist on two other particularities: transient loops and peaks of computation. Link state protocols do, indeed, have a transient state during the flooding of a new link state value. During this state, the databases are not synchronized. Even if this state is short, say a fraction of a second, there is a risk that the transient loops will occur and cause temporary congestion. We will see that the diffusing update algorithm (DUAL) embedded in EIGRP is free of these transient loops, although it has to introduce transient unreachabilities.

The second argument regards the "load profile" imposed by link state protocols. Each time the network map changes, all network nodes have to recompute their routing tables, which creates a "peak" of activity. Distance vector protocols, on the contrary, perform their computation on a destination-per-destination basis. If a link fails, one needs to recompute routes only for those destinations that were routed over this particular link. Moreover, this computation will be localized to one part of the network only—the routers that are "upstream" from the said link. This is particularly visible in case of "route flapping," when a link keeps failing at regular and short intervals; each "flap" will result in the flooding of a link state message to all routers in the network, which will have to compute again and again their complete routing tables.

For the sake of truth and fairness, one should observe that it is entirely possible to perform partial computations within link state databases. However, this is rarely implemented, and the proponents of EIGRP believe that their protocol, because of its "loop-free" property, is both simpler and more efficient than OSPF.

7.4.2 The DUAL Algorithm

Several researchers have tried to improve the distance vector technology. In the RIP chapter and in the IGRP section above, we mentioned algorithms like split horizon, triggered updates, source tracing, path holddown, and route poisoning. None of these, however, is entirely satisfactory. The source tracing algorithm requires nearly as much computation as OSPF, maybe more; the other algorithms either do not offer complete protection against loops or impose long unreachabilities—or both. The "distributed update algorithm" (DUAL), proposed by J. J. Garcia-Luna-Aceves [8], is a definitive improvement. That algorithm aims at removing transient loops from both distance vector and link state routing protocols. We will detail here the distance vector version that is implemented in EIGRP. The link state version is similar—it essentially freezes the routing tables during the flooding of link state updates in order to avoid incoherent decisions based on transient states.

DUAL is based on the "diffusion" algorithm for partial route updates proposed by E. W. Dijkstra and C. S. Scholten in 1980 [9], and on the remark that one cannot create a loop by picking a shorter path to the destination [10]. Suppose that each router i maintains for each destination j and for each of its neighbors k the following information:

d(k,j): the distance from k to j

l(i,k): the cost of the link between i and k

The information d(k,j) is obtained from the distance vectors advertised by the neighbors; the link cost l(i,k) is a local parameter. The router normally selects as next hop toward j one of its neighbors, say x, which minimizes the sum.

$$d(i,j) = l(i,x) + d(x,j)$$

A router that has a stable version of the routing table is said to be in "passive" state. Suppose now that this router receives a routing update—that either a link cost $l'(i,k)$ or a distance vector $d'(k,j)$ is updated. If the new cost is lower than the existing cost:

$$l'(i,k) + d'(k,j) < d(i,j)$$

then the router can simply adopt k as the next hop, update $d(i,j)$, and announce the update to the neighbors. There is no problem there, as one cannot create a loop by adopting a shorter route. If the new cost is larger than $d(i,j)$, one will generally not take any action, except if the neighbor concerned by the update is x, the selected next hop toward j. In this case, one will first look for "acceptable neighbors," using in fact the same selection process that we described in IGRP for the selection of an alternate path. A neighbor is acceptable if its distance to the destination is shorter than that of the local router:

$$d(k,j) < d(i,j)$$

where $d(i,j)$ is the "old" value, before taking into account the update. If there is at least one acceptable neighbor, the router selects the one that results in the lowest value of:

$$d'(i,j) = l(i,k) + d(k,j)$$

then updates the next hop for destination j and the value $d(i,j)$. It advertises the new distance to its neighbors. If there is no acceptable neighbor, the router must engage a "diffusion" computation. As long as the computation is not complete, it will "freeze" its routing table, or at least the route to the destination j. There were no loops before, so freezing the table cannot create a loop. It can, however, create a "black hole" if packets are sent toward a broken link, but this will last only for the duration of the computation.

In order to perform the diffusion process, the router sends a particular form of update called a "query" to all its neighbors, except to x, from which it received the update. That query mentions the destination j and the new distance $l'(i,x) + d'(x,j)$ and calls for a response: the new distance $d'(k,j)$ from the neighbor. The neighbors will first treat the message as a normal "update." If this update leaves them in a passive state, e.g., because they were not routing through i or because they could find an alternate neighbor, they reply immediately with the new version of their routing tables. Otherwise, they will themselves pass in "active" mode and propagate queries to all of their neighbors: this is the "diffusion" of the update along the network's graph.

A router that is in active mode may, in some cases, receive queries. It will update its tables, and send a reply. The reply will always mention the frozen distance—the value $l'(i,x) + d'(x,j)$. When a router has received the replies from all of its neighbors, it can switch back from active to passive mode. It will in turn reply to the router that initially sent it a query so that the "ebbing" of the diffusion occurs. Ultimately, the reply will arrive at the first router that detected the problem, e.g., a broken link—the network has converged.

7.4.3 Extending IGRP

Implementing DUAL required serious modification to IGRP. Since a router must keep in memory an up-to-date version of each neighbor's distance vector, the updates have to be acknowledged. In fact, one has to use incremental updates. Then, one has to distinguish between simple updates, sent by a router that has remained passive, and the queries that are sent by an active router waiting for a reply. The queries are not to be confused with RIP or IGRP's "requests," which are simple messages asking for information. Finally, as one implements incremental updates, one cannot rely on their periodic exchange to test a link's connectivity. For these reasons, EIGRP defines five message types:

☞ "Hello" messages are used for neighbor discovery.
☞ "Update" messages carry the modification of a passive router to the distance vector.
☞ "Query" messages carry the distance updates of an active router and trigger the "diffusion" algorithm.
☞ "Reply" messages are sent in response to queries.
☞ "Request" messages are similar to IGRP's requests.

The hello packets are multicast to all EIGRP routers in the network. They are sent at regular intervals, and the neighbors will reply by sending their own hello packets. This procedure is somewhat similar to the one of OSPF—it enables the EIGRP routers to test the validity of their connections. Updates and queries are generally transmitted through a "reliable multicast" procedure: they must be acknowledged. Replies and requests are generally transmitted through a "reliable unicast" procedure. Since 1996, cisco's implementations of EIGRP takes into consideration the available bandwidth when determining the rate of updates; they can be configured to only use a certain maximum percentage of bandwidth. The CPU and memory utilization have also been improved.

The "extensions" to IGRP are not limited to the implementation of the DUAL algorithm. The format of routing entries has also been updated to allow routing on arbitrary subnet masks or CIDR supernet masks, and the notation of external routes carries a "route tag" similar to the one of RIP-2 or OSPF for use by the external gateway protocols. Contrary to OSPF, there is no notion of "area" in EIGRP. However, subnets, and more generally "address prefixes," can be "aggregated" by some routers that will play the same role as area-border routers, perhaps in a more flexible way. Finally, one should note that the EIGRP documentation mentions a "compatibility mode" for easing the transition between IGRP and EIGRP.

7.5 Choosing Routing Protocols

GGP, Hello, RIP, IGRP, IS-IS, OSPF, and EIGRP were all considered state of the art at the time they were developed. It would be very surprising if, as time passes, the state of the art remains unchanged. It is indeed difficult to predict the future, especially as it has not happened yet. One may see a resurrection of old switching techniques like "flood and source route" or "hot-potato routing," where transmission efficiency is traded for faster route computation or for lesser memory requirements. One may see a larger reliance on "synchronized time" to increase the dynamic of routing updates. And one may also see brand-new techniques such as optical switching, which may mandate further progress in the computation of routes.

These developments are, however, likely to take several years. In the interim, the network manager has to choose between RIP, IGRP, EIGRP, IS-IS, and OSPF. In this and the two previous chapters, we have tried to explain the advantages and disadvantages of the distance vector and link state technologies and of particular implementations. RIP version 1 and the original IGRP are not capable of handling the new "classless" IP prefixes, and should not be used. RIP version 2, EIGRP, IS-IS, and OSPF version 2 are all capable of handling these prefixes. In addition, there are IPv6 versions of RIP and OSPF, while EIGRP and IS-IS can support multiple address families and could thus easily support IPv6.

Most experts will recommend the link state protocols; in fact, the IAB recommended the use of OSPF as the standard interior gateway protocol for IP networks. RIP version 2 should only be used on small networks, where no path will ever be longer than 16 hops. There was a debate for some time about the possibility of also recommending IS-IS, on the basis that it would facilitate deployment of the CLNP protocol in parallel with IP. But any idea of transitioning the Internet toward ISO-defined protocols has now vanished. Even before that, it was not clear that integrated routing would lead to better service than the "ships-in-the-night" approach where each protocol is served by a dedicated routing algorithm. However, the IS-IS working group is active, and IS-IS commands a respectable following among the operators of large backbone networks, in part because IS-IS was the original IGP chosen on the NSFNET.

The only real contender to OSPF today is probably EIGRP. We have seen that EIGRP includes corrections for the known deficiencies of distance vector protocols while trying to keep their simplicity. Keeping the simplicity, however, is not entirely obvious. Maintaining a complete memory of all neighbors' distance vectors probably requires as much in the way of resources as maintaining the link state database—maybe more—while the diffusion procedure certainly does not converge faster than the link state computations. In fact, one could well argue that the distance vector technology can become as reliable as the link state technology only by becoming equally complex. At this stage, the debate is more one of quality of implementation, ease of configuration, and level of standardization. The quality of the implementation matters a lot. If a router is too slow in detecting that a link has broken, it will keep using a broken route for a very long time. On the other hand, a router that does not use proper "qualification" procedures to detect that a link is oscillating between an "available" and "disconnected" state will induce very undesirable route flapping in the network. The quality of the management interfaces will also be a very important factor. This can be shown only by field tests and customer reports; there is certainly no way to assert in this book that the OSPF implementation by vendor X is better than that of vendor Y or than the EIGRP implementation by cisco.

On the other hand, there is always a good reason to insist on a "standard" protocol such as OSPF: vendor independence. IGRP and EIGRP are proprietary protocols; key elements of their operation are patented by cisco. Changing the routing protocol when the network is in operation is an "interesting" experience; deciding that one will use IGRP or EIGRP really means that one will use exactly one vendor. Choosing OSPF, on the contrary, means that one can buy products from several vendors and benefit from the competition.

References

1. V. Strazisar, "Gateway Routing: An Implementation Specification," IEN-30, Bolt Beranek and Newman, April 1979.
2. V. Strazisar, "How to Build a Gateway," IEN-109, Bolt Beranek and Newman, August 1979.

3. D. Mills, "DCN Local-Network Protocols," RFC-891, December 1, 1983.

4. "Intermediate System to Intermediate System Intra-Domain Routeing Exchange Protocol for Use in Conjunction with the Protocol for Providing the Connectionless-Mode Network Service (ISO 8473)," ISO-DP-10589, February 1990.

5. R. Callon, "Use of OSI IS-IS for Routing in TCP/IP and Dual Environments," RFC-1195, December 19, 1990.

6. Charles L. Hedricks, "An Introduction to IGRP," Center for Computer and Information Services, Laboratory for Computer Science Research, Rutgers University, August 22, 1991.

7. Dino Farinacci, "Introduction to Enhanced IGRP (EIGRP)," cisco Systems, July 1993.

8. J. J. Garcia-Luna-Aceves, "A Unified Approach to Loop-Free Routing Using Distance Vectors or Link States," *ACM SIGCOMM '89 Symposium*, September 1989.

9. E. W. Dijkstra and C. S. Scholten, "Termination Detection for Diffusing Computations," *Information Processing Letters*, Vol. 11, No. 1, August 1980.

10. J. M. Jaffe and H. P. Moss, "A Responsive Distributed Routing Algorithm for Computer Networks," *IEEE Transmission on Communications*, Com 30:7, pp. 1758–1762, July 1982.

Part III

Exterior Routing
Protocols

EGP: A First Step Toward the Global Internet

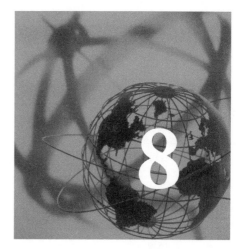

8

$\mathbf{I}$n the early 1980s the Internet was limited to the original Arpanet, its satellite extension Satnet, and a set of local networks directly connected to them by "gateways." As the network grew, it became necessary to adopt a hierarchical structure. The Internet was thus split into a set of "autonomous systems" (AS).

The "Exterior Gateways' Protocol" (EGP) was designed to enable the ASs to exchange routing information. EGP is still in use today, although it is being replaced by BGP. In this chapter, we will first describe the concept of AS, which was introduced by EGP and is also used with BGP. We will then review the design of EGP and study the general problem of computing routes between ASs. Finally, we will analyze the reasons why the EGP design proved to be limited and why a new protocol had to be designed.

8.1 Splitting the Internet into Autonomous Systems

In this section we will analyze why the growth of the Internet made it necessary to split the network into a set of independent entities. We will then introduce the definition of an autonomous system and the requirements for an EGP.

8.1.1 Enlarging the Internet

The early Internet grew out of the Arpanet and companion networks such as Satnet. At first it connected individual computers in research centers, and then it provided access to local networks. In the early 1980s, the Internet was a single network. All routers, which were then called "gateways," shared routing information through the same gateway-to-gateway protocol (GGP); the routing tables included entries and metrics for all the IP networks in the Internet.

This configuration caused a number of problems [1]. Obviously, the routing overhead increased with the number of connected routers; the size of the routing table increased with the number of connected networks. But the frequency of the routing exchanges also increased. The more numerous the routers and the links, the more likely it is that one of them will experience some trouble. Each time a link goes down, or up, the complete set of routing metrics must be computed again, which translates into many packet exchanges for a distance vector protocol like GGP.

But routing overhead was not the only consequence of managing a very large network. As the number of routers increased, so did the number of types of routers. Different machines from different makers with different software started to be used. All these machines used their own specific implementation of GGP, which made "maintenance and fault isolation nearly impossible" [1].

The large number of routers also made the deployment of new versions of the routing algorithm very difficult. As routing is effectively a single application distributed on all the routers, changing to a new version required effectively upgrading all sites at the same "flag hour." Past a certain network size, such upgrades become very acrobatic, and even more so if the routers are owned by different organizations and managed by different people. One begins to observe a strong pressure against any "gratuitous change"—in fact, against any change that is not clearly perceived as the remedy to a major failure. E. Rosen explains how the software became "too rigid and inflexible" [1].

It was obviously time to reform the "single network" model. The decision was made to split the Internet into a set of autonomous systems, each AS comprised of a set of routers and networks under the same administration. One of the ASs would be formed from the Arpanet and Satnet routers; it would be called the "core" and would play a "backbone" role in the Internet. All the other ASs would be called "stub AS." Each stub would have at least one router connected to at least one core router in order to obtain global Internet connectivity. Communication with remote stubs would normally occur through the core. These special routers, connected to other ASs, were called "exterior gateways" in 1982. They must exchange information in order to manage the connectivity: this is the purpose of the "Exterior Gateway Protocol" (EGP).

8.1.2 What Is an Autonomous System?

"A set of routers and networks under the same administration" is a very loose definition of an AS, and the concept is indeed very loose. The minimal AS is composed of exactly one router directly connecting one local network to the Internet, but there is no theoretical limit to the size of an AS—it can be a corporate network linking several local networks through a corporate backbone or a set of client networks served by one single Internet provider. From a routing point of view, the definition is quite simple: all parts of an AS must remain connected.

Internal connectivity means that all the routers within the AS must be interconnected. Two local networks that belong to the same organization but that rely on the core AS for connectivity cannot constitute a single AS. It also means that these routers must exchange routing information in order to maintain the connectivity. This is normally achieved by selecting a single routing protocol and running it between all the routers. In the 1982 terminology, routers inside an AS were called "interior gateways" and the protocol was an "Interior Gateway Protocol" (IGP). Examples of IGP in use today are RIP, OSPF, and IGRP; the protocol of choice in

1982 was GGP, the same gateway-to-gateway protocol that was used on the single Internet before the split into a set of ASs.

Each AS is identified by a 16-bit "AS number." This number is assigned by the numbering authorities, in much the same way as the Internet network numbers.

8.1.3 Exchanging Routing Information

Splitting the Internet into several ASs aims at lowering the routing overhead and at easing the network management; computing routes, distributing new versions of software, or isolating failing elements is easier when the number of links and routers is kept relatively small. However, connectivity must be maintained. The routing tables inside the AS should include entries covering all possible Internet destinations.

The routing tables are maintained by the IGP, but the IGP messages are only exchanged between interior gateways, that is between routers that belong to the AS. These routers can discover information only about the internal networks to which they are directly connected. They must get the information about exterior networks through a dialogue with exterior gateways, which are entry points in adjacent autonomous systems. The role of EGP is precisely to exchange this "reachability information." This information is very naturally a set of connected networks. Suppose that two ASs called X and Y are connected through the exterior gateways A and B.

A and B will use EGP to document the networks they can reach, such as the internal networks within X for A and those of Y for B. Once A has obtained this information, it can advertise it through the local IGP. If X uses RIP, A will prepare a distance vector with an entry for all the networks advertised by B and send it to its neighboring routers within X. If X uses OSPF, A will mention all these destinations in an exterior link state advertisement. Similarly, B will announce within Y that it has connectivity with the networks advertised by A.

8.2 Exchanging Information Through EGP

EGP organizes the exchange of "reachability" information between two adjacent ASs, or rather between two neighboring gateways. EGP is in fact composed of three separate procedures.

☞ The "neighbor acquisition" procedure determines whether two adjacent gateways agree to become neighbors.

☞ The "neighbor reachability" procedure monitors the link between the neighbors.

☞ The "network reachability" procedure organizes the exchange of reachability information.

In this section, we will detail the organization of the protocol.

8.2.1 The EGP Messages

The neighbor acquisition, neighbor reachability, and network reachability procedures are performed by exchanging EGP messages. All these messages are carried inside IP datagrams: the protocol number 8 has been assigned to EGP. They all start with the same 8-byte header.

```
 0                   1                   2                   3
 0 1 2 3 4 5 6 7 8 9 0 1 2 3 4 5 6 7 8 9 0 1 2 3 4 5 6 7 8 9 0 1
+-+-+-+-+-+-+-+-+-+-+-+-+-+-+-+-+-+-+-+-+-+-+-+-+-+-+-+-+-+-+-+-+
|  EGP Version  #  |     Type        |     Code      |   Info    |
+------------------+-----------------+---------------+-----------+
|         Checksum                   |  Autonomous System    #   |
+------------------------------------+---------------------------+
|       Sequence   #                 |     data  - - -           |
+------------------------------------+---------------------------+
```

The header carries a version number (currently 2), a checksum, the number of the autonomous system to which the sending router belongs, and a sequence number. The checksum is computed with the classic "complement-to-1-sum" algorithm also used by IP, TCP, and UDP; it protects the content of the EGP packet, from the version number to the last byte of data. The sequence number has different values depending on the particular packet type. Generally, EGP packets can be either queries or responses, and the sequence numbers will be used to correlate queries and responses.

The headers also contain "type," "code," and "information" fields. The type generally identifies the "subprotocol." All neighbor acquisition messages carry the type 3; all neighbor reachability messages carry the type 5. However, two types are allocated to the network reachability message—1 for updates, 2 for polls. The code field is generally used to identify a message within a subprotocol, such as to differentiate acquisition requests, confirmations, and refusals. The information field provides additional information within a message, e.g., refusal reasons.

The type 8 is used by error messages.

```
 0                   1                   2                   3
 0 1 2 3 4 5 6 7 8 9 0 1 2 3 4 5 6 7 8 9 0 1 2 3 4 5 6 7 8 9 0 1
+-+-+-+-+-+-+-+-+-+-+-+-+-+-+-+-+-+-+-+-+-+-+-+-+-+-+-+-+-+-+-+-+
|  EGP Version  #  |     Type        |     Code      |  Unused   |
+------------------+-----------------+---------------+-----------+
|         Checksum                   |  Autonomous System    #   |
+------------------------------------+---------------------------+
|       Sequence   #                 |     Reason                |
+------------------------------------+---------------------------+
|                  Error Message Header                          |
|           (first three 32-bit words of EGP header)            |
+---------------------------------------------------------------+
```

Error messages can be sent at any moment, in response to a wrongly formatted or unexpected EGP message. They carry an arbitrary sequence number, assigned by the sending router. The code field is always set to 0, the information field is not used, and the "reason" field is used to specify the error.

```
0  —  unspecified
1  —  Bad EGP checksum
2  —  Bad IP Source address in NR Poll or Response
3  —  Undefined EGP Type or Code
4  —  Received poll from non-neighbor
5  —  Received excess unsolicited NR message
6  —  Received excess poll
7  —  Erroneous counts in received NR message
8  —  No response received to NR poll
```

The error messages repeat the first 12 bytes of the received packet, i.e., the complete "header." The handling of the error will indeed depend on this header.

8.2.2 Neighbor Acquisition

Before exchanging any routing information—and indeed before using any routing information—the adjacent routers must agree to become "neighbors" for EGP. Becoming neighbors means that each AS will eventually agree to relay the adjacent AS's traffic. This requires some kind of formal agreement, maybe a contract, and certainly an explicit configuration. Classic implementations of EGP [2] can thus be parametrized by a list of "potential neighbors." The router will accept becoming neighbors only with the members of this list.

All neighbor acquisition messages share the same format.

```
 0                   1                   2                   3
 0 1 2 3 4 5 6 7 8 9 0 1 2 3 4 5 6 7 8 9 0 1 2 3 4 5 6 7 8 9 0 1
+-+-+-+-+-+-+-+-+-+-+-+-+-+-+-+-+-+-+-+-+-+-+-+-+-+-+-+-+-+-+-+-+
|   EGP Version    #   |       Type        |     Code    |  Info   |
+---------------------------------------+-----------------------+
|              Checksum                 |   Autonomous System   # |
+---------------------------------------+-----------------------+
|           Sequence   #                |   NR    Hello interval  |
+---------------------------------------+-----------------------+
|           NR poll interval            |
+---------------------------------------+
```

In the neighbor acquisition packets, the type is always set to 3. The code determines the particular packet.

```
Code  = 0   Neighbor Acquisition Request
Code  = 1   Neighbor Acquisition Reply
Code  = 2   Neighbor Acquisition Refusal (see Info field)
Code  = 3   Neighbor Cease Message (see Info field)
Code  = 4   Neighbor Cease Acknowledgment
```

The neighbor acquisition procedure is a very simple "two-way handshake." The router that wishes to become a neighbor sends a "neighbor acquisition request" to its partner, which will normally reply with an "acquisition reply," thus completing the acquisition procedure. The partner may also decide to refuse to become a neighbor and reply by a "refusal" message. The information field is set to 0 in requests and replies and indicates the "reason" in refusal messages.

```
0   Unspecified
1   Out of table space
2   Administrative prohibition
```

It may indeed happen that the router will not receive any reply or refusal—for example, if the partner is "down" or if one of the messages was lost due to a transmission error. Requests can be repeated at regular intervals, typically every 30 seconds. They carry a sequence number that is initialized to some random value when the router is initiated and is increased after each retransmission. Replies and refusals should repeat the sequence number of the request. The requestor should discard any response with a mismatching sequence number; it is probably an old message delayed or duplicated by the network.

The router that no longer wants to be a neighbor, e.g., because it is going down, sends a "neighbor cease" message, to which the partner replies with an acknowledgment. The information field of the cease message gives the reason for ceasing to be a neighbor.

```
0  Unspecified
1  Going down
2  No longer needed
```

The field is always set to 0 in the acknowledgment. As in the case of the initial exchange, cease packets carry a sequence number that must be repeated in the acknowledgment; cease packets should be repeated until an acknowledgment is received.

When a request/reply exchange has been successfully performed, the routers become neighbors. They can now run the neighbor reachability and network reachability procedures. Each of them should remember the "hello" and "poll" intervals that were announced by the neighbor during the initial exchange: they are important parameters of the neighbor reachability and network reachability procedures.

8.2.3 Neighbor Reachability

The purpose of the neighbor reachability (NR) procedure is to check that the link to the neighbor is still operational. In some cases, it is indeed possible to obtain this reachability information from the underlying network, although the underlying network's information should rather be taken as "negative only." For example, if two neighbors are connected through an ISDN network, failure to establish the connection certainly indicates that the neighbor is unreachable, but a successful connection establishment does not guarantee that the neighbor's routing functions are operational.

```
 0                   1                   2                   3
 0 1 2 3 4 5 6 7 8 9 0 1 2 3 4 5 6 7 8 9 0 1 2 3 4 5 6 7 8 9 0 1
+-+-+-+-+-+-+-+-+-+-+-+-+-+-+-+-+-+-+-+-+-+-+-+-+-+-+-+-+-+-+-+-+
|   EGP Version   #  |    Type:   5     |     Code     |   Status    |
+-+-+-+-+-+-+-+-+-+-+-+-+-+-+-+-+-+-+-+-+-+-+-+-+-+-+-+-+-+-+-+-+
|        Checksum        |     Autonomous System    #       |
+-+-+-+-+-+-+-+-+-+-+-+-+-+-+-+-+-+-+-+-+-+-+-+-+-+-+-+-+-+-+-+-+
|        Sequence   #      |
+-+-+-+-+-+-+-+-+-+-+-+-+-+
```

—   format of Hello and I-H-U messages   —

The network reachability protocol uses two kinds of packets—"hello" and "I heard you" (I-H-U). Both packets carry the type 5. Hellos are identified by the code 0; I-H-Us by the code 1. Both packets carry in the information field a "status" indication.

0—No status given
1—You appear reachable to me
2—You appear unreachable to me due to neighbor reachability protocol
3—You appear unreachable to me due to network reachability information (e.g., failure to
    establish a circuit)
4—You appear unreachable to me due to problems with my network interface

The router that wants to check the reachability of its neighbor will send hellos at regular intervals; the neighbor will send an I-H-U in reply to every hello that it receives. The hellos carry a sequence number, which is repeated in the I-H-U; mismatching replies will indeed be discarded.

Choosing the frequency of hellos is indeed a balance between two inconveniences—if the frequency is too low, link status will not be detected in due time while, if it is too high, one will end up consuming too much network and processing resources. This last danger can be alleviated somewhat by advertising a "minimum delay between hellos" during the acquisition procedure: this is the "NR hello interval" parameter of the acquisition messages. If the neighbor polls more frequently than this delay, it is legitimate to ignore its hellos. A typical hello interval is 30 seconds.

A single hello/I-H-U handshake is generally not deemed sufficient for declaring a link operational, and a single failed handshake is not sufficient to declare that a link is down. Such simplistic procedures would result in either declaring operational a link of poor quality or unduly declaring inoperational a link after a single transmission error. One particular pitfall to avoid is "oscillation" or "route flapping," i.e., changing the state of the link at short intervals. Each of these oscillations results in massive routing updates in each of the neighboring ASs, and thus in a very poor networking service!

The EGP reachability protocol tries to avoid this pitfall through a simple "dual threshold" procedure. A reachable neighbor is declared unreachable if fewer than i I-H-Us have been received in reply to the last n hellos. An unreachable neighbor is declared reachable only if at least more than j I-H-Us have been received in reply to the last m hellos. Fixing the values of i, n, j, and m is indeed a local decision; for the procedure to be effective, m should be larger than or equal to n, and the ratio j/m should be larger than the ratio i/n. The implementation described in RFC-911 considers that a neighbor remains reachable if at least one of the last four hellos was replied to and becomes reachable only if at least three of the last four hello exchanges were successful. This is equivalent to setting n and m to 4, i to 1, and j to 3 [2].

Although nothing forbids both routers from running the neighbor reachability protocol simultaneously, this is not needed. One may configure the EGP protocol in an "asymmetric" way, so that one neighbor is active and sends the hellos and the other one is passive and responds only by I-H-Us. The passive router can monitor the status passed in the hello packets. It will consider that the neighbor is reachable if the status mentions the value 1 (you appear reachable to me), unreachable otherwise.

8.2.4 Network Reachability

The purpose of the network reachability procedure is to exchange the list of networks that can be reached through each neighbor. The procedure is based on "polling"—each neighbor, at regular intervals, polls its partner for a list. As for the neighbor reachability procedure, the minimum value of this interval is fixed in the acquisition exchange: this is the "NR poll interval" of the acquisition message. This protects the routers against the possible overload caused by a silly partner.

```
 0                   1                   2                   3
 0 1 2 3 4 5 6 7 8 9 0 1 2 3 4 5 6 7 8 9 0 1 2 3 4 5 6 7 8 9 0 1
+-+-+-+-+-+-+-+-+-+-+-+-+-+-+-+-+-+-+-+-+-+-+-+-+-+-+-+-+-+-+-+-+
|    EGP Version   # |    Type:   2      |    Code           |    Unused         |
+-------------------------------------------------------------+
|         Checksum                      |    Autonomous System   #              |
+-------------------------------------------------------------+
|         Sequence  #                   |    Unused                             |
+-------------------------------------------------------------+
|                        IP Source Network                                      |
+-------------------------------------------------------------+
```

—   polling message   —

Polling messages are identified by the type number 2. The code field is set to 0, and the information field is not used. Polling messages carry a sequence number, which will be repeated in the responses, i.e., in the reachability messages. They also carry an "IP source network" identifier—the IP prefix of the network to which both routers are attached. This prefix will be padded with three, two, or one null bytes for class-A, -B, or -C networks.

The reachability message carries a list of reachable networks. It bears the type 1 and the code 0. It should be sent no more than a few seconds after receiving the poll; it repeats the sequence number of the poll. The polling router that does not receive a response after a reasonable delay should repeat its message, keeping the same sequence number, and the neighbor should indeed repeat its response. If no response is received after a certain number of repetitions, the polling router should consider that the neighbor has become unreachable or, more precisely, that there is no network reachable through this neighbor. No response is equivalent to an empty list of reachable networks.

The encoding of reachability messages, taken from RFC-888, is misleading as it indicates nonexistent 32-bit word boundaries [3]. In fact, the message is organized as an EGP header, followed by a network number identical to the one of the poll message and by a list of gateways and reachable networks. One would not understand this format if one does not realize that a single network, say an Ethernet, may connect several routers belonging to different ASs.

Suppose that, in the example above, the routers A, B, and C belong to the AS X, while the routers D, E, and F belong to the AS Y. Maintaining peer-to-peer neighbor relations between all routers would require nine independent EGP connections and is not very useful, as any of A, B, and C supposedly knows which networks within X are accessible through its partners—this information is present in the AS internal routing tables. The same is true for D, E, and F on AS Y. Thus, it is sufficient to distinguish only two exterior routers, say C and D, that will exchange reachability information on behalf of X and Y. If C would merely pass to D a list of networks reachable through X, D would have no solution but to pass all packets bound to these networks to C itself, which will then, in many cases, have to relay them to A or B. Relaying these packets twice over the connecting network is inefficient and causes delays. The reachability messages sent

0	1	2	3
0 1 2 3 4 5 6 7 8 9	0 1 2 3 4 5 6 7 8 9	0 1 2 3 4 5 6 7 8 9	0 1

EGP Version #	Type	Code	U	Zeroes		
Checksum		Autonomous System #				
Sequence #		# of Int Gwys	# of Ext Gwys			
IP Source Network						
Gateway 1 IP address (without network #)				1,	2 or	3 bytes
# Distances						
Distance 1	# Nets					
net 1,1,1	|||||||||||||||	|||||||||||||||		1,	2 or	3 bytes
net 1,1,2	|||||||||||||||	|||||||||||||||		1,	2 or	3 bytes
- - -						
Distance 2	# Nets					
net 1,2,1	|||||||||||||||	|||||||||||||||		1,	2 or	3 bytes
net 1,2,2	|||||||||||||||	|||||||||||||||		1,	2 or	3 bytes
- - -						
Gateway n IP address (without network #)				1,	2 or	3 bytes
# Distances						
Distance 1	# Nets					
net n,1,1	|||||||||||||||	|||||||||||||||		1,	2 or	3 bytes
net n,1,2	|||||||||||||||	|||||||||||||||		1,	2 or	3 bytes
Distance 2	# Nets					
net n,2,1	|||||||||||||||	|||||||||||||||		1,	2 or	3 bytes
net n,2,2	|||||||||||||||	|||||||||||||||		1,	2 or	3 bytes

—   Encoding of reachability messages (from RFC-888)   —

by C to D will, in fact, contain three lists of networks—one for each of A, B, and C. We will say that A and B are "indirect neighbors" of C.

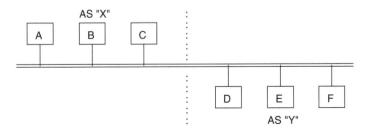

The header of the reachability messages includes a count of these lists, or more precisely a count of both the interior and exterior gateways mentioned in the list. EGP uses a hierarchical model; in this model, only the "core" was allowed to advertise exterior gateways. Each list will start with the network address of the router—or more precisely with the "host number" corresponding to the router within the connecting network, which can be 3, 2, or 1 bytes long depending on the network's class. It will then contain a number of sublists, in which the networks are classified according to their different "distances"; each network is represented by 1, 2, or 3 bytes of IP network number according to the IP network class. The interpretation of distances is largely conventional and will be discussed later; the only point mentioned in EGP itself is that a distance of 255 corresponds with an unreachable network.

Connectivity messages are normally sent as replies only to "poll" messages. They carry the sequence number of the poll message, and their information field is normally null. But poll messages can be spaced by a long interval, typically 2 minutes. If a change of topology occurs within this delay, some networks that were announced as reachable may suddenly become disconnected. Failing to pass this information to the neighbor will result in inadequate routing. The packets will travel along the old route before being discarded. In such events, the router is allowed to pass at most one "unsolicited" reachability message without waiting for the next poll. Unsolicited messages are characterized by the setting of the U bit, i.e., the most significant bit of the information field.

We may note that the "indirect neighbor" concept allows the network managers to run EGP from a different router than the one that is actually forwarding the packets, e.g., a computer that will be used as some form of "route server." This computer must indeed be tightly synchronized with the actual routers—for example, through management procedures.

8.3 Routes, Distances, and Loops

With EGP, the routers send and receive reachability lists. This information is used to update the routing tables in each of the neighboring autonomous systems.

In this section, we will study how these lists are built from the locally available routing information, and how the EGP information is used to compute distances and insert data in the routing tables. We will then detail why the limited loop control present in EGP mandated a carefully engineered Internet topology.

8.3.1 Advertising Destinations

Advertising that an IP network is reachable through a given router is the assertion of two propositions: that there is an internal path within the autonomous system toward this destination, and that the management of the AS agrees to relay packets on this path.

The first condition is obvious: there would be no point in advertising a nonexistent route. The second condition is perhaps difficult to understand if one sticks to the utopian community image of the early Internet, where everyone was supposed to pass everyone else's packets. Advertising a route to a destination means that exterior users will indeed use this route, and will send packets through it. The links that these packets will use are paid for by the local organization. In some cases—e.g., X.25 virtual circuits—the monthly invoices depend directly on the amount of traffic; letting more users send more data will directly translate to an increased bill! This "pay-per-use" form of billing is not generally the case. There is no reason to charge the local users of a local network inside a building. There is no "volume charge" on most leased lines; they have a fixed capacity and a constant price, whatever the traffic. But even if it doesn't have a direct effect on the bill, adding exterior traffic is not neutral. The exterior packets will compete for the same resources as the internal traffic. This will affect the quality of service perceived by the local users, and eventually it will trigger the installation of more powerful local networks or the renting of new lines that have an increased capacity.

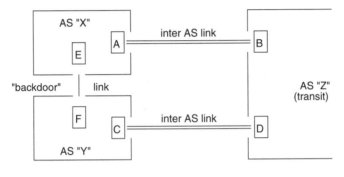

— Two ASs connected to one provider —

Let's consider the case of two autonomous systems, X and Y, connected to the same provider, Z. Both X and Y have probably passed a contract with Z, "buying" from it the Internet service, the Internet connectivity. Thus, Z will very naturally agree to route transit packets for X and Y. Part of their subscription fees will be used to procure the necessary transmission capacity within Z. Let's assume that X and Y belong to closely connected organizations. In order to speed up their exchanges, they may decide to establish a direct connection between themselves. This type of connection is often referred to as a "backdoor" link, the image being that two neighbors establish a discrete gate between their gardens so that they can communicate without going out on the street (without passing through the regular transit system).

Now let's consider the announcements that should be made by A, C, E, and F—the exterior routers within X and Y. In order for the backdoor to make any sense, E must announce to F reachability for all of X's IP networks, and F must do the same for Y's network. This reachability will be reflected in the routing tables, and the router A will now effectively be capable of reaching both X's and Y's networks. But A should normally not announce it. The agreement between X and Y is to establish direct connectivity for their own purposes, not to provide generic transit facilities! Similarly, C should announce only Y's networks.

In order to compute the EGP reachability messages, the routers must thus combine the list of networks that they may serve and the list of networks that they can reach. The first list is normally found in a configuration file provided by the AS's manager. It may, in fact, vary on a neighbor-per-neighbor basis. In our example, the link between X and Y could as well have been established using the main router A of X instead of an auxiliary router E.

The reachability information itself is derived from the internal routing tables, as computed by the IGP, such as RIP or OSPF. For each network that is present in the configuration file, the router will test the distance as indicated in the IGP routing tables. If that distance is infinite, the network will be advertised as nonreachable or not advertised at all.

8.3.2 Computing EGP Distances

Advertisements in RIP or OSPF carry both a network number or a subnet mask and a "distance" expressed according to some metric. As the ASs are free to implement their routing as they see fit, there is no reason to believe that their neighbors will use the same metrics. If one uses RIP, its metric is a hop count; if the other uses OSPF, its normal metric is an estimation of the transmission delay. The EGP protocol does in fact carry a metric—a single integer varying between 0 and 255—but the only thing EGP specifies is that the value 255 indicates an unreachable destination.

In fact, the main usage for this metric is to provide a handle for "preferred routes." Suppose that the autonomous systems X and Y are connected by one main link, say a T1 circuit between A and B, and by a backup link, say a 64-kbps circuit between C and D.

In this configuration, one should use a lower metric for the primary connection than for the secondary one. When receiving the announcements from X, Y will notice that the route through C is "longer." It will thus naturally send the packets bound to X through A. If the link between A and B fails, this will be detected by the neighbor reachability protocol: in the absence of a lower distance reachability through A, the routing tables within Y will be automatically updated, and the route through C will be used.

—   backdoor link: two routes are available   —

The distances can also be used to compare several paths to the same networks. Consider the case of the backdoor connection that we analyzed above. The networks within Y will be announced as reachable by C to D, which will thus announce this reachability within Z. As a consequence, these networks will be announced by B to A. This announcement will compete with the backdoor announcements by F to E. Since the purpose of establishing the backdoor connection was indeed to make sure that this route will be preferred to the normal transit through Z, one must make sure that the EGP distances announced by F are lower than those announced by B. This can normally be achieved by announcing shorter distances through F than through C, hoping that Z will not announce through B lower distances than those learned by D.

A strategy for allocating EGP distances was detailed in RFC-1096 for the early NSFnet backbone [4]. This network, which replaced Arpanet as the core of the Internet in the late 1980s, provided transit between "regional" networks in much the same way that the transit network Z provides connectivity to X and Y in the previous example. It was suggested that primary routers for regionals should announce a distance of 0, secondaries a distance of 1 or higher. The backbone always announced a distance of 128 for reachable networks, which facilitated the management of backdoors—the routers managing the backdoor just had to announce distances lower than 128.

8.3.3 Routing Tables

By running EGP, the routers acquire knowledge about exterior networks. They will insert this information in the local AS routing tables; more precisely, they will include "some" of it in the tables. In order to validate a route through a neighbor to a given destination, a number of conditions must be satisfied.

☞ The neighbor acquisition procedure must have succeeded.

☞ The neighbor must be reachable.

☞ The neighbor must have announced the destination.

☞ The local router must have determined that there is no "better" route toward the destination.

The first three conditions are easy to understand: it would be silly to forward packets toward a router that is not willing to relay them and, for example, has ceased to be a neighbor; over a link that is not operational; or toward a router that does not know about the destination. The fourth condition reflects the fact that several routes may well be available toward the destination. One should then pick the best one—in principle, the one with the lowest distance.

Picking the lowest distance is easy when all the exterior routes arrive at the same router. In this example, the backdoor link arrives at the same routers that handle the normal exterior links. They thus have no difficulty comparing status and metrics and picking the preferred route. But mandating that all links start from exactly one router would not be practical. In the normal configuration, the backdoor and the main router will communicate through some internal links, as in the example we used in the previous paragraphs. In order to enforce the choice of the best internal route, the EGP distances have to be translated into IGP metrics. How to do this is not specified in the EGP specification; in fact, it depends on the IGP that will be used.

all exterior links to the same router

If the AS uses OSPF, the routes obtained through EGP should normally be announced as "external link state records" by the border routers. We have seen in the OSPF chapter that the metrics used in these records are qualified by an E bit. If this bit is set, the metric is external and is supposedly larger than any internal value. This provides a very simple way to accommodate the EGP needs. The E bit will be set to 1, and the metric will be set to the EGP distance. The link state records will be flooded to all routers in the AS. When several routers advertise routes to the same networks, the shortest path will always pass through the one with the lowest external metric, i.e., the lowest EGP distance.

If the AS uses RIP, we have a much tougher case. RIP carries only one type of distance—the number of hops toward the destination. This distance, moreover, can take only a limited number of values—from 0 to 15 with RIP-2. One can indeed try to translate the EGP distances in a "number-of-hops" equivalent, but this is a thorny exercise. In order to guarantee that one path is preferred to another, we have to make sure that, for all routers in the AS, the number of hops on the "secondary" path is always larger than the number of hops on the primary one. The path length is the sum of the number of hops between the router and the external router and the initial metric derived from the EGP distance. The only safe way to guarantee the inequality is to set the initial metric for the secondary paths to a value equal to the "AS diameter"—the maximum number of hops between any two routers within the AS. This works only if this number is less than 8; otherwise, some routers will find that the distance through the secondary is infinite and will not be able to use the backup if the primary neighbor becomes unreachable. All this really means that one should not use RIP if the AS requires any form of fancy exterior routing!

In fact, using RIP in conjunction with EGP poses another problem—the transmission of external distances between external routers. In order to compute a reasonable value for the distance in their reachability announcements, the routers must know what value was received from the remote AS. When OSPF is used, this value is very simply flooded to all routers as an "externally typed" metric. This is not possible with the RIP metric. "Creative management" will be required.

Routes obtained through EGP should indeed be removed from the routing tables if the neighbor breaks the association by sending a "cease" message; if temporary unreachability is detected by the absence of timely responses to "hellos"; if the neighbor advertises the destination as unreachable (distance = 255); if the neighbor ceases to mention the destination in its reachability messages; or if the neighbor repeatedly fails to reply to poll messages.

8.3.4 An Engineered Topology

At first sight, EGP has many of the characteristics of a simple distance vector protocol: the updates carry lists of destinations and associated distances. One may thus be tempted to think that EGP could be used as a routing protocol operating at the AS level, e.g., computing EGP distances as the number of ASs between an exterior router and the destination. This does not work for many reasons, mostly underspecified rules for computing distances and slow convergency.

The distances announced through EGP reflect a combination of preferences and policies. In some extreme cases, such as the NSFnet backbone, the distances are constant: either 128 if the destination is reachable or 255 otherwise. Although there is a general understanding that one should not announce distances lower than the value that was received from the original neighbor, this is not really written within the protocol. Moreover, there is a strong requirement for "isolating the limited changes"—for not flooding the network with a set of routing messages after every little topology change within an AS. This is only required if the connectivity is lost. Finally, one will note that the infinity value is quite large: one would need 255 iterations before breaking a routing loop!

This large number of iterations will be made much worse by the polling nature of EGP. Updates are normally sent only after polls, typically every 2 minutes. Multiplying 2 minutes by 255 yields more than 8 hours—a very unacceptable duration for a routing loop! This clearly indicates that EGP was not designed as a general routing protocol. Its purpose is to provide "reachability" information so that packets are not sent on a route that does not lead to the destination. If a network is unreachable, it pays to avoid clobbering the Internet with doomed packets.

EGP was designed with a simple hierarchical topology in mind. Stub ASs should be connected to the backbone, which in 1983 was the Arpanet. It can be made to work in a more general topology, if this topology reduces to a loopless graph, i.e., to a tree. For example, EGP could work when the Internet consisted of a backbone—the NSFnet—which connected regional networks, which in turn connected university campuses and research organizations. For any of these hierarchical relations, EGP could support multiple path—typically a primary path and a limited number of backups. It could also, to some extent, support backdoor connections, if these connections were carefully engineered and were kept "strictly private," i.e., strictly for bilateral use. But EGP was certainly not designed to support a complex meshed topology where the unique backbone would be replaced by many competing commercial providers. In fact, for a limited transition period, the Arpanet and the NSFnet both had a backbone status in the Internet. This transition proved extremely painful!

8.4 The Limits of EGP

EGP was designed in 1983, and the Internet certainly did not stop growing at that point. More networks have been added which connect more diverse customers. Commercial usage and commercial provision of services have been encouraged. All this has resulted in unforecasted stresses on EGP and has showed new requirements, such as the need to avoid "false" information, to allow more complex topologies, and to enable some form of "policy routing."

8.4.1 Avoiding False Information

The initial experiences showed that the EGP protocol was quite fragile in at least one respect: a misbehaving exterior gateway could very easily inject false information in the network.

Suppose that a router belonging to the autonomous system X starts announcing that it has good connectivity to some networks within ASY. Moreover, suppose that it advertises lower distances than the proper routers of Y. The naive neighbors will immediately update their routing tables and send through X all the traffic bound to Y. This can have multiple consequences, from directing traffic on an inefficient route if a real path does exist between X and Y to "black holing" all of Y's traffic.

There is indeed no semantical difference between a correct EGP packet and one announcing excess reachability. Both are well formatted and include distances, network list, and so on. If one relied only on the EGP protocol, there would be precious little protection against such misbehaviors. They can result from plain mistakes, such as mistyping a configuration file, or from sheer malign intentions—e.g., if the exterior gateway has been subverted by a "cracker." But the packets can as well be entirely correct, and there can still be problems—e.g., if a very high-speed connection exists between X and Y so that Y will prefer using this high-speed path rather than a less capable direct connection.

The need to install a protection against such misbehavior was documented in the early plans for the establishment of the NSFnet backbone [4]. The only solution that could be implemented then was to require more administration, more manual configuration. For each connection between the NSFnet backbone and a regional network, an agreement must be reached, specifying which routers will connect the regional network and which ASs they will serve. The NSFnet also maintains a list of "configured networks"—a list of all the networks that may someday be connected to the backbone, as well as the corresponding AS numbers. When an NSFnet router receives a reachability message, it will check all the announced networks against this list. The advertisement will be accepted and eventually forwarded to only the internal routing tables if the network's AS number is one of those served by the gateway.

8.4.2 Policy Routing

The checks described in the previous section are mostly protections against rogue advertisements, making sure that a backbone does not suffer from a misbehaving neighbor. But the regionals themselves—and, in fact, any AS—have a similar problem as soon as they are connected to several backbones or as soon as they have several possible transit paths to reach a given destination.

Suppose that the research division of a commercial company is connected to the Internet through both a government-subsidized backbone network such as the NSFnet and a commercial IP provider, say BUSINESSNET, to avoid naming one particular company and offending its competition. It should use BUSINESSNET to reach its commercial partners and NSFnet to reach its "academic" partners. But the latter are also reachable through BUSINESSNET. The external router will receive EGP reachability announcements for these destinations from both the NSFnet and BUSINESSNET neighbors. It could simply "believe" the EGP information and pick whichever of the routers is announcing the shorter distance to the destination. However, these announcements are not coordinated, and there is no reason to believe that the distances are "comparable." Believing the EGP information will, in fact, lead to a random choice of the transit network!

Such a random choice is not very dangerous from a networking point of view—there is every reason to believe that both the NSFnet and BUSINESSNET are well behaved and that they are indeed ready to stand by their announcement and forward the packets to their destination. But there will be a marked impact on the company's finances, since BUSINESSNET probably charges for relaying packets while NSFnet does not. Leaving this to be decided by a random process is a form of Russian-roulette cost control that most accountants fail to praise!

The only answer, again, is "manual configuration." One must pass the information that, no matter what the distances announced by NSFnet and BUSINESSNET, NSFnet will always be the preferred route for the "academic" networks. Listing all such networks would, however, be a very lengthy exercise. There is no such thing as a "type-of-network" bit in the IP addresses. In fact, there is no clearly defined "type of network" either. Embarking on the definition of such information would lead to an interesting taxonomy of public and private universities, business and research units of commercial companies, and governments and not-for-profit institutions, to name a few variations. Our users will probably be better off by simply applying a "priority" between their network service providers, letting it be known that the routes through NSFnet, if they exist, should always be considered shorter than the routes through BUSINESSNET.

The particular comparison of BUSINESSNET versus NSFnet is just an example. If an AS is connected to several commercial providers, it will want to give priority to the least expensive, which may in fact vary over the course of time!

8.4.3 Topology and Routing Loops

EGP was designed for a very simple tree-structured topology that supposed the Internet was organized around a "core." With the increased commercial usage of the network, there can no longer be any such core. The latest iteration of such a backbone was the NSFnet. But the NSFnet was funded by the U.S. government and could be used only for research and education purposes. Commercial usage is not eligible for government funding and should use another route, provided by commercial networks. These providers have built their own backbones connecting their customers. During the same period, increased international usage has induced the birth of other backbones in various countries or regions, notably the EBONE in Europe.

The modern Internet is built from the meshed interconnection of all these backbones. EGP does not support this kind of topology, and the IETF has had to develop another protocol.

8.4.4 Message Size and Fragmentation

EGP messages are sent as IP datagrams. The complete list of reachable networks is sent in a single IP packet. The size of this list has increased continuously with the size of the Internet. Very early, the list became larger than the MTU available on most subnets. The fragmentation and reassembly procedure had to be used so that the EGP message could be transmitted as a sequence of IP fragments. But the initial packet can be successfully reassembled only if all fragments arrive at the destination—one missing fragment is sufficient to cause the loss of the whole message. Requests have to be repeated, which is very inefficient. In some cases, unreachabilities will be wrongly detected.

If EGP had not been replaced by BGP, a robust fragmentation procedure should have been added to the protocol.

8.5 Developing BGP

EGP was developed from 1982 to 1984, and was the exterior protocol of choice in the Internet until the end of the 1980s. But EGP today is pretty much a legacy of the old Arpanet days. The recommended protocol for exchanging information between ASs is BGP.

However, many of the concepts that were developed for EGP are still in use, notably the division of the Internet into autonomous systems and the separation of the routing functions between interior and exterior gateway protocol. In fact, BGP is an exterior gateway protocol—BGP is today's EGP!

References

1. E. Rosen, "Exterior Gateway Protocol (EGP)," RFC-827, BBN, October 1982.
2. P. Kirton, "EGP Gateway Under Berkeley UNIX 4.2," RFC-911, August 1984.
3. L. Seamonson and E. Rosen, "STUB Exterior Gateway Protocol," RFC-888, BBN, January 1984.
4. J. Rekhter, "EGP and Policy Based Routing in the New NSFnet Backbone," RFC-1096, February 1989.

With BGP
and CIDR
Toward the
World Wide
Internet

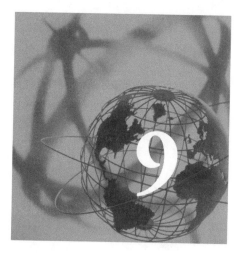

As the Internet grew, the limitations of EGP became unacceptable. There was a strong user demand to move away from the backbone-centered tree topology mandated by EGP. This led to the standardization of the Border Gateway Protocol (BGP) by the Border Gateway Protocol Working Group of the IETF.

The design of BGP underwent several stages. A first version of BGP was published in June 1989 as RFC-1105; a second version was published in June 1990 as RFC-1163; a third one in October 1991 as RFC-1267; the fourth version was published in July 1994 as RFC-1654, and revised in March 1995 as RFC-1771 [1, 2, 3]. These versions are often referred to as BGP-1, BGP-2, BGP-3, and BGP-4. We will describe only BGP-4 in this chapter, since this version has been in use in the Internet since 1995.

A key element of the BGP-4 design is the support for the Classless Inter-Domain Routing architecture (CIDR) that was introduced in 1992 to mitigate the rapid consumption of network addresses and to combat the explosion of the routing tables.

9.1 Exponential Growth and the Need for CIDR

The Internet was not initially designed for the large size that we now observe. Back in 1980 there were only a comparative few hosts. The address size was chosen because 32 bits appeared "natural," a nice even number that resulted in well-aligned packet formats. In fact, even the current separation of addresses into three classes was not present in the very early design; the 32 bits were separated into 8 bits indicating the "network" and 24 bits indicating the "host." The separation into class A, B, and C for large, medium, and small networks was added later, only after the managers of the network realized that they would soon have to accommodate much more than 256 sites!

Few systems can support such a rapid increase in size without stresses; the Internet is no exception. Three immediate dangers were outlined by the IAB in 1991: class B exhaustion, routing table explosion, and address depletion. The Classless Inter-Domain Routing (CIDR) was developed as an immediate solution to these problems, providing the Internet with enough breathing space so that we could wait for the development of a new version of IP [1,2]. CIDR has been presented as a cure for two of the most immediate dangers that the Internet faced. In this section, we will detail these dangers and explain how CIDR is supposed to cure them.

9.1.1 Class B Exhaustion

Network numbers come in three classes. An 8-bit class-A number allows for 24 bits of addressing—at most, 16,777,216 hosts. A 16-bit class-B number allows for 16 bits of addressing—at most, 65,536 hosts. A 24-bit class-C number allows 8 bits addressing—at most, 256 hosts. Phillip Gross, who was chairman of the IETF until April 1994, likened the situation to the well-known children's story about Goldilocks and the three bears. Class-A numbers were too scarce; one had to explain one's case to the Internet Assigned Numbers Authority (IANA) in great detail before obtaining such a number. Class-C networks were too narrow; many organizations had more than 256 hosts, or planned to have more. In any case, 8 bits did not provide much room for splitting the network into subnets. Class-B networks were "about right," and became very popular indeed.

But there are only 16,384 class-B numbers available, since the most significant and second most significant of the 16 bits are constrained to 1 and 0, respectively. By 1992, almost half of these had been allocated. If the same trend had continued, the last available class-B number would have been allocated in March 1994! Clearly, a solution had to be found.

9.1.2 Routing Table Explosion

As more and more networks get connected, the memory required for storing the routing tables grows. This memory requirement varies a lot with the routing protocol and with the router's architecture. In fact, the problem may appear in multiple ways. The phrase "routing table explosion" is merely a catchall term for all the problems posed by the manipulation of very large routing tables.

An early occurrence of routing problems caused by the growth was found several years ago in one of the transit networks when the number of connected networks passed a threshold of 4,000. The internal routing protocol of this network required the periodic transmission of complete routing tables, which were carried in a single IP datagram. As the size of the table grew, it had to be fragmented and sent in several consecutive packets. This exercised a bug in the router's network interface, which was configured to receive only four consecutive packets; new buffers had to be reallocated after four receptions, which took too much time to catch the fifth packet. As a result, some parts of the table were randomly lost, which resulted in routing instabilities.

A separate occurrence appeared in another brand of routers. In that architecture, the routing of packets used a forwarding table that listed the next hop for every known network. Because this table had to be accessed very frequently, it was implemented in fast memory within the interface boards themselves. This enabled local processing of the packet without relying on a central computer. It also enabled distributed forwarding without having to relay through the main memory, which is often a bottleneck. But memory is scarce on these boards and has to be allocated sparingly. When the board was designed, the engineers had taken no risk; choosing a table size of 10,000 entries when no known system had more than 2,000 connected networks appeared very safe indeed. When they realized that the 10,000 mark was to be passed in January 1993, the successors of these engineers knew they had an interesting problem to solve!

Modern designs solve this particular problem by storing a cache of only the most frequently accessed entries in the drivers. The reference version of the routing tables is computed by a "main processor," where memory is plentiful and programming is easier than in a real-time packet driver. This is where routing protocols such as BGP or OSPF are processed. But even with this hierarchical design, the increase in size of the routing table can stress the system's memory. Let's take the example of BGP. We will see that the size of the messages varies as a function of the number of ASs and the number of networks, the dominant term being proportional to the number of networks. But we will also learn that BGP applies "differential" transmission. The border routers are expected to keep a copy of the reachability lists and of the corresponding AS paths announced by all of their internal and external neighbors. Thus, the memory varies as a product of the number of destinations by the number of neighbors. Indeed, it depends on how much ancillary information is needed by the implementation, e.g., timers and pointers. Figures of several tens of megabytes have been quoted recently!

9.1.3 Classless Addresses

The CIDR design came from one observation: while many organizations possessed more than 256 computers, very few had more than a few thousand. It was thus suggested that, instead of getting one entire class-B address, such organizations would get the exact number of class-C networks that was sufficient for their needs.

There are many more class-C networks than class-B, more than 2 million, and one generally needs less than 8 or, at most, 16 class-C networks to satisfy the needs of an organization. Even if growth continues at the current rate, there will be class-C networks available for at least 5 years!

Organizations may still apply for a class-B network, but they will get one only if they really need it—that is, if they have to handle a large number of subnets (at least 32) and if they have at least 4,096 hosts to connect.

There are preciously few class-A numbers left, and they are not supposed to be allocated except to very large organizations that can justify several hundred locations and several hundred thousand hosts. In fact, the allocation of class-A networks cannot be done by the regional authorities. It is "at the IANA's discretion" [3]. In fact, the IANA has already started to allocate class-A networks to routing registries that will then allocate slices of addresses to actual networks, definitely blurring the difference between the class-A and the class-C.

Allocating several class-C numbers instead of one single class-B number cures the "class B exhaustion" problem, but it does little to solve the inflation of the routing tables. If we were not doing something radical, we would, on the contrary, increase the size of the tables! But the class-C network numbers allocated following the CIDR strategy are not "random"; they are contiguous and share the same "most significant bits"—the same prefixes. If the routing protocols were capable of routing on these prefixes, they would need only one entry for the block of network numbers—for the "supernet." Moreover, if we allocate the addresses intelligently, we may be able to perform a grouping by region, so that all network numbers within a given region share the same "prefix" and could be represented by a single entry in the routing tables of other regions. This is called "routing table aggregation."

9.2 The Concept of Path Vectors

There are many differences between EGP and BGP, but the most important innovation within BGP is probably the "path vector" concept, which enables loop prevention in complex topologies. In this section, we will present the rationales for defining this concept, how path vector protocols operate, what attributes BGP associates to paths, and what requirements this family of protocols imposes on internal communications within an AS.

9.2.1 From Distance Vectors to Path Vectors

The "distances" associated to destinations by EGP look very much like the metrics manipulated by distance vector protocols. However, we have seen that running an AS-level distance vector protocol is not realistic. There are many instances where the shortest path is not the preferred route—for example, if it goes through an expensive commercial service or an insecure academic association. In practice, the distances are used to advertise "preferences" for one or another transit route. If the shortest path is not always preferred, or if distances can be arbitrarily manipulated, we cannot guarantee any more that the Bellman-Ford algorithm will converge. The advertisement of "unreachable" destinations may be understood as an AS-level form of the split horizon procedure, but there is no notion of "counting to infinity" and thus no intrinsic protection against loops.

One could be tempted to solve the problem by using the more powerful link state technology. By distributing to all external routers a complete map of the Internet, one would let them perform loop-free computations of the shortest paths. This has, in fact, been tried in the "Inter-Domain Policy Routing" protocol (IDPR) which we will study in chapter 11. IDPR, however, had to solve the same "arbitrary distance" problem that also hinders the distance vector computation: each router will base its computation of the shortest routes on its local preferences for this or that transit network. As the packet progresses in the Internet, it will meet different routers that may have a different set of preferences (other "policies") and will have a different notion of the shortest path. The consistency of the computation cannot be guaranteed, and loops could again occur. In fact, to avoid loops, IDPR had to use explicit source routing—the packets were routed on interdomain paths that were explicitly specified as a list of successive relays, e.g., go from Nice to Los Angeles through Paris, New York, and Chicago, or something similar using network addresses. Establishing these paths, or even stating an explicit "loose source route" in every packet may be an adequate solution to some special requirements, but is generally perceived as causing too much overhead for all cases.

Another problem with the link state technology would be the need to broadcast a link state database to the whole Internet. Even if we only use AS-level granularity, this will be a fairly large object—there were more than 700 ASs registered in the Internet at the beginning of 1994. This is already much larger than the recommended maximum size of 200 routers for an OSPF area. The Internet is growing at a fast pace; even if routers are becoming more powerful, computing routes in such a centralized database may become very lengthy. The IDPR working group researched solutions for providing aggregation at a higher granularity than the AS, but this research has not given birth to industrial products.

When faced with the need to develop a successor to EGP that would handle arbitrary topologies, the designers of BGP had to solve this tough problem. Distance vector protocols fitted well with the classic hop-by-hop approach of the IP routing but did not offer enough protection against routing loops, while using a link state approach was deemed unrealistic. They solved their problem by resorting to a technology called the "path vector."

9.2.2 Path Vectors and Loop Avoidance

In a classic distance vector protocol, all the information about the route to a destination is concentrated in the "metric" value. This is insufficient for fast loop resolution. Various proposals had been made in the past to install additional protection by providing more information. For example, one could qualify all routes by a "previous relay" parameter, which immediately helps in destroying three-hop loops. One could also add a "first relay" parameter, which can be used by the "source-tracing" algorithm to reconstitute the path from the source and discover loops.

The approach implemented in BGP is even more radical. Each routing update will carry the full list of transit networks, or rather ASs, traversed between the source and the destination. A loop would occur only if one AS was listed twice, which would be an error. The loop-protection algorithm is thus very simple. When receiving a route advertisement, the external router will check that its own AS is not already listed in the path. If this is the case, it will refuse to use that path. Otherwise, it will stick the local identification in the path before advertising it further. This approach has one big advantage: it does not require that all relays use the same metrics, which would be problematic since they have different interests and make autonomous decisions. On the contrary, they are allowed to make arbitrary choices; if they update the path vectors according to the results of these choices, then the protocol guarantees that loops will be avoided.

Listing the complete path for each and every destination has one obvious drawback: it increases the size of the routing messages and generally the amount of memory necessary for running the protocol. This amount of memory increases with the number of networks in the Internet (N), as one must list one entry per network. One must also keep in memory for each of these networks the access path, i.e., a list of AS numbers. As all networks within an AS share the same access path, the number of paths is proportional to the number of ASs (A). The average length of the paths is equal to the average distance between two ASs, which depends indeed on the size of the Internet and on its topology; the classic assumption here is that the diameter of the Internet varies as the logarithm of the number of connected networks. If x is the memory required to note the presence of an AS in a path and if y is the memory required by a reachable destination, the memory requirement for running the path vector algorithm should vary as:

$$x.\ A.\ \log A + y.\ N$$

An estimated size of a complete routing table, as exchanged over the links by BGP-4, is given in RFC-1774. It is a function of three size parameters [10].

Number of routes	Mean AS distance	Number of ASs	Size in bytes
10,000	15	300	49,000
20,000	8	400	86,000
40,000	15	400	172,000
100,000	20	3000	520,000

The memory requirements within a router exceed those figures, as the router must keep such a list in memory for each of its peers. It must also store the list in an "easy-to-access" fashion, completing it with various indexes and access methods. The second point, with 20,000 networks, corresponds to the size of the Internet at the time of the edition of the RFC. By June 1999, the Internet had grown to about 60,000 routes, and the memory requirements of BGP-4 are rather large. However, the excess does not result so much from the path vector technology itself as from the need to list each and every network. We will see in a following section how this problem can be mitigated by "route reflectors."

9.2.3 Route Aggregation

Versions 1, 2, and 3 of BGP did not support "supernetting." A path described how to reach a set of class-A, -B, or -C networks. BGP-4 was introduced in 1994 in order to take full advantage of CIDR. This required two evolutions. First, instead of representing addresses as simple 32-bit numbers, such as 9.0.0.0, 128.96.0.0, or 192.4.18.0, one needs to introduce a prefix notation—the binary equivalent of 9/8, 128.96/16, or 192.4.18/24. Then, in order to reduce the size of the routing tables, one needs to support aggregation.

Take the example of a network provider managing the autonomous system T. The addresses of that provider's machines are chosen in one of two contiguous class-C networks, 197.8.0/24 and 197.8.1/24, which we can represent as a 23-bit prefix, i.e., 197.8.0/23. Two customers of that provider, the AS's X and Y, have been allocated the class-C addresses 197.8.3/24 and 197.8.4/24. In the absence of route aggregation, the AS T will announce 3 routes to its neighbor, Z:

```
Path1: through "T," reaches 197.8.0/23
Path2: through "T, X," reaches 197.8.2/24
Path3: through "T, Y," reaches 197.8.3/24
```

Announcing three paths, however, would do little for reducing the size of routing tables. What we clearly want to do is announce a single path, such as:

```
Path1: reaches 197.8.0/22
```

In this announcement, we have merged the prefixes used by T, X, and Y into a 22-bit prefix that serves them all. But we have a problem here—that of choosing the ASs that will be advertised in the path. We cannot just list T, because the loop detection property of the path vector protocol depends on the completeness of the path information. Omitting the information is not acceptable. But then, listing a complete path like T, X, Y is misleading—it appears as a three-hop path, which may induce remote ASs to make bad routing decisions. This has led the designers of BGP-4 to structure the "AS path" attribute into two components: an ordered list—AS sequence—and an unordered set—AS set. The path attribute, in our example, would thus be:

```
Path: (Sequence(T), Set(X, Y))
```

If Z wants to forward this path to one of its neighbors, it will have to place its own AS number in front of the AS sequence component, as in:

```
Path= (Sequence(Z, T), Set(X, Y))
```

The number of elements in the sequence component can be used to estimate the length of the path, for route selection purposes, for example. Both the sequence and set components are used for loop detection. An AS should not use a route when its own AS number is mentioned in either of these components.

Paths can, indeed, be aggregated recursively, e.g., at regional level, then at national and continental levels. In that case, the rule is very simple: the sequence component should be the intersection of all sequences, while the set components should contain all the ASs that are mentioned in any of the paths to aggregate yet are not present in the aggregated sequence. The reachability list will contain the union of all reachable prefixes.

9.2.4 Path Attributes

BGP-4 [8] handles paths between autonomous systems. These paths are described by a set of attributes, of which the "list of traversed AS" and the "list of reachable networks" are the most important. When several paths are available, adding other attributes will help the external routers to choose the best path. One could well envision qualifying the path with various metrics or policy notations. There are, in fact, several kinds of attributes.

Suppose, for example, that one wants to qualify the path by a bandwidth indication, e.g., the data rate of the slowest hop. This is a "transitive" attribute. Each router will receive a value from its neighbor, will update this value if the local link is slower than the received value, and will pass the result to its neighbors downstream. Not all attributes are transitive: one could, for example, attach to the path a "local preference" which is only meaningful within one autonomous system.

BGP-3 identifies all path attributes by a 2-octet code:

Octet 1: flags					Octet 2: type
O	T	P	E	reserved	Attr. type code

The first octet is used to pass four "attribute flags" indicating whether the attribute is optional (O = 1) or well known, transitive (T = 1) or local; whether the information is partial (P = 1);

and whether the attribute length is coded on 1 octet (E = 0) or 2. The lowest 4 bits of the first octet are always null. The second octet carries the type code. The "optional," "transitive," and "partial" flags are used to handle protocol extensions. A router that encounters an unknown attribute type checks the optional flag. It is a protocol error to not recognize an attribute that is marked as "well known," but routers are not expected to understand all the optional attributes. Optional non-transitive attributes provide optional information that is only pertinent to the local interconnection; such attributes, if not recognized, are silently ignored. Optional transitive attributes that are not understood are passed along the path, but in this case the "partial" bit is set, so that downstream routers understand that the attribute has only been "partially" evaluated.

Attribute	Type	Flags	Value
ORIGIN	1	Well known	IGP(0), EGP(1) or other (2)
AS_PATH	2	Well known	Autonomous systems in the path
NEXT_HOP	3	Well known	Address of next router
MULTI_EXIT_DISC	4	Optional, local	32 bit metric
LOCAL_PREF	5	Well known	32 bit metric
ATOMIC_AGGREGATE	6	Well known	Flags certain aggregations
AGGREGATOR	7	Optional, transitive	AS number and router ID.

The BGP-4 specification [8] lists 7 attributes. The origin attribute indicates whether the reachability information attached through this path was obtained through an IGP, i.e., provided directly by the relevant AS; through the old protocol EGP; or by some other means. The next-hop attribute plays exactly the same role as the indirect neighbor notation of EGP:

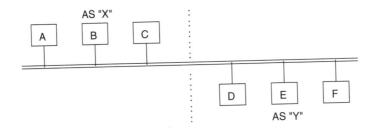

If a network connecting several routers is shared between two ASs, only two of them, one in each AS, need to "peer" using BGP. Suppose, for example, that the peering is between C and D. C may wish to indicate to D some paths for which the preferred first hop is, in fact, A or B. It will do so by adding to this path a next-hop attribute describing A or B. This attribute is indeed not a transitive attribute—there is no point in passing this information to the next router in the path.

The "multi-exit discriminator" is defined as a metric—the cost of using a particular router for reaching the next group. The set of paths exchanged by BGP routers internal to a given AS may include several almost identical paths, which only differ by the value of the multi-exit distance and next-hop attributes. The routers should indeed not aggregate these paths, since they should use the information to pick the "best exit point." These two attributes allow an AS to export limited topological knowledge internal to the AS to neighboring ASs.

The "local preference" attribute (code 5) is a metric used inside an AS to synchronize the route selection process of the border routers. This attribute may be tagged to a path by the "entry" border router. The various AS border routers may learn several paths that lead to the same routing prefixes. All these paths will be propagated inside the AS, but the border gateways will all select the path with the lowest local preference.

The "aggregator" attribute (type code 7) is inserted by the AS that made the decision to aggregate. It contains 6 octets—the 16-bit AS number and the 32-bit Internet address of the router that performed the aggregation. It is mostly used to facilitate troubleshooting—in case of a problem, one can immediately identify the system that performed the aggregation. The "atomic aggregate" attribute (type code 6) does not have any content; its length is always 0. It indicates that the router chose to pass an "aggregated prefix," i.e., one that is the union of several shorter prefixes. More specific routes may exist for some of these longer prefixes, but the router chose to "hide" them, so as to reduce the size of the AS path parameters.

9.2.5 Internal and External Peers

As in the EGP case, an external router that has learned of a path toward a given network should update the AS routing tables, either by inserting an external link in the OSPF database or by adding an entry in the RIP distance vector. But running BGP poses specific requirements. The path attributes must be propagated through the AS, and that cannot normally be done through the IGP alone. Consider the following connectivity diagram, where the AS Z is used as a transit between X and Y.

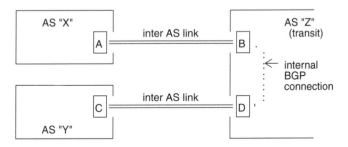

The AS path announced by A to B for the networks in X has just one entry—the AS X itself. The AS path announced by D to C should include both X and Z, but the main information available to D through the IGP is that routes to X's network are available. There may be some additional information, like a distance or the fact that the route originates from B, but that is not enough to propagate a useful BGP update message.

In order to solve this problem, BGP mandates that each external router establishes an "internal" BGP connection with all other external routers in the AS. These routers will be linked by a "fully connected graph." These internal connections will be used to propagate external routing information, independently of the IGP. They will also be used to get an agreement among

BGP routers on the best route toward a given external network, so that only the router managing this best route inserts information in the AS's internal routing tables through the IGP. The routers must be careful to maintain consistency between what they announce to their external BGP peers and what is actually used in the local AS. If the AS routers collectively decide to select another path for an external destination, that other path must be announced immediately to whoever is using the local AS for transit. Failure to do so might result in the formation of AS loops!

However, maintaining a fully connected graph is a very heavy requirement if we have a large number of external routers, as the BGP routers must keep in memory the full list of advertisements received from their peer. Some ASs are described in RFC-1773 [9] as containing 90 border routers in 1995, a number that has probably grown over the years. In fact, the requirement of a "fully connected graph" could destabilize a network, as the addition of any border router would impose additional processing and memory requirements to all existing routers. This is a major scaling issue. We will detail proposed solutions in the next chapter.

9.3 The Border Gateway Protocol

In this section, we will present the protocol—how it is run over TCP-IP; how messages are typed; and how the "open," "update," and "keep alive" procedures play the same role as EGP's "neighbor acquisition," "network reachability," and "neighbor reachability."

9.3.1 Running over TCP

A major design choice of BGP is that the protocol will be run over TCP. Exchanging connectivity information over a reliable transport protocol has a number of advantages and possibly a couple of drawbacks.

Delegating all "error control" functions to TCP makes the protocol much simpler; there is no need to design complex error recovery mechanisms as well as no need to couple the size of BGP messages with the size of IP datagrams. If we compare BGP to EGP, we can see, for example, that all EGP commands must be repeated if no response is obtained in some interval. The timer management must be incorporated within the EGP application, while there is no such need within BGP. This makes the EGP-state machine more complex, hence making the EGP code more difficult to debug and tune.

The timer management within EGP indeed plays a role, notably within the neighbor reachability procedure. The EGP application can keep a precise log of transmission errors and thus decide to consider the link "down" if too many hellos are left unanswered. With EGP we have "gradual" information, which can be expressed as, for example, a percentile. Using a TCP connection provides only a "binary" indication—either the link is broken, or it is functional. In fact, TCP will give an error indication only if one tries to send some data over a TCP connection and if these data are not acknowledged by the recipient after a long delay (after several retransmission attempts). To obtain in BGP the same functionality as the EGP's neighbor reachability procedure, one must thus send "probe" messages at regular intervals. If the link has gone down, TCP will not be able to transmit the probe messages and will signal an error. One can argue that posting probes at regular intervals over a TCP connection is simpler than the EGP equivalent of sending hellos and waiting for I-H-Us. On the other hand, as TCP is a very resilient protocol, one can be sure that some data will continue to pass even if the link is barely functional and the error rate quite high. One will not obtain the same precision as EGP's "I in N" evaluations. But there is no experimental evidence that this lack of precision poses severe problems—modern links tend to be either fully operational or fully broken.

The TCP design choice has also been criticized sometimes for its sensitivity to network congestion. Modern implementations of the TCP incorporate the "slow start" and "congestion avoidance" algorithm. These algorithms "sense the network" by monitoring packet losses. In a congested network, queues will build up, and eventually the saturated routers will have to drop packets. When losses are observed, TCP immediately reduces its rate of emission by shrinking the "congestion control window," which is the number of bytes that can be sent on a connection before an acknowledgment is received. The design is such that all TCP connections that share the same path will reduce their data rates equally, so that each connection gets a "fair share" of the resources.

This behavior of TCP is very desirable for normal connections. The network quickly reaches an equilibrium where all users get approximately the same amount of the resources. But consider the BGP connection—it may well be carrying the routing updates that are needed to cure the congestion. Slowing down this transmission is very counterproductive, because the routing protocol will thus converge very slowly. One may quickly jump to the conclusion that choosing to run the protocol over TCP was a fatal mistake. This is, however, shortsighted reasoning. Modern routers will tend to implement some form of "fair sharing" in any case, so that a station sending UDP packets or other forms of datagrams does not get more resources than a station using TCP. If one wants BGP packets to be processed faster, one must somehow mark them so that routers forward them with a higher priority. This marking can be done in many ways, such as by giving a higher priority to packets sent by routers rather than normal hosts, or by requesting TCP to mark the IP packets carrying the BGP connection with the "Internetwork control" precedence [5].

The choice of running over TCP has an effect on the volume of data exchanged between the routers. As messages are reliably transmitted, one can use "incremental updates" instead of retransmitting the whole tables at regular intervals. EGP requires that the routers send complete "reachability" messages listing all reachable networks every 2 minutes. BGP requires that only a fraction of the information that changed be transmitted. After an initial phase during which full tables are exchanged, BGP will require only a trickle of information—average data rates as low as 5 bps have been measured. This very low requirement has a very beneficial impact on network congestion!

9.3.2 The BGP Header

TCP provides for a "reliable byte stream" between the connected programs, while routing protocols like BGP actually exchange routing messages. The BGP protocol must thus include a "delimitation" function that will separate the byte stream in a set of independent messages. This is done very simply by attaching before all BGP messages a fixed-length "header" that includes the length of the routing message.

Marker (16 bytes)	
Length (2 octets)	Type (1 octet)

The receiving stations will have to read only the 19 bytes of the fixed-length header, then receive the "length" bytes that constitute the message—or, rather, length minus 19, as the length field of the BGP header counts all the bytes in the message, including the header itself. The next byte in the stream will be the beginning of the next message's header.

The last byte of the header is the packet type. The packet types are as follows:

1. OPEN
2. UPDATE
3. NOTIFICATION
4. KEEPALIVE

The 16-byte "marker" is designed to be used for security purposes. The particular algorithm that should be used to generate this marker is to be negotiated during the initial exchange, but no security algorithm is described in RFC-1267. One of the roles of the marker within the routing header is to provide a level of "redundancy" in the framing procedure. If, for some reason, the length of the messages is not correctly computed, the headers will end up being "misaligned." As a result, the length field will contain some random value. Suppose, for example, that the partner sends a 255-byte-long update message and that programming errors or a malfunctioning TCP code have caused a misalignment of 1 byte. Instead of receiving the 19-byte configuration:

```
0                       1
0 1 2 3 4 5 6 7 8 9 0 1 2 3 4 5 6 7 8
+-+-+-+-+-+-+-+-+-+-+-+-+-+-+-+-+-+-+-+
|H H H H H H H H H H H H H H H H|L L|T| .
```

the station will receive:

```
0                     1
0 1 2 3 4 5 6 7 8 9 0 1 2 3 4 5 6 7 8
+-+-+-+-+-+-+-+-+-+-+-+-+-+-+-+-+-+-+
|H H H H H H H H H H H H H H H L|L T| .
```

The place of the length field is occupied here by the less significant byte of length and the type byte. Instead of receiving the hexadecimal value 00FF (255), the station will receive FF02 (65,282). In the absence of sanity checks, the station would then settle for receiving a 65,263-byte message, which might indeed take a very long time! In order to maintain a high degree of resilience, the stations must thus make a number of sanity checks on the message. The length must fall within an acceptable range (between 19 and 8,192 bytes), the type code must have an acceptable value (between 1 and 4), and the marker must have the value mandated by the security algorithm. This algorithm, however, may well mandate that the marker be a cryptographic checksum of the message that can only be checked after complete reception.

If at any time within the connection one of these checks fails, the receiving station should signal the error to its partner by sending a "notification" message and should then close the connection.

We will now detail the BGP procedures.

9.3.3 Initial Exchange

The routers that support BGP normally wait for BGP connections on port 179. A router that wants to establish an association will first open a TCP connection toward that port on the peer router. Once the connection has been set, each side sends an OPEN message to negotiate the association's parameters.

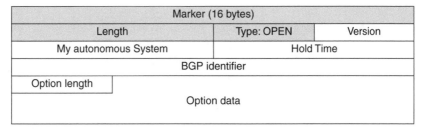

The parameters of the OPEN message are the BGP version number, the AS number of the sending router, a "hold time" (a number of seconds used by the "keep-alive" procedure), an "identifier," and a set of options. The "autonomous system" parameter is set to the AS number of the sending router. The identifier field carries one of the IP interface addresses of the BGP router. Each router must choose one identifier and use it for all BGP associations, regardless of the interface used to transmit the BGP packets. The option data contain a set of options, each encoded as a one-octet type, a one-octet length, and a variable length value. The only option defined in RFC-1771 is the authentication information (type 1), which contains a one-octet authentication code and variable length authentication data.

The authentication code specifies the type of authentication that will be used and determines the form and the meaning of the authentication data. The authentication code also determines the content of the marker field—or, rather, the content of the marker fields in the next messages; the marker of the open messages is always set to all 1s. RFC-1771 [8] does not define any standard value for the authentication code, which means that the connection peers have to agree on code and values by some nonstandard exchange, if they use the option at all. In fact, the BGP working group observed that protecting the BGP packets would not be very useful if one does not also protect TCP. We will present in section 9.3.7 a proposal to secure the TCP connection through an MD5 authentication option.

A connection is successful if the two peers exchange OPEN messages and agree on the BGP version and BGP hold-time that they will use in the remainder of the connection. There are many reasons why an initialization request could go wrong—notably if a collision is detected, if the version number is not supported by the peer, or if the authentication fails.

Connection collision occurs when both BGP peers attempt to set up a connection simultaneously, e.g., just after the link between them has been reconnected. Two TCP connections may be established and one will have to be closed. The decision to close a connection occurs just after the reception of an OPEN message. Duplication will be detected by the station if the "identifier" of the peer is already associated with an established connection. In that case, the station compares this identifier (considered as a 32-bit unsigned integer) to the local identifier. If the remote value is larger, the new connection is confirmed and the old connection is terminated, and vice versa.

The connection can be accepted only if both ends support the same BGP version. This version number is passed in the OPEN message. If the version number that is received is not equal to the version number that was sent, the connection must be terminated. The notification message will indicate the reason for termination and an acceptable version number, lower than or equal to the received number. This lower number will then be used in a new connection attempt, with increased chances of success!

In the absence of collisions or version conflicts, the local station must "authenticate" the remote peer before deciding that it wishes to establish an association with it. Establishing a BGP association is, indeed, subject to the same restrictions as becoming a neighbor under EGP—there must be some a priori agreement between the ASs for accepting to relay transit traffic. Classic implementations, as in the EGP case, are parameterized by a list of "potential neighbors." When receiving an open request, the BGP station will check that the incoming AS is "acceptable," that the identifier is well formed (is a valid address), and that the authentication codes and data have a valid value. If one of these conditions fails, the connection is terminated.

In BGP-4, the opening procedure negotiates the hold-time value, which defines the number of seconds that may elapse between the reception of two consecutive KEEPALIVE or UPDATE messages. The BGP program must use the lower of its own "configured" value and the value announced by the peer. The negotiation may even result in a zero hold time. Rejecting a connection is done by sending a notification message explaining the error, then closing the TCP connection. Accepting a connection is done by sending a "keep-alive" message.

9.3.4 Updates

Once the connection has been established, the BGP stations will start exchanging "updates," which play the same roles as EGP "network reachability" messages. The update messages are composed from a standard BGP header followed by a set of path attributes and a list of reachable networks.

Marker (16 bytes)	
Length	Type: UPDATE
Unfeasible routes length	
Withdrawn routes (variable length)	
Path attributes length	
Path attributes (variable length)	
Network Layer Reachability Information (variable length)	

The UPDATE message contains two optional parts, a list of "unfeasible" routes and updated information on one specific path. The 16-bit "unfeasible routes length" states the length in octets of the "withdrawn routes"—routes that were previously advertised as reachable through some path, but are no longer. A single update message may inform of the withdrawal of several routes, which may have been attached to several different paths. Previous versions of BGP did not support this feature; each path had to be updated in turn, and unreachable networks had to be reported as an attribute to the updated paths.

The remainder of the UPDATE message reports information on one single path. All the attributes refer to that path, and the networks are those that can be reached through it. The path attributes are encoded in the "type, length, value" format that we presented in the previous section, together with the list of standard path attributes, e.g., origin, AS path, neighbor, and inter-AS metric. All of these fields have an arbitrary alignment. One should certainly not deduce from the figure above that the network layer reachability information is aligned on a 32-bit boundary. Both the withdrawn routes and the reachability information are represented by lists of routing prefixes. Each prefix is encoded as a one-octet length field, indicating the length of the prefix in bits, and a variable number of octets encoding a sufficient number of address bits—4 octets if the length is between 25 and 32, 3 if the length is between 17 and 24, 2 if the length is between 9 and 16, and 1 otherwise.

Just after initiating the connection, each router sends to its partner a list of proposed paths, using as many UPDATE messages as necessary. The routers are expected to memorize the paths provided by their partners. After the initial exchanges, this information will not be repeated, and the routers will send updates only for the paths that changed.

The handling of updates is very similar to the handling of distance vector algorithms. When an update is received, the path is compared to the current path used for reaching the advertised networks. If the new path is shorter than the old path, the routing tables are modified and corresponding updates are sent to the BGP neighbors (the definition of "shorter" is discussed in section 9.4.4). The tables are also modified if the new path is received from the "currently selected" neighbor for the destination, particularly when the neighbor announces that this path is now unreachable. In that case, the last advertisements from all other neighbors are compared, and the best path is selected.

After a change in the routing tables, the corresponding update message is propagated to all the neighbors, with one exception: if all border routers within the AS form a "connected graph," there is no need to repeat an update received on an internal connection to any other internal connection.

Two different forms of "sanity check" must be done before choosing to route packets on a path received in an update message. First, one must run the path vector loop protection—i.e., consider as "unusable" any path that the local AS is part of. Using such a path would result in a loop. Second, one must check that the path is "stable"—that it does not oscillate too rapidly between reachable and unreachable states. In practice, one has to "hold down" the path for some delay before validating it.

9.3.5 Keep-Alive Features

As was the case with EGP, there is a need for BGP routers to constantly monitor the reachability of their neighbors. We have seen in the introduction that TCP will provide such information only if the link is actually used, i.e., if data are sent. This is not, in fact, completely true. TCP users may enable a particular TCP "keep-alive" feature that triggers the periodic probing of the connection by the TCP program. BGP does not use this feature; it relies on the periodic sending of BGP packets. These packets may well result from "natural" traffic, such as updates. But there is no guaranteed rate of update messages. Such messages are triggered only by changes in the routing topology.

In order to obtain a sufficient rate of probing, the BGP stations will occasionally send KEEPALIVE messages. These messages are composed simply of a 19-byte BGP header.

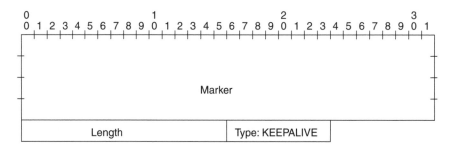

However, merely sending regular probes does not provide a complete guarantee that the association is functional. One must also check that messages are arriving regularly from the peer. During the opening exchange, the BGP stations have announced a hold time, i.e., the maximum delay during which the peer should have to wait between successive messages. Failure to receive a message during this delay will indicate that the peer has ceased to function properly, even if the TCP connection may remain operational.

As the transmission delay of a TCP connection is anything but constant, the sending station has to send messages more frequently than the hold time indicates. Sending an average of three messages during this period is considered adequate. This typically results in sending messages every 2 minutes.

This feature is extremely unwelcome when the link is through a public switched network such as X.25 or ISDN. The price of an X.25 virtual circuit is generally a combination of the volume of data exchanged over the network and the duration of the connections. The price of an ISDN circuit is entirely dependent on the duration of the connections. In an attempt to minimize the bills, routers will typically hang up the circuit in the absence of traffic; they will set it up again if they notice that packets have to be transmitted. By sending regular keep-alive packets, BGP would force the circuits never to hang up or to be reinstalled frequently, thus seriously increasing the network charges.

The hold-time value is negotiated during the opening exchange. Negotiating a zero hold time implies that KEEPALIVE messages will not be exchanged at all. This minimizes the traffic generated by BGP. After the initial connection, we will observe only update and notification packets. But it also suppresses the testing of the link's availability, which must be performed by other means. It is suggested that we use "lower-layer" signals, such as signalling messages received from the public network, and link the fate of the underlying TCP connection to the availability of the public network [8].

9.3.6 Error Notifications

If a BGP station receives an ill-formatted or otherwise erroneous message, or if it fails to receive any message during a period longer than the hold time, it will report the error to its peer by sending a notification message, then gracefully close the TCP connection.

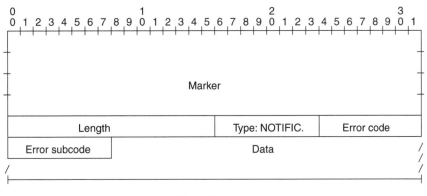

— The NOTIFICATION message of BGP —

Within the notification messages, the 19-byte BGP header is followed by an error code, an error subcode, and a variable amount of data, the length of which can be deduced from the message length. Several error codes and subcodes have been defined. These are shown in the table below.

Error Code	Subcode	Symbolic Name
1	Message Header Error	
	1	Connection Not Synchronized
	2	Bad Message Length
	3	Bad Message Type
2	OPEN Message Error	
	1	Unsupported Version Number
	2	Bad Peer AS
	3	Bad BGP Identifier
	4	Unsupported Optional Parameter
	5	Authentication Failure
	6	Unacceptable Hold Time
3	UPDATE Message Error	
	1	Malformed Attribute List
	2	Unrecognized Well-Known Attribute
	3	Missing Well-Known Attribute
	4	Attribute Flags Error
	5	Attribute Length Error
	6	Invalid ORIGIN Attribute
	7	AS Routing Loop
	8	Invalid NEXT_HOP Attribute
	9	Optional Attribute Error

Error Code	Subcode	Symbolic Name
	10	Invalid Network Field
	11	Malformed AS_PATH
4	Hold Timer Expired	
5	Finite State Machine Error	
6	Cease	

The "finite-state machine" error was not mentioned in the previous paragraphs. It corresponds to the reception of an unexpected message—for example, an UPDATE before the OPEN has been accepted.

The "cease" error is not necessarily an error. It is sent whenever the BGP station wants to terminate the association, such as when it is going down.

9.3.7 Securing the TCP Connection

The BGP connections are a critical component of the Internet service and, as such, a potential target for hackers and other malevolent pirates. In the recent past, we have witnessed several hacker attacks that exploited the lack of protection of TCP connections:

☞ The SYN flooding attack tries to bring down a server by forcing it to create a very large number of "half open" connections.

☞ The RST attack tries to break down a connection by sending a reset packet.

☞ The DATA insertion attack tries to insert a forged packet into the TCP stream.

☞ The "hijacking" attack tries to substitute a third party for the original partner of the connection.

The effect of these attacks on the BGP/TCP connection could be quite nefarious. Bringing down the router would essentially disconnect a whole network. Bringing down the connection would cause the BGP partners to remove the routes advertised on the connection, thus disconnecting whole sets of networks. Hijacking the connection would allow the insertion of bogus routes, creating loops and black holes or capturing the traffic bound to some target networks.

The TCP MD5 Signature Option detailed in RFC-2385 [15] is an attempt at protecting the TCP connection used by BGP. This option is, in nature, quite similar to the MD5 protection options defined for RIP and OSPF, but it is implemented at the TCP layer. The basic idea is to define a TCP option that will carry an MD5 checksum:

IP Header (20 bytes)
TCP "fixed" header (20 bytes)
TCP options, including MD5 checksum
TCP payload (BGP)

The MD5 checksum is computed by the sender over a concatenation of the TCP pseudo-header, which includes the source and destination addresses; of the TCP header, excluding options and assuming a checksum of zero; of the TCP payload; and of a secret or password known to both the sender and the receiver. The signature value is recomputed by the receiver using the same algorithm. Packets whose signatures do not match the computed value are silently ignored. Packets that do not include the signature option are also ignored.

The TCP MD5 checksum option has been hastily deployed in order to protect operational routers against attacks. It certainly offers a much greater level of protection than the simple password incorporated at the BGP level. It is, however, judged rather weak by security experts: the IESG message in RFC-2385 states that "it is understood to have security weaknesses against concerted attacks."

Another way to protect the TCP connection would be to run TCP on top of a secure IP connection, using, for example, the authentication service [16, 17].

9.4 Synchronizing with the IGP

We presented the requirement of the path vector protocols in the beginning of this chapter. We noticed that the BGP external routers must use internal connections to exchange the path vector information within the same AS, and that they must synchronize their updates with the modification of the local routing tables.

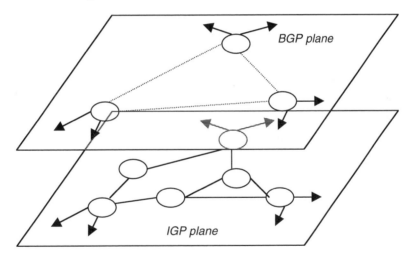

We can represent the relation between the BGP and the IGP as a relation between two planes. In the BGP plane, border routers learn paths from routers in neighboring ASs through BGP, select a path to remote destinations through the BGP "decision process," and synchronize with each other through internal BGP connections. In the IGP plane, border routers announce external routes and learn about internal connectivity. BGP and IGP should be maintained consistently, in order to provide stable routing while enforcing the AS's policy.

9.4.1 Interconnection Policies

The Internet was first developed to fill the needs of academic users, whose budgets often could not allow for extensive continental or transoceanic links. Some nice "big daddy" had to come in and fork over the money—typically, a governmental organization such as the NSF in the United States or a ministry of education or research in other countries. Government funds have this strange inconvenience that they are tightly controlled by various forms of parliaments that may impose very strict conditions on the way the money will be spent. In these early days of the Internet, these restrictions were known as "Acceptable Use Policies" (AUP). For example, as the NSF grants were meant to foster science, the NSFnet AUP insisted that the network would be used only for scientific purposes.

Today's networks are typically commercial enterprises, which very seldom care about restricting what the customer will transmit and to whom. On the other hand, commercial networks need to get revenues for their investments, and as such will not necessarily agree to freely relay third parties' traffic:

☞ The basic arrangement is between a provider and its customer, to provide access to the Internet through a default route.

☞ Small providers will buy "transit" services from larger providers. These larger providers are often known as "backbone" providers.

☞ Large providers will typically decide to "peer" with each other. Limited peering provides connection to the addresses directly managed by the peer, such as its internal addresses and its direct clients. Full peering provides transitive interconnection.

☞ Providers may negotiate "backup" agreements, to maintain connectivity in case of partial failure.

These agreements are typically specified in contracts that must be enforced by the border routers:

☞ The contract with a customer will be enforced by accepting only the paths that lead directly to that customer, and by exporting only a default route.

☞ Transit services are provided by only announcing routes for the destinations listed in the transit agreement.

☞ Limited peering will be enforced by announcing routes to the local AS or to its direct customers. The border router may also be programmed to only accept routes that lead directly to the partner or to one of its customers.

☞ Full peering is provided by typically removing all restrictions.

☞ Backup agreements are typically enforced by assigning a low preference to the imported routes, so that other paths will be preferred if they are available.

The border routers will typically be programmed with large configuration files detailing the exportable routes. For each BGP peer, the configuration files will determine which routes can be imported and which routes can be exported.

9.4.2 The Decision Process

The BGP decision process is composed of three phases:

☞ Evaluate the paths that have been learned from external routers.

☞ Select the most appropriate path for each destination.

☞ Advertise the path to neighbors.

The evaluation process performed in the first phase will be based on a combination of path information, such as the content of the AS path, local information, such as the bandwidth of the connection to the path's next hop, and local preferences. The information will be combined in a "local preference" metric. The first phase of the evaluation is in fact independent of any configuration, because it simply aims at removing unacceptable paths from any further configuration. Unacceptable paths are:

☞ paths that include a mention of the local AS in the AS path,

☞ paths that do not conform to the AS policy, and

☞ paths that have not been qualified as "stable."

We can imagine several strategies based on the information present in the path. In particular, we can use the number of ASs in the path as a metric; this is a very crude metric, yet it has some reasonable correlation with the real world.

We can also complement the path information with some administrative data. We can assign "weights" to some ASs, in order to assert our preferences and to represent our policy constraints. It would probably suffice to assign such weights to a small number of providers. We can indeed also assign "heavy" weights to the ASs that we don't want to see in transit. Then, we could compute a metric that is the sum of the weight of the ASs in the path, or 1 if the AS is not explicitly weighted. We will have to make sure that the same weights are used by all our border routers.

There are, in fact, criteria other than the number of ASs in the path or the AS weight. In particular, some paths result from aggregation. Merely counting the ASs in the AS_SEQUENCE component would be an underestimation, but counting the ASs in the AS_SET would lead to an overestimation. It is reasonable to apply some form of weighting against such paths—for example, consider that any aggregated path transited through a fraction of the ASs in the AS_SET.

The metric derived from the path information can then be combined with local information, such as information on the bandwidth and cost involved in reaching the next hop, in order to obtain the "local preference" metric, which can then be incorporated as a path attribute before transmitting the path to the AS's border routers through internal connection.

Once the evaluation has been completed, we can enter the second phase. At this point, all border routers have received a copy of all the valid paths and must coherently select a single route for each destination. When more than one path is available, the selection proceeds as follows:

1. Remove from consideration the paths whose next-hop neighbor is unreachable.
2. Retain the paths with the best value of the "local preference."
3. If multiple paths are tied with the same local preference, select the path with the lowest MULTI_EXIT_DISC parameter value.
4. If multiple paths are still tied, select the external path announced by the external neighbor with the lowest BGP identifier.
5. If multiple paths remain tied, select the external path announced by the internal neighbor with the lowest BGP identifier.

Earlier versions of BGP did not define the local preference attribute, which meant that network managers had to carefully program all border routers with the same evaluation algorithm;

failure to do so would result in different decisions, and maybe loops or black holes. Using the BGP-4 "local preference" attribute guarantees that border routers will arrive at consistent decisions and all select the same "next hop." However, in order to guarantee that this consistent decision is also the desired decision, one must still guarantee that border routers perform consistent evaluations, using the same administrative weights, algorithms, and so on. In practice, this is a very time-consuming and error-prone task.

The path evaluation is performed each time border routers receive new information, such as new path updates, for example. When they receive an indication of unreachability for external prefixes, the routers will remove the corresponding paths from the list of available paths and perform a new selection. If a new path is available, they will select it. If no new path is available, the destinations have become unreachable.

9.4.3 Exporting Routes in the IGP

Consider first the "normal case" of an AS that runs OSPF. Several "border routers" are connected to the backbone area. They are importing and exporting routes between BGP and OSPF.

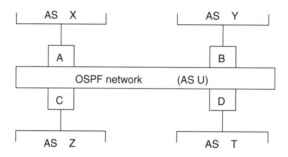

Running BGP in these conditions is relatively simple. The four border routers, A, B, C, and D, exchange the AS path information through internal BGP connections. They must indeed control the information that they import and export, according to the local policies—we discussed the requirements of EGP in the previous chapter, and we will describe the handling of policies in the next section.

The routes are imported into OSPF through external link state records, which are advertised by the border routers and are identified by the destination's IP address. These records are indeed advertised by the border router that is in direct contact with the external path and not by a random router that learned the route through an internal BGP connection. The routers must fill up the metrics and the "route tag" of the record.

Network mask		
E,TOS=0	0	TOS 0 metric
External route tag (0)		
E,TOS=x	0	TOS x metric
External route tag (x)		
- - -	- - -	- - -

Normally, one does not use multiple metrics for external connections, except maybe if some routes are not adequate for a specific type of service. BGP does not support type-of-service routing. The specification of the interactions between BGP and OSPF [6] provides a simple default metric—the bit E should be set, and the metric itself should be set to 1. More sophisticated policies could be used, for example, by letting the backup border routers advertise larger metrics, according to their degree of preference.

The specification also provides a standard formatting of the "route tag."

```
 0                   1                   2                   3
 0 1 2 3 4 5 6 7 8 9 0 1 2 3 4 5 6 7 8 9 0 1 2 3 4 5 6 7 8 9 0 1
+-+-+-+-+-+-+-+-+-+-+-+-+-+-+-+-+-+-+-+-+-+-+-+-+-+-+-+-+-+-+-+-+
|a|c|p|l|      ArbitraryTag       |       AutonomousSystem      |
+-+-+-+-+-+-+-+-+-+-+-+-+-+-+-+-+-+-+-+-+-+-+-+-+-+-+-+-+-+-+-+-+
```

The first bit of this format is "arbitrary." It is set to 1 to distinguish the standard encoding from previous proprietary conventions implemented by some router manufacturers. The other elements of this format are the "completeness" bit (c), the "path length" (pl), a tag, and the number of the AS to which the route leads. In our example, the routes are learned from BGP and are thus "complete" (c = 1). The path length will be set to its maximum value, 2 ('10'), as the path always has at least two components: the remote AS and the local AS.

When routes become unavailable, the border routers should remove the corresponding announcements.

9.4.4 CIDR and the IGP

The external routing information provided by BGP-4 is composed of variable-length prefixes. In order to exploit this information, the internal gateway protocols must also be able to carry variable-length prefixes. We have seen that RIP-1 and IGRP cannot; RIP-2, OSPF, IS-IS, and EIGRP, on the other hand, are all capable of handling subnet masks. The only difference between CIDR's supernet masks and these subnet masks is a number of bits; this does not change the protocol.

However, there is a more subtle difference—the fact that the masked subnets generally belong to the AS itself and are not "overlapping." Given one station address, it belongs to exactly one of the subnets. But let's now consider another example, in fact an extension of the test network that we used in the exposition of the aggregation problem. The only difference between this topology and the previous example is that we now have a direct connection between Y and Z.

All the border routers use BGP-4, and Z will receive the following two paths from T and Y.

```
Path(T):  (Sequence(T), Set(X,Y)), Reaches 197.8.0.0/22
Path(Y):  (Sequence(Y)), Reaches 197.8.3.0/24
```

Suppose now that a router in Z wants to send a packet to a host in Y, say 197.8.3.99. The address of that host is matched by both path(T) and path(Y), which means that we could use either of them. But the two paths are not equivalent. In fact, the whole set of addresses that matches the second prefix is entirely included in the set that matches the first one. We will say, according to the BGP-4 vocabulary, that the two paths overlap and that the second path is "more specific." It provides more precise information over a narrower set of addresses. When a single router advertises several overlapping prefixes, the most specific information should always be trusted. In the CIDR documentation, this is explained by a simple rule: "the longest match wins."

In fact, it is always safe to let the longest match win, even when the information comes from different routers. We know for sure that this subset of addresses is reachable, while it may well be temporarily disconnected from the larger set described by the shorter prefix. This would be, for example, the case of a subscriber that just switched providers without renumbering.

—   a counter-example to the longest-match rule   —

However, that rule may have a few drawbacks, as a more specific path is not necessarily "shorter." It is easy to provide a counter-example. In that case, the two paths are:

```
Path(T):  (Sequence(T), Set(X, Y)), Reaches 197.8.0.0/22
Path(W):  (Sequence(W, V, Y)), Reaches 197.8.3.0/24
```

The second path is still more specific, but it is longer. We are thus left with two problems: deciding which path to follow and finding a way to insert it into the routing tables and to propagate through the IGP. The first decision is entirely within BGP. The "decision processes" must select the best path as a function of the path length, e.g., the number of ASs in the sequences, of the various preferences and weights, of the policies. We will not have many problems if they decide to follow the "least specific" path. It will suffice to enter exactly one address and mask pair in the IGP tables. We should however do this only in well-controlled cases, as it is an exception to the longest-match rule. Let's consider the other case, i.e., when the most specific path is retained. This corresponds to our first example, a direct connection between Y and Z.

Passing the two prefixes to the IGP would be reasonable if the IGP was ready to find several overlapping prefixes in the tables and if it had a predictable strategy, e.g., to always route according to the most specific information, to implement the "longest-match win" rule. This may well happen in a revised version of OSPF. The OSPF working group of the IETF is working on it. But this is not necessarily the case today; overlapping prefixes were not part of the IGP's specifications. The only solution then is to break the overlapping prefixes into a set of independent values. In our example, we will proceed as if we had, in fact, received:

```
Path(T): (Sequence(T), Set(X,Y))
Reaches 197.8.0/23, 197.8.2/24
Path(Y): (Sequence(Y)), Reaches 197.8.3/24
```

This indeed has an impact on the announcement that the AS will send to its own neighbors. We will have two possible choices, to forward the deaggregated routes or to regroup them and export only the aggregation of these routes. This is very easy in our example, as Y is already part of the set component of Path(T). The path exported by Z will be:

```
Path(Z): (Sequence(Z), Set(X,Y,T)), Reaches 197.8.0/22
```

However the fact that we performed an "invisible" aggregation should be signaled by inserting the "atomic aggregate" and "aggregator" attributes in the path's attribute list.

9.4.5 Exporting Routes to Neighboring ASs

The whole purpose of BGP is to control the exporting of routes to neighboring ASs, in order to verify three properties:

☞ that the export of routes is consistent with the local AS's policies,

☞ that only reachable routes are actually exported, and

☞ that the routes are exported with consistent information.

The consistency with the local AS's policies is enforced by screening the list of selected paths and comparing it to the peering conditions that are specified in configuration files. It will only export routes that meet the transit or peering agreements.

Before announcing any path, the border router will check that the path is still available, i.e., that the internal border router selected as the path's entry point in the domain is still reachable through the local IGP. If the path ceases to be available, the border router will have to either switch to an alternate path, or to announce that the path's routes have become unreachable.

The path information will be updated in order to reflect the local decision. The AS_SEQUENCE component of the AS_PATH will be completed by a notation of the local AS, the LOCAL_PREFERENCE attribute will be removed, and the MULTI_EXIT_DISC attribute will optionally be set to a configured value. If several paths have been aggregated within the domain, the AGGREGATOR attribute will be set, as well as the ATOMIC_AGGREGATE attribute if more specific paths have been fused into less specific ones.

9.4.6 What If a Neighbor Does Not Use BGP-4?

The previous section presented the "favorable" case, where all the border routers use BGP-4. But in some cases the neighbors don't support BGP-4 and run an earlier version of BGP, or maybe even EGP. We will then have a mix of technologies.

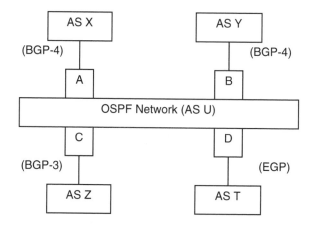

The mix of technologies poses two problems. Older versions of BGP do not support CIDR, and thus cannot export the subnetted or supernetted routes that BGP-4 carries, while EGP does not support the notion of AS_PATH, and thus does not provide any of the loop control supported by BGP.

When BGP-4 was introduced, there were some plans to use "reverse aggregation" in order to facilitate the interoperation with BGP-3 during a transition period. For example, suppose X announces a BGP-4 path:

```
AS_PATH: X, reaches 197.8.0/22
```

C could have announced to Z a "deaggregated" path that explicitly lists the four class-C networks included in the route prefix 197.8.0/22:

```
AS_PATH: X, reaches 197.8.0.0, 197.8.1.0, 197.8.2.0, 197.8.3.0
```

Indeed, the example we used was small enough to be explained easily; real-life examples may result in very large expansions! Basically, by doing this deaggregation, we are reenabling the famous routing table explosion that we wanted to avoid. We may even have a worse result than if we had not aggregated in the first place, as some prefixes may encompass the whole range of addresses that is managed by a provider, although only a fraction of that range is actually allocated. Translating to BGP-3 also supposes that one converts the BGP-4 AS_PATH information, which is organized into "sequence" and "set," into a simple list of AS numbers, losing a lot of the precision introduced in BGP-4 and potentially leading to wrong decisions if the BGP-3 AS reinjects the learned path into another BGP-4 domain.

EGP poses an even worse problem, as it does not carry any path information, and thus does not offer any protection against loops.

In practice, all networks should now have transitioned to BGP-4. EGP, or earlier versions of BGP, can only be encountered in "leaf" ASs that simply connect to a provider, but do not relay packets between several ASs. In this case, the provider's border routers will apply a simple strategy. They will only accept local routes from Z or T, announcing reachability to all or part of these ASs, and they will only export to Z or T a single "default" path, 0.0.0.0/0.

9.4.7 Complex Autonomous Systems

In the "pure" Internet architecture, there should be exactly one IGP per AS. However, the real world has its constraints. A domain that is transitioning from RIP to OSPF, for example, will have some OSPF areas attached to some RIP domains. In fact, the most important characteristic is that an AS has a single administration and appears to the external world as a coherent entity. Mixing several IGPs within an AS is not desirable, but it has to be supported, as in the following diagram.

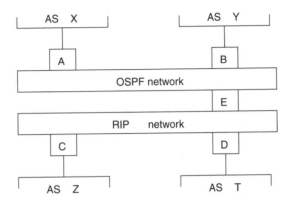

The router E will have to translate information between OSPF and RIP. In one direction, it will simply construct a distance vector that lists the destinations present in the OSPF link state database and the distances derived from the shortest-path evaluations. In the other direction, it will have to insert external link state records in the database both for the internal networks of the RIP area and for the external networks advertised by C and D.

RIP passes very little information about external routes. RIP-2 entries include only a 16-bit external route tag, which is set to 0 for local destinations and to the neighbor's AS number otherwise. This information will be used to construct the route tag of the OSPF external link state records. The AS number will be copied from RIP's route tag. The "completeness" bit of these records will always be null: the information is not sufficient to construct a reasonable AS path. The path length will be set to 0 if the AS number is unknown, to 1 otherwise.

The border gateways X and Y will receive this information through OSPF. They will advertise routes with the origin attribute set to EGP. The AS path will be composed of the local AS number and of the advertised AS number, if it is present.

9.5 Growing Pains

BGP solved one of the Internet problems—moving from a tree topology organized around a single backbone network to a general mesh topology. CIDR was a brilliant example of "just-in-time" development by the IETF. The allocation of "blocks of C" was operational in 1992, just in time to avoid the death of the Internet by class B exhaustion. BGP-4 was deployed in the spring of 1994, just in time to avoid the death of the Internet by explosion of the routing tables. But as the Internet continues to grow, the limits of the BGP technology translate into increased stress in the network operation.

Running BGP requires a very large amount of manual configuration, in order to express adequate routing preferences and transit and peering policies. Configuration errors can snowball into Internet-wide routing incidents. In short, the Internet is experiencing growing pains, which we will detail in the next chapter.

References

1. K. Lougheed and Y. Rekhter, "A Border Gateway Protocol (BGP)," RFC-1105, cisco Systems, T. J. Watson Research Center, IBM Corp., June 1989.

2. K. Lougheed and Y. Rekhter, "A Border Gateway Protocol (BGP)," RFC-1163, cisco Systems, T. J. Watson Research Center, IBM Corp., June 1990.

3. K. Lougheed and Y. Rekhter, "A Border Gateway Protocol 3 (BGP-3)," RFC-1267, cisco Systems, T. J. Watson Research Center, IBM Corp., October 1991.

4. Y. Rekhter, "BGP Protocol Analysis," RFC-1265, T. J. Watson Research Center, IBM Corp., October 1991.

5. Y. Rekhter, "Experience with the BGP Protocol," RFC-1266, T. J. Watson Research Center, IBM Corp., October 1991.

6. K. Varadhan, "BGP OSPF Interaction," RFC-1403, January 14, 1993.

7. Y. Rekhter and T. Li, "A Border Gateway Protocol 4 (BGP-4)," RFC-1654, July 1994.

8. Y. Rekhter and T. Li, "A Border Gateway Protocol 4 (BGP-4)," RFC-1771, March 1995.

9. P. Traina, "Experience with the BGP-4 Protocol," RFC-1773, March 1995.

10. P. Traina, Editor. "BGP-4 Protocol Analysis," RFC-1774, March 1995.

11. V. Fuller, T. Li, J. I. Yu, and K. Varadhan, "Supernetting: An Address Assignment and Aggregation Strategy," RFC-1338, June 1992.

12. V. Fuller, T. Li, J. I. Yu, and K. Varadhan, "Classless Inter-Domain Routing (CIDR): An Address Assignment and Aggregation Strategy," RFC-1519, September 1993.

13. E. Gerich, "Guidelines for Management of IP Address Space," RFC-1466, May 1993.

14. Y. Rekhter and T. Li, "An Architecture for IP Address Allocation with CIDR," RFC-1518, September 1993.

15. A. Heffernan, "Protection of BGP Sessions via the TCP MD5 Signature Option," RFC-2385, August 1998.

16. S. Kent and R. Atkinson, "Security Architecture for the Internet Protocol," RFC-2401, November 1998.

17. S. Kent and R. Atkinson, "IP Authentication Header," RFC-2402, November 1998.

Growing Pains: From CIDR to IPv6

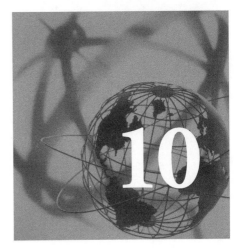

10

$\mathbf{T}$he Internet is growing, and it is growing fast—the number of connected hosts is doubling almost every year, while the volume of traffic is doubling every 6 to 10 months. This growth has been sustained for several years, and all measures indicate that it may well continue at the same rate for another five years, at least. Internet providers must invest continuously to build up network capacity, but they also have to cope with a side effect of the growth, the strains it places on the routing fabric.

10.1 Addresses, Networks, and Routing Tables

Nobody knows exactly how large the Internet is, how many Internet users there are worldwide. The very high growth rate that it has enjoyed makes all measurement attempts approximate at best, since the numbers may well change during the measure. In my opinion, one of the most significant measures is the number of hosts registered in the domain name system. This number is not directly related to the number of users: for example, there are 18 million AOL users, but AOL declares fewer than 2 million addresses. However, the size of the address space is a good indication of the size of the routing problem, because the routing system must guarantee that all the registered addresses will be reachable. (The numbers between 1991 and July 1996 come from the DNS studies conducted by Network Wizards; those between September 1996 and June 1999 from the Netsizer service, www.netsizer.com; and the numbers between 1999 and 2001 are interpolations.)

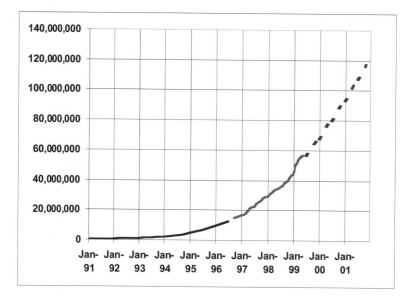

Thanks to CIDR and to network aggregation, the number of routes that have to be propagated by BGP does not grow quite as fast as the number of hosts. As shown in the following figure, the number of routes grows almost linearly over time, while the number of hosts grows exponentially. But the growth is still very fast. There were almost 60,000 routes declared in the BGP routing tables in June 1999. (The chart is drawn from numbers collected by Erik-Jan Bos and Geoff Huston and published at http://www.telstra.net/ops/bgptable.html.)

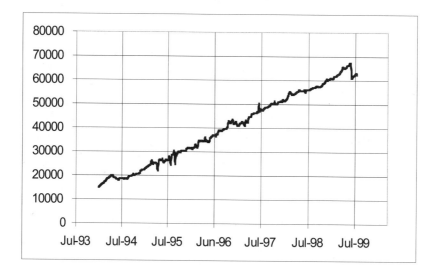

The growth in routes and networks has some very direct consequences on the load of the system. Obviously, routers need to manage ever larger tables. But the memory effect is probably not quite as important as the traffic effect: more networks mean more routing traffic.

10.1.1 Routing Instabilities

In a communication to the 1997 ACM/SIGCOMM conference[1], Craig Labovitz et al. reported their finding after the analysis of nine months of BGP traffic. In short, they found many more updates than would have been required for a normal operation of the network. The Internet, at the time, included about 1300 autonomous systems, 1500 paths, and 45,000 prefixes. Most paths remain available for relatively long periods, as shown in Paxson's study [2]; thus, a normal figure would have been somewhere between 10,000 and 100,000 updates per day. Instead, Labovitz et al. observed 3 to 6 million updates per day. This had a dramatic impact on Internet service, as routers spent precious computing resources handling these unnecessary updates, not to mention the traffic overhead. Moreover, in some routers, updating the routing tables required flushing a "route cache" in the route processors, which resulted in temporary slowdown. Too frequent updates could, in fact, result in loss of service.

Most of these updates were pathological, redundant messages that did not reflect changes in the network topology. A table presented by Labovitz et al. [1] shows a partial list of updates on February 1, 1997. The actual provider names have been replaced by anonymous letters, and the updates are categorized as either route announcements (i.e., actual path updates) or route withdrawals. The "unique" column lists the number of updates that would have been necessary if withdrawals and announcements were not duplicated in unnecessary, redundant messages.

Network	Announce	Withdrawn	Unique
A	1,127	23,276	4,344
B	0	36,776	8,424
C	32	10	12
D	63	171	28
E	1,350	1,351	8
F	11	86,417	12,435
G	2	61,780	10,659
H	21,197	77,931	14,030
I	259	2,479,023	14,112
J	2,335	1,363	853

The very large number of duplicate withdrawals was clearly due to bugs. In fact, the majority of the announcements resulted from hardware and software bugs in several popular routers. Faulty hardware could, for example, detect a connectivity loss when in fact the line was only temporarily unavailable for a few milliseconds. Faulty software would fail to keep proper track of previously sent withdrawals and would repeat them "just in case." These problems have since been corrected, but other, more systematic problems remain. In a consecutive study, Craig Labovitz and his partners studied the behavior of three "backbone" ISPs between November 1997 and November 1998 [3]. They were able to look both at the OSPF and BGP level.

The OSPF reports showed that outages were due to the expected mix of scheduled maintenance, power outages, fiber and circuit cuts, and hardware and software problems. The majority of outages were detected in the customer networks that the ISP served, rather than in the backbone itself: backbone routers, for example, would typically be located in operation centers equipped with back-up power, and would not be subject to power failures. Another characteristic was the random distribution of the outages, which did not exhibit any specific frequencies.

On the other hand, BGP outages, which are characterized by the unavailability of interdomain paths, showed a very clear periodic behavior, including a component with a period of 7 days, and another with a period of 24 hours. In fact, the frequency of updates was, by and large, correlated with the volume of traffic, and would increase during the typical busy hours. This behavior contradicts the theoretical notion that updates would be triggered by the loss of links, by hardware or software failures in the routers. If that was true, the behavior of BGP would have mimicked that of OSPF!

The most likely culprit for the outages observed in November 1998 is network congestion. As the web traffic continues to grow, network links are very often congested. This means that the BGP packets, which are carried by TCP connections, may easily be delayed when the TCP connection "backs off" to ease congestion at a bottleneck link. This back-off may result in the failure to transmit keep-alive messages at the specified interval, which leads to the categorization of a border router as "down" when it is merely experiencing congestion. This bad diagnostic can have a snowball effect. First, the routes that were transiting through the "down" router will be replaced or removed, creating a spike of BGP traffic. Soon after that, the "down" router will try to reestablish the BGP connection, and will send a complete update, listing all available paths. This exchange of traffic will contribute to the congestion, and also to the overload of downstream routers that receive the sequences of updates. The downstream routers may in turn become congested and fail to send keep-alive messages at the specified interval, amplifying the initial problem.

The congestion is more likely to affect internal BGP connections, because these connections transit through several interior routers, while external BGP connections are typically through a single hop. A possible cure deployed by some routers is to increase the priority or "precedence" of the IP packets that carry BGP traffic, ensuring that they will be transmitted normally even during congestion. That cure will ease some of the problems reported by Labovitz et al. [3], but would still leave an open vulnerability. If routers start to receive too many updates, if they cannot get enough processing resources, they may take too long to send the keep-alive messages and trigger the same kind of cumulative failures.

10.1.2 Controlling the Rate of the Advertisements

Interdomain routing is, in effect, a distributed application performed by the routers of tens of thousands of Internet Service Providers. Just as the OSPF flooding process distributes link state information to all the routers in an area, the BGP update process distributes reachability information to all border routers. Indeed, the BGP update is not a full flooding process. Updates that only affect a secondary path, one which has not been retained by an intermediate domain, do not get propagated. But, on the other hand, a multihomed AS that can choose between several paths toward a given destination will receive as many copies of each update that the destination triggers. Local updates are propagated at least once to all border routers in the Internet.

If each of the about 60,000 entries in the routing tables would only be updated once a week, each router receives about 6 updates per minute, a reasonable proposition. But the experience shows that a small fraction of the routes contribute an inordinate amount of updates. This phenomenon, informally known as "route flap," can be caused by software or hardware bugs, by the interaction between BGP and network congestion described in the previous section, or by local decisions.

Whatever the cause of a route flap, it is necessary to mitigate its effects. If a misbehaving router sends too many updates at too short intervals, its neighbors that try to process all the updates will exhaust their computing resource and may fall into a congested state that triggers further instabilities. A solution, proposed in RFC-2439 [4], is to limit the rate at which updates are accepted for any given path. Limiting the rate obviously diminishes the responsiveness of the protocol and should be done with caution. In practice, one should ensure:

- ☞ that if a path remained stable for a long time and just changed once, the update will be propagated quickly;
- ☞ that if a path oscillates rapidly, updates will be suppressed and the path will be declared unreachable;
- ☞ that if an alternate path exists, the oscillating path will be damped more aggressively than if it was the sole path to the destination; and
- ☞ that damping does not affect the internal BGP connections, as it is important that all routers within an AS keep a coherent view and advertise the same path for any given destination.

BGP-4, as specified in RFC-1771 [5], contains a partial provision against route flaps. Border routers are expected to wait some minimal delay between consecutive announcements and another, shorter delay between successive route originations. The standard interval values are set to 30 seconds for the advertisement interval, to 15 seconds for the origination interval. These intervals achieve one important result: routes that just changed are more likely than others to change again at a brief interval. Waiting for 15 or 30 seconds allows routers to "pack" consecutive updates, thus diminishing the global load. But such delays are far too short to solve the damping problem. Let's suppose that 20% of the 60,000 interdomain paths advertised in June 1999 exhibit some instability. A 30-second interval still means more than 400 advertisements per second, and many more for multihomed networks. This is already too much for some routers!

The basic idea of RFC-2439 is to associate to each path a "figure of merit." The figure of merit is computed as an exponentially smoothed average of the number of updates received in the recent path. Specifically, the following formula is used:

- ☞ On reception of an update, increase the figure of merit by one.
- ☞ At regular intervals, multiply the figure of merit by a coefficient K, $0 < K < 1$. The actual value of the coefficient will be lower if the path is available and is the only path to the destination than if it is not available, or if alternate paths exist.

Paths that remained stable for a long time will have a figure of merit near zero, while paths that exhibit high instability will have a higher figure. Routers would then refrain from advertising, or using paths whose figures of merit exceed a threshold value—a value of 2 is suggested in RFC-2439 [4].

10.1.3 Controlling the Source of the Advertisements

We already observed the similarity between OSPF flooding and BGP updates. As in OSPF, information that originates from any border router gets propagated to the whole set of routers in the Internet, which will then base their route computations on this information. Needless to say, inaccurate information results in inaccurate routing. A classic example of failure occurs when a leaf network misconfigures its addresses. The perennial "network legend" used to be that some brainy but careless MIT alumni would use the MIT class-A address in their network, then connect to their ISP. The ISP would pick up the address, advertise it to the whole world through BGP, and subsequently receive traffic for the MIT class-A address that will, essentially, go down a black hole.

Such examples may well be apocryphal, but a real-life incident did occur on April 25, 1997. A small Virginia ISP misconfigured one of its border routers. That router would essentially receive all the path announcements from its neighbor, remove the AS_PATH information, and replace it with a single element, as if the destinations were directly accessible through that ISP. It then reannounced the modified routes to its neighbors. As a consequence, many networks sent their entire Internet traffic to the Virginia ISP, effectively disconnecting the Internet for up to two hours.

The only ISPs that did not suffer from the incident were the ones that exercised caution and refused to believe or accept the modified path. In fact, similar incidents had been happening before, albeit at a lower scale, and work was already underway to provide a method for systematically controlling the veracity, or at least the plausibility, of route announcement. To be precise, three methods have been proposed. One possible way to check whether routes are acceptable is to compare them to a registration database, into which each ISP would document the network that it serves and the autonomous systems with which it peers. The Internet Route Registry (IRR) was set up to that effect. It continues and incorporates an earlier effort, the Route Arbiter Database (RADB) that was set up by Merit for the NSF. The IRR, is in fact, a collection of databases maintained by regional networks and organizations such as Merit for the original RADB, Réseaux IP Européens (RIPE) for the European networks, Cable & Wireless, ANS, Level3, and Bell Canada. A complete listing of Internet Registries is available on the web [6]. All entries follow a common format, specified in RIPE report 181 [7]. Entries in the database describe networks, the routes that link networks and autonomous systems, autonomous systems and their readiness to accept routes from other systems. Network operators that want to use the IRR services will get copies of the databases, in order to collate the various entries. They can then check the plausibility of announcements by checking the correlation between the AS_PATH information and the advertised routes. The last domain in the AS_PATH, or at least one domain in the AS_SET component of the AS_PATH, should match one of the ASs declared in a route entry for the reachable prefix. One could then, in theory, verify that the path itself is plausible by checking that each component of the AS_SEQUENCE has declared its readiness to accept routes from the other components.

There are, however, two practical problems with the IRR approach. One is the declarative nature of the databases. Domain managers have to feed their information into the regional bases. Some will do it, but many won't, or won't do it in time. This leaves holes in the data set, routes for which no declaration is registered. Paths that lead to nonregistered routes cannot be verified.

This also causes some of the information to be obsolete. If obsolete information contradicts a valid path, that path may be rejected, leading to an unnecessary lack of connectivity.

A possible way to alleviate the load of the registration procedures would be to use the domain name system instead of a special purpose database. The domain name system is, in fact, a database distributed over thousands of Internet servers. It is already used to provide information about addresses, and it would be possible to provide information about prefixes as well. In a proposition submitted to the IETF, Tony Bates, Randy Bush, Tony Li, and Yakov Rekhter propose to create a special DNS tree to hold domain information. The information on a prefix such as 10.1.128/20 may be encoded under a DNS name such as 128/20.1.10.bgp.in-addr.arpa. The routers that receive a path could use the DNS to retrieve the AS records associated to the advertised prefixes, and to check that the path only contains prefixes that can legitimately be announced by the neighboring AS. Using the DNS has two advantages:

☞ Because the DNS is a distributed system, the information could be managed directly by the owner of the prefix.

☞ Because the DNS information can be secured through electronic signatures [8], the router can check the source and the veracity of the information.

But a similar or better level of security can be achieved without having to query the DNS each time a border router receives a path announcement. In a contribution to the IETF, Sandra Murphy analyzes the security of BGP [9] and proposes a set of possible improvements:

☞ The originating AS could certify the validity of the announcement by attaching a digital signature attribute to the path information. The digital signature would attest to the identity of the AS that inserted the network information. Certificates could be also attached to attest that the AS is authorized to announce this network.

☞ If aggregation occurs, the aggregator could insert a digital signature attesting to the origin of the aggregation, and possibly a certificate attesting to its right to aggregate.

☞ A digital signature could be inserted by each relay, attesting to the veracity of the path.

These concepts form the basis of a "secure BGP" that has still, however, to be developed. The potential problem here is the overhead of signatures, in terms of both transmission volume and computation overhead. To be reasonably secure, key lengths of a thousand bits should be used. In 1999, exponentiation of such numbers still requires a significant amount of time, maybe one tenth of a second. This would seriously limit the rate of update transmissions. However, the potential benefit is very large, and the performance of computers increases every year. We may see such solutions become routine in a few years.

10.2 The Structure of Interconnections

The Internet may appear to be thriving, but the system is experiencing tensions. The initial interconnection structure, based on public exchange points, is being questioned by large operators for a mix of business and technical reasons. The business reasons have, in fact, pushed a small number of providers to develop very large networks that cover whole continents, and that may well evolve to cover the whole world. Managing these networks and their interconnections poses specific problems.

10.2.1 From Public Exchanges to Private Peering

The original NSFnet plans called for a set of five Network Access Points (NAP) through which regional networks would connect to the NSFnet and to alternative commercial networks. The exchanges would complement an existing set of interconnection points such as the Commercial Internet Exchange (CIX) and the two Federal Internet Exchanges (FIX), FIX-East and FIX-West. Similar exchanges would be developed in the other countries, allowing for local connections of Internet providers.

An exchange typically is a computer center in which each participating network provider brings a router. These routers are connected to a "neutral" interconnection system provided by the exchange. The interconnection normally is not provided by a router, because of policy considerations. An exchange is a place where multiple providers come and interconnect, but these interconnections still result in most cases from bilateral contracts between every two pairs of connected networks. Each of these "peering agreements" is materialized by at least one BGP session between the routers belonging to the network. If the exchange network was materialized as a single router, this router would route all packets bound to a given destination to a single path, regardless of peering contracts. In fact, an exchange built around a high-speed router would act as a transit provider. The BGP sessions would be established between each network and the exchange's router.

In the most common setup, the exchange network is provided using "layer 2" switching technology. That technology must provide enough bandwidth to accommodate the aggregate traffic of the participating network interconnections. Various technologies have been used over time:

☞ The first exchanges were build around a 100-Mbps FDDI ring. That technology was adequate when the network connections ran at T1 or E1 speed—i.e., 1.5 or 2 Mbps. It is inadequate now.

☞ Several exchanges were built using an ATM switch or a network of ATM switches. That technology is capable of providing OC3 or maybe OC12 connections, and proved hard to develop initially, as ATM switches did not have adequately sized buffers, and were lacking adequate queue management techniques. These problems have now been fixed.

☞ Other exchanges have been built using switched Ethernet technology, at speeds such as 10 Mbps, 100 Mbps, or 1 Gbps.

In the future, we may see exchanges using even more advanced technology, such as optical fibers and Wave Division Multiplexing. Exchanges played an important role in the development of the Internet, allowing hundreds of networks to connect in a single place. Several exchanges developed additional services, such as access to route information registries, name servers, and cache servers. However, the whole notion of exchanges is being questioned by the largest Internet providers, who attack it for a mix of business and technology reasons and who prefer to use private interconnections.

The business reason is rather easy to explain. When they join an exchange, network providers sign a contract that, in effect, forces them to exchange traffic with all other exchange members. This is very advantageous for small providers, who, by getting access to an exchange point, get access, in effect, to the whole Internet, without having to pay an interconnection fee to larger providers. But it is equally disadvantageous for the large providers, who feel their networks provide the bulk of the Internet's transit capacity, and who would normally charge for their services. However, this problem could be solved by slightly modifying the exchange connection rules. Just because a connection takes place in an exchange point does not mean that it has to be free. The technical problems, on the other hand, cannot be dealt with by simply rewriting a contract. Exchanges, by their very nature, become focal points for congestion. The congestion can happen at the routing level, at the access level, and eventually in the exchange itself.

The routing problem may become very hard if a single router has to manage the peering with hundreds of partners. The memory requirement increases, because BGP requires that routers maintain a complete copy of the announcement received from each peer. The rate of announcements also increases with the number of peers, possibly leading to saturation of the local processing resource. As fledging networks connect to the exchange, some inexperienced operators will fatally make mistakes, which can easily generate abusive messaging and processing loads.

The access link between the exchange and each network is shared by sources in all peering networks. If one of the source networks sends an inordinate amount of traffic, the access link will become congested. This congestion will then be shared by all the peering networks. It is theorically possible to use techniques such as weighted fair queuing to diminish the effect of this problem; we will present these techniques in chapter 14. But these techniques are hard to deploy at high speed. Moreover, the network access router has only indirect control of the amount of traffic that it will accept from the peering partners. BGP allows routers to limit the range of destinations that they announce to partners, following the policy specified in the peering agreements. However, a misconfigured peer can send traffic for destinations that were not announced. Routers are typically not configured to check the source of the packets. If a destination was announced to peer A but not to peer B, that destination is in effect usable by peer B as well. The potential for errors, and possibly also for abuse, is quite high.

We explained above that exchanges typically are built around the fastest local network technology that is available when they are created. However, as the traffic increases at a very high rate, the exchange network needs to be continually upgraded, and access routers need to be often replaced by more powerful models. This is, by nature, a discontinuous process. The consequences, if the exchange networks become congested, are very scary. Thousands of networks will be congested, and a large fraction of the Internet will experience poor service.

Private interconnections, in practice, do not suffer from the same problems. Because they are used only by a pair of networks, there will be only one BGP connection to maintain, typically with another well-operated, large network. The capacity can be provisioned to match the planned traffic between the two networks. Moreover, if the traffic increases, it is possible to multiply the number of private connections in order to split their loads, while multiplying the number of exchange points would be a complicated process.

10.2.2 Managing a Large AS

Large networks that cover a whole continent need to manage a large number of interconnections, and may thus include a very large number of border routers. A value of more than 100 would not be surprising. Maintaining such a large number of routers increases the burden of internal BGP connections. The first problem is that BGP, in theory, requires a full mesh of interconnections, and the second problem is that the frequency of updates will increase with the number of connections.

Maintaining a complete mesh of connections means that each time a new border router is added to the network, all other border routers will have to be configured to establish a BGP session with that border router. The memory and process requirements of each border router will be proportional to the number of border routers in the whole network, which will clearly pose a scaling problem. RFC-1966 [11] proposes to reduce this burden by introducing route reflectors, routers that act as relays for routing updates. Routers are grouped in clusters that only communicate with the other internal BGP routers through a small number of reflectors. The reflectors communicate with the other internal BGP routers, or with other reflectors. In order to avoid loops that could be caused by misconfiguration, RFC-1966 introduces two new BGP attributes, an ORIGINATOR_ID (code 9), identifying the routers that created the path, and a CLUSTER_LIST that identifies all clusters that the internal path traversed. Clusters are identified by the 32-bit identifier of their main reflector. Paths shall never be advertised back to their originator within a cluster, and clusters should not accept paths from other clusters if their identifier is already present in the router list.

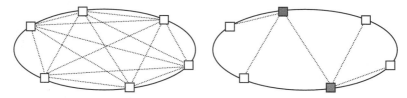

I-BGP connections, with and without reflectors

RFC-1965 [10] proposes another way to organize the routing within a large domain. It introduces the concept of "confederation" that was first developed in the Inter-Domain Routing Protocol (IDRP) [12], a protocol developed to play the same role of BGP in the ISO/CLNP framework. For some time, many interdomain routing experts believed that IDRP could one day replace BGP. This did not happen, but many of the IDPR concepts, such as confederation, are being retrofitted into BGP.

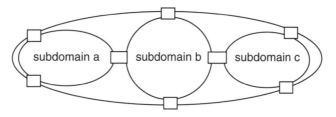

AS as confederation of subdomains

The basic idea of confederation is to consider a large domain as a collection of smaller domains. This naturally brings the advantages of clustering, since the full mesh of IGP only has to be maintained within a subdomain, or between the internal border routers of the subdomains. Another advantage is that it is possible to perform address aggregation within a subdomain. Given proper address allocation, local customers of a subdomain can be represented by a single address prefix in other subdomains, thus diminishing the size of the internal routing tables. Again, care must be taken to avoid the possible effects of misconfiguration. RFC-1965 proposes to modify the structure of the AS_PATH attribute, adding an AS_CONFED_SET and an AS_CONFED_SEQUENCE component to represent the traversal of domains, in addition to the AS_SET and AS_SEQUENCE that represent the traversal of ASs.

In order to deal with alternate paths, large domains also require consistent parameterization of the LOCAL_PREFERENCE attribute. For example, if a customer network is multihomed, it can be reached through the direct path, i.e., through its normal connection to the local ISP, through a back-up connection, through another ISP, or perhaps through another "customer-supplied" path. This requires manual configuration of the local preference, a task that providers would like to automate. In order to solve this problem, RFC-1997 proposed to add a COMMUNITY attribute to BGP [13, 14].

10.2.3 Interconnection Between Large ASs

Suppose that networks A and B cover the same geographical area. Connecting these two networks through a single peering point would not be very efficient, as all the traffic would have to be routed back and forth through that point. Suppose, for example, the two networks both serve North America and peer in Washington, DC. Traffic between two users located in the same city, say Los Angeles, will have to be hauled back and forth through Washington, DC!

A single point of interconnection is not very efficient

A simple improvement is to establish multiple peering points between the two networks. However, in a classic BGP configuration, all the routers that belong to the same AS will advertise the same routes. The internal configuration of each network is hidden through address aggregation. As a consequence, the interior routing protocols in network A can only consider that all gateways to network B are at an equal distance to all destinations announced by B, and vice versa. Suppose that the networks A and B, instead of peering only in Washington, DC, now also peer in Los Angeles and Chicago. The problem we mentioned in the previous paragraph is solved: a connection between two users located in Los Angeles will only use the Los Angeles gateway. But consider a TCP connection between x, connected to network A in Washington, DC, and y, connected to network B in Chicago. The packets sent from x to y will be routed by the IGP of network A toward the nearest point of access to B, Washington, DC, and will move from there to y. In the reverse direction, the packets sent by y toward x will be routed through the Chicago access point to A, and from there to x. This asymmetric routing is often called "hot potato routing."

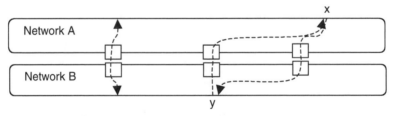

Advertising the same information leads to hot potato routing

Whether hot potato routing is good or bad depends on the nature of the interconnected networks. In the case of two large transit networks with balanced interconnections, the consequences probably are not very important, as asymmetries in one direction will be compensated by asymmetries in another direction. The consequences may, however, be quite drastic if one of the networks specializes in "web hosting" services, providing high-speed connection to a set of web servers, often concentrated in a single computer center.

servers

Asymmetric routing and server farms

Web servers are characterized by a highly asymmetric traffic pattern. They receive short commands and respond with large quantities of text, images, and video. Asymmetric routing guarantees that, even if the network provider took pains to provide high-speed connections and a large number of interconnection points, the outgoing traffic will be concentrated on a single gateway. The solution to this problem requires cooperation from network A, which will have to program its border routers to announce multiple paths, with properly configured MULTI_EXIT_DISC parameters.

10.3 Routing Table Aggregation and Address Allocation

The growth of the Internet routing table can only be achieved if addresses are aggregated—that is, if multiple long prefixes can be represented by a single short prefix. Address aggregation also concurs to a reduction in the number of updates propagated through the Internet, as the path leading to the aggregate will tend to be more stable than the path to individual components. But routing table aggregation can be achieved only if the addresses are assigned in a coordinated fashion. In this section, we will present this coordination and the other problems that need to be solved, such as the relationship with the providers and the need, at some stage, to engage in address renumbering.

10.3.1 Coordinated Address Allocation

The aggregation of addresses by common prefixes is facilitated by the regional scope of the current address assignment authorities. One of the first actions of the coordinators has been to lay out an addressing plan by continents, allocating to these continents a range of class-C addresses [17]:

Multiregional	192.0.0.0–193.255.255.255
Europe	194.0.0.0–195.255.255.255
Others	196.0.0.0–197.255.255.255
North America	198.0.0.0–199.255.255.255
Central/South America	200.0.0.0–201.255.255.255
Pacific Rim	202.0.0.0–203.255.255.255
Others	204.0.0.0–205.255.255.255
Others	206.0.0.0–207.255.255.255

The continent-level authorities then delegate a fraction of their share to lower-level authorities. For example, the European authority is the "network coordination center" of RIPE; it delegates slices of its spaces to national authorities, such as FRNIC in France. Other regional authorities are the American Registries for Internet Numbers (ARIN) and the Asia Pacific Network Information Center (APNIC).

If the plan is followed, we can hope that all the European networks will be represented by exactly one entry in the routing tables of other continents—that is, a 7-bit prefix corresponding to all IP addresses included between 194.0.0.0 and 196.0.0.0. But there are still some debates going on about, among other things, the "provider" or "geographic" nature of the addresses. In fact, as the Internet grows, the registries have started to allocate addresses in new ranges. The typical process is for IANA to delegate an address range to a regional registry, which then subdelegates it through either national registries or network providers.

10.3.2 Provider and Clients

Until 1992, the Internet network numbers had no relation at all to the network's topology. This is both an advantage, as it provides flexibility, and an inconvenience, as it is the main cause for the explosion of the routing table. A coordinated assignment strategy will obviously have to remove some of the flexibility in order to deflate the tables, but the real question is, how much? There are two responses to this question, called "provider addressing" and "geographical addressing."

The Internet's topology bears little relation to geography. It is expressed in terms of links, routers, and connections. All of these are laid down by Internet providers. Two organizations that are neighbors in a given city may be either very near or very far apart in terms of Internet distance. They will be very near if they subscribe to the same provider, quite far apart if they don't. In the latter case, the packets will have to travel to the point where the two providers interconnect, which may be in the same city, in the same region, or maybe only near some national "Internet interconnection." There were examples, in June 1994 in France, of providers interconnected only through a European gateway. If a client of A sent a packet to a client of B, the packet would go from Paris to Amsterdam and back!

The only strategy that guarantees all the benefits of "routing table aggregation" is thus called "provider allocation" [4]. Each Internet provider receives a slice of the address space and "sells" the network numbers to its clients. As a result, all of the clients' addresses share the same prefix and can be aggregated as one single entry in the other providers' routing tables.

But suppose now that an organization wishes to switch from provider A to provider B. If it keeps the address that was assigned by A, it obliges provider B to announce this "exception" to all other providers. Failure to do so would result in all the traffic being directed to the old provider, A. All of a sudden, we have added an individual entry for the organization in all these routing tables, and the benefits of aggregation have been lost. We may, perhaps, tolerate this disorder during an interim period, but the organization will eventually have to change its Internet address for a new one allocated by B.

We will see in the next paragraph that changing an Internet address is not always very easy. If changing providers means that we will have to renumber, we may think twice and compare the benefits of a slightly lower tariff or a slightly better service with the administrative cost of address renumbering. This may have a freezing effect on competition, something many of us are quite reluctant to accept.

The "provider addressing" strategy has a logical consequence—addresses are really owned by the provider. This, in a way, locks the client in the provider's arms and is a big departure from the current situation, where addresses are owned by the clients. Today, because I own my address, I need only to sign a contract to change providers. I may have several simultaneous subscriptions to different providers and select the best provider for any particular destination; I may even change the routing as a function of the time of the day if the providers have a service that varies with time. I cannot do the same with provider addressing.

Geographical addressing is an alternative to provider addressing that leaves the ownership of the addresses to the clients, yet still allows some aggregation. Address slices are allocated to regions or cities; the clients receive addresses within these regions. The providers will have to maintain detailed tables for the cities they serve, but we will probably have a good aggregation at the higher level of the hierarchy—by region, by country, or by continent. Many experts assert, however, that the geographical addressing would not provide sufficient aggregation; the "detailed tables" could be so large that the providers would not be capable of handling them.

10.3.3 Will We Need to Renumber?

The provider addressing strategy just described results in address aggregation only if the users that move from one provider to another do change their addresses. With the current technology, changing a machine's address rates from relatively easy to almost undoable [19].

Changing your address means that you will replace the old value in all the places where this value is stored. In theory, if one uses state-of-the-art technology, there are only two such places: the master file of the BOOTP or DHCP server and the database of the DNS server. If one updates the BOOTP or DHCP file, the address will be updated the next time the host is initialized; if one updates the DNS, all our partners will get the new address the next time they query the DNS.

Things, however, are not so easy. Consider first the host "reinitialization." It may be standard practice in some places to power down your personal computer when you leave the office, but that is not always the case. My workstation, for example, has been up for the entire last month. There are many programs that can take advantage of the night, such as automatic backup of the hard disk. It is also a good time to receive mail from your friends from other continents. And many people do work at night, through modem connections. All these hosts that stayed up will have to be rebooted explicitly. Then it is often the case that these hosts, which are rarely rebooted, do not use BOOTP or DHCP. We will have to configure their addresses manually.

On most systems, it is almost impossible to change the IP address without rebooting. This is very annoying, as it implies that the servers running on these systems will have to be stopped. In some cases, doing a clean stop may be a very lengthy operation, as one has to stop the system according to very precise procedures in order to guarantee a clean restart. Even if one could change the IP address without rebooting, one will not be able to keep the TCP connections; the TCP context is identified by a combination of TCP ports and IP addresses.

Until all hosts have migrated to the new address, we will have a mix of old and new addresses on the local subnet. This is annoying, though not fatal. The routers will have to be programmed to announce these two networks. The most annoying side effect is that two hosts that do not belong to the same IP subnet may need to send their packets to a router to communicate. Hopefully, this situation will not last very long.

Once we have accomplished this transition and updated the DNS server, we might think we are finished, but this is only "almost true." For one thing, the DNS uses "replication" and "caching" to enhance reliability and response times. This means that there are copies of the old addresses in the "secondary servers" and in an unpredictable number of caches all over the Internet. We can probably trigger an update of the secondary servers; in any case, they will get the new values during their next scheduled update. But we will have to wait for the caches to time-out, which can take a few days, if we have not taken the precaution to initialize the DNS records with short TTL values.

Then there is the problem of all those applications that use Internet addresses directly, that think it is smart to write down your address in a file somewhere so that they don't need to use the name server. This is a thoroughly bad idea, but software engineers are people, and people are human. They have bad ideas, and it is quite difficult to drag them away from using them. The only thing one can hope is that they will learn. Maybe by reading this book.

In summary, renumbering is difficult today, network managers with hands-on experience will tell you. This does not bode well for a strategy that would rely on frequent renumbering for routing table aggregation, but time will tell. It may well be the case that someone will come out with a very clean implementation that combines the DNS and the DHCP server, which entirely parameterizes the old and new addresses, which allows us to keep both addresses for a transition period so that we don't have to reboot or break the TCP connections. They may even allow us to keep two addresses forever, so that one can buy Internet services from multiple providers. Who knows? Until now, the Internet has survived because smart people came out with smart solutions. As the size of the network increases, the supply of smart people is certainly not diminishing!

10.3.4 The NAT Alternative

The Network Address Translation technology was developed for networks that don't want to be fully connected to the Internet, and that accept having all their outgoing traffic "rewritten" by an address translation gateway. When the NAT technology is used, the "partially connected" network uses "private addresses"—that is, addresses that are not routable in the Internet. A set of such addresses has been set aside in RFC-1597 [20] and RFC-1918 [22]. One of the network addresses that was so set aside was "network 10," the class-A network that was initially allocated to the Arpanet and that was not used anymore after its decommissioning.

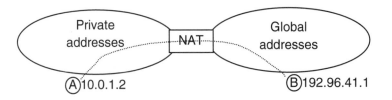

The reserved addresses cannot be used in the global Internet, which means that host B of our example will never be able to send a packet toward the private address 10.0.1.2 of host A. To communicate, these two hosts must rely on the address translation service of the NAT gateway. The communication will typically proceed as follows:

1. A decides to contact B and sends a packet from source address 10.0.1.2 (private) toward the destination address 192.96.41.1.

2. The NAT intercepts the packet and translates the address 10.0.1.2 into a global address, such as 192.1.2.3, taken out of a pool managed by the NAT. The packet is then relayed toward B.

3. B receives the packet and replies by sending a packet from 192.96.41.1 toward 192.1.2.3.

4. The NAT intercepts the packet, realizes that the address 192.1.2.3 has been reserved as a translation of 10.0.1.2, and performs the reverse translation.

5. A receives the packet. Successive packets will undergo the same translation, as long as the NAT remembers that 10.0.1.2 maps to 192.1.2.3.

The translation, however, is not quite so simple as just managing a cache of addresses and rewriting headers. First, one must deal with the TCP and UDP checksums, which protect not only the data but also the source and destination addresses. The checksum must be updated to reflect the address translation. Then, the NAT must deal with applications that directly manage addresses. FTP, for example, routinely sends over its control connection the addresses and ports that will be used for its data connections. This means that the NAT has to recognize the applications that are being used, and that it shall in some cases translate parts of the packet content in addition to the packet header.

On the surface, NATs may look attractive. The network can use a large address space, and will not normally need to renumber, even if it changes providers. But these arguments are very shortsighted, as explained in RFC-1627. At the time of e-commerce, corporations often have to establish business relations with their customers and providers, which is not facilitated by the use of private addresses. If two organizations are using the same private addresses, any direct interconnection is going to be awkward, at best. Then, if two corporations that used the same private addresses merge, the network administrators will be confronted with a serious nightmare.

The worst effect of NAT is on network security. In fact, NAT vendors often say that the use of private address space provides some level of security, because machines are not readily accessible to the outside. This is, at best, a half truth. As soon as a privately addressed host has contacted an outside host, the NAT establishes an address mapping that can then be used to send packets inside the private network. The security will at that point rely on the scanning of inappropriate packets by the NAT box, not on the fact that the addresses are private. This scanning of packets is exactly the same as performed by ordinary firewalls, and the NAT will not provide a better level of security than these ordinary firewalls. But firewalls also allow hosts to build up additional security by using end-to-end encryption, while NATs don't. NATs are incompatible with IP security, because IP security protects the packet header as well as the packet content— one of the services of IP security is to verify the origin of the packet, and NATs are essentially lying about this origin. Then, NATs have to examine the content of the packet to track addresses, and they cannot do so if the packets are encrypted.

I would never recommend relying on the NAT technology. Just do the paperwork and get unique addresses.

10.4 Is IPv6 the Solution?

The next generation Internet Protocol, IPv6, was specifically designed to ease the Internet's growing pains. The larger addresses would enable more hosts to connect to the Internet, and the addresses would be structured hierarchically in order to lower the size of the routing tables. Many ISPs have been reluctant to embrace IPv6, even if this did not slow down the evolution of BGP-4, which has become multiprotocol capable in order to support IPv6 and possibly other protocols.

10.4.1 A Larger Address Space Is a Two-edged Sword

The main advantage of IPv6, its larger addresses, is viewed with some suspicion by the practitioners of interdomain routing. They note that the growth of the routing table has only been controlled through harsh discipline imposed by the address registries, and that IPv6 has the potential of loosening that discipline. If addresses are plentiful, then it will be more difficult for the registries to invoke scarcity and to restrain users.

These fears are not necessarily well founded. The IETF has proceeded with great care to define a "provider-based" address structure for IPv6. The aggregatable structure allows for several levels of hierarchy, such as link, site, intermediate provider, and top-level provider. Only 13 bits have been allocated to the top level of the hierarchy, which should, in theory, limit the global routing tables to 8,192 entries, at least until someone decides to open up that field.

The real test, indeed, will only come from experience, to see whether the users can accept provider-based addressing. IPv6 contains much better support for this than IPv4. Automatic address configuration should make renumbering easy, especially if it is combined with automatic update of routing prefixes in routers. The support of multiple simultaneous addresses should release the need for multihoming, one of the main sources of entropy in the routing tables. In between, one can only prepare for the deployment of IPv6.

10.4.2 Extending BGP for IPv6

BGP-4, as defined in RFC-1771 [23], only supports the old IP protocol, IPv4. For this reason, the IETF initially thought to base IPv6 interdomain routing on IDRP [12], which was thought easier to extend to a multiprotocol environment. This initial project was however abandoned, mainly because there is much more experience available today with BGP than with IDRP. Transitioning to a new IP is hard enough without having to learn yet another routing protocol. The IETF eventually developed a "multiprotocol" version of BGP-4. This version, documented in RFC-2283 [24], will be able to support several protocols in addition to IPv4. It assumes that all BGP routers will be IPv4 capable, which will certainly be true at least during a transition phase. It also assumes that the decomposition in Autonomous Systems will be maintained irrespective of the protocol that is being used, i.e., that the AS number will not depend on whether the AS runs IPv4, IPv6, both, or even other protocols.

To develop multiprotocol capabilities, BGP-4 has to be extended. BGP-4 uses IPv4 addresses in three places:

☞ The network layer reachability information (NLRI) found in path announcements and route withdrawals is expressed as a set of IPv4 prefixes.

☞ The aggregator attribute contains an AS number and the IPv4 address of the aggregating router.

☞ The next-hop attribute contains the IPv4 address of the router that serves the path.

One may observe that in the aggregator attribute, the IPv4 address is used solely as an identifier. As long as BGP-4 routers are IPv4-capable and have unique IPv4 addresses, there is no need to change the syntax of that attribute. One may also observe that the next hop attribute is always used in conjunction with a list of reachable domains. In order to forward IPv6 packets, one needs to know the IPv6 address of the next hop, and the same will be true for any address family.

RFC-2283 extends BGP by defining two new path attributes: the Multiprotocol Reachable NLRI (MP_REACH_NLRI, code 14) and Multiprotocol Unreachable NLRI (MP_UNREACH_NLRI, code 15). The MP_REACH_NLRI attribute contains a list of one or many address family reachability data sets, each composed of an address family identifier followed by next-hop information and a list of prefixes. The MP_UNREACH_NLRI address family unreachability data sets, each composed of an address family identifier and a list of prefixes.

In each of these attributes, the address family is identified by a 16-bit address family, registered with the IANA, and by a one-octet "subsequent address family" qualifier. The following table lists the address family numbers that were defined by the IANA in July 1999. In addition to IPv4 and IPv6, the list includes several proprietary protocols that are often used in corporate networks, as well as several ITU-defined address plans.

Number	Address Family Description
0	Reserved
1	IP (IP version 4)
2	IP6 (IP version 6)
3	NSAP
4	HDLC (8-bit multidrop)
5	BBN 1822
6	802 (includes all 802 media plus Ethernet "canonical format")
7	E.163 (telephone numbers)
8	E.164 (SMDS, Frame Relay, ATM)
9	F.69 (Telex)
10	X.121 (X.25, Frame Relay)
11	IPX
12	Appletalk
13	Decnet IV
14	Banyan Vines
15	E.164 with NSAP format subaddress (UNI-3.1)
65535	Reserved

The subsequent address family code further qualifies the type of reachability information carried in the attribute, defining whether the addresses are used for unicast routing (code 1), for multicast forwarding (code 2), or for both (code 3).

Each prefix information is composed of a one-octet length field that provides the length of the prefix in bits, followed by the minimal number of octets necessary to encode the prefix.

The next-hop information is composed of the next-hop address, encoded as a one-octet length field followed by a variable length value, and of a variable number of "subnetwork point of attachment addresses" (SNPA). In pure Internet technology, one would have called these fields "subnetwork addresses." They are, for example, the Ethernet addresses of the next hop. The SNPA acronym is carried over from the OSI terminology used in IDRP. The presence of these subnetwork addresses is optional. In IPv6, these addresses can be obtained through the next-hop discovery protocol.

Using the BGP-4 multiprotocol extension to carry IPv6 extension is fairly straightforward. The only problem that was debated was whether the next-hop information should carry a global address or a local scope address. Global addresses can be used in all conditions but are subject to renumbering, while local addresses can only be used within one link (link local) or within a site (site local) but will not be affected by renumbering. For some time, the working group debated the use of site local addresses for the internal BGP connections. The idea was not adopted, because there is no clear relation between a "site" and an autonomous system. What was adopted was a possibility to encode either a global address or the combination of a global address and a link local address in the next-hop information, so that routers that happen to be on the same link can use the link local address and not be affected by renumbering operations. The use of BGP-4 for IPv6 is detailed in RFC-2545 [25].

10.5 Waiting for the New IP

Despite spectacular incidents, the interdomain routing architecture has been able to cope with the growth of the Internet. The whole process relies heavily on manual configuration of routing parameters in "BGP configuration tables," which requires very skilled operators. As the Internet continues to grow, as we transition toward a multiprotocol environment, BGP probably will continue to evolve and new parameters will be defined. It will certainly be many years before we see a complete transition to IPv6, and many more years before a new routing technology appears.

References

1. C. Labovitz, G. R. Malan, and F. Jahanian, "Internet Routing Instability," Proceedings of ACM/SIGCOMM 1997, *Computer Communication Review*, Vol. 27, No. 4, October 1997.

2. V. Paxson, "End to End Routing Behavior in the Internet," Proceedings of ACM/SIGCOMM 1996, *Computer Communication Review*, October 1996.

3. C. Labovitz, A. Ahuja, and F. Jahanian, "Experimental Study of Internet Stability and Wide-Area Backbone Failures," *Proceedings of IEEE/INFOCOM '99*, March 1999.

4. C. Villamizar, R. Chandra, and R. Govindan, "BGP Route Flap Damping," RFC-2439, November 1998.

5. Y. Rekhter and T. Li, "A Border Gateway Protocol 4 (BGP-4)," RFC-1771, March 1995.

6. Listing of Internet Routing Registries, http://www.merit.edu/list-of-routing-registries.html

7. T. Bates, E. Gerich, L. Joncheray, J-M. Jouanigot, D. Karrenberg, M. Terpstra, and J. Yu, "Representation of IP Routing Policies in a Routing Registry," RIPE report RIPE-181, October 1994. Also, RFC-1786, March 1995.

8. D. Eastlake, "Domain Name System Security Extensions," RFC-2535, March 1999.

9. S. Murphy, "BGP Security Analysis," work in progress, June 1999.

10. P. Traina, "Autonomous System Confederations for BGP," RFC-1965, June 1996.

11. T. Bates and R. Chandra, "BGP Route Reflection: An Alternative to Full Mesh IBGP," RFC-1966, June 1996.

12. C. Kunzinger, Editor, "Inter-Domain Routing Protocol," ISO/IEC 10747, October 1993.

13. R. Chandra and P. Traina, "BGP Communities Attribute," RFC-1997, August 1996.

14. E. Chen and T. Bates, "An Application of the BGP Community Attribute in Multi-Home Routing," RFC-1998, August 1996.

15. V. Fuller, T. Li, J. I. Yu, and K. Varadhan, "Supernetting: An Address Assignment and Aggregation Strategy," RFC-1338, June 1992.

16. V. Fuller, T. Li, J. I. Yu, and K. Varadhan, "Classless Inter-Domain Routing (CIDR): An Address Assignment and Aggregation Strategy," RFC-1519, September 1993.

17. E. Gerich, "Guidelines for Management of IP Address Space," RFC-1466, May 1993.

18. Y. Rekhter and T. Li, "An Architecture for IP Address Allocation with CIDR," RFC-1518, September 1993.

19. H. Berkowitz, P. Ferguson, W. Leland, and P. Nesser, "Enterprise Renumbering: Experience and Information Solicitation," RFC-1916, February 1996.

20. Y. Rekhter, B. Moskowitz, D. Karrenberg, and G. de Groot, "Address Allocation for Private Internets," RFC-1597, March 1994.

21. E. Lear, E. Fair, D. Crocker, and T. Kessler, "Network 10 Considered Harmful (Some Practices Shouldn't Be Codified)," RFC-1627, June 1994.

22. Y. Rekhter, B. Moskowitz, D. Karrenberg, G. de Groot, and E. Lear, "Address Allocation for Private Internets," RFC-1918, February 1996.

23. Y. Rekhter and T. Li, "A Border Gateway Protocol 4 (BGP-4)," RFC-1771, March 1995.

24. T. Bates and R. Chandra, "Multiprotocol Extensions for BGP-4," RFC-2283, February 1998.

25. P. Marques and F. Dupont, "Use of BGP-4 Multiprotocol Extensions for IPv6 Inter-Domain Routing," RFC-2545, March 1999.

Policy Routing

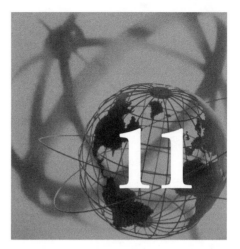

$\mathbf{I}$n its broadest sense, policy routing refers to any form of routing that is influenced by factors other than merely picking the shortest path. The most common reason to do policy routing is to accommodate "acceptable-use policies" and to select providers. But other reasons may exist, such as finding a path that provides a particular quality of service.

11.1 The Objectives of Policy Routing

The requirement for policy routing really appeared with the "commercialization" of the Internet. Users of the early Internet did not care much about the route that was used for carrying their packets. The network was perceived as "free," a "public good" that should simply be shared evenly. But commercial users could not benefit from public subsidies and thus could not use the "default" route through the "academic" backbones. They had to alter the shortest path to take into account a policy requirement, or, in other words, route the packets through a network that accepted commercial traffic. This could take some truly amazing forms, such as when two users could send some of their traffic, such as the coordination of an experiment, over the academic network, but when the same users had to send another conversation, such as a discussion about a commercial contract, over an "AUP-free" network.

The requirement for policies then became more and more sophisticated. Merely finding one acceptable route is not enough when you are charged for your traffic. You may want to switch to another provider between 1:00 P.M. and 3:00 P.M. to benefit from better rates. Or you may want to specify entirely the list of providers that is used for a given connection so that it meets throughput or delay requirements.

Policy routing, in fact, goes beyond the strict notion of *acceptable use*. The term has come to encompass both contractual notions, such as the choice of providers, and quality of service considerations, such as finding a path that would be adequate for a high-bandwidth videoconference. It turns out that quality of service and policy compatibility can all be expressed as a set of desired path attributes. Policy routing will search for a path that meets all requested attributes.

11.2 Provider Selection

The first form of policy routing is the selection of an appropriate provider. We have seen in chapter 9 that BGP allows managers to "weight" their different providers, so that the one with the lowest tariffs or best services is generally preferred. But BGP can perform a selection only between the routes that are presented by the directly connected providers. There are many cases where the user is connected through a regional network that is itself connected to multiple providers. We will see that one cannot rely only on BGP in those situations, that one has to use "tunnelling" to establish a "virtual link" toward the selected provider. Then, we will see that the tunnelling approach can be generalized and allows for the setup of arbitrary "source-initiated routes" between autonomous systems. We will present the current state of the "Source Demand Routing Protocol," which is being developed by an IETF working group.

11.2.1 The Regional Network Problem

The development of regional networks can be traced back to a policy decision by the NSF to provide a backbone service only for academic users. Universities could not connect directly to the backbone; they had to group themselves into regional associations so that the NSFnet had to deal with only one regional partner, the regional network.

Some regional networks were truly commercial, but many were organized according to a local version of the "information highway" paradigm. The regional authorities would subsidize an infrastructure in an effort to foster the local economy through electronic communication. This is certainly not an irrational idea—better communication with local universities and local research centers would certainly help regional industries to develop new products, educate their workforce, and create jobs and wealth. One can indeed debate whether the creation of a local monopoly is the correct model for developing any new technology; free-market economists would observe that competition should be the rule. In fact, many of the regional networks that started as not-for-profit associations are turning into strictly commercial enterprises; we began seeing the first takeover bids in June 1994.

But subsidized regional networks have an interesting problem. They generally operate under a very simple charter drafted by regional authorities, mentioning that all regional organizations can connect. It doesn't matter whether they are commercial or educational, for profit or not for profit; the regional network should let everybody connect. But this simple charter cannot be transitively passed to the transit providers. The academic backbone network accepts only traffic related to education and research; the commercial transits accept only traffic from their subscribers. Moreover, the "public" regional networks generally have to guarantee that they do not privilege one particular transit provider over the other. A subsidized local monopoly should not interfere with the free market. Now, let's consider a test case.

Provider selection: the desired picture

The regional network R0 has a de facto monopoly in the region. Its three subscribers, user1, user2, and user3, use R0 to communicate among themselves but buy their "long-haul" services from three different transit providers, Tr.1, Tr.2, Tr.3. We will make the hypothesis that all three users exchange data with the same destination D. This really implies that there are three routes between D and R0. As IP routing considers only the destination address, BGP can provide only a very partial solution to this problem.

The only possible action BGP can take is to "filter" destinations. It is easy for each of the transit networks to announce to D only the customers that they agree to serve. R0 announces to each of Tr.1, Tr.2, and Tr.3 that the destinations user1, user2, and user3 are reachable through an AS path composed of R0 alone, but Tr.1 will announce to D that user1 is reachable through the AS path Tr.1, R0. Tr.2 and Tr.3 can take similar actions. However, R0 has to pick exactly one route toward D, which results in an asymmetrical situation.

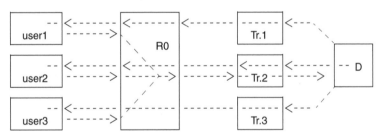

Provider selection: what BGP can achieve

The traffic from D to user1 flows through the provider Tr.1, which user1 selected, but the traffic in the reverse direction flows through Tr.2, the default transit picked by the regional network. There may be cases where this is just fine, e.g., if the quality of service of Tr.2 is sufficient. However, it is contradictory to the golden rule: user1 should really use only the resources that it paid for—those of provider Tr.1.

11.2.2 BGP in a Tunnel

One possible solution to the provider selection problem could be to install multiple routing tables within the regional network, so that the routes become a function of both the destination and addresses. This is, however, a major change in the routing protocols. Moreover, it is only a partial solution as users may in some case have agreements with more than one provider, such as for backup reasons. One will pretty soon have to use "artificial intelligence" techniques within the routing processes, which will not be a guarantee of high performance and simple management.

A simpler solution is to establish a "virtual link" between the user and the provider, tunnelling IP in IP [1]. Suppose that a station U1x within the domain user1 wants to send a TCP-IP packet toward Dx within the domain D:

IP header

This IP packet will naturally be forwarded to the border router of the AS user1, say U1br. If that border router simply forwards the packet to the border router of the regional network R0, the packet would eventually be routed through Tr.2. But U1br will instead "encapsulate" the packet by prepending a new IP header:

U1br $\rightarrow$ T1br, ip-ip	U1x $\rightarrow$ Dx, tcp	tcp header + data

IP header(1)   IP header(2)

This IP header is bound to the border router T1br, i.e., the border gateway between Tr.1 and R0. As the protocol type is set to IP in IP, T1br will decapsulate the packet and forward it through Tr.1 toward the final destination.

The encapsulation that we saw here amounts to creating a virtual link. That virtual link has essentially the same properties as any link between two routers—one can use it for routing, and one should also check that it is available. A good way to do this is simply to run BGP over the tunnel, e.g., between U1br and T1br. That way, one will check that the data will flow between the two routers and one will also exchange the path vector information, independently of the policies enforced by R0. This is almost equivalent to establishing a physical link between user1 and Tr.1, and one gets pretty much the "desired policy" that we expressed previously.

Provider selection: the "tunnelling" solution

There will however be some differences between this and an ideal solution. Encapsulation creates a sizable transmission overhead and requires more processing in the border routers than simple forwarding: the decapsulation program generally does not belong to the router's fast path. Encapsulation also creates some strange failure modes, such as when the normal path within R0 is replaced by a backup. Although the link is not entirely broken, it suddenly starts operating at a very reduced capacity. It is possible to get some protection against this problem by monitoring the AS path—the path that R0 announces to U1 for the destination Tr.1. If rerouting occurs, the AS path will mention several unexpected relays!

11.2.3 UNIFY, IDRP, and SDRP

The tunnelling technique we just discussed is in fact just a special case of policy routing, because it selects only one particular provider in the path. One may wish to constrain more points in the path or to select the whole path. There are two different reasons for doing so—"provider selection" and "quality of service selection."

The provider selection is merely a generalization of the tunnelling technique. Two system managers may decide to select the particular path that should be used for exchanging data between them, regardless of the decisions made by the intermediate domains. They will establish a source-initiated route between two border routers of their respective domains; the packets will then flow over that route, much in the same way that packets flew between two border routers in our tunnelling example.

The quality of service selection could be used in relation to "resource reservation." If an application needs special guarantees, it may place reservations at some places in the network where the congestion is most likely to occur. But it generally cannot predict that the packets will be routed along that path. It must in fact "pin" the route by explicitly specifying the path.

The "Source Demand Routing Protocol" (SDRP) is developed within the IETF to fulfill these demands. It is interesting to note that SDRP was initially conceived as a complement to the OSI's "Inter-Domain Routing Protocol" (IDRP), within the "UNIFY" architecture. IDRP is very similar to BGP, to the point that there was at one point a consensus within the IETF working groups not to develop a version 5 of BGP but, rather, simply to use IDRP. The architects of IDRP, BGP, and SDRP are in fact very often the same persons. IDRP includes several enhancements to BGP-4, such as the support of multiple-addressing families and variable address lengths or the organization of ASs into "confederations," which are used to aggregate the AS path information.

The idea of UNIFY, as presented by Deborah Estrin, Yakov Rekhter, and Steven Hotz [2], is to distinguish the "normal" routing from the "special" routing that is affected by policies. One may invest in the permanent computation of routes for the "normal" routing, using a combination of exterior protocols, such as BGP or IDRP, and interior protocols, such as OSPF. But it would be a waste of resources to do the same investment for special routes, which are used only in rare cases. The responsibility of computing special routes will thus be left to the originators. These routes will be expressed as a sequence of relays through the network. The forwarding of packets will be assured by the normal routing. The SDRP is used to express these special routes. SDRP is thus a complement to IDRP or BGP, enabling the implementation of arbitrary policies.

11.2.4 Source Demand Routing

The work on "Source Demand Routing" (SDR) [3] aims at defining a mechanism for route selection. The SDR packet comprises three parts:

Delivery Header (IP header)	SDRP header (route information)	SDRP payload (data packet)

The "forwarding header" is a normal IP header that specifies the next hop in the path. The SDRP payload carries the data that should be delivered to the end process. The SDRP header carries the route information.

—   The SDRP header   —

The most important parameter in this header is probably the "source route." The IP header specifies a destination IP address. When the destination receives the packet, the content is passed to the SDRP process, as indicated by the IP protocol type. The router will at this stage progress the source route; it replaces the IP destination field by the next element in the source-route specification, as indicated by the "next-hop pointer," increments that pointer, decrements the SDRP hop count, and forwards the packet. In fact, if the hop count is null, we detect an SDRP error; the packet is not forwarded, and an error message is generated instead.

Similarly, if the next-hop pointer was larger than or equal to the "source-route length," the packet should not be forwarded. It has reached the end of the source-initiated route. At this stage, one looks at the "payload type." If this is set to 1, the payload is a complete IP packet. We are using SDRP between two border routers in a way very similar to simple encapsulation. The inner packet is thus forwarded. Any other value indicates a protocol type. The IP-level protocol type is replaced by that value, and the packet is processed as if the SDRP header was absent.

We can observe, however, that the SDRP header is much more complex than a simple source-route parameter. This complexity comes from several causes, such as the need to provide for efficient error recovery, the parameterization of "loose" and "strict" routes, and a desire to support the setup of paths.

If an error occurs during the relaying of an SDRP packet, the router that detects the error will send back an ICMP report. This report carries the incoming IP header and the first 8 bytes of the content; it will be sent back to the source router that sent the initial packet. It is important, for precise error processing, to be able to retrieve precisely the route where the error occurred. This is why the fifth to eighth bytes of the SDRP header carry a "source-route identifier" that is set by the source router and uniquely identifies the source route for that router. In addition, the hop count contained in the second byte enables the router to understand where the route went wrong.

Because SDRP wants to provide interdomain routing facilities, including only router addresses in the source route may be too strict. We want to say that the packet should go through RENATER, then EBONE, then NSFnet, i.e., specifying the network that is traversed. But we don't necessarily want to say which of the relays between RENATER and EBONE should be used. It is probably a good idea to let the network's routers pick the best path at any given time. SDRP provides a special address format to achieve this result. If the IP address in the source route is of the form 128.0.x.y, then its last two bytes encode an AS number. The SDRP processes should not copy this address in the IP header. They should use the information provided by the BGP processes to retrieve the IP address of the nearest border router of the specified AS, and use that address.

There is, however, one pitfall in this form of domain routing. Suppose that a user specified a source route in terms of domains, e.g., A, B, C, and D in the following diagram:

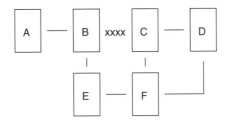

Suppose now that the link between B and C breaks. If the SDRP process in B blindly follows the source route, the packet will be routed toward a router in C by the alternate path through E and F. It will thus effectively be routed through A, B, E, F, C, and D, which is clearly suboptimal. For this reason, SDRP defines the concept of "loose" or "strict" source routing. The status of routing is indicated by the S bit in the first octet, which mandates strict routing if set to 1. In our case, if the strict bit had been set, the router in B would determine that C was no longer "adjacent" after the loss of the link. It would refuse to forward the packet and send instead an error report.

Two other flags, D and P, are used to differentiate data packets (D = 1) from control packets and to indicate that the source route is being "probed" (P = 1).

The working group is still studying some possible adjunctions to the SDR protocol, notably a setup procedure in which intermediate routers could "memorize" the source route, thus allowing the packets to carry a much shorter SDR header. The "source protocol type" will differentiate between packets that are explicitly source-route packets (SourceProtoType=1) and packets sent along a memorized route (SourceProtoType=2). The "probe" bit is set by the source router to test the possibility of a setup. If an intermediate router agrees to "set up" the route, it leaves the bit unchanged. If it disagrees, it resets the bit to 0. If all routers agree, the final destination notifies the initial source; the route is set.

Control packets are used mostly for reporting incidents and managing the source route. The information is carried in the "target router," "prefix," "prefix length," and "notification" fields. We have already seen some possible incidents, such as when a strict source route was refused because two domains were not adjacent. There are other incidents as well—for example, "policy violations." The encapsulation technique should be handled with care, as it allows users to bypass the routing and the controls. It is legitimate for intermediate relays to check that the source router is allowed to use their resources and to refuse to forward the packet if they feel that a local policy is being violated.

11.3 The IDPR Approach

At the same time that BGP was designed and deployed, another working group of the IETF worked on a very different approach to interdomain routing, called "Inter-Domain Policy Routing" (IDPR) [4, 5, 6]. This acronym should not be confused with IDRP, OSI's Inter-Domain Routing Protocol. The phonetic spelling of IDPR is generally "I-Dee-Pee-aaR", while IDRP and SDRP are spelled "I-Dreep" and "S-Dreep." Didn't I mention already that internauts like acronyms?

BGP uses a path vector technology, which one can understand as a natural evolution of the distance vector protocols. IDPR, on the contrary, follows the link state technology. It is a very complex protocol, even more complex than OSPF. We will not attempt to present all its details, as it is not used much in today's Internet, but we will concentrate on the main lines of its design: the maintenance of a "network map," the computation of policy routes from this map, and the setup of paths through the interconnection of ASs.

11.3.1 The AS-Level Map

It would be entirely unrealistic to represent the whole Internet in a single link state database. There are far too many links; we would not be able to complete a shortest-path computation in a decent interval. However, the Internet is composed of the interconnection of autonomous systems. These ASs provide natural aggregates for a "high-level" map, where the nodes would not be the routers but the ASs themselves would be, and where the only links that we will consider will be those linking the ASs.

In fact, even listing all ASs and all links between the ASs might result in too large a database. One may want to perform further aggregation. More precisely, one may want to consider only those ASs that perform "transit" services: the provider networks. If we do that, we are left with a relatively small set of domains, maybe a few hundred. There will be several tens of thousands of stub or multihomed ASs, but they will all be at the "periphery" of the network.

The map defined for IDPR considers two kinds of objects: "domains" and "virtual gateways." A domain is an AS. A virtual gateway is the set of "policy gateways" (i.e., border routers) that links two ASs. Combining several pairs of policy gateways in one single virtual gateway reduces the amount of information to be stored in the database and also increases the stability of the connections. The virtual gateway will remain up as long as a sufficient fraction of the policy gateways are up. However, there may be several virtual gateways between two domains. If, for example, domains have different interconnection points at different geographical locations, it is reasonable to preserve them as distinct virtual gateways.

A domain is identified by its AS number. A virtual gateway is identified by a pair of AS numbers and a "virtual gateway number." The two other objects that we need to identify are the policy gateways and the "route servers" (i.e., the systems that hold a copy of the database and can use it for computing routes). Both are identified by the combination of their AS number and a local identifier assigned by the domain's administrator.

The database holds "status" information about virtual gateways and "configuration" information about domains. The status information describes essentially whether a virtual gateway is up or down. The configuration information describes the domain's transit policy in terms of "restrictions," "quality," and "cost." The restrictions are lists of source and destination patterns that can use the domain. They can be completed by "temporal specifications" (definitions of the time interval during which the restriction applies) and by "user class specifications" defining the set of user classes to which the restriction applies. Restrictions can also be applied to virtual gateways—a particular set of sources may be authorized to transit through the domain without being capable of using a particular connection.

IDPR includes a flooding protocol, similar to that of OSPF, for distributing the database information to all database servers. However, the maintenance of the database is supposed to be much simpler than in the case of OSPF, because the "time to live" of the information is supposed to be much longer. The configuration information is expected to be fairly static; RFC-1479 suggests using a time to live of 530 hours—more than three weeks. The "dynamic" information is also quite stable, as it describes virtual gateways that can be redundant collections of policy gateways. The suggested value for the time to live is here 25 hours. This is much longer than OSPF's time to live, which is 1 hour.

Apart from the increased time to live, we have a couple of interesting differences between the OSPF and the IDPR approaches to database organization and update propagation. The OSPF routers are all under one single authority—the domain's manager. They can thus trust each other, and the security requirements boil down to fending off intruders by proper authentication procedures. IDPR routers, on the contrary, are located all over the Internet. It is essential that the information flooded into the database be properly authenticated. The flooding procedure involves timestamp and digital signatures to authenticate the information being flooded and to protect the infrastructure against resubmission of stale messages.

Yet another difference is the requirement for consistency. Within one OSPF area, it is essential that all routers maintain synchronized copies of the database. Any discrepancy is likely to result in incorrect route computations and maybe in loops. This goal is almost unachievable in a very large system that covers the whole Internet. We will see that IDPR uses "source-specified routing," similar to SDRP, which removes this need.

11.3.2 Shortest AS Paths

The IDPR routes are computed by route servers. The route servers may be colocated with the policy routers, but they can also be separate agents, such as workstations that simply listen to the flooding protocol and acquire a copy of the interdomain policy database.

IDPR routes are computed "on demand," as a function of a requested profile. A route request lists the source, the destination, and the requested "quality-of-service" and "monetary constraints." Suppose, for example, that the database describes the following map:

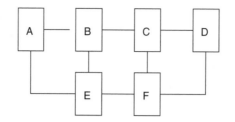

We want to set up a path between A and D that guarantees a certain quality of service, e.g., a throughput larger than 1 Mbps. The first thing we will do, from a conceptual point of view, is remove from the map all the ASs and all the virtual gateways that do not meet the constraint. For example, we may have to remove the domain E because the routing restrictions do not allow sending traffic to D through E. Then, we may also have to remove the virtual gateway between C and D because its throughput is lower than 1 Mbps. We will end up with a subset of the graph:

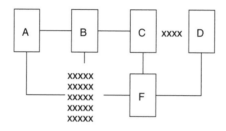

Given that subset, we will compute the policy route that meets the requirements: i.e., A, B, C, F, D. Note that one does not need to derive the subset of the database before starting the route computation. It is fairly easy to modify the shortest-path-first algorithm to take into account the policy constraint. Each time we add a link, or rather a virtual gateway, into the set of "links to be evaluated," we simply have to check that the link meets the policy requirements. Everything we said about the shortest-path-first algorithm remains valid. In particular, it is possible to find multiple possible routes that lead to the same destination.

We should note that the policy-route computation cannot, in fact, be entirely identical in all IDPR route servers in the Internet. The restrictions are not determined entirely by the transit network. We have to combine the "public restrictions," which are announced by the policy gateways and are flooded to all route servers, with the "local preferences," which are set by the local administrators and are generally kept secret. The local preferences will be expressed in terms of acceptable transit networks, requested services, or acceptable costs. They will definitely influence the computation of the routes.

Thus it is not necessary to enforce a strict alignment of the databases. In fact, if we consider that a route server serves only one specific domain, we can take advantage of the local preferences and the local knowledge to reduce the size of the database. There is no need to store information about a remote AS if that remote AS is never going to authorize the transit of the local users' packets.

The nonalignment of the databases precludes the usage of hop-by-hop routing techniques similar to those of BGP or OSPF. Within OSPF, each intermediate router performs a route computation based on its local copy of the database; since the databases are identical, all the computations yield consistent results and the hop-by-hop relaying works. As the IDPR routers no doubt benefit from identical databases, they must use source-specified routes similar to the ones of SDRP.

11.3.3 Forwarding Packets with IDPR

Within IDPR, the establishment of a policy route between a source and a destination follows three phases.

1. The source queries the local route server and obtains the description of one or several policy routes.
2. The source requests from the local "path agent" the setup of the corresponding path.
3. Once the path is established, a data packet can be forwarded.

In fact, the setup of the path is not necessarily done by the source itself. The source may be an ordinary host that is not aware that policy routing is taking place. The path agent would be a sort of "default policy router." Packets will be sent to that path agent using normal IP forwarding. The characteristics of the path will be derived from the source and destination addresses of the packets. The path will be established between the source's path agent and the destination's path agent. A single path may in some cases serve several sources and several destinations that belong to the same domains.

The path setup is the establishment of a virtual circuit. A path is identified by the concatenation of the AS number of the source, the identifier of the originator's policy gateway, and a 32-bit "local path identifier" specified by the originator. Within these 32 bits, 2 bits indicate the "direction." One can establish paths that allow transfer of data from the originator, to the originator, or in both directions; the policies of the intermediate networks may be such that only one direction of transmission will be authorized. The path-control messages can travel in both directions. They allow managers to set up, tear down, or repair a path.

The initial setup request progresses hop-by-hop from policy gateway to policy gateway. Each intermediate hop checks that the request is compatible with the domain's transit policy and may "refuse" the establishment if this is not the case. As the path is expressed in terms of virtual gateways, one must determine at each hop the actual destination among the set of policy gateways that constitute the virtual gateway. If they agree with the requested policy and if they can find a successor, the policy gateways must memorize the path identifier and the associated actions. The path will be established when the setup message reaches the target domain. At this point, an "acceptation" message will travel back to the source, signalling that the path is now available. The data packets that flow on this path will be encapsulated within a path header containing the path identifier. They will be relayed among the path, from policy gateway to policy gateway, until they reach the destination.

When the path is established, the list of virtual gateways is transformed into one specific list of policy gateways. It may happen that some of these policy gateways become unavailable or unreachable. The "repair" procedure attempts to reestablish the path by choosing another policy gateway within the same virtual gateway. If it fails, or if the path is no longer needed, the path will be torn down.

The route servers may respond with multiple routes that lead to the destination. This is the equivalent to OSPF's "equal-cost multipath." Path agents may decide to establish several paths and spread the traffic over these paths for better performance or better reliability. However, this possibility is merely mentioned in the IDPR documentation; there is no evidence that it has been implemented or tested.

11.3.4 Experience with IDPR

Among the procedures that we have presented in this chapter, only the simple "provider selection by tunnelling" is used today, and that usage is still extremely limited. Neither SDRP nor IDPR is used outside experimental circles. The SDR working group, in fact, is still working on the finalization of SDRP and of the associated policy description language. IDPR became, in July 1993, a "proposed standard" for the Internet, but there has not been any large-scale deployment, let alone usage. The extreme complexity of the IDPR protocol is probably sufficient to explain this slow deployment. We can say that is more complex than the sum of OSPF and BGP. The demand for policy routing is not so pressing that networks will all of a sudden decide to make such an investment.

One can also observe that the virtual-circuit nature of the IDRP paths is largely a departure from the standard IP architecture and from what the end-to-end principle suggests about "states in the network." The justification for this path setup procedure is the large overhead that would result from explicitly sending the complete path information in every packet; this is, in fact, a very debatable point if we consider the amount of signalling that is necessary for setting up, tearing down, or repairing paths.

There is, however, one very interesting aspect in the IDPR architecture, i.e., the split of function between the route server and the actual packet forwarding. All the traditional routing architectures assume that the routes are computed in real time by the routing agents themselves. This ties the routing function to the forwarding routers. There is no particular reason to colocate the route servers and the border routers; the only gain would be a reduced overhead of the flooding protocol, but that is not a large overhead in any case. Having separate route servers allows the use of dedicated computers for this service. It is both scalable, as one can add an arbitrary number of such computers, and flexible, as one can very easily change the computation algorithm or the local preferences. In fact, we may observe that this separation is quite old, as it was already possible with EGP to decouple the "EGP entity" and the actual forwarding routers; however, EGP was not attempting to memorize a full network map.

11.4 Multi-Protocol Label Switching

In 1996, an Internet start-up company called Ipsilon introduced a new technology, IP switching [7,8,9,10]. The key idea of the technology was to build cheaper, faster IP routers by harnessing the switching power of the ATM technology. Indeed, in this industry, cheaper and faster really means cheaper and faster than the competition, and the competition indeed woke up with its own answers, such as cisco's "tag switching" proposal [11]. These propositions were the starting point for what is now known as Multi-Protocol Label Switching (MPLS).

The basic premise of MPLS is that packets will be routed based on a short label, similar to an ATM virtual circuit identifier. This was supposed to have two advantages:

☞ Because labels are shorter than IP addresses, the packets could be forwarded at a faster rate.
☞ Because labels are independent from IP addresses, the packet could follow a different route than the default shortest path computed by IP routing, thus allowing for policy decisions.

We will present the MPLS development and review the MPLS claims in the next section.

11.4.1 Label Switching

Label switching is characterized by the possibility to execute routing decisions based on the compact information contained in a short binary label. In many respects, this is similar to the forwarding process of classic virtual circuit switched networks such as X.25, ATM, or frame relay. Label Switching Routers (LSR) will maintain label switching tables that associate an incoming label to a routing action, typically the forwarding on an interface with a different label value. Suppose, for example, that in our five node test network, we set up two Label Switched Paths from A to C and A to E, both through B:

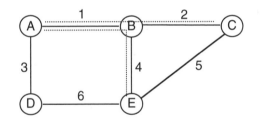

A will attach to the packets a label that determines their routing, such as 100 for the packets bound to C and 101 for the packets bound to E. B will have to maintain the knowledge in its routing table that packets received with label 100 on link 1 should be forwarded with label 107 on link 2, and that packets received with label 101 should be forwarded with label 109 on link 4. C, in turn, will have to remember that packets received with label 107 on link 2 have reached their final destination.

MPLS, however, is more than just another virtual circuit switching procedure. After all, if that was all that was needed, we could have used frame relay or ATM. The main characteristic of MPLS is that it is integrated with IP routing and also has provisions for interdomain routing. In our example, we have defined two virtual circuits, but we are supposed to operate a network where all destinations are reachable. MPLS has a provision for that. The specification reserves the label value 0 to indicate a packet that carries an IP packet and should be routed according to the IP destination address. It also reserves the value 2 for IPv6.

In the IP architecture, the routing is organized according to several levels of hierarchy. Autonomous systems are interconnected through border routers and may be split into several routing areas. Suppose that we want to establish a virtual circuit that crosses several independent domains. One obvious possibility would be to establish a path that crosses all of these domains. Each router would forward the packet with the label expected by its immediate neighbor. Most Internet paths cross 10 to 20 routers, so this means that we will have to establish a chain of 10 to 20 labels. Such a chain would probably be very fragile: it would be broken if any of the 10 to 20 intermediate paths gets broken. This is much more fragile than classical IP, where local routing procedures would immediately repair the routing tables. To obtain a reliability comparable to that of IP, MPLS proposes to use not one single label but, rather, a stack of labels, each in its own "plane." Suppose, for example, that we have to establish a 6-hop path through two domains, A and B. The forwarding will proceed as indicated in the following table:

Router	Action	Label 1	Label 2
A.1	Sends packet to A.2.	101	35
A.2	Examines Label 1, sends to A.3.	112	35
A.3	Examines and removes label 1. Examines label 2, sends to B.1.		77
B.1	Examines label. Updates, inserts label 1, sends to B.2.	93	201
B.2	Examines label 1, relays to B.3.	37	201
B.3	Receives packet.	—	—

Suppose now that the link between A.2 and A.3 is lost. The virtual circuit will be rerouted locally, to replace the intermediate router A.2 by A.4. The new forwarding will be:

Router	Action	Label 1	Label 2
A.1	*Sends packet to A.2.*	*99*	35
A.4	*Examines Label 1, sends to A.3.*	*113*	35
A.3	Examines and removes label 1. Examines label 2, sends to B.1.		77
B.1	Examines label. Updates, inserts label 1, sends to B.2.	93	201
B.2	Examines label 1, relays to B.3.	37	201
B.3	Receives packet.	—	—

The MPLS working group is still working on the details of the protocol, but the standard label format will probably follow the structure below:

Label (20 bits)	Exp (3 bits)	S	TTL (8 bits)

According to this format, the label is encoded on 20 bits. The S bit indicates whether the label is the last one in the stack. The TTL is used, as in IP, to detect possible loops and to remove packets that have exceeded their time to live. Three bits have been reserved for experimental purposes, possibly to implement preference levels compatible with the differentiated services that we will present in chapter 14.

11.4.2 Proposed Usage of MPLS

The initial rationale for label switching was performance, the possibility of developing fast routers. It is obviously simpler to check a label against a flat table detailing a small number of paths than it is to compare an IP address against a complete routing table. From there, intuitive reasoning would deduce that MPLS routers would be faster and less expensive than classical IP routers. The intuitive reasoning, however, is probably wrong. The current generation of "backbone" IP routers can route millions of packets per second. They support speeds up to 2.5 Gbps (OC48) without using label switching. In fact, researchers have argued that IP routing could be performed easily at even higher speeds [12]. This was not obvious in 1996, when Ipsilon introduced IP switching, but it became clear once routers started to integrate dedicated routing components and processors. In this environment, the complexity of the table look-up operation matters less than the location of the table. If the table is located "on board," it can be accessed at the very high speed of the component's internal clock. The look-up is slowed down only if the table has to be accessed from external memory. One could think that tables of labels would be shorter, and thus that MPLS would have a performance advantage, but research in table architecture has shown that even the complete backbone routing tables can be arranged to fit in the cache of a Pentium processor, let alone a special purpose component [13]. The growth of the routing table appears to be linear in time, while the capacity of components is expected to double every 18 months, following Moore's law. There is thus every reason to believe that label switching will not have any significant performance advantage over classical IP routing.

As the performance argument faded, the proponents of label switching have put forward three possible applications for MPLS:

☞ to implement policy-based routing,
☞ to enable traffic engineering, and
☞ to isolate interior routing from the vagaries of interdomain routing.

Implementing policy-based routing with MPLS would follow the same algorithms that were developed for IDPR, replacing IDPR's virtual gateways with label switching routers. The link state data base of protocols such as OSPF or IS-IS can be used to compute paths that meet a specified policy requirement. As in IDPR, one would only consider the links that meet the specified requirements, and would then compute the shortest path that would use only these paths. The computation would provide a list of routers that the path should traverse. This explicit path would then be passed to the label path setup protocol. OSPF or IS-IS can indeed not be used at the interdomain level, where one would probably have to rely on an IDPR-like database of AS capabilities. This, however, is still very much a research topic.

Traffic engineering, in circuit-switched networks, is traditionally done by identifying traffic flows between specific sources and destinations, by obtaining statistics on the volume of each of these flows, and then by arranging these flows on a set of network paths that maximize network utilization. One can indeed obtain statistics in an IP network as well, but traditional IP forwarding does not lend itself well to traffic engineering, because the path depends solely from the destination address, not from the combination of the source and destination. With MPLS, one can apply the traditional traffic engineering technique to compute and set up label switched paths, and one can then assign traffic to these paths based on the combination of destination address, source address, and possibly other information such as port numbers. The packets will be spread under the various paths according to the specified patterns, leading to better network utilization.

We have seen in the previous chapter that route flapping was one of the major problems posed by interdomain routing. Route flapping translates into modifications of the interior routing protocols and can easily overload all the routers in a network. It is possible to use MPLS to isolate the interior and exterior routing protocols. A domain manager could, for example, establish a full mesh of label switched paths between all the domain's border routers. Transit traffic would be routed on these paths. The routing decisions of the border routers will determine which path gets used for what set of addresses, without having to interfere with the interior routing. The label switched paths will only have to be rearranged if the interior conditions change.

11.4.3 Establishing MPLS Paths

One could in theory use a variety of ways to establish the label switched paths. It would for example be conceivable to let a network configuration center compute all the paths, with the exception of the default labels for IPv4 and IPv6 routing that would be preconfigured in each router. The configuration center could then use a management protocol such as SNMP to program the labels in each of the network's routers.

In practice, it seems more reasonable to use a dynamic protocol, just like it seems more reasonable to use a dynamic protocol for IP routing. Two approaches have been explored by the IETF. The first approach is to extend the resource reservation protocol, RSVP, in order to set up the paths and simultaneously reserve the path's resource. (We will present RSVP in chapter 14.) The second approach is to design a completely autonomous Label Distribution Protocol (LDP). The design of LDP has to satisfy multiple constraints:

☞ The protocol should be autonomous, which implies that it should enable autoconfiguration and neighbor discovery.
☞ The protocol should be robust, it should handle topology changes and not cause loops.
☞ It should be possible to set up the path according to a broad range of criteria.

LDP is still a work in progress, but we can already see its broad lines. The protocol contains a discovery procedure through multicasting Hello messages, followed by adjacency control procedures to establish, keep alive, and eventually tear down relations between routers. The path establishment procedures will include a loop detection algorithm, based on a path vector attribute that will carry the list of routers in the path.

Paths that are affected by a link failure will be withdrawn. One could imagine, as in all circuit switching networks, a correction procedure that would reconstruct the fractions of the paths that were torn down, but it is probably simpler to just restart their initialization from the path's source.

There is an obvious tension in the route set-up procedure between the various ways MPLS could be used. On one hand, one could imagine that a configuration manager has entirely determined the list of routers on the path, and simply requests the establishment of the corresponding labels. At the other extreme, one could imagine that the path initiator simply asks to set up a path toward a specified destination, expecting that label switching routers would set up a path that follows the IP routing tables. One could also specify the destination and a set of quality of service criteria, and to let label switching routers discover and set up a path that meets the criteria. In fact, LDP lists a catalogue of possible routing criteria, such as:

☞ IPv4 address,

☞ BGP next hop,

☞ OSPF router ID,

☞ OSPF border area router,

☞ Explicit path, expressed as a list of router addresses,

☞ Aggregate group, expressed as a list of prefixes,

☞ Specific flow, expressed as a combination of source, destination, and other header parameters such as ports,

☞ Multicast group, or combination of source address and multicast groups, for multicast routing.

The design of LDP is debated quite intensely in the IETF. The current documents are all drafts. A final version will certainly be published some time after the release of this book.

11.5 The Future of Policy Routing

The past attempts at policy routing have not been successful. MPLS could perhaps succeed where IDPR and SDRP failed, but success is by no means guaranteed. Out of the problems that MPLS addresses, many can be solved by other means. We already mentioned that any performance advantage of MPLS over classical IP routing has essentially vanished. Of the three remaining advantages, the isolation of interior routing and interdomain forwarding is somewhat fuzzy. Its value could be reduced by techniques such as BGP route flap damping. Then, the traffic engineering advantage could disappear if techniques such as Optimized Multi-Path can be successfully developed. If OMP automatically maintains network utilization toward an optimal point, there will not be much interest in technologies based on statistics and manual configuration. Finally, policy routing itself is quite debatable.

Policy-routed paths are typically set on demand. The path is chosen as a function of the network conditions that prevail at the time of the demand. Yet, if the path is maintained for a long time, these conditions are bound to change, and the path will soon cease to be optimal. We will see an hysteresis effect, where old paths keep using tortuous routing and may degrade the overall network performance. This effect disappears if each path only uses a tiny fraction of the network resource, and if paths are set up and torn down frequently. But then, one could wonder whether any special routing was needed for these tiny paths. It is entirely possible that a better network usage will be found through a combination of OMP and the resource reservation techniques that we will present in chapter 14.

Finally, we may observe that policy routed paths may be easy to set up within a single network, but that any set up in an interdomain configuration will encounter the mix of business and technical difficulties that doomed IDPR.

References

1. Y. Rekhter, "Selecting an Indirect Provider," work in progress, April 1994.

2. Y. Rekhter, D. Estrin, and S. Hotz, "Scalable Inter-Domain Routing Architecture," Proceedings of ACM SIG-COMM '92 Conference, *ACM Computer Communication Review,* October 1992.

3. Deborah Estrin, Daniel Zappala, Tony Li, and Yakov Rekhter, "Source Demand Routing: Packet Format and Forwarding Specification," work in progress, September 1993.

4. M. Steenstrup, "IDPR as a Proposed Standard," RFC-1477, July 26, 1993.

5. M. Lepp and M. Steenstrup, "An Architecture for Inter-Domain Policy Routing," RFC-1478, July 26, 1993.

6. M. Steenstrup, "Inter-Domain Policy Routing Protocol Specification: Version 1," RFC-1479, July 26, 1993.

7. P. Newman, G. Minshall, T. Lyon, and L. Huston, "IP Switching and Gigabit Routers," *IEEE Communications Magazine*, Vol. 35, January 1997.

8. P. Newman et al., "Ipsilon's General Switch Management Protocol Specification Version 1.1," RFC-1987, August 1996.

9. P. Newman et al., "Ipsilon Flow Management Protocol Specification for IPv4," RFC-1953, May 1996.

10. P. Newman et al., "Transmission of Flow Labelled IPv4 on ATM Data Links," RFC-1954, May 1996.

11. Y. Rekhter, B. Davie, D. Katz, E. Rosen, and G. Swallow, "Cisco Systems' Tag Switching Architecture Overview," RFC-2105, February 1997.

12. C. Partridge et al., "A 50-gb/s IP Router," *IEEE/ACM Transactions on Networking*, Vol. 6, pp. 237–248, June 1998.

13. M. Degermark, A. Brodnik, S. Carlsson, and S. Pink, "Small Forwarding Tables for Fast Routing Lookups," *ACM Computer Communication Review*, Vol. 27, pp. 3–15, October 1997. ACM SIGCOMM '97, September 1997.

Part IV
New Developments

IP Multicast Routing[1]

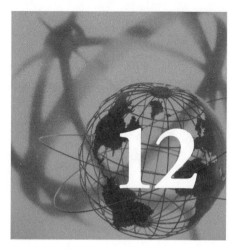

$\mathbf{T}$oday, most Internet applications are so-called *unicast* because they use a point-to-point transmission infrastructure. The usage of point-to-multipoint transmission was limited to local network applications due to the natural broadcast capabilities of LANs. But during the past few years, we have observed the emergence of new applications that use *multicast* transmission to enable efficient communication among a group of hosts (instead of two hosts). These applications require "multicast routing"—sending an IP packet to a "group" address so that it reaches all the members of the group, which may be scattered throughout the Internet.

In this chapter, we present the usage of IP multicast by applications, as well as the requirements of ISPs and their customers that motivate its deployment. Then, we review the various multicast routing algorithms and protocols that are used in the Internet and their characteristics. We also present the emerging standards for multicast routing over the Internet. Next, we describe experiences deploying multicast, including the MBONE—the experimental "multicast backbone" that has been deployed over the Internet to test new multimedia applications using multicast technology. Finally, we discuss the future of commercially deployed multicast, what issues have stalled its progress, and the provision of Internet-wide multicast connectivity.

12.1 Benefits of Multicast

The deployment of IP multicast is driven by a number of important Internet applications and services that require point-to-multipoint delivery. These applications and services cannot scale to thousands or millions of receivers with multiple point-to-point, unicast streams. In this section, we present examples of some important properties of multicast routing that enable or improve applications' performance. Multicast facilitates resource discovery and minimizes the network

---

1. This chapter was written in collaboration with Christophe Diot and Brian Levine.

load of file transfer, multimedia streaming applications, and distributed conferences. Finally multicast enables large-scale gaming sessions on the Internet.

It is therefore important to understand that multicast is a service that is most beneficial to users that source information (e.g., content providers) and to ISPs and carriers. Multicast reduces the time it takes to send data to a large set of receivers and reduces the network capacity required to deliver information to a group of receivers. For carriers and ISPs, multicast represents an opportunity to reduce network load and end-to-end delay. For receivers, it is unimportant whether data is delivered via unicast or multicast services.

12.1.1 Multicast and Resource Discovery

The first usage of multicast in local area networks was probably for "resource discovery" using the broadcast capabilities of this kind of network. We have seen examples of such usage in the presentation of RIP and OSPF. If an OSPF router wants to find out which other OSPF routers are present on a local area network, it simply broadcasts a hello packet to the conventional "all OSPF routers" address. That address is fixed. It has been assigned by the IANA; it is known in advance and is encoded in the OSPF program. On a network with no broadcast capabilities, the alternative would be to send the hello packet to each neighbor separately, requiring routers to be configured with a list of neighbors' addresses. Broadcasting allows the router to discover this list with a single transmission and lessens the burdens of the administrator.

The use of the "all RIP routers" address by RIP-2 is similar. But the usefulness of multicast is not limited to routing protocols. Take the case of the "bootstrap" protocol (BOOTP), which is used to load stations with an initial value of the system parameters. By definition, the station that runs this protocol is "bare." It may even be delivered and operated right out of the box! By sending a multicast packet to the conventional "all bootstrap servers" address, the station can automatically discover the local server. In fact, if there are several servers on the local cable, it will receive responses from all of them. But that is not very important; picking any of them is good enough. Automatic configuration will occur, without requiring the intervention of a system manager.

In all these examples, the "OSPF hello," "RIP responses," or "bootstrap requests" are simply broadcast on the local network. To extend such resource discovery capability to network interconnection, the introduction of multicast routing is needed. Consider the example of a station willing to discover the local domain-name server on a network made of various Ethernets interconnected by routers. There is typically less than one server per cable. Simply sending a packet to "all name servers on the cable" would not be very productive. To actually reach the servers, the packets have to be relayed by routers and multicast by these routers on remote cables.

There is some danger in the relaying of multicast packets. If there are several routers on the cable and if special care is not taken, they will all relay the packets again and again. In this way, it is easy to create not only a multicast loop but a multicast avalanche, bringing the whole network to a stop as it is quickly filled to capacity. The whole purpose of multicast routing is precisely to achieve delivery of multicast packets in a "careful" way, without loops and without excess transmissions.

But let's come back to the DNS example. Sending to a conventional address like "all name servers on the network" would probably achieve the desired result, but it will unnecessarily involve all of the organization's name servers while, in fact, what we are looking for is "the nearest name server." A very popular algorithm is to execute an "expanding-ring search," which is a sequence of "scope-limited" broadcasts, using the "time to live" (TTL) field of the IP header as a scope-limiting parameter.

1. Set d = 1.
2. Send a packet to the group address, with TTL = d.
3. Wait for a delay T. If a response arrives, select the server, exit.
4. If no response arrives, increment d, T. If d is larger than the "network diameter," we have failed. Else, repeat step 2.

The TTL is decremented at each relay, and a packet with a null TTL is not forwarded any further. In fact, in the case of point-to-point transmission, the router that realizes that the TTL is now null is supposed to send back an ICMP message (TTL expired). The IP multicast specification introduces an exception to this rule. A multicast packet whose TTL has expired is simply dropped; no ICMP (or IGMP) packet is sent.

12.1.2 Transmitting Files

Let's consider again the example network we used for explaining RIP and OSPF. Suppose that we want to send a copy of a file from node C to nodes A, B, D, and E:

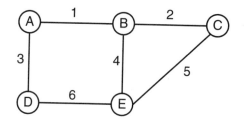

We can achieve this either by a set of four point-to-point file transfers or by multicasting the file to all nodes at the same time. Using point-to-point transfers may appear simpler, as one will be using well-tuned and well-understood software, such as "ftp." But let's now analyze the number of times the file travels on each of the network links. Multicast is clearly more efficient, because any given link is used only once. This efficiency increases with the size of the network and also with the number of recipients; the 50% advantage shown in our small example is probably an underestimate.

		Using point-to-point (unicast)					Using multicast
	For	A	B	E	D	Total	
Link	1	1				1	1
	2	1	1			2	1
	5			1	1	2	1
	6				1	1	1
		2	1	1	2	6	4

Multicast file transfer is not standard software today, unlike TCP-based software. The fundamental challenge in providing reliable multicasting is managing the feedback from receivers as they request retransmissions of lost data and acknowledge data that are received correctly. In our example, nodes A, B, D, and E will all send messages to C when they detect part of the file was lost in transit. These lost parts must be resent by C. As we add more receivers for C, the number of messages sent to C when data is lost in the network will increase as well. The type of service is called "reliable multicast." Numerous protocols have been developed to manage reliable multicast data transfer. Some of these reliable multicast protocols are soon to become IETF standards.

One should not think that multicasting files and data reliably is a marginal application—distribution of weather maps or lost credit card numbers immediately come to mind as real-life examples. Multicast file transfer services can also support efficient web caching, distributed databases, and remote logging.

Related to file transfer are "push applications," which allow individual users to select automatic delivery of information from a variety of content bundles, called "channels." This information is then automatically spooled and pushed to users at regular intervals. PointCast is an example of an existing push application. This application is always downloading information, even if the user is otherwise occupied and not actively reading the information. Because of this, the impact of unicast bandwidth demand for PointCast and others like it has been substantial and troublesome for corporate networks. Companies that provide push technology are looking for ways (like multicast delivery) to conserve bandwidth to keep corporations from banning these applications entirely.

12.1.3 Conferencing

The first diffusion of the "soundtrack" of a conference over the Internet occurred during the spring 1992 IETF conference in San Diego. The first diffusion of a video signal took place during the next IETF conference, in Boston. Since then the technology has matured, and several videoconferencing applications have been made available to the Internet. "Netcasting" is now an expected feature of the IETF meetings that enables hundreds of participants worldwide to follow the debates and ask questions through the Internet. The IETF is certainly not the sole user of this technology. Various universities and research centers have multicast their conferences, seminars, and workshops. Tele-teaching is another very popular conferencing application on the Internet, and many universities worldwide use this application.

These multimedia transmissions take advantage of the high processing capabilities of modern workstations, which include dedicated hardware. The audio and video signals are digitized and compressed by the source station, which sends them as a sequence of UDP packets to a "group address"—an IP address that identifies the conference session. Listening stations "tune in" by asking to receive packets sent to that group. They generally decode the audio on the workstation's sound interface and display the video in a "window" on the workstation's screen.

In fact, the IETF netcasting is a very asymmetric application. The conference speakers are listened to and their slides are viewed by a large number of recipients who will merely ask some questions at the end of the talk. But the technology can also be used for smaller "electronic meetings," in which participants see and hear each other and generally share an electronic "whiteboard" in the same way that participants in a face-to-face meeting use a whiteboard. Each of them can draw or write on the board; their drawings or writing will appear to all of their colleagues.

Conference applications are multiple media, multiple recipients, and multiple sources. But these applications, which appear to be many-to-many, are in reality likely to be few-to-few, or few-to-many because of social issues.

An important characteristic of conferencing application is variable membership. Every conference speaker will tell you that, if the room is large enough, people will be coming in and going out at any time. Indeed this varies with the size of the group. Students in a classroom generally arrive on time and seldom leave before the end of the class. It is also quite obvious that, when a TV program is seen by hundreds of thousands, some listeners will tune in or out at any moment during the show.

This variable membership is much easier to handle with multicast transmission and group addressing. If we used a set of point-to-point addresses instead, then each arrival and departure would translate into a set of "signalling" messages that would have to be sent to all the potential sources!

12.1.4 Streaming Audio and Video

Audio and video distribution, also referred to as webcasting, involves one source sending real-time audio and video over the Internet to one or more receivers simultaneously. Many web sites have already made video distribution an integral part of their content.

With the deployment of high-bandwidth access technologies to the home, TV and radio on the Internet become very attractive applications. Providing content on the Internet is much cheaper than deploying a broadcast-TV channel. There are two network architecture paradigms for media streaming: a hierarchy of servers that relay media to interested receivers using point-to-point transmission, or a source using multicast transmissions to reach all receivers. The advantages of the server-based architecture are its robustness and an easier access control to the content. But on very large events, it has proven to be inefficient for two reasons:

☞ There can be a significant delay between the time when information is delivered to receivers located close to the sender and the time it is delivered to receivers further down the tree hierarchy.

☞ The bandwidth used to transmit the information is significant.

Multicast solves such problems. The challenge with multicast is to protect the source from being jammed by malicious senders. Access control and data encryption can provide such protection. Multicast consequently offers a scalable alternative to hierarchical, server-based architecture in the case of very large groups. In the case of small groups, it is unclear if the cost of multicast is worth the bandwidth gain.

12.1.5 Interactive Applications

Longer-term, applications with more interaction among users will appear. These applications exist already in the military domain with Distributed Interactive Simulation (DIS) and

High Level Architecture (HLA) IEEE standards. DIS and HLA can be used, for example, to organize a "digital battlefield" environment. Applications with significant interaction between users will appear in the public domain with the deployment of shared virtual worlds and distributed games. Multiplayer games have many of the same requirements of DIS and HLA applications. Games on the Internet have the potential to manage a larger number of concurrent participants than government-sponsored simulations. The scale of the multicast groups for these applications is highly likely to be tightly tied to social and human-factors issues, and does not necessarily entail large-scale many-to-many multicast. A large number of linked few-to-few groups may be satisfactory.

Multicast is a mandatory technology to allow such interaction because of its scalable dissemination of data and because it minimizes delay among participants: In an interactive application, all participants must have received and displayed any action played by any other participant within 150 ms; otherwise, the action loses its real-time quality. Such property is difficult to realize with point-to-point dissemination of data.

Together with real-time interaction among users, very large interactive applications have other requirements that make them complex to deploy with a classic point-to-point communication infrastructure:

☞ Fast leaves and joins of multicast groups. Joins should be almost instantaneous and may occur at the rate of hundreds per second.

☞ Thousands of simultaneous multicast groups. For example, each "room" in a virtual world may be mapped to its own multicast group.

☞ Partial reliability to ensure low packet loss.

One solution often used to manage these requirements is to use a "broadcast and filter" approach such as in USENET. Therefore, due to the large number of participants, not all players in the session can see each other. This results in a disparate receiver interest in application events that makes the broadcast and filter approach extremely inefficient.

Another interesting area of interactive applications is serverless games. In serverless architectures, participants multicast to each other their current application states and are able to synchronize without a centralized server. The success of this mechanism is a function of the latency between participants, which is dependent on the multicast topology connecting members. Large latencies in packet delivery require the group to be broken up into divisions. Partitioning of group members is a strong trend in large-scale applications. Here, the latency is the partitioning factor; for USENET, DIS, and games, partitioning based on content increases efficient data distribution. Packets are "addressed" toward interested hosts using separate multicast groups within a single application session.

12.1.6 Issues with Deploying Multicast

The applications that are driving multicast are one-to-many and few-to-few currently. As of yet, many-to-many applications have not gained popularity or received much attention. Providing a many-to-many service is difficult and, as we will see later, ISPs and carriers find multicast an attractive service to offer when it is easy to deploy and manage.

The phenomenal growth in the number of businesses connected to the Internet has been driven by unicast-based email and web applications. However, general users of the Internet acting as receivers will not drive Internetwide multicast connectivity. The use of multicast results in bandwidth savings that make it an attractive service mainly to sources and administrators of low-capacity domains, such as corporate networks. Internet receivers do not care whether they receive their audio streams from unicast or multicast. As receivers, they require the same amount of bandwidth. Moreover, users will find unicast delivery a more stable service at this point.

Sources require multicast so that they may scale their services to extremely large audiences. Low-capacity domains require multicast only when many redundant high-bandwidth streams threaten the capacity of incoming links. For example, many employees in a company may choose to all receive unicast streams of a popular video event, overwhelming the incoming bandwidth capacity.

Today, multicast is included with the standard set of protocols shipped with commercial routers, but most Internet Service Providers (ISPs) have not yet enabled the service in their networks. A number of issues have stalled the widespread use of multicast, which we discuss later in this chapter. The main problem is that multicasting on the Internet does not meet the requirements of a commercial service. At its core, however, multicast relies on a routing protocol. We explain the mechanisms of multicast routing in the next section.

12.2 Multicast Routing

We have seen in the previous section that there is a large potential demand for multicast transmission. However, the introduction of multicast routing in the Internet is recent. In this section, we will review several multicast routing algorithms, starting with the simplest algorithms intended for use in broadcast LANs, such as "flooding" or "spanning trees." Then, we present more advanced routing techniques, such as "reverse path forwarding," "Steiner trees," and "center-based trees." Afterwards, we describe the actual multicast routing protocol standards used on the Internet that are based on these routing algorithms.

There are a number of key challenges that must be met by a multicast routing algorithm to be applicable to the Internet. It must route data only to group members, optimize routes from the source to receivers, maintain loop-free routes, and not concentrate all multicast traffic on a subset of links. Furthermore, the signalling in creating and maintaining a group must scale well with a dynamic receiver set. These criteria will be discussed for each of the algorithms described in the following sections.

12.2.1 Flooding

We have already encountered one multicast propagation technique when studying the OSPF protocol: link state updates are flooded to all OSPF routers in an area. Flooding is probably the oldest and simplest multicast routing algorithm. Apart from OSPF, it is also used for the propagation of the "Usenet news" messages, which are flooded to all news servers within a "distribution group."

There are several variants of the flooding algorithm, but they all share the same general principle. A node in the network will receive a packet that was sent to a multicast destination. It will first try to ascertain whether this is the first reception of this particular packet, or whether this is a duplicate. If it is a first transmission, it will transmit a copy of the packet on all (except the incoming) interfaces, ensuring that the packet eventually reaches all network destinations.

The key to any flooding implementation is indeed the test for "first reception" in order to avoid loops. OSPF solves this by looking in the link state database; if the received link state update is newer than the local value, the database is updated and the packet is forwarded. Usenet news also uses this comparison with a local database. All news's messages have a unique identifier, which can be used as a key for accessing the database. If the message is already present in the database, it is not transmitted any further. Otherwise, it is added to the base and forwarded. But accessing the database can be costly, and the news service speeds up the test by carrying "trace" information in the messages. The trace field lists the names of all the hosts that have already seen the message. This field is checked upon receipt of message; if the local host is present in the traces, the message is not processed any further. It is also present when forwarding; if a neighbor's name is already present in the trace, there is no need to forward the message to that specific neighbor.

OSPF and news implement "application-level flooding," but it would not be very difficult to implement an equivalent protocol at the IP level. The only requirement would be that one maintains a list of recently seen packets, e.g., the identifiers of all the packets that have been received in the last two minutes, assuming that two minutes is the "maximum lifetime" of a packet. The "route-recording" option could be used to perform checks similar to the news traces, and the TTL value could be used to limit the scope of the flooding. This would be very simple, but would not be very effective.

☞ The very nature of the flooding algorithm requires that one maintain a list of "last-seen" packets. This list can be fairly long on a high-speed network.

☞ The "last-seen" lists guarantee that a router will not forward the same packet twice, but it certainly does not guarantee that the router will receive a given packet only once.

The flooding algorithm is used mostly when the main requirement is robustness, and when a more sophisticated multicast technique is not possible. It does not depend on any kind of routing tables, and one can easily show that in the absence of transmission errors the packet will be received by all destinations for which at least one path exists. But it is quite greedy on both memory resources, as it needs one entry per packet, and transmission resources, as it will use all available paths instead of just one. Flooding is also better described as a broadcast protocol, as all hosts on the network receive the flooded data.

12.2.2 Spanning Trees

A more efficient solution than flooding is the "spanning tree" technique, which is used, for example, by "media-access-control (MAC) bridges." In order to avoid loops, one will simply build up an "overlay" network by marking some links as "part of the tree" and other links as "unused." The set of selected links forms a loop-free graph, or a tree; it spans to all nodes in the network, thus the name, spanning tree. If we take again our small test network as an example:

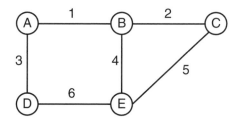

we can build a spanning tree by selecting the links 1, 2, 3, and 4.

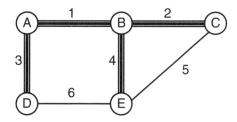

Once a spanning tree has been built, the propagation of multicast packets becomes very simple. When a multicast packet is received, it is immediately forwarded to all outgoing links that are part of the tree except the incoming link. Since the tree is loop-free, we guarantee that the packet will not loop; since this is a spanning tree, we guarantee that the packet will reach all destinations.

As mentioned above, the spanning-tree technique is used by IEEE-802 MAC bridges. The spanning tree is built up at network initialization, first by selecting a "main" bridge that becomes the center of the network, then by marking the links that are on the shortest paths between any other bridge and that center.

One could easily use a spanning-tree technique for propagating IP multicast packets within an AS. The spanning-tree technique is robust and does not require much memory: one needs only a boolean variable per network interface to mark it as "on" or "off" the tree. But the basic spanning tree has two drawbacks: it does not take into account group membership, and it concentrates all the traffic into a small subset of the network links.

Suppose that on our test network a specific group includes only the nodes A, B, and C; the packet will nevertheless be propagated to the nodes D and E, because they are part of the spanning tree. Suppose then that another group includes only nodes C, D, and E; the packets will be propagated on links 1, 2, 3, and 4—on all of the spanning tree. This is very inefficient, because using only 5 and 6 would have resulted in faster propagation. Also, not using links 5 and 6 concentrates the traffic on links 1, 2, 3, and 4, which become more rapidly overloaded and prone to congestion. For this reason, one prefers algorithms that compute "group-specific" graphs and try to make an efficient use of network resources.

12.2.3 Reverse-Path Forwarding

"Reverse-Path Forwarding" (RPF) is due to the work of Y. Dalal and R. Metcalfe; it was revised by Steve Deering [1] to avoid duplicates on multi-access links. The RPF algorithm takes advantage of the IP routing table to "orientate" the network and to compute an implicit spanning tree per multicast source. In its simplest form, the RPF algorithm works as follows:

1. When a multicast packet is received, note source (S), interface (I).
2. If I belongs to the shortest path from S, forward to all interfaces except I.
3. If the test in step 2 is false, refuse the packet.

The advantage of this simple form is that RPF does not require any more resources than the normal "unicast" routing table; if one knows how to compute the route toward S, then one can safely process multicast packets received from S. One should note, however, that for maximum efficiency one should not use the unicast routing table itself. One should compute the shortest path from the source to the node rather than the shortest path from the node to the source. When links are not symmetric, one must thus use the "forward-path" metric to compute multicast-specific routes.

   Then one can easily be more efficient if one is able to look "one step further"—i.e., to know whether the local router is on the shortest path between a neighbor and the source before forwarding a packet to that neighbor. If this is not the case, there is no point in forwarding packets that will immediately be dropped by the next router. This one-step-further information is sometimes easy to extract from the route computation process, for example, by using the link state database in OSPF. It does not require more than one bit of additional storage per source and interface in the routing table, and is thus a classic extension of an RPF implementation.

   Reverse-path forwarding results in a different spanning tree for each source. The consequence is that each router has to store "state" information on a per-multicast-group per-source basis. In other words, the amount of memory used in the routing tables is on the order of the number of groups times the number of sources in each group. In our example, multicast from A, C, and E will use three different trees in our test network.

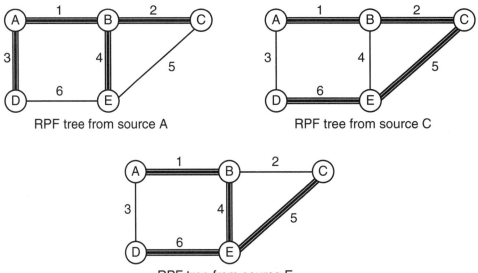

RPF tree from source A

RPF tree from source C

RPF tree from source E

These trees have two interesting properties:

☞ They guarantee the fastest possible delivery, as multicasting follows the shortest path from source to destination.

☞ Because a different tree is computed for each source, the packets are spread over multiple links resulting in better network utilization.

We can immediately note, however, a problem with the simple form of RPF: group membership is not taken into account when building the tree, and packets are simply flooded to the whole network—or at the very least as far as the initial TTL permits. In fact, it is easy to modify RPF in order to take into account group membership in the "leaves" of the network—the subnets that connect only "subscribers" and do not participate in multicast routing. We will see in Section 12.4 that the Internet group membership protocol (IGMP) enables the router to know whether there are group members or not in a leaf. If not, it is easy to avoid multicasting the group's packet on these leaves. This is called "truncated broadcast." But truncated broadcast is only a partial solution. The group membership is not taken into account when building the branches of the tree.

12.2.4 RPF and Prunes

The "pruning" variant of RPF was proposed to take into consideration group membership in basic RPF algorithm and to reduce flooding of data in the network. The idea is to complete the basic RPF by somehow memorizing the group membership and to forward a packet only if there is a group member down the tree. This will result in minimal trees but requires very dynamic updates. Group memberships may vary rapidly, and the trees computed for all sources should be modified.

The pruning option of the RPF algorithm is thus better described by "flood and prune." When a multicast transmission starts from source S, the first packet is propagated to all the network nodes: this is the flooding. The nodes that are at the border of the network (i.e., nodes that have no point behind them in the RPF tree) are called leaf nodes. The leaf nodes will all receive the first multicast packet. If there is no group member attached to the leaf node, the node does not need to receive further packets. It will thus send back a "prune message" to the node that sent the packet stating, "Don't send further packets from source S to group G on this interface I."

The intermediate routers that receive the prunes memorize them. If they have received a prune message through all the interfaces on which they forwarded the first packet and if there is no local recipient, they have no need for receiving from this source further packets for that group. They will forward the prune command up the RPF tree. Eventually, the tree will include only the branches that lead to active recipients.

There are two obvious drawbacks in the flood and prune algorithm:

☞ Packets are flooded to the whole network on a periodic basis.

☞ All routers must keep state on a per-group and per-source basis, even if they are not part of the spanning tree.

The state that must be kept is transient; it varies with the membership of the group and with the network topology, each of which may vary in the course of time. The states are thus kept for a limited lifetime, a duration that supposedly matches the rhythms of topology and membership changes. When this time has elapsed, the prune messages are removed from the local memory. The next packet is again multicast to all destinations and will, if necessary, trigger the emission of new prune messages.

Periodically sending packets to the whole network might be reasonable for a local domain, but it is not something that should be routinely repeated in the whole Internet, with its millions of connected computers. The amount of memory required of routers must also scale to support a connected Internet. For flood-and-prune protocols, the amount of memory grows as the product of the number of sources and the number of groups. Furthermore, routers that are not on the multicast tree must keep prunes in memory. Both numbers grow with the size of the network; if the number of groups becomes very large, there is a risk of heavily taxing the resources available in network routers.

12.2.5 Steiner Trees

We have said that one of the challenges in the construction of a multicast route is to optimize the tree given some network metric. We have explained that RPF algorithm computed a minimum delay tree for each source in a multicast group, at the expense of network resources. A minimum-cost Steiner tree is constructed by an algorithm that globally optimizes the network resource used to multicast data in a group, possibly at the expense of the delay among group members [41]. Let's take again our test network and consider a group where the recipients are A and D and the source is C. The RPF tree is thus:

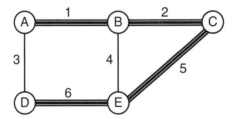

This tree uses four network links, but it is indeed possible to build a graph that also connects C to A and D and uses only three links:

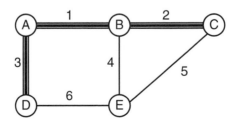

This tree is "slower" because packets for D have to be relayed on three links instead of two, but it is more efficient in the sense that it uses fewer network resources.

The Steiner problem is known to be NP-hard. Its formal expression is "given a set N of n points in the Euclidean plane (the network nodes and hosts), the shortest network interconnecting N is called a Steiner Minimal Tree (SMT)," or:

Given $G = (V, E, d)$ a distance graph, and a set S

V the set of Vertices; E the set of Edges

d a distance (or cost) function on E

S a subset of V

A minimum-cost Steiner tree is a tree of G that spans S with a minimal total distance on its edges.

Steiner trees minimize the number of links that are needed to connect the members of a group within a graph. This is an interesting network property because, if we consider the total amount of resources used by a large number of groups, using fewer resources eventually minimizes the risk of congestion. However, Steiner trees have a set of characteristics that make them difficult to implement in a real network with dynamic membership:

☞ Steiner trees can be computationally intensive.

☞ Designing a Steiner tree requires the knowledge of the full network topology.

☞ As in the spanning tree algorithm, there is a traffic concentration on a subset of the links.

☞ Group membership cannot be changed without recomputing the total tree. Consequently, the multicast route used by members that do not leave the group is changed any time a member joins or leaves the group. This is an unacceptable property.

The following example illustrates this latter issue. If the members are not only A, D, and C but also A, D, E, and C, the minimal tree becomes:

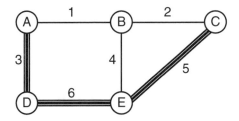

Then, if we add B to the recipient set, the minimal tree becomes equivalent to the RPF tree:

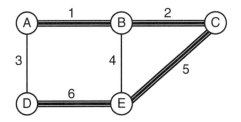

We observe that, at each of these stages, the routing has changed widely. This instability, together with the absence of a general-case solution for large networks, makes the minimum-cost Steiner tree more a mathematical construct than a practical tool, theoretically attractive but difficult to use in real networks. In fact, we do not know of any routing protocol based on the minimum-cost Steiner tree algorithm that has ever been deployed in the Internet.

12.2.6 Center-Based Trees

In the analysis of the flood and prune strategy, we have seen that it suffers from two defects: a periodic transmission to all network sites in order to trigger the pruning, and the need to keep states for all active groups and sources in all the network routers. Tony Ballardie proposed the "center-based tree" algorithm as a potential solution to these problems [2].

As the name implies, building a center-based tree starts with choosing a "center," i.e., a fixed point in the network that will be the center of the multicast group. The recipients will then send "join" commands toward the center. In other words, a center-based tree uses "explicit signalling." These commands will be processed by all intermediate routers, which will mark the interface on which they are received as belonging to the group's tree. The routers need to keep state information on a per-group basis, listing all the interfaces that belong to the tree. If the router that receives a join command is already a member of the tree, it will mark only one more interface as belonging to the group. If this is the first join command that the router receives, it will forward the command one step further toward the center.

There is no requirement that the originators of the multicast packet belong to the group. If they don't, their packets will simply be forwarded toward the center until they reach the first router that belongs to the group's tree. At this stage, the packet will be "intercepted" and the multicasting will proceed along the center-based tree in the same way it progresses along a spanning tree. In fact, the center-based tree technique is equivalent to building "a spanning tree per group." This tree is the same for all sources, which has the advantage over RPF of requiring only one state per group in each router involved in the tree instead of one state per pair of groups and sources in each router of the network. However, it suffers the potential disadvantage that the path between some sources and some receivers may be suboptimal.

The main problem of the center-based tree algorithm is the choice of the center. Choosing a center to optimize the delay among participants is a bad idea. First, this problem is NP-complete. Second, the group membership being dynamic, the center would not remain optimal for long. Simpler solutions are to choose the center close to the sender when the multicast group is a single sender; or to have network nodes specifically configured to act as static centers, such as routers that border a domain.

The principal advantage of a center-based tree is that it limits the expansion of multicast transmissions to precisely the set of all recipients. This is in stern contrast with RPF, in which packets are sent to the whole network and all routers have to keep state about all ongoing multicast sessions. This is due to the explicit-join nature of the signalling used in the center-based tree. The second advantage of the center-based tree algorithm is that its center-based "shared" tree uses only per-group resources at routers, as compared to per-source, per-group resources required for "source-rooted" flood-and-prune trees.

In the center-based tree algorithm, data forwarding can be of two natures: unidirectional or bidirectional. In unidirectional trees, all packets converge to the center before being forwarded to all group members, including the sender. This approach has two drawbacks: it concentrates the traffic around the center, and it increases the end-to-end transmission delay. But it is simple to implement. A solution to avoid this concentration issue is to have more than one active center in the tree. Bidirectional trees allow data to be forwarded from the sender directly to the receivers, not necessarily going through the center before reaching some receivers. This approach results in shorter delay and less concentration, even if concentration remains more important than in per-source trees.

12.3 Multicast Routing Protocols for the Internet

A number of standard multicast routing protocols have begun to appear for use on the Internet. Today, specifications exist for DVMRP, a multicast version of OSPF, and PIM. DVMRP is a result of early multicast routing efforts. MOSPF provides routing facilities within an AS of limited size; the emphasis is on efficient route computation. "Protocol Independent Multicast" [5] was intended as a generic solution to multicast routing, including interdomain multicast routing issues. An interdomain solution must tackle problems like the explosion of router memory that a very large number of groups could utilize, or the need to perform ISP selection and policy routing. We will see that PIM comes in two variants, called "dense" and "sparse," which correspond roughly to flood and prunes and to unidirectional center-based trees. Because of some limitations of the above routing protocols, a number of other proposals have been designed to enable the deployment of multicast in the Internet, awaiting standards agreement. These include MSDP, BGMP, and CBT, all of which we discuss in the next section.

12.3.1 Distance Vector Multicast Routing Protocol

The "Distance Vector Multicast Routing Protocol" [4] is the first multicast routing protocol ever deployed in the Internet. It was originally implemented as a program called "mrouted" that runs on Unix machines. DVMRP is a very simple distance vector routing protocol, quite similar to RIP. DVMRP computes the "reverse paths" used by the reverse-path-forwarding algorithm. The multicast routers exchange distance-vector updates that contain lists of destinations—or, rather, potential sources—and distances. As for RIP-2, the distances are expressed as hop counts and the sources are combinations of IP addresses and subnet masks. There are, however, a few differences with RIP-2, i.e., DVMRP's use of reverse-path distances and the handling of tunnels. The DVMRP updates are sent not only over the multicast-capable interfaces, but also over all the tunnels that start from the multicast router. These tunnels must be explicitly configured by the router's administrator. Each tunnel has three parameters: the destination router, a cost that is used to compute the DVMRP distances, and a "threshold." With DVMRP, the routers can tell, for each source network and each neighboring router, whether that router considers them as the previous hop from the source. This is advertised in the same way that RIP-2 advertises next hops.

The forwarding process uses the reverse-path forwarding algorithm. When an mrouted process receives a multicast packet from an interface or a tunnel, it checks in the DVMRP routing table whether that interface or that tunnel is on the shortest path from the source. If this is not the case, the packet is dropped. Otherwise, it is forwarded to all multicast-capable interfaces and all tunnels for which the local router is the previous hop from the source. At this stage, the router also applies two checks: a verification of the multicast packet TTL and a check for group membership.

12.3.2 Multicast Extensions to OSPF

MOSPF takes advantage of the presence of a "network map" in the link state database [6, 7]. It complements the database with a new type of link state records—i.e., the group memberships—so that OSPF routers can essentially perform the RPF and prune computations "in memory" without ever actually having to flood the first packet of a group transmission.

Suppose that an OSPF router receives a multicast packet from the source S toward the group G. This router relies on the link state database to compute the "shortest-path tree" that links the source S to all the destinations within the area, using the "forward" metrics—the metrics of the links that start from S toward the group. It then uses the group membership information to prune the branches of the tree that do not lead to any group member. Finally, it forwards the multicast packet over only those of its outgoing interfaces that belong to the pruned multicast tree, which we will call the "source-based tree."

However, there are a number of special cases that make this computation slightly more complex than what we just explained. One must allow for an incremental deployment of the multicast facility; take into consideration the partition into areas and the need to support "external" multicast; and solve the "equal-cost multipath" ambiguities.

During the deployment phase, some routers, but not all, will be capable of multicast routing. The capability to perform multicast routing is marked by a bit in the router's "option" flag:

					M	E	T

If the bit M is null, the router cannot do multicast. It must be ignored in the computation of the source-based trees. Note that MOSPF does not include any provision for setting up tunnels—the reasoning is that this is only a transition tool and that very soon the majority of the area's routers will be multicast-capable.

The group memberships are defined by a new link state record in which a router responsible for a subnet will list all the groups that have at least one member in the subnet. The area-border routers will summarize the memberships of their areas and will advertise over the backbone a group membership record that lists all the groups for which at least one member exists in the area. If an area has several area-border routers, all these border routers will be considered group members over the backbone. But this will not result in duplicate transmission, as one can use the cost advertised in the "summary links" to compute an RPF tree that starts from the source when the source does not belong to the area.

Indeed, the external router cannot advertise all the groups that have been defined on the whole Internet. The number of such groups can be far too large, while only those groups that have local members need to be represented in the database. The solution is simple: by default, the external routers will be considered as members of all the groups. They will be part of all the source-based trees computed in the backbone. For the same reason, the area-border routers will be part of all the groups belonging to their areas.

The equal-cost multipath procedure of OSPF results in an interesting problem: if the routers simply pick at random one of the equal-cost paths, there is no guarantee that they will all pick the same. They would thus compute different source-based trees, which would lead to incoherent decisions. For this reason, the MOSPF specification includes an equal-path resolution algorithm that privileges broadcast networks as well as paths serving multiple members.

MOSPF is a very powerful protocol, which some may find a bit too powerful. It requires that one performs one shortest-path computation for all multicast sources—in fact, for each combination of source and group. There are potentially as many sources as hosts in the area, and the number of groups itself is likely to grow with the size of the AS. As a result, the number of computations that follow any routing update is likely to grow as the square of the size of the area. As the cost of each computation is of the order of 0(N. log N), there is a potential for saturating even the most powerful of the router's CPUs.

The solution suggested by MOSPF is to do the computation "on demand," when the first packet arrives from source S to group G, then to memorize the results in a cache, which will be flushed if the database is updated. This simple optimization has not been sufficient to make MOSPF a simple and scalable protocol. The complexity of MOSPF has contributed to the fast deployment of PIM.

12.3.3 Protocol-Independent Multicast, Dense Mode

Protocol-Independent Multicast (PIM) currently is the most popular multicast routing protocol in the Internet. PIM has two modes of operation: sparse and dense [8]. The adjectives "dense" and "sparse" refer to the density of group members in the Internet. Suppose that we take a random sampling of the Internet (i.e., that we pick a sample "area"). A group is said to be *dense* if the probability is high that the area contains at least one group member, even if that area is reasonably small. It is said to be *sparse* if, on the contrary, that probability is low. Dense groups have a large number of members—an example might be the multicasting of the IETF conference, which is followed by a large number of network specialists all over the world. Sparse groups, on the other hand, have few members who are present only in a small number of places—an example could be a conference of the IAB, which is attended only by its 12 members worldwide. Indeed, dense and sparse are just two extreme situations; one could imagine groups which are semi-sparse or medium-dense. PIM consequently offers the capability to locally switch from sparse mode to dense mode, and to use both modes in the same multicast group. But before going further, let's first describe the dense mode.

A dense group is very close to a LAN: almost all hosts in the area are interested in the multicast information. It consequently makes sense to use a simple and robust routing protocol such as flood and prune. The weak point of the flood and prune algorithm is that each branch of the RPF tree will have to be tested periodically, which amounts to broadcast test packets at regular intervals. If the group is dense and the receivers are located in a single domain, this is quite acceptable: the proportion of branches that have to be pruned is low. The dense mode of PIM is thus an implementation of this strategy.

PIM is simpler than DVMRP because it does not mandate the computation of specific routing tables. The multicast routing is independent from the point-to-point routing protocol; it simply supposes that such a protocol exists. A consequence of this independence is that PIM routers do not try to compute multicast-specific routes. They suppose that the point-to-point routes are symmetric. The precise way that PIM implements RPF and prunes is as follows:

1. If a router receives a multicast packet from source S to group G, it first checks in the standard unicast routing table that the incoming interface is the one that is used for sending unicast packets toward S. If this is not the case, it drops the packets and sends back a "prune(S,G)" message on the incoming interface.

2. The router will then forward a copy of the message on all the interfaces for which it has not already received a "prune(S,G)" message. If there are no such interfaces (i.e., if all the interfaces have been pruned), it drops the packet and sends back a "prune(S,G)" message on the incoming interface.

Note that the first packet effectively will be flooded on all interfaces. Doing otherwise would suppose that one could obtain "downstream" information from the unicast routing protocol and would thus break the "protocol-independence" hypothesis. In fact, PIM-dense is an extremely simple protocol that can be implemented with minimal effort. It simply supposes that routers are capable of memorizing, or rather caching, the "prune" messages in a context associated to the "source/group" pair. But even this is optional; the router that is lacking memory resources can decide to drop the "least recently used" contexts. The only problem will be that a few more packets will be flooded than necessary; if that number grows too large, the group will automatically be reinserted in the "recently used" list.

The only tricky points are the handling of equal-cost multipaths and of broadcast networks. The PIM specification proposes a very simple solution to the equal-cost multipath problem—to accept multicast packets only from the equal-cost neighbor that has the largest IP address. For broadcast networks, we have to solve the problem that occurs when several routers are connected to the same cable.

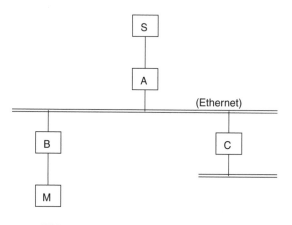

— PIM-dense: several routers on the same cable —

The source S sends a packet to the group G. That packet is received by the router A, which forwards it over the Ethernet. It is received by the routers B and C. B forwards it on its second interface to the group member M. C notices that there is no group member connected to its second interface, so it decides to prune the group. It sends a prune (S,G) to A. If A believes the prune message, the router B and the group member M will never receive the following packets sent by S!

The PIM specification suggests a simple precaution against this problem. The prune messages are always sent to the "all-routers" multicast address (224.0.0.2). They will be received by A and B. When A receives the prune, it does not apply it immediately, but simply schedules the group for deletion. When B receives the prune, it will send a "join" message to the same all-routers multicast address; A will thus cancel the prune. Since these messages are multicast to all routers, even if many of them are in the same situation as C, only one will have to send a "join"; A will not receive a tempest of "join" messages.

Another problem may occur if several routers are connected to the same broadcast network. Two of them, or maybe more, may well receive the packets from the source through different paths. An example is given in the multiple-path diagram.

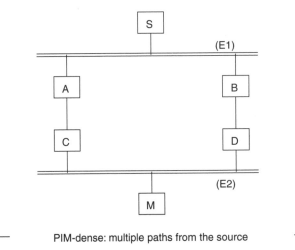

PIM-dense: multiple paths from the source

The source S sends a first packet toward the group G on the Ethernet segment E1. The packet is picked by the routers A and B, each of which forward a copy of it to C and D. Both C and D send a copy of the packet on the Ethernet segment E2. The group member M receives two copies!

In fact, both C and D will notice that there is a problem if they have kept some state information for the pair "source=S, group=G." Both will receive the copy of the packet that the other router sent over E2. Because the state information mentions, for each of them, that these packets are forwarded on the interface E2, they notice immediately that another router is active on the same link. They will thus send an "assert(S,G)" packet to resolve the "collision." The assert messages carry the distance between their senders and the source. A router that receives an assert packet compares this distance with its own. If the distance is shorter, it prunes the interface from the list of selected interfaces for the group and source. The assert, prune, and join packets are defined as extensions of the basic IGMP protocol.

12.3.4 Protocol-Independent Multicast, Sparse Mode

The PIM-dense specification is simple and easy to implement, but it does not suit the needs of sparse groups. Just because three internauts wish to engage in an audio conference is not a good reason to flood the whole Internet with one new packet every minute, and to keep states in all the Internet routers. Suppose that a few thousand of these conferences were in progress; using PIM-dense would create sufficient background noise to saturate most Internet connections! In this situation, one must reverse the default behavior. Packets should not be flooded to the whole network; they should be sent only to the members that have "explicitly" notified their interest in the group.

The "PIM-sparse" algorithm [9] uses the unidirectional variant of the center-based tree algorithm that we presented previously. In fact, PIM-sparse does not use the notion of center, but that of "rendezvous point." To each sparse group is associated one or more rendezvous points (RPs). The receivers join the group by sending a join message to the RP. This message is processed by all the routers between the member and the RP, which all cache a "status information" for the group. Let's consider our "test" network for an example. The RP for the group G is C:

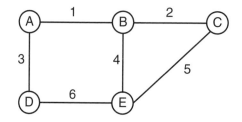

D joins the group by sending a join packet toward C, using PIM as the protocol to join to the RP. The join packet is, in fact, sent to E—the next hop toward destination C. The join packet mentions the group address, G, and the address of the RP, C. It is relayed by E toward C. At this stage, the RP tree is:

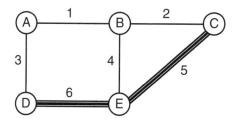

Now, the source B starts sending toward the group G. That source has no idea of who the group members are; it knows only the RP. It will thus encapsulate its first packet in a "register" command that is sent to the RP. As a result, the RP will send a join packet toward that source, adding a new root to the RP tree. The RP will resend the source's packet on the RP tree. The first packet sent by B will thus use the following path:

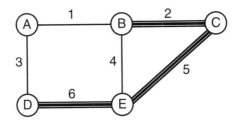

This is not exactly optimal, but the traffic is "contained." As in the center-based tree case, it is not sent to any router that is not located between one member and the RP. The next packets may well continue on the same suboptimal path, but any of the routers in the path may also decide that they are really seeing many packets from this particular source. Suppose, for example, that D wants to get better service; it will send a join on the direct route to B and a prune toward the RP. The path used for the next packets sent by B will thus be:

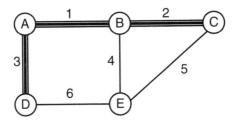

The packets now follow the direct path between B and D. If there were more members in the group to join B directly, the packets would follow the reverse-path forwarding tree that starts from B and covers all recipients. This would be as efficient as if the group used PIM-dense. Note that B still sends one copy of its packets to the RP—there may be other members in the group besides those who joined directly. Also note that the RP tree is not torn down; it can still be used for other sources.

Switching from sparse mode to dense mode is realized in practice by choosing the value of a parameter that defines when a group is dense enough to move to per-source tree.

From a data-forwarding standpoint, only the second step of the transmission (from the RP to all receivers) can be considered a real multicast transmission. This inefficiency has led IETF to study a bidirectional version of PIM that would allow data to be forwarded to all group members directly from the sender, not necessarily going through an RP. This optimization should solve the concentration and delay issues, but will be more complex to implement.

12.4 Internet Multicast Today

Multicast was first deployed to support experimental research. It was called the MBONE, or "Multicast Backbone." It was quickly discovered that although routing is an essential piece of providing a multicast service, there are many other challenges that make up a complete multicast service. In this section, we provide a brief history of the MBONE and the lessons learned. Then, we review the current standards that support Internetwide connectivity, including interdomain routing algorithms.

12.4.1 The Experimental Multicast Backbone

The MBONE is an "overlay" network on the Internet that started in 1992 to enable early usage of multicast applications without waiting for the full availability of Internet multicasting standards.

The approach was to start with a simple experiment in order to deploy some test applications and to learn the technology. That experiment concerned only a small fraction of the Internet routers—a limited subset of the topology. The MBONE uses "tunnels" to link "multicast island" domains, areas of the Internet where the multicast service is supported. Tunnels are virtual links through the general IP network. DVMRP, the multicast routing protocol used in the MBONE, was designed to use its own routing protocol, independent of the global Internet routing, in order to account for the tunnels.

Multicast sites send and receive multicast packets in a "native" form:

s → g, ip	S → G, udp	udp header + data
Ethernet header	IP header	

In this packet, the IP destination address G is a class-D group address. It has been translated to the Ethernet group address g according to the rules specified in RFC-1112. To run the MBONE experiment, the station's networking software had to be upgraded in order to:

☞ support transmission to and reception from class-D addresses,

☞ enhance UDP so that it can send to and receive multicast packets, and

☞ support the Internet Group Management Protocol (IGMP).

The first part of this update really concerns the low-level transmission software. The local network controllers must be programmed to listen to multicast group addresses, and the ARP address resolution must be bypassed to use the class-D-to-IEEE-802 address translation instead. The second and third parts are complementary. By default, a UDP interface (e.g., a UDP "socket") allows a program to receive the packets bound to one of the host's IP addresses and to the UDP port associated with the socket. It takes an extra system call to also receive the packet sent to a particular multicast group and port, which is not necessarily equal to the socket's port. Many programs on the same host may well be listening to the same multicast transmission. Multihomed hosts should select the particular interface by which they want to send and receive from one particular group. An attempt to use several interfaces for the same group would result in duplicate transmissions or duplicate receptions. The same socket system call by which a program connects to a group triggers the emissions of IGMP "membership reports." IGMP is used by hosts to inform edge routers that they are interested in a particular multicast group. We explain the operation of IGMP shortly.

Once the stations have been upgraded, they can exchange multicast traffic among themselves, but only within their multicast island. Initially, an island comprises exactly one local network. In order to participate in the MBONE, one must attach at least one multicast router to the local network and establish a link between that router and at least one other remote router already connected to the MBONE. If these two routers are "adjacent," the multicast traffic will flow in parallel with the IP traffic. The separated islands are simply merged into a larger multicast-capable archipelago. But in general, MBONE traffic must cross several routers that are not yet multicast-capable. The first version of the MBONE software achieved this with IP-level source routing, inserting the IP address of the remote router as a "source route" between the source and the group address using IP header option processing. This posed severe performance problems. The latest version uses encapsulation.

Source:R1, Dest:R2, Protocol: IP in IP	Source:S, Dest:G, Protocol: UDP	UDP header and data
IP header (1)	IP header (2)	

The IP multicast packet from source S to group G is sent in a tunnel between the multicast router R1 and R2. The MBONE map thus consists of a set of tunnels connecting multicast routers and linking multicast-capable local networks.

Because early on a multicast routing facility was not available in the generic routers, that function was provided as a part of the experiment. Members of the Internet's end-to-end research group have provided extensions to various versions of the UNIX operating system as "freeware." The extensions are composed of:

☞ host extensions for supporting IP multicast, IGMP, and UDP; and
☞ the "mrouted" program that could turn a UNIX workstation into a multicast router.

The *mrouted* program implements DVMRP.

Today, the MBONE is still operational, but multicast connectivity is beginning to see native support from Internet routers. Next, we describe the architecture that is being shipped with routers from vendors.

12.4.2 The Current Architecture

The de facto multicast architecture in routers today is based on DVMRP, MOSPF, or PIM. IGMP is used by hosts to announce their interest in receiving a multicast to edge routers. IGMP version 1 (IGMPv1) [3] was proposed in conjunction with DVMRP. IGMP version 2 (IGMPv2) [11] adds fast termination of group subscriptions and is now an IETF standard. As we saw in the last section, DVMRP and MOSPF are limited in applicability to smaller networks, while PIM is used both in local area networks and in the public Internet. For interdomain use, PIM requires that the group-to-Rendezvous-Point mapping must be advertised to all hosts on the Internet. The Multicast Source Discovery Protocol (MSDP) has been designed to distribute this mapping via TCP connections to other domains. MSDP runs over the Multicast Border Gateway Protocol (MBGP, also called BGP+) [1], which is a set of multicast extensions for BGP version 4 that separates unicast and multicast policy.

In the near future, interdomain multicast is expected to be managed by the Border Gateway Multicast Protocol (BGMP) [13]. BGMP is an interdomain protocol used to manage interoperability between multicast routing protocols in different domains. It uses bidirectional shared trees between domains and operates more efficiently than the MSDP/MBGP combination. The remainder of this section discusses IGMP, MSDP, and BGMP in detail.

The following figure illustrates the IP multicast architecture. Interdomain support, if present, is based on MSDP/MBGP or BGMP, which rely on BGP. Multicast routing trees within domains are built by PIM (dense and sparse modes), or by other protocols like DVMRP. Connections between hosts and edge routers are managed by IGMP.

Transport Level Support	Reliable Multicast	Group-Key Distribution	MASC AAP MAAS MZAP SDAP	SDR SDP SAP	(No address allocation Unreliable No receiver auth.)
	IGMP				
Intra-domain Routing	PIM SM/DM, DVMRP, MOSPF, etc.				
Inter-domain Routing	MBGP MSDP	BGMP	(No inter-domain support)		
	BGP				
	IP datagrams				

The logical layout of the IP multicast protocol architecture

The upper level of the figure represents various functions not provided by the IP multicast architecture that may be provided at the transport layer. We review these issues in the next section. We have already mentioned the provision of reliable multicast protocols in section 12.1. Currently, any host can send data over any multicast group, even if the group is in use by another session. Multicast address allocation ensures that addresses can be reserved by sessions to avoid collisions. Multicast address allocation, if present, is handled by a set of six Multicast Address Allocation Architecture (MAAA) protocols or by the session announcement protocols (SDR, SDP, and SAP). Group-Key Distribution protocols manage shared encryption keys across large receiver sets to provide receiver authorization services.

12.4.3 Internet Group Membership Protocol

The only difference between a point-to-point IP packet and a multicast packet is the presence of a "group address" in the destination field, using the class-D format. The specification of "Host Extensions for IP Multicasting" by Steve Deering [3] defines how these group packets are sent and received on IP interfaces.

There are no specific extensions to IP that must be made for the reception of multicast packets on point-to-point lines (i.e., unicast IP interfaces). Packets are simply framed into whatever format is mandated by the technology and sent. However, on broadcast networks, it is important to send only one copy of the multicast packets for multiple receivers.

There are two kinds of broadcast networks: those that support only "global broadcast," in which case the multicast packets are sent to all the stations on the network; and those that support more specific group addresses, in which case one must derive the network-layer group address from the IP class-D address. A slice of the IEEE-802 local networks addressing plan has been reserved to that effect. If the local network supports IEEE-802 addresses, the group address is derived from the IP address by placing the low-order 23 bits of the IP address into the low-order 23 bits of the Ethernet multicast address 01-00-5E-00-00-00 (hex). There is no need to perform any ARP; the translation is automatic.

But if the host merely programs its local network interface, it will receive only those multicast packets that are sent by group members on the same local network. Packets from remote sources must be relayed by routers, which will forward them on the local network only if they know that there is at least one recipient for the group on this network. The Internet Group Membership Protocol (IGMP) solves this problem. IGMP is used by routers to discover what groups have interested member hosts on each network to which they are attached. IGMP version 2 is defined in RFC-2236. (Version 1 was defined as an appendix to the DVMRP specification and can be found in RFC-1112.)

IGMP is implemented directly over IP (protocol type 2) and is composed of four messages: "general membership query," "group-specific membership query," "host membership report," and "leave group." Routers use general query messages to learn which groups have members on an attached network. Group-specific queries are used to learn if a particular group has any members. All messages have the same format.

Version	Type	Code	Checksum
Group Address			

The "version" field indicates the version number of the protocol. It is currently set to 2.

The type field is set to 0x11 in membership queries, to 0x16 in reports. Other types are used by extensions to this protocol, for example, to implement the Distance Vector Multicast Routing Protocol (DVMRP) between MBONE routers or for the PIM protocol. The code field is used by DVMRP. It is set to 0 in the membership queries and membership reports. The checksum is computed with the standard "complement to 1 sum" algorithm of IP and protects the whole IGMP message.

Multicast routers send periodic queries to the "all-systems" static multicast address (224.0.0.1), using a TTL of 1 so that the queries are not propagated outside of the local network. More precisely, one router per subnetwork performs this task. If multiple IGMP routers are present, the router with the lowest IP address is elected. The group address is left at 0 in the queries; that field is used only in replies. The hosts that receive these queries reply with one report message per group. IGMP takes precautions so that all hosts do not reply at the same time, which would generate massive collisions on the Ethernet cables. Routers don't need to know precisely the list of members for each group; they only need to know the list of groups for which there is at least one member on the network. Accordingly, collisions between membership reports are avoided by delaying replies at hosts by random interval timers. Each host that must reply to a query with a report will first wait a random delay. If, during that delay, another report is heard for the same group, the local reporting is canceled. Otherwise, the report is sent to the reported group address; all group members will hear it. All multicast routers will also hear it, because these routers listen to all group addresses.

If a router does not receive any reports for a particular group before a certain timeout, the router assumes the group has no local members. In this case, the router does not need to forward multicast arriving from remote domains for that group onto the attached network.

Note that hosts can send an immediate unsolicited membership report upon joining a multicast group. When hosts leave a group, they send a leave-group message to the "all-routers" static multicast address with a TTL of 1. When a router receives the leave-group message for a group that has group members on the reception interface, it sends a group-specific query message periodically for a short time. If the router does not receive a membership report by the time the last query message expires, it can be assumed that the group has no local group members.

IGMP protocol is used on point-to-point connections between hosts and routers. This protocol could also be used between routers, but more sophisticated multicast routing algorithms are used instead.

IGMP version 3 (IGMPv3) [14] allows receivers to subscribe to specific sources of a particular multicast group. It is still a work in progress.

12.4.4 Interdomain Routing

PIM, MOSPF, DVMRP, and CBT are just a few of the multicast routing protocols that have been proposed or are in development. Any autonomous domain may choose to use any multicast routing protocol. But getting such a piecewise and varied deployment of different protocols to interoperate is a challenge. Therefore the IETF would like to standardize one interdomain multicast routing protocol so that new intradomain protocols need only interoperate with one other protocol.

Drawing a distinction between intra- and interdomain routing also makes management simpler for ISPs and carriers. This allows them to hold different policies for intra- and interdomain routing of traffic. In the remainder of this section, we discuss two interdomain routing protocols. The first is MSDP, which aims to connect PIM domains together. MSDP is meant as an interim solution until BGMP, a more robust interdomain protocol, is deployed between domains.

12.4.5 MSDP and MBGP

One problem with using protocols that are based on cores or rendezvous points is that the multicast session is dependent on the correct operation of a single node. If the core or RP dies, then the entire session may collapse. Receivers in domains outside the core's domain are helpless to try to solve the problem, which is an issue that upsets ISPs. Furthermore, if there are no receivers in the domain that holds the core, then the ISP that manages that domain must carry traffic despite the fact it has no paying customers. Such problems are referred to as "third-party dependencies."

The Multicast Source Discovery Protocol (MSDP) was introduced to stop third-party dependencies between PIM domains. Although MSDP is only at the Internet draft stage [12], it is widely used. MSDP solves third-party dependencies by building shortest-path routing trees from RPs in remote domains directly to sources.

In MSDP, neighboring domains announce sources to each other using *source activation* messages. Fortunately, neighboring domains are connected in a graph by MBGP (BGP with multicast extensions). MSDP operates at RPs and between domains using TCP links. RPs flood source activation messages to all other MSDP domains. Similar to DVMRP flooding, MSDP ensures that loop-freedom is preserved by using a "peer-based reverse-path-forwarding check." If an incoming source activation message is not received from the peer that is the next hop toward the originating rendezvous point of the message, it is dropped. Otherwise the source activation message is forwarded to other neighbors. The MBGP routing table is examined to determine what peer is the next hop toward the originator of the message.

If interested receivers are present for an announced source, then the RP would have an active group shared-tree entry in its routing tables. When receivers are present that are interested in a particular source, the RPs then join on the shortest path to the source (not the source's RP!). It is possible for edge routers to join directly to the source rather than receive packets through their own RPs.

TCP is used in MSDP for two reasons: first, to ensure that the policy information in source activation messages is delivered before data; second, because the information sent may be too large for a single UDP datagram. MSDP occasionally carries multicast data on the TCP connections to avoid the delay in transmitting data while session activation messages are propagated. But, although RTCP and many reliable multicast applications perform multicast roundtrip time estimations with low-rate session messages, if a TCP retransmit timer is used, then RTCP will return unrepresentative results for the high-rate data flows. For this reason, MSDP version 2 can optionally use unreliable datagram tunnels between peers. Unfortunately, MSDP does not scale due to its periodic flood-and-prune mechanism. However, it does eliminate the problems related to RPs that are not located in a source's domain.

The PIM/MSDP/MBGP combination is just one step above the MBONE tunnel/ DVMRP technology. Packets are not flooded through the entire Internet and prune state is not present in routers that are not part of the multicast tree. However, MSDP does not really solve third-party dependencies so much as prevent the use of shared trees between domains. The purpose of using cores and RPs was to support shared trees, but MSDP relegates PIM to using shared trees only with local domains. It allows only per-source trees between domains. We discuss more problems with PIM/MSDP in the next section on the future of multicast. First, we discuss BGMP, a more sophisticated interdomain protocol.

12.4.6 BGMP

The Border Gateway Multicast Protocol is standardized by the IETF to provide a more stable and scalable solution to the problems of interdomain routing. BGMP builds bidirectional shared trees between domains. BGMP always operates between border routers, and never RPs, cores, or source. BGMP uses explicit join mechanisms to construct the shared tree between domains, but in some situations will construct shortest path branches between domains. Inside domains, any multicast routing protocol can be used: PIM, DVMRP, MOSPF, etc.

When border routers learn from the intradomain protocol there are hosts interested in sending or receiving data on an interdomain multicast group, they send join messages toward the "root domain" of a multicast group. The route domain is essentially the core of the multicast group (except in BGMP, in which no specific router is the core); any border router of the root domain suffices.

How does BGMP know what is the root domain for a specific group? Any method can be used, but the specification expects the use of the set of Multicast Address Set Claim (MASC) protocols, which is also a work in progress. MASC is a separate protocol that allows domains to claim temporary "ownership" of ranges of address. MASC-based address ownership is performed in hierarchical blocks so that BGMP routers can aggregate group-to-domain tables.

How does BGMP know the next border router on the path to the root domain? BGMP relies on the network of BGP peers used to distribute unicast routers.

In sum, BGMP routers send join messages to the next BGP peer on the path to the root domain for each group that has subscribed receivers. When the peer receives the join message, it sends the join message to its peer that is nearer to the route domain. This process continues on from r-router-peer to border-router-peer, forming a shared tree. Data sent over the tree are forwarded on all existing outgoing interfaces: no reverse path checks are performed. For example, a BGMP bidirectional tree of domains is illustrated in the figure below. Receiver x in domain D sends data that are forwarded by its border router d1 to its neighbor b2, and then on to the rest of the tree. However, in domain C, DVMRP is used and packets from x that arrive on border router C1 are dropped because the shortest reverse path to x is through router c2 (shown in dashed lines).

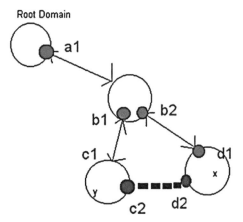

Two options are available in BGMP to resolve this problem. The default solution is for c1 to encapsulate packets from x and tunnel them to c2. C2 decapsulates the packets and distributes the data natively to the rest of the domain. But because routers are not optimized to perform encapsulation, a second choice exists. C2 can form a source-specific (really domain-specific) shortest path tree directly to d2.

12.5 IP Multicast Deployment Issues

Since its introduction, IP multicast has seen slow commercial deployment in the Internet. Although it has been available through the experimental MBONE for a number of years and is now supported natively by routers from vendors, it is just beginning to see commercial support from carriers, ISPs, and common operating systems. There are basically two reasons for this slow deployment: a modest customer demand and thus modest business motivation, and the relatively high cost of deploying multicast.

The most apparent benefit of multicast today is to reduce the amount of bandwidth required to transport data to multiple recipients. Longer term, it may also be used to minimize network delays in interactive application sessions. Multicast services are currently significantly more expensive than the unicast service, in terms of deployment, installation at customer premises, and management. Consequently, multicast makes sense today for an ISP or corporate network only when the bandwidth savings are higher than the deployment and management costs. This is multicast's deployment "sweet spot." Because multicast is more complex and more difficult to manage than unicast, it is only cost effective for an ISP to deploy multicast and manage it for customers when doing so saves significant bandwidth. The sweet spot is where the additional cost of providing the service is outweighed by the gained performance benefit.

Consequently, there is an incentive for ISPs and content providers to support small group sessions with unicast rather than multicast. For example, Broadcast.com follows this philosophy. Web events where the expected audience is small are supported by unicast connections because the bandwidth saved is not worth the overhead of multicast management. For events as large as the Victoria's Secret fashion show, which attracted 1.5 million visitors in the spring of 1999, multicast bandwidth savings were sought whenever possible. Such a large audience has the potential to overwhelm any large collection of servers and available network bandwidth, making multicast a profitable and useful service for both servers and the network.

The sweet-spot principle predicts that while the multicast architecture remains complex, it will not be widely deployed. In the short term, there are several issues that must be addressed before multicast can be routinely used:

☞ The standards for interdomain multicast routing must converge toward a stable and efficient solution.

☞ One must find a controlled way to allocate multicast addresses in the Internet.

☞ One must resolve the contradiction between the current open multicast model and commercial imperatives.

☞ One must resolve the security issues relative to open membership.

We will see that a transition to IPv6 could help solve some of these problems.

12.5.1 Domain Independence and Management

ISPs are having a difficult time managing multicast, although it is yet to become a popular service. While intradomain multicast is relatively easier to deploy, providing interdomain multicast is complicated. Interdomain multicast precludes complete control of the network, which makes it difficult to debug problems. This is important with protocols like BGMP or MSDP/MBGP, which involve contact with other domains.

For applications with many low-rate sources, like distributed games and DIS applications, it is more efficient to have all sources share a single bidirectional tree. Such trees are more efficient in terms of the amount of state at routers (although not with the data carried to receivers). Protocols like PIM and CBT were designed to support bidirectional trees.

However, ISPs using PIM, or other RP/core-based protocols face a number of problems regarding domain independence. As we mentioned earlier, many third-party dependency problems are present when RPs manage sources in other domains.

☞ Traffic sources in other domains potentially require traffic controls, such as rate or congestion control.

☞ An ISP that relies on an RP located in another domain has very little control over the service that its customers receive via the remote RP.

☞ ISPs do not want to be the core of a session for which they have no receivers, as it is a waste of their resources.

In addition to the problems above, using an RP or core requires advertisement of the address of the RP or core in a scalable fashion with low latency.

Specific to PIM are problems due to the difference in its deployment as compared to its intended design. PIM uses RPs so that applications with multiple low-rate sources can benefit from shared trees. However, deployed PIM never uses shared trees for transport for two reasons: MSDP and incorrect variable settings.

First, MSDP prevents the use of shared trees between domains. This is because when remote RPs receive source activation messages, they join directly to the source and not to the RP of the source. Even when two sources are colocated in the same domain, RPs in remote domains will form two separate per-source branches, one to each source. Accordingly, MSDP defeats the shared-tree support in PIM between domains. Note that having RPs join to the remote source's RP would not create "true" shared trees as CBT or PIM-sparse mode builds. The links between RPs would actually be tunnels; traffic toward two domains would be sent separately even if they shared a common path.

Second, although PIM specifies that receivers should only switch to a dense-mode per-source tree when the rate of a source passes a threshold, in practice multiple vendors have set the default setting of the threshold to zero. With such a setting, the following steps occur in deployed PIM. Receivers begin by joining to an RP's sparse-mode tree. Next, receivers immediately learn of all other participants in the session. Finally, receivers immediately form dense-mode per-source trees to each participant in the session. Therefore, in practice, PIM does not construct shared trees within domains for the purposes of transporting data.

PIM was designed to support both dense-mode per-source trees and sparse-mode shared trees. The deployment of PIM and MSDP defeats these design goals: deployed PIM is de facto a per-source protocol that suffers from the problems of shared-tree protocols, such as third-party dependencies and RP advertisement. This set of problems disconnects the deployed architecture from the intended designs.

Our best hope for solving these contradictions is the standardization of BGMP, which could include optional support for bidirectional trees. This standardization will probably trigger the evolution of intradomain protocols toward better support for bidirectional trees.

A related problem is network management for multicast routing, which refers to debugging problems that occur with the multicast tree during transmission and monitoring utilization and operation patterns for network planning purposes. The current set of tools for debugging multicast are all freeware developed as needed by MBONE users. Commercial toolkits for multicast network management await widespread deployment of multicast. However, such tools are a crucial part of multicast deployment since deploying multicast without them is likely to generate less than satisfactory customer experiences.

The current set of programs available for multicast management includes Mrinfo, Mtrace, RTPmon, Mhealth, Multimon, and Mlisten. Also available is the RouteMonitor, which is a tool that measures the stability of routes on the MBONE [29]. RouteMonitor counts the number of times distance metrics for each DVMRP router change in a given period. An MBGP RouteMonitor is under development. Robust versions of these tools will be needed by ISPs that deploy multicast routing.

12.5.2 Address Allocation and Address Control

Address allocation plays a key role in the deployment of unicast routing. Addresses may be allocated to users by the registries or delegated by providers, but addresses will only become useful in the Internet if at least one provider agrees to relay packets toward them, and also to insert a corresponding routing entry in its BGP announcements. On the other hand, address allocation to multicast groups in the experimental MBONE was essentially random. An application could literally pick whatever class-D address it saw fit. There were, in fact, attempts at coordination, but these attempts were enforced only by peer pressure, not by any routing mechanism.

Because there is no method of allocating addresses uniquely in the current model, the IETF is experimenting with static allocation of blocks of multicast addresses. This scheme is often referred to as GLOP [31]. This experiment should last until May 2000, when it is expected that protocols developed under the IETF Multicast Address Allocation Architecture (MAAA) [23] will be implemented. BGMP relies on MAAA protocols to designate the cores of multicast groups and to solve address allocation.

As the current multicast address space is unregulated, nothing prevents applications from sending data to any multicast address. Members of two sessions will receive each other's data if separate addresses are not chosen. A lack of address allocation mechanisms poses no threat to ISPs, other than that of dealing with angry customers and carrying unwanted data. However, address collision poses a serious inefficiency risk for multicast receivers and can create application inconsistencies. This is because packets from other sessions must be processed and dropped.

A proper allocation scheme would have a number of properties.

☞ No single user could disrupt service to other users, for example, by allocating all addresses.
☞ No (or negligible) delay in address allocation so as not to delay applications.
☞ Low complexity of implementation.
☞ High scalability to interdomain environments.
☞ Efficient utilization of the address space.
☞ Long-term scaling to millions of multicast groups.

Due to the very small number of groups that current routers can support, the chance of an address collision is very limited right now. The chance that any two of 48K addresses collide in the IPv4 multicast address space is 25%. However, the average multicast-capable router sold and deployed today has memory available for only 1–2K (source address, group address) entries. For the 268 million class-D multicast addresses available, the chances of collision are limited to less than 0.05% for memory that can hold 2K addresses. However, if multicast were to become more popular (and routers reserved more memory for multicast addresses), the problem of multicast allocation will become a serious issue. For routers with memory that can store 32K addresses, the chances of a collision when all addresses are used increases to 11.75%. Our figure shows the probability of a collision of addresses given a limited amount of router memory (in units of addresses).

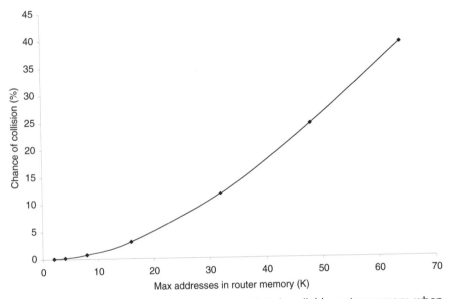

The chance of address collision in IPv4 with restricted available router memory, when all memory is allocated.

Currently, there are four alternatives to the current model for address allocation.

1. The Multicast Address Allocation Architecture (MAAA) [23]
2. Static allocation and assignment [31] (referred to as GLOP)
3. Per-source (or channel) allocation as proposed by the Express [25] model
4. IP version 6 (IPv6) addressing [15], which we will detail later

MAAA's design emphasized the efficient use of a dynamically allocated address space at the cost of complex design. GLOP uses autonomous system (AS) numbers as the basis for restricting addresses available to domains. GLOP is a short-term experiment to be reviewed in May 2000. IPv6 drastically increases the address space at the expense of changing IP packet structures, although IPv6 was designed to be incrementally deployed in the Internet. IPv6 is a major rework of IP but does provide sufficient unique addresses to make address allocation easy. IPv6 and

Express solve all requirements, requiring a change in current packet-header formats for IPv6, and the deployment of IGMPv3 for Express.

MAAA is complex. It consists of three protocols connecting hosts, domains, and multicast address allocation servers. Hosts request addresses from servers using the Multicast Address Dynamic Client Allocation Protocol (MADCAP) [32]. The servers inform each other of claimed address blocks using the Address Allocation Protocol (AAP) [22]. The allocation of addresses between domains is handled by the Multicast Address Set Claim (MASC) [19] protocol. Other protocols exist for managing the address space within the domain, such as the Multicast Zone Allocation Protocol (MZAP) [24]. Even if MAAA scalability issues can be solved by an appropriate implementation, MAAA does not solve the problem of the reduced number of multicast addresses available in the current addressing scheme.

Express [25] is an alternative to the IP-multicast model that uses a per-source, *channel-based* model. Each channel is a service identified by a tuple (S, E), where S is the sender's source address and E is the express destination address (i.e., a class-D address). Only S may send to (S, E) because receivers subscribed to (S,E) are not subscribed to (S',E), for some other host S'. Thus, data transmitted from two sources to the same address E is only sent to receivers subscribing to both sources. Similarly, a proposal called "Simple Multicast" designates addresses as a (core, class-D address) model for the purposes of core advertisement for shared trees [33]. The scheme in Simple Multicast is not meant to address source authorization. Regardless of purpose, such a tuple solves the allocation problem as address allocation is local to the core or source S listed.

One small problem with Express results from each host using a different multicast address (unlike the current model, in which even per-source trees have the same class-D address). The session can no longer be identified by a common address among sources. For example, in a distributed game many users are the sources of data. This problem can be solved at the application level by using an alternate identifier.

12.5.3 Open Multicast Model and Commercial Imperative

We have already discussed the multicast architecture. Let's review the IP-multicast service model. It is an *open* service model. No mechanism restricts the hosts or users from creating a multicast *group*, receiving data from a group, or sending data to a group. As with all IP datagrams, multicast datagrams are best-effort and unreliable. Each multicast group is named by a class-D multicast address. To receive data from the multicast group, hosts must join the group by contacting their routers using IGMP. Once a host joins a group, it receives all data sent to the group address, regardless of the sender's source address.

Hosts can send to a multicast group without becoming a receiver; such hosts are often referred to as *non-member senders*. Multiple senders may share the same multicast address; whether those sources share a single multicast routing tree or have separate trees leading to the receivers is dependent on the multicast routing protocol. Senders cannot reserve addresses or prevent another sender from choosing the same address. The number of hosts joined to a group as receivers is dynamic and unknown. The status of entities (i.e., sender, receiver, or both) is unknown. In sum, an IP-multicast group is not managed.

The classic argument for the open multicast model is that it is not possible, in practice, to prevent relaying of packets by third parties. This is true even for unicast transmissions that can be rather easily wiretapped, and is even more obvious for multicast trees, where wiretap or uncontrolled multicast forwarding can happen through any branch of the tree. The MBONE model was thus that receivers, and nobody else, would decide which source they intended to listen to, and that efficient access control would have to be based on encryption: anyone could try to receive a multicast transmission, but only authorized receivers would receive the group's key.

In practice, this model does not quite fit the classic commercial imperatives of network providers. The providers would typically like to sell multicast availability as a premium service. This implies having a way of controlling, at a minimum, who is authorized to send data to a group, as well as the possibility to bill for the service. The lack of access control functions presents a danger for companies providing content over multicast groups as well as for receivers who pay for a given service. Just as web sites require protection from hackers attempting to change the content of a site, multicast-based content providers require access controls as protection from outsiders launching a number of possible attacks, including:

☞ Flooding attacks, in which high-rate, useless data are transmitted on the same multicast group causing congestion and packet loss. Flooding attacks prevent reception of data by valid receivers.

☞ Collisions of sessions. Due to the lack of group creation controls, two sessions using the same address can interleave their data.

☞ Drowning out of authentic sources with alternate data, changing the content of the session. This is also a source of lost revenue.

Without access control mechanisms, such attacks are trivial to implement. One enhancement over current IP group management is IGMP version 3 [14], which provides source pruning for specific multicast groups, as well as source-specific joins. IGMPv3 prevents data from entering the backbone when the routing protocols support this option. Unfortunately, it is not possible to prune sources or have source-specific joins in shared-tree protocols such as PIM-Sparse mode, CBT, or BGMP. In addition, attacks may still be possible in the backbone with IGMPv3 when even one receiver does not prune all noisy or malicious sources. Note that IGMP version 3 is still under development.

12.5.4 Dynamic Receivers and Group Security

Unauthorized reception of multicast data, including pay-for content such as pay-per-view events, represents a source of lost revenue for content providers. According to the current model, any receiver can join any group, as long as they can learn the group's address.

Providing security for multicast-based communication is inherently more complicated than for unicast-based communication because multiple entities participate, most of which will not have trusted relationships with each other. Future multicast security should provide four distinct mechanisms: authentication, authorization, encryption, and data integrity. Authentication is the process of forcing hosts to prove their identities so that they may be authorized to create, send to, or receive data from a group. Authorization is the process of allowing authenticated hosts to perform specific tasks. Encryption ensures eavesdroppers cannot read data on the network. Data integrity mechanisms ensure that datagrams have not been altered in transit.

The current IP multicast service and architecture do not provide authentication or authorization for sources or receivers. Encryption is an application- or transport-level mechanism. Data integrity is provided only by standard IP security mechanisms. Solutions to this problem include solutions at the application level and at the network level.

Encryption is often cited as the appropriate mechanism to preserve data privacy at the application level. Unfortunately, for large heterogeneous groups, application-level key management is, at best, a partially solved problem. For example, sending a secret key to each member of a very large group is a self-defeating proposition: a secret that is shared by a million machines is hardly a secret anymore. To maintain scalability in the presence of a large receiver set, rekeying must be done on portions of the tree [34,39,30]. For example, the proposed Iolus protocol [30] protects data from unauthorized receivers with data encryption. Unlike normal multicast delivery, Iolus has the drawback that packets may cross some links more than once.

Secure multicast services are network-level solutions to ensure that multicast tree construction and delivery services are restricted to authenticated and authorized hosts. Such protocols are therefore more resistant to attacks, such as denial-of-service and theft-of-service attacks. For example, Keyed-HIP (KHIP) [34] is a proposed network-level security scheme that restricts sub-branch construction to unauthorized domains and hosts. KHIP provides transmissions and receiver access control, as well as data integrity. Each packet is encrypted to ensure data integrity.

KHIP uses a bidirectional, core-based multicast routing tree and lacks facilities for excluding specific sources from the tree. In fact, all bidirectional shared-tree protocols break down into the same state as per-source trees when individual sources must authenticate for each receiver. Cain has suggested placing authorization mechanisms at the edge of the network to maintain per-group in the presence of receiver-specific source prunes [40]. However, such a scheme maintains security at the edge routers. If the edge routers are bypassed, then unauthorized transmissions will enter into the backbone. The advantage of such a scheme is that it keeps complexity on edge routers and out of the backbone.

One very serious unresolved issue with multicast security is the location of access lists. One simple model is to place control of authorized receivers at the (primary) source of a session. Such a model does not resolve who authorizes sources within domains—presumably, system administrators would handle it—or interdomain authorization. One alternative to source-based authentication would be to use authentication servers.

12.5.5 Is IPv6 the Solution?

One of the design goals of IPv6 was to include multicast as part of the base standard, not as an add-on. Instead of having a separate group membership discovery, the IPv6 equivalent of IGMP will be part of ICMPv6, and will be expected to be present in all IPv6 hosts and routers. The set of ICMPv6 messages that enable "multicast listener discovery" (MLD) [42] are the multicast listener "query," "report," and "done," which are roughly equivalent to IGMP membership query, report, and leave.

IPv6 Multicast routing will be similar to IPv4 multicast routing. The multicast extensions to OSPF are carried over in OSPFv6, and PIM can be implemented trivially using algorithmic extensions to MLD. The multiprotocol extensions to BGP are used to support both IPv6 and BGMP.

The most visible innovation in IPv6 will be the size and the structure of the multicast addresses. We saw in chapter 4 that the addressing format includes provision for very large multicast addresses:

8 bits	4 bits	4 bits	112 bits
11111111	Flags	Scope	Group ID

In fact, these addresses introduce at least two new capabilities, as well as the possibility of future extensions. The first new capability is the very large address size. The IPv6 addressing scheme offers 2^{112} multicast addresses for world use, driving the chances of collision to near zero. For an IPv6 router with space for 1024K addresses, the chance of a collision is less than 10^{-28}. The second new capability is the insertion of a scope field, which can be used to limit the distribution of some multicast groups, thus providing a limited but practical way to manage the membership of a group.

Furthermore, the combination of flag fields and a large address size allows for experimentation of new multicast routing paradigms, such as Express or simple multicast. An Express-like scheme can be used in IPv6 by splitting the 112 bits of address between a 64-bit routing prefix that identifies the domain of the source and a 48-bit group identifier within this domain. Domains could claim implicit ownership of address spaces. The ownership of multicast addresses within a domain could be managed with AAP or a similar protocol. Flags could be used to specify whether the group's traffic is expected to follow a per-source tree, a centered tree, or a bidirectional tree. Using IPv6 could satisfy most, if not all, of the properties of a good allocation scheme and is already supported by vendors and the IETF.

12.6 The Future of Multicast Routing

There has been a long effort since Deering's first specification of multicast routing, and support for the service exists now in many commercial routers. However, to provide a multicast service, one has to implement a complex protocol architecture not limited to a single routing protocol. Issues like address allocation, domain isolation, access control, and security have to be provided for multicast to become a commercial service.

Multicast services are already being deployed in 1999 by some ISPs, such as Sprint and UUNet. But multicast has not matured yet enough to be widely used. This is partially because of the lack of scalability of the current protocol architecture, but this is also due to the absence of leading application. We have shown that the first application to benefit from a multicast communication infrastructure will be the one with a large number of users, yet this is the most difficult to support, as it immediately requires one to solve interdomain routing and access control problems. The current IP-multicast architecture deployed by carriers and ISPs to compensate for these issues is complex and has limited scalability.

Another practical problem hampering the deployment of multicast is the relatively cutting edge nature of the multicast products, which are typically found only in the most recent models of routers and network access servers. But many ISPs still use old routers and access servers, for which multicast upgrades may not be available. These equipments typically start their life in the most demanding parts of the network and, as they age, are typically pushed toward the edges of the network, where they can still match the limited bandwidth demand. Deploying multicast immediately would imply their brutal decommission and require immediate capital investment for their replacement.

Research efforts are currently trying to address the scalability issues by providing a simpler architecture. PIM bidirectional, Simple Multicast, and EXPRESS are part of this effort. IPv6 might offer a unique opportunity to introduce these research efforts in a new scalable architecture without compromising current effort to increase the stability and the scalability of the current IPv4 multicast protocol architecture. The future of multicast routing relies on these efforts, and also on the capacity of the network providers to define business models that can fund the deployment of the service.

References

1. T. Bates, R. Chandra, D. Katz, and Y. Rekhter, "Multiprotocol extensions for BGP-4." IETF, Request for Comments 2283, February 1998.

2. T. Ballardie, P. Francis, and J. Crowcroft, "Core Based Tree (CBT), An Architecture for Scalable Inter-Domain Routing," ACM-SIGCOMM '93 Conference, September 1993.

3. S. Deering, "Multicast Routing in a Datagram Internetwork," Ph.D. thesis, Stanford University, California, 1991.

4. S. Deering, "Host Extensions for IP Multicasting," RFC-1112, August 1, 1989.

5. S. Deering, C. Partridge, and D. Waitzman, "Distance Vector Multicast Routing Protocol," RFC-1075, November 1, 1988.

6. S. Deering, D. Estrin, D. Farinacci, V. Jacobson, L. Ching-gung, and W. Liming, "Protocol Independent Multicast (PIM): Motivation and Architecture," work in progress, March 1994.

7. J. Moy, "Multicast Extensions to OSPF," RFC-1584, March 24, 1994.

8. J. Moy, "MOSPF: Analysis and Experience," RFC-1585, March 24, 1994.

9. S. Deering, D. Estrin, D. Farinacci, and V. Jacobson, "Protocol Independent Multicast (PIM), Dense Mode Protocol Specification," work in progress, March 1994.

10. S. Deering, D. Estrin, D. Farinacci, V. Jacobson, L. Ching-gung, and W. Liming, "Protocol Independent Multicast (PIM), Sparse Mode Protocol Specification," work in progress, March 1994.

11. W. Fenner, "Internet Group Management Protocol, Version 2," IETF Request for Comments 2236, November 1997.

12. D. Farinacci, Y. Rekhter, P. Lothberg, H. Kilmer, and J. Hall, "Multicast Source Discovery Protocol (MSDP)," IETF Internet draft, draft-farinacci-msdp-*.txt, June 1998.

13. K. Kumar, P. Radoslavov, D. Thaler, C. Alaettinoglu, D. Estrin, and M. Handley, "The MASC/BGMP Architecture for Interdomain Multicast Routing," in *Proc. ACM SIGCOMM 98*, September 1998.

14. B. Cain, S. Deering, and A. Thyagarajan, "Internet Group Management Protocol, Version 3," IETF Internet draft, draft-ietf-idmr-igmp-v3-*.txt, February 1999.

15. S. Deering and R. Hinden, "Internet Protocol, Version 6 (IPv6) Specification," IETF Request for Comments 2460, December 1998.

16. S. Deering, D. Estrin, D. Farinacci, V. Jacobson, G. Liu, and L. Wei, "PIM Architecture for Wide-Area Multicast Routing," IEEE/ACM Transactions on Networking, pp. 153–162, April 1996.

17. S. Deering, D. Estrin, D. Farinacci, V. Jacobson, A. Helmy, D. Meyer, and L. Wei, "Protocol Independent Multicast Version 2 Dense Mode Specification," IETF Internet draft, draft-ietf-pim-v2-dm-*.txt, November 1998.

18. D. Estrin, D. Farinacci, A. Helmy, D. Thaler, S. Deering, M. Handley, V. Jacobson, C. Liu, P. Sharma, and L. Wei, "Protocol Independent Multicast Sparse-Mode (PIM-SM): Protocol Specification," Internet Engineering Task Force (IETF), RFC-2362, June 1998.

19. D. Estrin, R. Govindan, M. Handley, S. Kumar, P. Radoslavov, and D. Thaler, "The Multicast Address Set Claim (MASC) Protocol," Internet draft, draft-ietf-malloc-masc-01.txt, August 1998.

20. D. Farinacci, Y. Rekhter, P. Lothberg, H. Kilmer, and J. Hall, "Multicast Source Discovery Protocol (MSDP)," IETF Internet draft, draft-farinacci-msdp-*.txt, June 1998.

21. R. Finlayson, "IP Multicast and Firewalls," IETF Internet draft, draft-ietf-mboned-mcast-firewall-*.txt, November 1998.

22. M. Handley, "The Address Allocation Protocol," IETF Internet draft, draft-ietf-malloc-aap-*.txt, August 1998.

23. M. Handley, D. Thaler, and D. Estrin, "The Internet Multicast Address Allocation Architecture," IETF Internet draft, draft-handley-malloc-arch-*.ps, December 1997.

24. M. Handley, D. Thaler, and R. Kermode, "Multicast-Scope Zone Announcement Protocol (MZAP)," Internet draft, draft-ietf-mboned-mzap-04.txt, June 1999.

25. H. Holbrook and D. Cheriton, "IP Multicast Channels: EXPRESS Support for Large-Scale Single-Source Applications," to appear in *Proc. ACM SIGCOMM '99*, September 1999.

26. Internet Assigned Numbers Authority. *http://www.isi.edu/in-notes/iana/ assignments/multicast-addresses*. (See also *http://www.isi.edu/in-notes/iana/assignments/ single-source-multicast.*)

27. K. Kumar, P. Radoslavov, D. Thaler, C. Alaettinoglu, D. Estrin, and M. Handley, "The MASC/BGMP Architecture for Interdomain Multicast Routing," in *Proc. ACM SIGCOMM 98*, September 1998.

28. Maestro BOF. 45th IETF Meeting. Oslo, Norway. IDMR Working group. July 1999.

29. D. Massey and W. Fenner, *RouteMonitor*. Available from *http://ganef.cs.ucla.edu/~masseyd/Route*.

30. S. Mittra, "Iolus: A Framework for Scalable Secure Multicasting," In *Proc. ACM SIGCOMM '97*, September 1997. ACM.

31. D. Meyer and P. Lothberg, "Static Allocations in 233/8," Internet draft, draft-ietf-mboned-static-allocation-*.txt, May 1999.

32. B. Patel, M. Shah, and S. Hanna, "Multicast Address Dynamic Client Allocation Protocol," IETF Internet draft, draft-ietf-malloc-madcap-*.txt, May 1999.

33. R. Perlman, C.-Y. Lee, A. Ballardie, J. Crowcroft, Z. Wang, T. Maufer, C. Diot, J. Thoo, and M. Green, "Simple Multicast: A Design for Simple, Low-Overhead Multicast," Internet draft, February 1999.

34. C. Shields and J. J. Garcia-Luna-Aceves, "KHIP—A Scalable, Efficient Protocol for Secure Multicast Routing," to appear in *Proceedings of ACM Sigcomm '99*.

35. C. Shields and J. J. Garcia-Luna-Aceves, "HIP—A Protocol for Hierarchical Multicast Routing," in *Proceedings of the Seventeenth Annual ACM Symposium on Principles of Distributed Computing*, Puerto Vallarta, Mexico, June 1998.

36. C. Shields and J. J. Garcia-Luna-Aceves, "The Ordered Core Based Tree Protocol," in Proceedings of the IEEE INFOCOM97, Kobe, Japan, April 1997.

37. T. Speakman, D. Farinacci, S. Lin, and A. Tweedly, "Pragmatic General Multicast," Internet draft, January 1998.

38. D. Waitzman, C. Partridge, and S. Deering, "Distance Vector Multicast Routing Protocol," IETF Request for Comments 1075, November 1988.

39. C. Wong, M. Gouda, and S. Lam, "Secure Group Communications Using Key Graphs," in *Proc. ACM SIGCOMM '98*, pp. 68–79, September 1998.

40. B. Cain, "Source Access Control for Bi-Directional Trees," 41st IETF meeting. March 30-April 3, 1998; Los Angeles, CA, USA.

41. F. K. Hwang, D. S. Richards, and P. Winter, "The Steiner Tree Problem," North-Holland, 1992.

42. S. Deering, W. Fenner, and B. Haberman, "Multicast Listener Discovery (MLD) for IPv6," work in progress, June 1999.

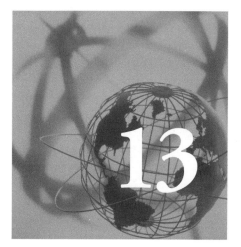

Mobility

In the long run, it may well be the case that all computers will be mobile. Even so, they will have to be connected to the Internet. Therefore, the Internet Protocol had to be extended to support mobility.

13.1 Mobile Hosts

The original Internet was designed in the late 1970s. Computers then were relatively heavy objects that were often stored in dedicated rooms; mobile computers existed, but were used mostly in special applications, such as in armored vehicles or in aircrafts. The need to support mobility in the Internet became pressing only with the advent of portable computers.

In this chapter we will review the objectives of IP mobility and then present the basic model and the corresponding protocols that were developed by the "mobile IP" working group of the IETF. This development is by no means complete. We will also detail the way in which the new versions will have to be improved.

13.2 The Objectives of IP Mobility

Mobile computing is a very large concept. In fact, there are three different forms of mobility: portable computers, which are transported and connected from remote locations; mobile computers, which stay connected during their movements; and mobile networks. In this section, we will expand these definitions, examine the transmission technologies that are used for enabling mobility, and finally cite the requirements for IP mobility that were agreed to by the mobile IP working group of the IETF.

13.2.1 Portable Computers

Portable computers have most probably been the fastest growing segment of the computer market in recent years, second only to the growth of the Internet. There is a clear synergy between portability and connectedness—the portable device is used by frequent travellers to acquire and process information, while the network is precisely the place where they want to find or export this information.

A typical day for the owner of a portable computer might include a visit to a friendly site, then a trip to the airport, yet another of those long waits in the lounge while the flight keeps being delayed, a plane trip, another car ride, and a stop at the office. In all these locations, there may be a need to be connected. One may want to plug the computer in the friendly site's local network and exchange information; one may want to use a portable phone and a modem to send some urgent messages from the taxi; one may want to connect to a pay phone in the airport to immediately start processing the backlog of electronic mail that has accumulated in the home office. One will eventually connect the portable computer to the home-office local network to backup the portable disk.

Fulfilling these needs is obviously useful, and several solutions already exist. One can use "dynamic configuration" protocols to acquire a temporary address in a remote network; one can plug a modem into a portable phone or a pay phone; one may even find a 64-kbps ISDN pay phone in some places, at least in Japan. These solutions are useful, but they are only partial. They generally imply the use of temporary addresses that describe the location of the computer—a remote local network, a data server connected to a telephone exchange. The TCP connections are identified by a pair of IP addresses and ports. Using temporary addresses implies that these connections will not survive the temporary attachment. In some cases, the temporary assignments may pose security problems, since there is little difference between a remote computer that uses dynamic configuration to connect to the local network and a bona fide local computer. Then, there is the privacy requirement: because the temporary address embeds an identification of the temporary location, it is possible to derive from this address the whereabouts of the mobile user, thus adding yet another set of digital fingerprints in our Big-Brother society!

Portable computing, as described here, is in fact only a first step toward mobile computing, which some researchers prefer to describe as "ubiquitous computing."

13.2.2 Mobile Computing

In the previous section, our mobile-computing scenario used fairly static technologies: local networks and plugs, telephones and modems. Obviously, there can be a better link between a portable computer and a cellular phone, and that link actually has existed for quite a long time. It is called "packet radio." Do you remember the "ALOHA" experiment that opened the road to shared-access local networks such as Ethernet? It was already a packet radio network.

The principle of packet radio is simple. A number of computers share one radio channel, one wavelength, in much the same way that stations connected to an Ethernet share a cable. One particular channel is used only in a limited area—a "cell"—just like cellular telephony. On each cell, a main station is connected to the Internet infrastructure and is capable of relaying IP packets between the radio channel and the Internet. It signals its presence by emitting a "beacon." When the mobile computer moves, it will listen continuously to a set of wavelengths, trying to pick the main station that sends the clearest signal.

The whole purpose of the mobile IP technology is to enable this transition from cell to cell, called "roaming," while keeping the mobile unit connected to the Internet. The mobile computer will keep the same IP address irrespective of its location so that TCP connections, which are identified by the address and port pairs, can be maintained.

13.2.3 Various Transmission Technologies

For the sake of presentation, we spoke only of radio channels in the previous paragraph. This certainly is not the only enabling technology for IP mobility. In fact, there are at least three competing solutions.

- ☞ Sharing a radio frequency through packet radio
- ☞ Sharing a radio wave band through spread spectrum
- ☞ Using infrared transmission

The packet radio technique is very similar to the Ethernet case—instead of sharing a cable, one shares a radio channel. This is, however, slightly more complex, because one cannot use the classic CSMA-CD protocol, which is based on a principle of "listen before sending, listen while sending." Listening before sending is known as "pure CSMA" and is easily implemented, but "listening while sending" for "collision detection" is nearly impossible, because the local emission overpowers the remote signals by several orders of magnitude. Pure CSMA is slightly less efficient and more prone to collisions than CSMA-CD. Several designs have been tried, such as inserting random delays in the CSMA protocol, completing it with some form of acknowledgments and repetition, or switching from CSMA to a more organized access such as "time division" or "slot reservation."

Radio channels are prone to various forms of "noise." Signals may be echoed by large buildings; remote stations may interfere with each other; various forms of electronic signals can add noise to the transmission. One can attenuate this problem by diminishing the distance between the stations, hence reducing the size of the cells. But this requires a larger number of "main stations" and makes the network more expensive to build. The spread spectrum technology is an elegant way to solve this problem. Each bit to be transmitted is split into a number of tiny time or frequency intervals according to a pattern that is characteristic of the sender. By averaging the received signal according to the same pattern or "signature," the receivers will extract the sender's emission out of the random noises caused by other senders, echoes, and parasite signals. Several mobile IP systems have been built using simple implementations of this technique.

Infrared transmission has also been used for many "indoor" mobile systems. Infrared transmission has several advantages over radio. It does not propagate to very long distances and thus cannot easily be heard outside of a building. It is less prone to interference than radio and thus is not usually subject to the same form of "bandwidth regulation"—there is no risk that a malfunctioning infrared transmitter can cause havoc in a nearby air-traffic control radar. Small-distance infrared transmitters are probably easier and thus less expensive to build than radios. A popular design is the installation of infrared receivers in the ceilings that communicate with mobile laptops lying on desks. Sharing an infrared channel between several stations poses almost the same problems as sharing a radio channel, and the same solutions, such as CSMA, can be used.

13.2.4 Moving Networks

Mobility is not limited to portable computers carried by high-tech owners. As computers become cheaper and smaller, one may expect to see more and more of them in places that seem unlikely today, e.g., in cars. There are already computer-controlled antilock brakes. What about a braking system controlled completely by a computer, or maybe two for redundancy, then another for regulating the engine, and yet another for managing the information display? We will certainly need something more elaborate than a speedometer and a fuel gauge in the twenty-first century cars! These computers will obviously have to communicate between themselves, for example, to reduce speed if the temperature of the braking devices is not nominal. They will also have to communicate with the infrastructure, e.g., to update the map of the city with the location of the most recent traffic jams.

This is not pure fiction. The transmission of data between Formula 1 racing cars and the pits is routinely used by the crews to monitor the engines. Manufacturers are working on "local area networks" to reduce the large amount of cabling used in cars, and systems where the car receives "navigation data" from the infrastructure are already on display. But let's not look only at cars. Computer networks are already present in planes, trains, and ships. Connecting these networks to the Internet is just a natural follow-on—your car will be able to send a status report to your mechanic; truck drivers will keep in touch with their companies and receive new freight assignments.

For the networker, this adds one dimension to the mobile IP challenge: we need to manage "mobile networks" as well as "mobile hosts." We may even have to manage "recursive mobility"— a mobile computer may connect to the plane's or car's local networks. Instead of merely updating the position of one object, one will constantly have to update the route to that object.

13.2.5 The Requirements

When the IETF mobile IP working group started to work, one of its first tasks was to delineate a set of "user requirements" for a mobile IP solution. These requirements are derived from the expected usage that we analyzed previously.

1. A mobile host should be capable of continuing to communicate, using the same IP address, after it has been disconnected from the Internet and reconnected at a different point.
2. A mobile host should be capable of interoperating with existing hosts, routers, and services.

The first requirement is dictated by the need to maintain TCP-IP connections while the mobile host is roaming from cell to cell. Keeping a single IP address is essential because this address identifies the TCP connection. The second requirement is dictated by the need for "gradual deployment." There would be little advantage in IP mobility if one could not connect to existing servers using existing networks. Waiting for the whole infrastructure to be updated is utterly unrealistic in a million-computer Internet!

These two requirements are essential, but a few other "soft requirements" were also listed by the group.

1. No weakening of IP security
2. Multicast capability
3. Location privacy

The general feeling is that there is little security in the Internet today, but there is a trust that if one sends a packet to address X it will indeed arrive at the addressed host. Mobility poses an obvious question there. If I can take my portable computer to any Internet location and use my home address, there is an implicit risk that some hacker will configure his or her portable with my address and pretend to be me. Whatever solution is chosen must at least guarantee that, if all the routers between the mobile host and the destination are trustable, then there is no way for the hacker to perpetuate the intrusion.

Multicasting poses another kind of problem. We have learned in the previous chapter that the classic solutions to multicast routing are "reverse-path forwarding" and "core-based tree." In one case, loop protection is based on computing the fastest reverse path to the source address. This is obviously difficult if the source is constantly moving. In the other case, data distribution is based on the maintenance of a graph of routers that are members of the group; when receivers move, this graph will have to be updated constantly. Yet the new wave of Internet applications is largely based on multicasting; one should make sure that these applications also work on mobile hosts.

We have already mentioned the fears of an electronic Big-Brother society and the risk of leaving "digital fingerprints" by displaying the location of a mobile computer. Keeping one single IP address for the mobile computer eases this fear somewhat, but the risk still exists, e.g., by letting observers trace the routes to the mobile. There should be a means of hiding mobile location information from other hosts.

13.3 Architecture/Terminology

Several competing designs have been proposed to the mobile IP working group. The first practical problem was that these designs used very different terminologies—for example, base station and home base could easily be very different objects. The basic model for supporting mobility in the Internet is presented in RFC-2002 [3]. We will present the model and the "dogleg routing" problem.

13.3.1 The Basic Model

The basic model uses the following terminology:

☞ Mobile Node (MN) has a registered Home Address in a Home network, and obtains a care-of-address (COA) when it visits a Foreign network.

☞ Home Agent (HA) belongs to the Home network and serves the Home Address.

☞ Foreign Agent (FA) serves visiting Mobile Nodes.

☞ Corresponding Node (CN) exchanges data with the MN and may be either mobile or fixed.

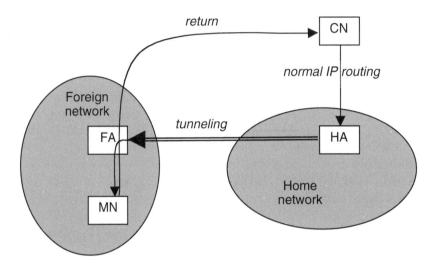

A mobile node (MN) will roam from place to place and will obtain connectivity through a foreign network. In this foreign network, it may obtain help from a foreign agent. The way the MN obtains connectivity is not specified in the architecture. It may be through a radio or infrared channel, or maybe by letting the mobile unit temporarily plug into a local network. The foreign network is connected to the Internet and can exchange data with regular Internet hosts.

Since there is no requirement that the MN have dialogues only with fixed Internet stations, we use the name "correspondent node" (CN) instead of "fixed node" for the MN's partner. When a CN wants to send data to an MN, it simply formats a regular IP packet using the CN's address as the source and the MN's permanent address or home address as destination. These packets will arrive, using normal IP routing, to a very special router, the "home agent" (HA).

From a routing protocol point of view, the HA behaves as if it is connected directly to the MN, e.g., an Ethernet segment behind the HA attached to the MN. The MN's home address will be assigned within the subnet space of that "virtual Ethernet." An HA will generally serve several MNs.

The HA must keep track of the current location of the MN it serves. This location is represented by the care-of address (COA), normally the address of the foreign agent that serves the MN in the foreign domain. When the HA receives a packet from the CN to the MN, it encapsulates it in a new IP envelope.

Source=HA, Dest=COA, protocol=IP in IP (4)	Source=CN, Dest=MN, protocol=TCP.	TCP header + data
New IP header	Original IP packet	

The new header carries as source address the HA address and as destination the COA address. The packet's "payload" is the original IP packet from CN to MN, including both the header and the data part. The "protocol" field in the new header indicates "IP in IP," i.e., a tunnelled packet. There are many ways to design the encapsulation procedure. The figure above shows the headers specified in RFC-2003 [4]. The new packet is posted on the Internet and will arrive at the foreign agent. The FA will recognize an address that it manages (COA) and will know from the protocol field that it should decapsulate the packet carried in the data part. If the MN has not moved, the FA can forward the packet on the foreign network using, for example, a local radio or infrared channel.

There is no problem going in the other direction. The MN simply formats a normal IP packet with its own source address and the CN's address as destination. It forwards it to the base, which relays it toward the CN using normal IP routing.

The path from MN to CN is shorter than the path from CN to MN, which has to go through the HA. In the worst case, if an MN based in Paris is visiting San Francisco and wants to communicate with a CN in San Francisco, the packets from CN to MN will have to go from San Francisco to Paris and back. This asymmetric procedure is known as "dogleg routing," something many experts don't like.

13.3.2 Requirements of Basic Model

The basic model presented above implies a set of basic requirements. The HA must be able to "announce" that it is the router for the MN, and it must keep track of the MN's location. The MN must be able to "discover" the base and must "register" so that the base agrees to serve as a relay for its packets.

One possibility is to let the HA behave as a proxy for an MN that has left its original location. Suppose, for example, that the home network is an Ethernet, and that the HA is a host connected to the same segment as the MN, when the MN is home. We will have two modes of operation. When the MN is home, it will directly receive the packets sent on the local network. When the MN is at a foreign location, the HA will respond to address resolution requests on behalf of the MN, using "proxy ARP," and will capture the packets bound to the MN.

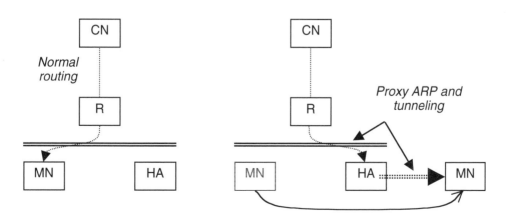

The proxy ARP solution has the big advantage that it allows any node to become mobile, while behaving strictly like a fixed host when at its nominal location. One should note that the home agent function can easily be performed by a router connected to the network, resulting in better performance. For nodes that are truly mobile and have no natural fixed location, one can use a "virtual network" solution. The home addresses belong to a subnet managed by the HA, but this subnet has no physical instantiation. The HA announces the MN through the local routing protocol, such as OSPF or RIP. Everything is set up as if the HA is a gateway to a virtual Ethernet.

The second requirement of the basic model is that the HA must keep track of the MN. This implies that signalling messages will have to be exchanged either between the FA and the HA or between the MN and the HA. These messages will have to be somehow secured so that an intruder cannot just signal to the HA his or her own location as the new position of the MN!

For the MN to discover the base, one will use an "advertisement" protocol. There was a debate in the working group whether to use a media-specific solution or a generic IP-level solution. The group eventually chose the latter.

Once the MN has discovered the FA, it must register with it. Just suppose that the MN simply transmitted the "care-of" address to the HA without telling the base. The HA would send encapsulated packets to the base, which would decapsulate them and send them back to the HA using normal Internet routing. One needs an "exception" there: the base must realize that the MN is now connected to it. Thus, one needs an explicit negotiation between MN and base.

13.3.3 Moving from Network to Network

The whole purpose of mobility is to allow the MN to move from cell to cell, from network to network. Short distance mobility is generally solved by lower level protocols that allow a group of cells to behave as a single network. The MN will not know a priori that it has moved—most MNs are not using the global positioning satellite system, or at least not yet. The MN will discover that it is moving by listening to advertisements from the foreign agents, and it will discover that it is back home by receiving advertisements from the home agent.

Through the advertisement protocol, the MN has discovered the IP and "media" address of the new FA. It must now register with this new FA and obtain its agreement to relay packets, as well as the COA address. Then it will have to communicate the new COA to the HA so that new packets get relayed through the new base.

However, we also have to take care of packets that are already in transit between the HA and the former base. If cells are sufficiently narrow, the MN may still be hearing the former base and may perhaps receive these packets, but we should not count on that. Switching cells may well imply that the MN is switching to a new frequency, that the MN may be moving too fast, or that the infrared signal of the new base may well be overpowering the one of the former base. In general, we should assume that packets that are not routed to the current FA will be lost.

Early versions of the mobile-IP specifications included a redirection procedure. The MN would keep a list of the recently visited FA, and would inform them of its new position. But the working group could not agree on a redirection design that would eliminate risks of loops as well as security concerns. Without precautions, it would be easy for a hacker to send a "redirection" message to the current FA and to capture the MN's traffic! This could be prevented by setting up a security association between the MN and each FA, but that would be an additional requirement. In most cases, the only security association is between the MN and the HA.

13.3.4 What If There Is No Foreign Agent?

In some cases, mobile nodes may connect to foreign networks that do not comply with the Mobile IP specifications and do not include any foreign agent. The MN may obtain IP connectivity nevertheless, using protocols such as DHCP or PPP to obtain a temporary IP address, in the address space managed by the foreign network. The MN can then use this temporary address as its temporary care-of address, effectively subsuming the functions of the foreign agent. The packets sent by the HA will be tunneled all the way to the MN. This degenerate mode of IP mobility has a few inconveniences:

☞ Tunnelling all the way to the mobile is not efficient when the last hop is a narrow radio link. It is more efficient for a foreign agent to remove the tunnelling overhead before transmitting the packet on the last hop.

☞ Allocating addresses to visiting hosts implies a higher rate of consumption of the IP address space, thus precipitating exhaustion of the IP address space.

☞ Using the mobile as its own FA means that the FA will disappear from the Internet as soon as the mobile moves to a new location, and that packets in transit will be irremediably lost.

For these reasons, visiting hosts should always try to locate a foreign agent, even if they can acquire an address in the foreign network. The degenerate mode may however be a practical solution when the last hop is a fast connection, such as a high-bandwidth local area network, and when the MN remains a long time at the remote location.

13.4 Protocols and Conventions

Once a common model was agreed upon, the working group set up to define a protocol. They took advantage of the experience gained by the mobile IP pioneers [1, 2] and eventually came out with one single protocol. In fact, it was not easy to come to an agreement; they had to leave out a number of possible optimizations. Each time they had to choose, they tried to choose the simplest solution. They felt it was important that they rapidly agree on a proposed standard and deploy IP mobility.

The protocol, as defined in RFC2002 [3], has two main phases: discovery and registration. It also includes a redirection procedure for notifying the former base after an MN has moved.

13.4.1 The Discovery Protocol

Foreign agents and home agents will often be implemented as special processes within routers. The agent discovery protocol is thus defined as an extension of the router discovery protocol that we presented in section 3.5.2 of chapter 3.

To signal their positions, the home agents and foreign agents multicast at regular intervals an agent advertisement message. This message is actually defined as an extension to the ICMP router advertisement message. In addition to the standard router advertisement fields such as router address, the agent advertisement and prefix length extensions contain the following information:

- ☞ A sequence number.
- ☞ The life-time of registration.
- ☞ A set of flags indicating whether registration is required, whether the agent is ready to serve as a home agent or as a foreign agent, whether it is busy, whether the agent supports minimal encapsulation according to RFC-2003 [4] or the Generic Routing Encapsulation (GRE) defined in RFC-1701 [5], and whether the header compression defined by Van Jacobson will be used.
- ☞ A list of at least one care-of address. We should note that the COA addresses are not necessarily equivalent to the router address advertised in the classic router advertisement messages.
- ☞ The length of the prefixes advertised in the standard part of the router advertisement message.

The MN will listen to the advertisement to determine whether it has moved to a foreign network, and in some cases whether it has returned to its home network:

- ☞ An MN detects that it has moved when it stops receiving advertisements from the selected agent, or when it can determine from the router address and prefix length that the current network is not the same as the previous one.
- ☞ An MN detects that it is back home when it receives advertisements from its home agent.

An MN that detects a move should start the registration procedure for the new location. An MN that is back home should cancel its registration with the home agent in order to resume direct IP routing.

The sequence number is used by the MN to detect possible "reboots" of the agent. The registration procedure results in the acquisition of information on the MN by the agent; if the agent is rebooted, it will lose its memory and thus all traces of the registration. When an MN remains in a network, it will have to monitor the sequence number of its current agent. When they are initiated, agents set the sequence number to zero. The sequence number is incremented by one for each advertisement, until it reaches 65,635 (0xFFFF), after which the sequence number is reset to 256. The MN should normally receive sequence numbers that are larger than the previous value. If a sequence number is lower than the previous value but larger than 255, the MN detects a sequence number rollover. If the sequence number is lower than the previous value and lower than 256, the MN detects that the agent has been reinitialized and immediately restarts the registration procedure.

Periodic broadcast of information is a simple and efficient way for agents to advertise themselves. However, there is a limit to the frequency of this broadcast—the radio channels very often have a limited bandwidth, and it would be counterproductive to saturate them with repeated beacons. In several implementations of mobility, the MN can detect that it has changed cells through media-level information, e.g., by monitoring the energy of signals received on different frequencies. Instead of waiting for the periodic advertisement, this MN can "solicit" the information by sending an explicit message to the "all-bases" address. The solicit message is identical to ICMP router solicitation, and must be sent with a TTL set to 1.

The agent will respond to the MN solicitation with an advertisement. This advertisement, unlike periodic broadcasts, is sent to the point-to-point address of the solicitor.

13.4.2 The Registration Procedure

Once the MN has discovered a new foreign agent, it will have to register with this new agent, acquire the COA address, and transmit the COA address to the HA. The registration protocol combines these functions into four messages.

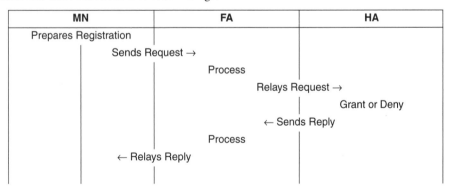

There is an obvious alternative to this choice—first to have an exchange between the MN and the FA, so that the MN acquires a COA address, and then to have an exchange between the MN and the HA. But this would imply twice as many transmissions between the MN and the FA, since the FA would, in any case, have to relay the packet from the MN to the HA. On a narrow radio channel, having exactly one exchange instead of two is a sizable advantage.

Both the request and reply messages are transmitted over UDP (port 434) and have simple structures. The request message contains:

☞ a message type (request, 1);

☞ a set of flags, indicating whether the FA is colocated with the MN, as well as the preferred encapsulation;

☞ the requested lifetime of the registration, set to 0 if the MN requests the cancellation of a previous registration;

☞ the home address of the MN, the HA address, and the COA;

☞ a 64-bit request identification; and

☞ a set of extension parameters, including the authentication extensions.

The reply message contains:

☞ a message type (reply, 3);

☞ a reply code, indicating whether the request was granted or denied and, in the latter case, whether it was denied by the FA or by the HA, and for which reason;

☞ the accepted lifetime of the registration, which may be lower than the requested lifetime;

☞ the home address of the MN and the HA address;

☞ a 64-bit request identification that will be used to correlate the reply with the request; and

☞ a set of extension parameters, including the authentication extensions.

The main problem when designing a mobile registration protocol is security. The request will carry the new COA, and it is imperative to protect against two types of attacks:

☞ Rogue agents may pretend to be an FA when, in fact, they have no relation with the FN and simply want to impersonate it and capture its traffic.

☞ Malicious agents may replay old registration messages, effectively cutting the MN from the network.

The first type of attack can only be thwarted by using an effective authentication mechanism, such as the one implemented by the Mobile-IP authentication extension. The extension carries a security parameter index (SPI) and a variable length authentication field. The combination of the SPI and the agent address (HA, COA, or MN) identifies a security context, whose parameters are a shared secret, and a signature algorithm, such as "keyed MD5." The authentication field is obtained by combining the protected data and the shared secret through the algorithm. In fact, the same message can contain several authentication fields. It must always contain an "MN to HA" authentication, but it may also contain an "MN to FA" or an "FA to HA" authentication. Each field protects the message bytes up to the authentication parameter.

The authentication extension is used to prove the origin of the message, and also to prove that the parameters were not modified in transit. To obtain protection against replay attacks, the agents must guarantee that no two requests will contain the same identification. Two methods are specified. The first one uses 64-bit NTP timestamps, while the other is based on random numbers that are supposed to be used only once (also known as *nonce*) and is covered by an IBM patent. When the timestamp method is used, the HA will only accept messages whose timestamp is larger than any previous timestamp used by the MN. It will also reject messages when the timestamp is not close enough to the current time. Normally, the timestamp in the reply is set to the value in the request, but if the message was rejected because the timestamp was not properly synchronized, the most significant 32 bits of the message will carry the "time at the call" agent, with a precision set to the second. In all cases, whether random numbers or timestamp are used, the least significant 32 bits of the reply's identification will match the least significant 32 bits of the request's identification. The FA will use these 32 bits to match requests and replies. The authentication procedure seals the MN parameters settings, which the FA will thus not be able to change. In consequence, the MN must first listen to the FA advertisement and select values for the flags, the lifetime, and the COA that are compatible with the advertisements. If the MN uses "out of range" values, the FA will have no choice but to reject the request.

When the HA receives the request, it checks the authentication and the identification parameters. If the message is authentic and the identification is acceptable, the HA accepts the requests, sends a reply, and starts tunnelling MN-bound packets toward the FA, using the care-off address.

Requests and replies can be lost. If the MN does not receive a reply within a reasonable delay, it will have to repeat the request, using a new identification. The FA will never initiate or repeat messages on its own—its role in this procedure is essentially passive, relaying requests and replies.

13.4.3 Encapsulation Procedures

There are many ways to design encapsulation procedures. Indeed, mobile-IP is not the only Internet extension that uses tunnelling: we have already seen that tunnelling could be used to establish virtual links between disconnected areas of the same network, or to carry multicast packets across networks that are not multicast-capable. Tunnelling, in fact, is a generic solution to "exception routing." Mobile-IP provides a choice between three encapsulation procedures:

☞ A basic procedure, defined in RFC-2003 [4].
☞ A minimal encapsulation, defined in RFC-2004 [5].
☞ The Generic Routing Encapsulation (GRE) defined in RFC-1701 [6].

GRE is a general purpose encapsulation procedure that was developed by cisco before Mobile-IP. According to GRE, a small GRE header is interposed between the "delivery header" and the original IP packet:

Source=HA, Dest=COA, protocol=GRE (47)	Encapsulation parameters	Source=CN, Dest=MN, protocol=TCP	TCP header + data
New IP header	GRE Header	Original IP packet	

The GRE header contains a set of parameters, including the following:

☞ A protocol type that identifies the type of the encapsulated packet. The protocol type follows Ethernet conventions. GRE can be used to carry not only IP, but any other protocol that could be carried over an Ethernet.
☞ An optional 16-bit checksum.
☞ An optional 32-bit sequence number.
☞ An optional 32-bit key, used to authenticate the source of the packets.

☞ An optional routing field, which can be used to implement source routing.

☞ A set of flags, identifying which of the optional fields are present.

GRE generality is useful in many situations when tunnelling is used for interconnection or policy routing. However, in the case of Mobile-IP, simpler solutions can be used. In its most basic mode, the GRE header reduces to a 32-bit word containing the flags and the protocol type. The basic encapsulation procedure defined in RFC-2003 [4] is simpler: there is no intermediate header, simply a delivery header followed by the original packet.

Source=HA, Dest=COA, protocol=IP in IP (4)	Source=CN, Dest=MN, protocol=TCP.	TCP header + data
New IP header	Original IP packet	

One may, however, observe that in many cases it is possible to deduce some fields of the inner header from the content of the delivery header. For example, fields such as packet length, header checksum, or even some of the addresses often are redundant. The minimal encapsulation specified in RFC-2004 [5] replaces the inner header with a compressed header, for transmission efficiency:

Source=HA, Dest=COA, protocol=Min.Encaps (55)	Compressed header	TCP header + data
New IP header	Original IP packet	

The compressed header contains:

☞ the protocol type of the encapsulated packet, TCP in our example;

☞ the destination address of the encapsulated packet;

☞ optionally, the source address of the encapsulated packet, if it is not equal to the source address of the delivery header; and

☞ a 16-bit checksum that protects the compressed header against transmission errors.

When receiving minimally encapsulated packets, the FA will reconstitute the original header by combining the compressed header's information with the fields in the delivery headers. Some fields, such as header checksum, will have to be computed based on the new values.

The discovery and registration procedures allow the MN, FA, and HA to negotiate the type of encapsulation that they will use. They must all support the basic "IP-in-IP" encapsulation, but they may additionally support GRE or the minimal encapsulation.

When either GRE or IP-in-IP is used, the HA and FA must be careful to handle the TTL in a way that reduces the possible effect of loops. Suppose, for example, that an FA receives a tunnelled packet for an MN that is known to have left the foreign network. The FA could simply forward the packet to the MN, using generic IP routing. The packet would then most probably make its way back to the HA. If the HA has kept the old, erroneous COA registration, it will probably tunnel the packet back to the same FA. The basic precaution in both cases is to make sure that the packet's TTL is decremented before encapsulation. The tunnel is considered a "single-hop" path. Decrementing the TTL and discarding packets whose TTL is null ensures that looping packets will eventually be removed from the Internet.

13.4.4 Broadcast and Multicast

If the MN had remained in its home network, it would have received the broadcast packets sent over that network, and it could have subscribed to multicast groups. The HA can, indeed, capture copies of the packets that are broadcast or multicast on the home network and tunnel them toward the MN, but doing so poses two problems. The first one is quite obvious: subscribing to many multicast groups can generate a lot of traffic. Sending individual copies of multicast packets to individual MNs is much less efficient than multicasting a single copy over the home network. The second risk is that of mixing the scope of the broadcast.

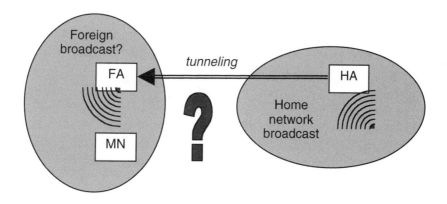

If the HA captures a packet bound to the local broadcast address, 255.255.255.255, and simply tunnels it to the FA, the FA will broadcast it on the foreign network, which is definitely not what was supposed to happen. In fact, the FA will probably simply refuse to rebroadcast the data.

The mobile-IP registration procedure allows the HA to discover whether the MN is using the service of an FA, or whether the MN and COA are colocated. If the tunnel actually ends in the MN, there is no harm in tunnelling the broadcast packet directly to the MN. On the other hand, if the FA and the MN are distinct, the HA should use a double encapsulation:

Source=HA, Dest=COA, protocol=encaps	Source=HA, Dest=MN, protocol=encaps	Source=CN, Dest=broadcast, protocol=UDP	UDP header + data
New IP header	double encaps	Original broadcast packet	

The broadcast packet is encapsulated in a packet bound explicitly to the MN, which is sent encapsulated in a packet bound to the FA. The FA will transmit the copy to the MN. There will not be any broadcast on the foreign network.

The same solution could be applied to multicast. The MN could tunnel IGMP messages to the HA, in order to remotely subscribe to multicast groups managed by the home network. However, in many cases, it could be more efficient for the MN to simply subscribe to the multicast groups in the foreign network. That way, if many visiting nodes subscribe to the same groups, only one copy of the multicast packets will be sent on the foreign network.

13.4.5 Mobile Networks

Throughout this section, we described the mobile as a mobile *node*, not a mobile *host*. In fact, nothing prevents the mobile node from acting as a router. Many cars, for example, already are equipped with internal computer networks, as different embedded computers manage the dashboard, the engine, the brakes, and the sound system. We can easily imagine connecting this network to the Internet by adding another computer that would manage a wireless connection and act as a mobile router.

Using mobile IP, that computer will present itself as a mobile node in the wireless cells that it visits. It can then maintain an explicit tunnel with the home network, possibly a network managed by the car's manufacturer, or maybe by the car's owner, and remain so connected to the Internet.

Suppose now that a passenger plugs a laptop into the car's dashboard. The wireless router that connects the car to the Internet will behave as a foreign agent for the laptop, allowing it to connect to the laptop's home network—for example, to the passenger's office.

13.5 Further Refinements

The mobile-IP group took many shortcuts in order to converge. Many refinements will have to be addressed in further versions of IP mobility. The refinements fall under three general umbrellas: more robustness, more efficiency, and more security.

The basic design that we exposed in Section 13.3 calls for a single agent talking to a single HA. This is not very robust because the HA becomes a dreadful "single point of failure." One should be able to duplicate the HA or, better still, to distribute its functionality on a network of servers. This is also not very efficient because all changes of bases have to be reported back to the HA. One should be able to cluster bases so that only moves from cluster to cluster have to be reported to the HA, not moves from base to base. An alternative is to be able to organize informal networks of wireless stations, using what is commonly known as "ad hoc networking." Then comes the problem of dogleg routing. If a CN and an MN start exchanging high volumes of data, dogleg routing will be felt as a very unreasonable penalty. We should be able to eliminate it, but we should not compromise the network's security.

13.5.1 Multiple Home Agents

The single HA model has the obvious advantage of simplicity but the no-less-obvious inconvenience of fragility. Should the HA fail, the MN becomes unreachable. Let's consider again the virtual Ethernet metaphor that we used to describe the basic model. If that was an actual concrete Ethernet, we could engineer more redundancy by connecting several routers to this cable.

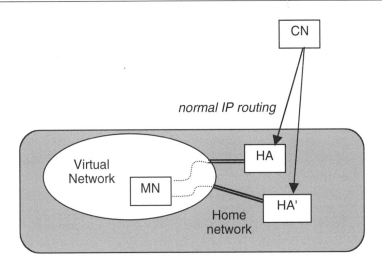

Should one of the routers fail, the routing protocol would quickly propagate the information and update the routing tables. But if we try to copy this design by adding a new HA to the virtual Ethernet, we immediately stumble on the format of the registration messages: they carry only one HA address.

There certainly are solutions. For example, one could think of a variation of the OSPF protocol. The set of HAs will elect a designated HA, in the same way routers on an actual subnet elect a designated router. This primary router will be in charge of capturing the packets sent to the conventional HA address and inserting "mobile location" records in the area database. These records will be flooded to all the routers in the area, so that any of the area's routers could locate the MN, capture packets bound to it, and tunnel them to the current agent. It should be noted that one of the early mobile IP designs supported the "virtual subnet, multiple HAs" concept [2].

13.5.2 Clusters of Foreign Agents

The main reason we would want to support "agent clustering" is best explained by the "bicycle-in-a-corridor" scenario. Let's first imagine a very large university, one with a lot of alleys between the buildings and many corridors in the buildings. A bright young French student is visiting this superb California university. He carries his laptop on the backpack of his bicycle, and while he is riding his laptop is busy fetching all the latest French news through its IP-over-infrared interface. Infrared communications have a very short range—say, three meters. Therefore, every three meters, one needs to connect to a new cell. Now, if we apply the basic model of Section 13.3, we observe that we will have to execute a handshake between the American bicycle and bases and the French HA every three meters. This is certainly suboptimal!

There are, however, solutions to this problem. Suppose that, instead of equating the COA address and the agent's address, one uses a special COA address that means simply "any router in this area" and that, by some "magic," all these routers can forward packets to the mobile node. There will be no need to advise the HA when an agent changes, as long as the mobile unit remains in the same area. Designing the magic should not be too difficult—algorithms to that effect were part of at least two of the original mobile IP proposals [1, 2]. In the particular case where the routers are running OSPF, it is conceivable to design a new link state record describing the mobile's position. New values of this record will be flooded each time the mobile unit changes bases.

Indeed, the effect of such an improvement on the registration protocol will have to be studied in detail. In particular, one must be sure that the HA still receives regular location messages. One must also resolve the mobile identification problem; in the basic design, the identification is performed by the HA.

13.5.3 Mobile Ad-Hoc Networks

There are some quite large radio frequency bands that have been set aside for public use, with minimal constraints on the emitters, besides the maximum authorized power and maybe the requirement to use spread spectrum modulation. What happens if many users decide to buy wireless devices, if the number of mobile nodes increases? Are we going to witness another "tragedy of the commons," where overgrazing, or rather overoccupation of the public radio bands, would lead to a lack of service for everybody? In a communication to the 1996 Sigcomm conference [7], Tim Shepard analyses this problems and concludes that, in fact, the waveband can remain useful, if we adopt some precautions. When the density of stations increases, the global level of noise caused by multiple spread spectrum emissions also increases. However, as the Earth is not flat, each station has a limited horizon, and the overall level of noise is determined by the number of stations within that horizon, or in fact by the density of the stations. On the other hand, the level of the signal is determined by the distance between the communicating stations. Even if the noise increases, we can maintain a reasonable signal-to-noise ratio if we reduce the distance between stations, which is possible because the density of stations increases.

A consequence of the reduced useful distance is that packets will have to be relayed by several stations. One needs then to define a way to organize these stations into a routing domain, so that packets can be transmitted to the global Internet. The IETF has set up a working group, MANET, to study a routing protocol that would enable Mobile Ad-Hoc networking, in which participating stations cooperate in order to achieve global connectivity [8]. In fact, the scope of the working group is not restricted to radio transmission. Ad-hoc networks could use a mix of technologies, including radio, infrared, and fixed lines. Ad-hoc networking is an interesting research problem. It combines the classic requirements of routing research, such as finding short paths in robust ways, with the particular requirements of mobility support, such as security, the need to preserve battery life, and the prevalence of one-way connectivity.

Classic routing algorithms such as RIP or OSPF are probably not the best solutions to the ad-hoc network problem. RIP may not converge fast enough to accommodate the high rate of topology changes that is expected in these networks. OSPF will react to each topology change by flooding the updated link state records to all the network's nodes, which may cause an important overhead, especially for nodes that have a limited battery resource. The old military networks used to solve this problem by using algorithms such as hot potato routing and also combinations of flooding and traces. In hot potato routing, the nodes send the packet to a random neighbor. If that neighbor happens to be the final destination, the transfer is complete. Otherwise, the neighbor will in turn pick a random neighbor. Doing so, the packet will explore at random all network paths. In practice, hot potato routing can be combined with local knowledge, so that if a node actually knows the path to the destination, it sends the packet on that path, not at random. However, the hot potato routing will often stop and fail if the destination cannot be found in the allocated TTL.

In the flood and trace algorithm, a node would send the packet to all its neighbors, recording all intermediate steps in the packet header. The trace in the packet that first reaches the destination is the shortest path from the source to that destination. The destination will reply, either through a known path or through the flooding mechanism if it does not know any path to the source. The reply will contain a copy of the path from source to destination. The source can then use this path in the next exchanges, as long as the path remains available. When a source suspects that a path is no longer valid, it resumes the flooding procedure. Flooding, just like hot potato routing, can be combined with local knowledge, so that a station that receives a flooded packet stops the flooding and forwards the packet on the known path. The flood and trace algorithm is very robust, but may also be very greedy in a large network.

The MANET working group has not produced final results at the time of this writing. They are considering various proposals, such as modifications of the link state and distance vector algorithm.

13.5.4 Dogleg Routing Elimination

Let's consider again our French student riding his bicycle on a California campus. Suppose now that, instead of fetching the French news, his laptop is fetching documentation in the local library. According to the basic model, the packets sent from the library to the laptop are first routed to the HA address in France, then tunnelled back to the agent and routed to the mobile host. Obviously, one is tempted to believe that one could do better than shuffling packets on another continent in order to cross a campus.

In mobile IP parlance, this is known as "dogleg routing elimination." This is not a very difficult problem conceptually—one could easily imagine that the MN would send redirection messages to the CN, informing it of its present location. Such a solution was present in one early mobile IP proposal that used source routing. The packets sent by the MN to the CN were source routed through the agent. The CN would automatically reverse the source route and send the packets to the MN using a source route through the agent. However, this poses some efficiency and security problems.

The MN will have to send redirection packets or source-routed packets to all its CHs after each change of agent. If these packets get lost or delayed, the CHs will continue sending their traffic to the old agent. This will certainly result in increased delays and probably also in an increased rate of packet losses. Then one has to consider the signalization overhead: if the MN is moving fast, it will keep sending redirection packets to the CN after all the frequent changes of agent. If the communication between MN and CN is not very active, there may well come a point where this signalization overhead exceeds the advantages of eliminating dogleg routing.

But the real issue is security. Using redirection or reversing source routes opens a security hole; an intruder could easily send a redirection packet to a CN and capture the connection between the CN and the MN. It is easy to imagine that the MN will share a secret with the HA, but much less easy to believe that it will also share a prearranged secret with all possible CHs. In practice, dogleg routing will be eliminated only if trusted "authentication" mechanisms become available.

Note that there may be good reasons to keep the dogleg routing even if all due authentication mechanisms are present. Letting the CN know the current position of the MN in some cases may be perceived as a violation of privacy.

13.5.5 Source Address Verification

A number of "hacker" attacks are facilitated by the possibility to spoof the address of another host. Disguising the packets under a false source address helps hide the attacker's identity in flooding attacks; helps in targeting third parties' replies in the so-called "smurf" attacks; and may even help in gaining privileges in some other attacks. As a result, many network managers have started to implement source address filtering, to check that the source addresses are genuine, or at least plausible. Source address verification:

☞ is often performed in firewalls, to check that no outside packets are allowed to carry the source address that belongs inside the protected network;

☞ can sometimes be implemented between providers and customers, to check that the packets sent by the customer into the Internet only use source addresses that belong to the customer network; and

☞ could in the future be implemented at peering points between providers, to check that the packets sent by the provider belong to a network that the provider serves.

Source address verification is incompatible with the current specification of Mobile-IP, whose entire design lays on the desire to use the same source address, whatever the mobile's location. If we wanted to allow source address modification, we should modify Mobile-IP implementations so that packets originating from the source address are always tunnelled to the home agent, which would forward them onto the Internet. This is actually what is done in many "virtual private network" configurations, in order to connect the home computer's telecommuters to the corporation's network, through the firewall. Protocols such as L2F and L2TP were designed to that effect.

RFC-2344 [10] specifies how the Mobile-IP architecture can be extended to support source address verification. Foreign Agents that are capable of tunnelling packets back to the HA advertise that possibility through special flags in the agent advertisement message. The MN that does not want to run afoul of source address verifications selects a capable agent and requests "reverse tunnelling" to the HA.

13.6 Mobility and IPv6

The requirements and architecture of Mobile-IPv6 are essentially the same as those of Mobile-IPv4. Stations must be able to keep communicating using their home address even if they are moving, and to do so will have to enlist the services of home agents. They will have to communicate their care-of address to the home agent through appropriate registration messages. The implementation, however, differs in many respects:

☞ The discovery mechanism is performed naturally through the IPv6 neighbor discovery and address configuration mechanisms.

☞ The use of security enables the mobile nodes to notify their COA not only to the home agent, but also to the corresponding nodes.

☞ The use of the source routing header allows for efficient encapsulation.

The actual design of Mobile-IPv6 is still a work in progress. The following description is based on a June 1999 draft [9].

13.6.1 Discovery

Discovering the characteristics of a local link is an integral part of IPv6 neighbor discovery mechanisms, as we saw in Sections 4.4 and 4.5 of chapter 4. By listening to router advertisements, the stations can learn the prefixes that have been assigned to the link through which they are connected. This can help them detect whether they are still connected to their home network, or whether they are visiting a foreign network.

A station that is visiting a foreign network can use the address configuration procedures of IPv6 to obtain an address on the foreign link. There is no need, as in IPv4, to let foreign agents use a single care-of address for many mobile nodes. In mobile IPv6, colocation of the MN and the FA is the rule, and there is no need to deploy any FA.

The only problem that remains is the discovery of the home agent. This requires a slight modification of the router advertisement formats: the inclusion of a bit indicating a router's willingness to serve as a home agent.

13.6.2 Binding Updates

The registration of the care-of addresses is performed in IPv6 by means of the Binding Update destination option. This destination option header that contains the binding update option can be "daisy-chained" into any packet bound to the home agent. It will typically follow a security header, AH or ESP: the security option is necessary to authenticate the source of the packet. There are four destination options defined for mobile-IPv6:

☞ the binding update, which informs about the new COA;

☞ the binding acknowledgement, which acknowledges reception of the COA;

☞ the binding request, a simple option to request information about the current COA; and

☞ the home address option, which identifies the home address of the mobile node.

The binding update contains a list of optional components. In many cases, it will not contain the actual COA, which will instead be transmitted in the source address of the IPv6 header. It will definitely not contain the home address, which will be transmitted in the home address option. It also will not contain the security parameters present in the IPv4 registration messages, because the AH or the ESP guarantees the authenticity of the message and provides protection against replay attack. The update will contain a set of flags, indicating which optional elements are present; a lifetime, indicating the expected duration of the binding; and a sequence number, to avoid the potential confusions caused by out-of-order delivery.

The HA that accepts the update will respond by an acknowledgement. The acknowledgement will repeat the sequence number of the update, allowing the MN to match update and acknowledgement. It will contain a code indicating if the binding was accepted or the reason for which it was rejected, the lifetime for which the update was accepted and a suggested update refresh period. The acknowledgement may also include a list of available home agents.

Binding updates are not necessarily sent only to the home agent. They may also be sent to corresponding nodes.

13.6.3 Encapsulation

Instead of using ad-hoc encapsulation, mobile-IPv6 will use the standard routing header that we presented in section 4.3.2 of chapter 4. Packets bound to the MN will be sent on a two-hop source route, the first hop being the COA and the last hop being the home address of the MN.

While using the routing header instead of an IP-in-IP header is a relatively minor change, the home address destination option represents a much more substantial improvement. Let's consider its use in a communication between a CN and an MN, assuming that the CN initiates the connection:

☞ The CN sends a packet toward the home address of the MN.

☞ The HA, using neighbor discovery, intercepts the packets bound to the MN. It rewrites the header, inserting a routing header to direct the packet toward the COA.

☞ The MN receives the packet through its COA. It processes it and sends a response.

☞ The source address of the response is sent to the COA. The home address is inserted as a destination option. If there is an available security association, the MN inserts an AH or an ESP, and a binding update destination option. The packet is sent to the CN.

☞ The CN receives the response. Using the home address destination option, it identifies that the packet actually comes from the MN. Using the binding update, it validates the COA. The next packet to the MN will include a routing header, specifying the two-hop route through the COA. It will also include an AH and an ESP, and a binding acknowledgement.

The source of any further packets from the MN will be the COA, while the home address will be carried as a destination option. For the duration of the COA binding, further packets from the CN will include the routing header. The MN will have to refresh the binding at regular intervals, and will also have to update it in case of changes. Using the COA as the source address guarantees that the MN traffic will always be compatible with the source address verification procedures.

13.7 The Future of Mobility

We are only now seeing the beginnings of mobile computing. IP extensions for mobility are being standardized, and the real deployment is slowly starting. Wide-area wireless data services are becoming available. This is certainly a very promising technology. Many experts are convinced that tomorrow's computers will all be mobile! The current protocols have been designed in a very conservative fashion, so as to work in the current Internet. To gain the advantage of mobility, one will probably have to update the routing protocols so that they will allow multiple home agents and clusters of bases. One will also have to enhance the security of the Internet, so that one identifies the mobiles in a trusted manner. This enhancement may well come from a transition to IPv6, which will provide extensive support for both mobility and security.

We will also have to solve some delicate problems posed to TCP by the mobile environment. TCP includes algorithms, for timer computation or congestion avoidance, that try to estimate the throughput of the connection and its transmission delay from past measurements. But, in a mobile environment, throughput and delay may quickly vary. Roaming from one cell to another often causes temporary losses of connectivity. TCP will react by reducing its sending rate to a minimum. When the connectivity is reestablished, that sending rate will increase, but it will increase slowly. If it is not reestablished soon enough, there are some risks that the connection will break. In short, implementing a mobile IP is only a first step; we will also have to adapt the transmission control algorithms.

References

1. F. Teraoka, Y. Yokote, and M. Tokoru, "A Network Architecture Providing Host Migration Transparency," *ACM SIG-COMM '91 Conference*, September 1991.

2. J. Ioannidis, D. Duchamp, and G. Q. Maguire, Jr., "IP-based Protocols for Mobile Internetworking," *ACM SIG-COMM '91 Conference*, September 1991.

3. C. Perkins, Editor, "IP Mobility Support," RFC-2002, October 1996.

4. C. Perkins, Editor, "IP Encapsulation Within IP," RFC-2003, October 1996.

5. C. Perkins, "Minimal Encapsulation Within IP," RFC-2004, October 1996.

6. S. Hanks, T. Li, D. Farinacci, and P. Traina, "Generic Routing Encapsulation (GRE)," RFC-1701, October 1994.

7. T. J. Shepard, "A Channel Access Scheme for Large Dense Packet Radio Networks," minutes of SIGCOMM 1996 Conference, *ACM Communication Review*, vol. 26, October 1996.

8. S. Corson and J. Macker, "Mobile Ad Hoc Networking (MANET): Routing Protocol Performance Issues and Evaluation Considerations," RFC-2501, January 1999.

9. D. B. Johnson and C. Perkins, "Mobility Support in IPv6," work in progress, June 1999.

10. G. Montenegro, "Reverse Tunnelling for Mobile IP," RFC-2344, May 1998.

Network Service Quality and Resource Reservation[1]

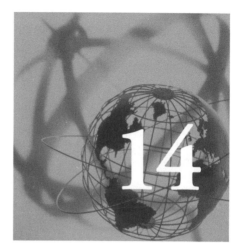

The Internet protocol is based on the datagram paradigm. Packets are routed independently of each other, without any concept of "connection." There is no notion of "quality of service." The throughput is not guaranteed; the transmission delay is not bounded. The network is simply expected to make its "best effort" to satisfy its clients—i.e., to render a service proportional to the client's investment (if the network has been equipped with faster lines, we expect shorter response times).

Many authors assert that the simple best-effort service is ill-fitted for the new multimedia applications. Sending voice and video in real time requires the guarantee that the data will flow at a stable rate, with a constant or almost constant delay. This is why the telephone network uses a "circuit switching" paradigm: each time you start a phone conversation, the telephone network reserves a "circuit," in fact a sufficient share of every transmission link on the path between the two partners.

Faced with the demand for new transmission facilities, during the early '90s the Internet research groups initiated several efforts. The first response was a demonstration that the asynchronous-packet switching technology can indeed provide guarantees of services if sufficient resources are available along the paths of real-time data flows. As a follow-up, effort was launched to develop quantitative Quality-of-Service (QOS) definitions and "resource reservation" protocols, so that strict application requirements could be satisfied, if needed. In parallel, other teams started to experiment with multimedia applications on the existing Internet, demonstrating that the supposedly strict requirements are in fact much more flexible than expected, with little user perceivable quality degradation.

Both the new QOS definitions and a reservation protocol, RSVP, became proposed Internet standards. However what followed the standardization was not a rapid deployment as originally expected. Instead, during the process of developing these standards various doubts were

1. This chapter has been written in collaboration with Lixia Zhang.

developed about the complexity of implementation and the scalability in real deployment. Since late 1997 another effort took off which aims at defining differentiated services for aggregate traffic flows. We will detail these developments in this chapter.

14.1 Queues and Delays

Today, most Internet routers operate in a strict "first-come, first-served" fashion. Packets arriving from the input lines are immediately examined by the routing process and queued on an outgoing interface. They are then transmitted in the order of arrival. This behavior has the advantage of being easy to understand and implement, but we will show that the delays will then vary as a function of the network load. There have been attempts to solve the problem by changing the routing algorithms, but we will see that they are not entirely convincing. At the end of this section, we will present the end-to-end "congestion avoidance" algorithm that is used for "standard" traffic, along with its limitations.

14.1.1 The Basic Quality of Service

The modelling of networks uses a special branch of mathematics—the "queuing theory." We will not suddenly dive into heavy usage of calculus, but simply recall the major results of the theory.

A router that operates according to the first-come, first-served policy can be modelled by a "one-server queue."

$$\text{arrivals} \Rightarrow \boxed{| \; | \; | \; |} \Rightarrow \text{service}$$
$$\text{queue}$$

A packet that is ready for transmission is a "client" of the server. It "lines in the queue" behind the clients that have already arrived. The most common simplification assumption is Poisson's hypothesis, that clients can arrive at any time, independent of past events. Under this assumption, the "state" of that server is determined by the number of clients in the queue. The actual number of clients is a random variable. Its distribution depends on the "load"—i.e., the ratio r of the arrival rate to the service rate; the probability of having n clients in the queue is

$$p(n) = (1 - r) \times r^{n}$$

The queuing delay is a function of the number of packets in the queue and of the service time of an individual packet. If "μ" is the service rate, then the average queuing delay t and its variance v are

$$t = \frac{1}{(1 - r)\mu}$$

$$v = \frac{1}{(1 - r)\mu^{2}}$$

Both numbers increase very rapidly with the load of the server. The numbers observed in the network in fact depend on the precise shape of the "offered load." The Poissonian hypothesis is not always, and maybe never, verified. The response curve of a given network will be affected by the "burstiness" of the traffic: if the offered load can vary sharply in short intervals, both the average delay and the standard deviations will be larger than those of Poissonian traffic of equivalent load. But the general rule will hold: if the traffic increases, the delay becomes longer and more variable. Indeed, if the load exceeds the server's capacity, the queue can increase infinitely. The server will not have so many buffers and will be forced to drop packets. The only ways to restore lower delays are to increase the server's capacity or to reduce the load.

Increasing the capacity requires investments, such as buying more powerful equipment or wider transmission trunks. Network managers must get a value of the average load, either through traffic measurement or through a statistical analysis. They will then use this value for dimensioning their network and deciding on the necessary investments. But this is a long-term process. In the short term, the network capacity is fixed, and the only solution is to adapt the load.

14.1.2 Can We Solve Congestion Through Routing?

Let's go back to our test network:

There are two paths between A and E, either through B or through D. We have seen that RIP routers will pick one of these paths more or less at random, while OSPF will spread the traffic equally over both paths. In either case, the decision is determined by "static" variables, the number of hops for RIP, the data rate of the links for OSPF.

Suppose now that link number 6 is heavily loaded by local traffic between D and E. The users will experience longer delays between A and E if the router sends their packets over the path A, D, E rather than A, B, E, so it appears natural to modify the routing algorithm and to take the link's load into account when computing the routes. This implies that the link metric is a function of the link's load. The precise way to implement a load-dependent metric varies with the protocol. With RIP, one could possibly affect a metric of 2 or 3, instead of 1, to the links that are very loaded or almost saturated. With OSPF, one would probably change the throughput metric to take into account the available throughput. We saw in chapter 7 that IGRP already includes an indicator of the link's load in its multicomponent metric. Once we have included the indication of the load in the metric, the shortest paths computed by the routing protocols will naturally use the less loaded links, e.g., A, B, E.

But the load of a link is a dynamic variable. It must be reassessed at regular intervals. For example, if the local activity that overloaded link 6 stops, then the load-dependent metric of that link will decrease. The node D will send a new distance vector or advertise a new link state. This will result in new routing tables.

In fact, this kind of dynamic route computation was tested in the early Arpanet, and people did not like the resulting instability of the routing. One must realize that the routing protocol is a way to "control" the network. We are trying to achieve closed-loop control by observing the status of the network and by deriving in real time the best routes for that status. The first problem is that the network load may vary rapidly, faster than the time it takes to compute the new routes. We have to consider the classic theory of control, which tells us that one can do closed-loop control only if the control loop reacts faster than the changes in the controlled object. One cannot arbitrarily shorten the control loop. There is a limit to the acceptable frequency of routing updates and route computation! As a result, one will have to average the load over a relatively long period, at least several minutes, in order to "stabilize" the load metric.

The second problem is the interaction between the control and the observed variable. Suppose that we increase the metric of link number 6 between D and E. The route A, B, E becomes shorter and receives all the traffic between A and E. As a result, this route becomes more loaded, while some load is removed from the alternate path A, D, E. The next time, the load metric of A, D, E will perhaps become lower than the one of A, B, E. The traffic will move back to this path. But then, the very fact of moving this traffic causes the load metric of A, D, E to increase, and the one of A, B, E to decrease! The traffic will keep moving back and forth between the two paths. This kind of oscillation certainly does not increase the quality of service. It is caused by the "all-or-nothing" routing decision—if a link becomes overloaded, all of its traffic is moved away to another link, which in turn will become overloaded. The solution to this problem is that one should move only a fraction of the traffic. This is possible if one is using protocols that allow spreading the traffic over paths of equal length. Normally, the traffic is shared evenly over the equal-length paths; one can take the load into account in order to slowly tune the proportion of traffic that is sent over each of the links.

There is a third problem. Suppose that link number 6 is heavily loaded. If we simply increase its metric, we may observe that the path D, A, B, E just became shorter than the direct connection D, E. According to the previous rules, we could spread the traffic from D to E over these two paths, but this is not necessarily a good idea. The path D, A, B, E requires more network resources per individual packet than the direct path. The traffic that we derived will compete with the "natural" load of those links. We may have provided a better service for the applications sending from D to E, but we have degraded the service provided to the other users. In short, we have spread the congestion!

For these reasons, load-dependent routing was seldom used in the Internet. The only way to implement it "without risk" is as a complement to the spreading of traffic over "equal-cost" routes. The routes will be computed using static parameters, such as nominal bandwidth. The load will be measured with precautions, averaging over a long delay. Then, the dynamic load measurements will be used to compute which share of the traffic will be sent over each of the equal-cost routes. This is what the "optimized multipath" algorithm that we discussed in chapter 6 tries to achieve. Implemented properly, dynamic load balancing may result in a better usage of the network resources. In any case, load balancing is not a way to eliminate congestion. One has to reduce the incoming traffic.

14.1.3 End-to-End Control

In the Internet, the load reduction is obtained by a "congestion avoidance" algorithm that was inserted by Van Jacobson in TCP in 1988.

When a host starts a TCP connection, it should take care not to perturb the network. It should use only a minimal TCP "congestion window," allowing at most one unacknowledged packet in the network, regardless of the credits sent by the receiver. This is called "slow start." Then, each time an acknowledgment is received, it will increase that limit by one, which effectively results in doubling the congestion window size every acknowledgment delay, or *round-trip time* (RTT). It will send one packet, receive one acknowledgment, and thus increase the window to two packets. After sending those two packets, it will normally receive two acknowledgments, and thus increase the window to four, and so on. This periodic doubling results in an exponential increase of the transmission rate and should not be continued indefinitely, as one would no doubt congest the network. It ceases either when one notices a packet loss, in which case one has to go back to the beginning, or when one reaches a certain "threshold," at which point one starts using linear increments, adding one packet to the window every round-trip time.

The gradual window size increase will eventually lead to congestion, which will trigger the loss of a packet. Congestion may also result from other causes, such as an increase in network usage by other sources or a change in the routing toward a narrower backup channel. Van Jacobson decided to play it safe: if it notices a packet loss, the TCP connection will immediately back off to the minimal window of one packet. It will then restart the slow-start procedure. However, before backing off, the sender takes note of the throughput (or, rather, the congestion window that was in use at the time of the congestion). The new threshold for switching from the exponential to the linear phase will be set to half of this value.

When Van Jacobson and Sally Floyd evaluated the behavior of the slow start and congestion algorithm through experiments and simulations, they noticed an undesirable synchronization effect. TCP connections that shared the same congested link would tend to observe congestion and loss of packets at the same moment, and thus increase and decrease their congestion window size in quasi-synchronicity. Analysis showed that this was caused by the way routers managed their packet queues. Whenever demand exceeded capacity, the queues would fill up until they reached their maximum size, at which point all incoming packets would be dropped—this behavior is known as "drop tail." Sally Floyd proposed to force a better behavior by ensuring that the dropping of packets begins before the queue actually fills up, and also by choosing the dropped packets through an explicitly random algorithm, in order to forcibly remove the synchronization effect. The proposed queue management algorithm is called "Random Early Drop" (RED) and is described in RFC-2309. According to RED, routers associate a "packet drop rate" to each queue. The rate is null when the queue length is lower than a threshold value. It increases gradually with the queue length, and is obviously set to 100% when the queue reaches its maximum size. All simulations and controlled experiments so far show that this mechanism is generally preferable to the "drop tail" behavior. It breaks synchronizations, which ensures a better usage of the network. It also provides early warning of congestion well before the queues are full, so that at least some TCP connections will reduce their window size. This results in smaller average queue sizes, and thus smaller end-to-end transmission delays.

14.1.4 The Limits of End-to-End Control

The introduction of the slow-start algorithm in TCP was great progress. In 1988, before the introduction of this algorithm, the network was heavily congested. The 64-kbps links that were used at that time could not cope with the growing traffic. With the mere change of a couple of lines in the implementations, the situation changed radically. The network became stable again, the load matched the resources, and the delay stayed within acceptable limits.

There are, however, some limitations to the end-to-end approach. Most of the critics concentrate on the "fairness" of the algorithm. There is no evidence that all users will get a fair share of the resources. Many theoretical studies, simulations, and measurements have shown that the behavior of end-to-end algorithms is itself very dependent on the response time of the network. If two clients share the same congested path, the one that is the nearest to the bottleneck will track the resource more accurately and will end up getting a larger share.

Moreover, the end-to-end approach assumes that all users cooperate and that they implement the congestion avoidance algorithm, reducing automatically their sending rate when they observe that the path to the destination is getting congested. There is no protection against the "bad boy" who does not "play by the rules." For example, the real-time applications like audio or video, if not implemented properly, can be among the bad boys. Unlike the polite TCP connections with Slow-Start, they may send data at an almost constant bit rate despite long delays and packet losses, effectively depriving other users of their expected share of the bandwidth.

We have exposed one consequence of the end-to-end principle—that users should not trust the network. But the opposite is equally true: networks should not trust their users, either. If they want to provide guarantees of services or at least some level of fairness, they should engineer for it. We will show some possible policies in the next section.

14.2 Queuing and Scheduling

The "fair queuing" algorithm was developed as a way to impose some fairness in the switching process. But the fairness requirement can be interpreted in many ways—a variant is the case of sharing links paid for by two or more organizations, where each party's fair share should be proportional to its payment share. This requires a "weighted" variant of the fair queuing algorithm, where each organization is given a share

The "weighted fair queuing" algorithm can also be used to support real-time applications. A recent theoretical result demonstrates the possibility to obtain precise quality-of-service guarantees through a weighted fair queuing mechanism.

We will describe these three algorithms in turn in this section.

14.2.1 Fair Queuing

Traditional datagram switches, as we mentioned above, switch packets independently. There is no memory of the past history, no state in the network. The principle of fair queuing, as developed by A. Demers, S. Keshav, and S. Shenker [1], is precisely to introduce some state in the switches by separating the incoming traffic into well-identified "flows" and guaranteeing to each flow an equal share of the transmission capacity.

Traditional queuing: one queue per output line

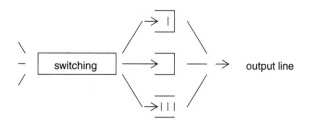

Fair queuing: one queue per flow

Once flows have been identified, one must make sure that each of them receives a "fair share." One should first define what "fair" means. Demers, Keshav, and Shenker use the following definition, which is derived from previous work:

1. No user receives more than it requests.
2. No other allocation scheme satisfying condition 1 has a higher minimum allocation.
3. Condition 2 remains recursively true as we remove the minimal user and reduce the total resource accordingly.

In short, this means that we will define a "maximum share" of the resource, P, so that any user that requests less than P will be satisfied, and so that all other users will get exactly P. The authors propose to use a "fluid" model to obtain that result. They consider a "hypothetical service discipline," where the server visits each queue in "round-robin" fashion, and transmits exactly one bit from each active queue. The duration of each round will be equal to the quotient $N(t)$ of the number of active queues at time t by the link's data rate, C. Let $R(t)$ denote the number of rounds that took place between 0 and t:

$$\frac{dR(t)}{dt} = \frac{C}{N(t)}$$

In the simplest form of the fair queuing algorithm, one will associate to each queue x the values $S(x,i)$ and $F(x,i)$ of $R(t)$ at the beginning and at the end of the transmission of the packet of rank i from that queue. Let t_i and P_i denote the arrival time of the packet and its length. Fair queuing will be achieved if:

$$S(x,i) = \text{MAX}\ (F(x,i-1),\ R(t_i))$$

$$F(x,i) = S(x,i) + P_i$$

In reality one cannot transmit the packets "one bit at a time," mixing bits from the various queues. This hypothesis is useful only for the presentation of the algorithm. But the authors observe that quantities such as $N(t)$ depend only on the packet arrival times. It is thus possible to compute the successive values of $R(t)$ and $F(x,i)$ when the packets arrive. One can then associate with each packet the value $F(x,i)$ that is computed when it arrives and use it to define the sending order of packets.

One can demonstrate that this algorithm almost meets the fairness criteria that were stated above. In fact, the only difference with the "perfectly fair" queuing is due to packet transmission—the queue that just transmitted a packet is slightly "in advance" by at most one packet worth of data. The algorithm can also be used to identify the queues that should be penalized in case of congestion—those with the largest value of $F(x,i)$. This will penalize the bigger users, giving them an incentive to reduce their traffic.

The implementation of fair queuing assumes that one can effectively separate the traffic into well-identified flows. This is quite difficult in an IP network. Various definitions have been proposed, e.g., "all packets from the same source address," "all packets with the same source/destination pair," "all packets belonging to the same TCP connection." Each of these definitions has its own set of problems. Classifying by source address, for example, appears quite fair in a world of personal computers and workstations. Each machine is generally operated by exactly one user, so that the policy results in equally sharing the network resource between the users. But suppose that the network also comprises a small number of service machines (e.g., mainframes). Since each mainframe has exactly one IP address, it will receive exactly the same share as the average PC, which is probably not what network administrators will describe as fair.

Classifying by TCP connection will solve the mainframes' problem. But there is no identification of the TCP connection inside the IP header. One has to look inside the packets. Even when one is not religious about layering, this approach is not to be encouraged. Several applications use UDP instead of TCP, others transmit encrypted packets, and some use IP fragmentation. Relying on the "source/destination pair" is a good compromise if one wants to look only at the IP header. This approach gives an advantage to the stations that manage several connections, which is reasonable for mainframes that manage connections with all of their terminals, but it may unduly privilege the multitasking workstations that can, for example, request several file transfers in parallel.

Some implementers have observed that, even if one considers only the address pairs, the number of flows to manage can become very large, something like a product of the number of servers multiplied by the number of clients. This could translate into very large tables, maybe exceeding the link drivers' memory, maybe requiring very long visiting times. A "statistical" version of the fair queuing algorithm has been developed to solve this problem by managing only a small number of queues and by a random assignment of flows to these queues. Suppose, for example, that we identify flows by the pair of source and destination addresses. We can compute a "hash code" of these addresses, a "pseudo-random" number. If we want to manage only 32 queues, we will consider only 5 bits of this random number and will attach the packets to the queue according to these bits. By managing a counter for each queue, we will guarantee that each group of flows gets the same share of the transmission resource. This provides some level of isolation. As long as one shares a queue with "well-behaved" flows, the service is fair. In order to guarantee that the long-term sharing is also fair, even if some flows are ill-behaved, one has to periodically "shuffle" the queues. This can be done by changing the computation of the pseudo-random number or, in our example, by changing the set of 5 bits that one will consider. Such shuffling of the queues, however, may lead to packets being served out of order. For example, if a flow is originally mapped to the first queue, which is large in size, and after a shuffling is mapped to the tenth queue, which has only a few packets in it, then later packets from this flow will be served out of the tenth queue while some earlier packets are still waiting at the end of the first queue.

14.2.2 Weighted Fair Queuing

Weighted fair queuing was presented by Lixia Zhang [2] almost simultaneously with the proposal of Demers, Keshav, and Shenker. Weighted fair queuing is, in fact, a modern denomination; the algorithm proposed by Lixia Zhang to achieve this result was called "Virtual Clock." The objectives of fair queuing and virtual clocks were somewhat different. In one case, the goal was to share the resource fairly between a variable number of users. Now, we deal with well-identified data flows, which have been established through some management procedure. We want:

1. to support the diverse requirements of various applications and provide them with adequate resources,
2. to monitor effectively the resources used by the various applications,
3. to provide "fire walls" among individual flows, and
4. to preserve the full flexibility of packet switching.

Management procedures have defined for each flow an "average data rate" (ARi), corresponding to its "nominal usage." A virtual clock (VCi) is associated to each flow. It is set to the real time when the flow is created. In the simplest version of the algorithm, VCi is incremented each time a packet is received for the flow i. The increment is:

$$d = \frac{P}{AR_i}$$

i.e., the duration of the transmission of a packet of length P on a virtual link of rate ARi. The packet is stamped with the new value of VCi; packets are transmitted by increasing the order of these stamps.

The value VCi is used both for ordering the packets for transmission, according to the flows' data rates, and for monitoring the resources actually used by each flow. If a flow has been sending faster than the allocated rate ARi, then its virtual clock will be larger than the real time, and vice versa if it has been slower. Some differences are unavoidable. The production of data is a random process that the packet transmission through the network may further randomize. One could expect that, over some short intervals, the allocated rate will be exceeded. We need to wait for a "decent interval" before checking the behavior of a flow. That interval varies with the applications; in the virtual clock proposal, an average interval (AIi) is associated to each flow. We can then obtain the average numbers of bits per interval by multiplying AIi and ARi. When we have transmitted that many bits over the flow, we will compare the virtual clock and the real time:

1. If the virtual clock is "late," it is reset to the real time.
2. If the virtual clock is "too far ahead," control actions must be taken.

However, it is difficult to quantify what we mean by "too far ahead." In this algorithm, the advances of the virtual clock are maintained over successive intervals. But the number of excess packets per interval is a random variable, and the "accumulated advance" is thus the sum of independent random variables. On average, these variables are null, but the variations will be accumulated. If one waits long enough, one can be sure that the virtual clock will exceed any preset threshold value. The problem can be solved by imposing restrictions on the source, a "user behavior envelope," so that a source will never send more than AIi times ARi bits in the average interval.

Because average intervals have to be rather long, we will observe another problem. A source that would have remained "silent" during the first part of an interval will accumulate "credits." It will then be possible for this source to send a long burst of packets without being interrupted by the other flows, which will disturb these other flows. Lixia Zhang proposes to solve this problem by introducing for each flow an "auxiliary virtual clock" (auxVC). When a packet arrives, the following actions are taken:

$$auxVC = MAX \text{ (real time, auxVC)}$$

$$VCi = VCi + \frac{P}{ARi}$$

$$auxVC = VCi + \frac{P}{ARi}$$

The auxiliary clock is used to "stamp" the packets. We will transmit the packets by the order of increasing stamp values; in case of congestion, we will destroy the packets that have the largest stamps. The auxiliary clock cannot fall behind the real time, so that no flow can artificially build up credits by remaining silent. The main virtual clock is used only for monitoring the flow, to check that it does not exceed the allocated data rate.

14.2.3 Shared Links

Fair queuing is an attempt to give to each user a fair share of the resources; weighted fair queuing aims at serving each application according to its needs. But fairness has many facets, and individual users are not the only ones that can claim a share. Consider the transoceanic connection problem. Transoceanic links are expensive. It takes a long time to lay a transmission cable between two continents or to launch a new telecommunication satellite. The resource is limited by the data rate of the existing cables and by the bandwidth of the existing satellites. When an organization has to build a worldwide network, these links account for more than a fair share of the budget. But the price of these links is not strictly proportional to the data rate. As for other goods, it is more economical to buy in bulk. It is more economical thus to pool resources with other organizations and to buy a "fatter pipe" than individual budgets could have afforded.

Once several organizations have bought a fat pipe, they have to share it among themselves. They could indeed use some form of data rate dividers, such as "link multiplexers" based on time division. But one can do better by using packet transmission techniques. Suppose that at a given time one of the syndicated organizations has little traffic to send, less than its share of the link. With link multiplexers, that remaining share will be wasted. With packet switching, it can be allocated to the other organizations, which will at that time benefit from a better response time. It is thus natural to place a packet switch at each end of the fat pipe and to link this switch to the networks of the sharing organizations.

The two routers must manage one separate queue per organization, so as to give to each organization a fair share of the pipe. In our simple example, they can deduce the organization's ownership of a packet from the link over which the packet was received. But this simple approach would be unpractical if the organizations were also sharing a connection network. In general, the relevant queue must be deduced from the source address.

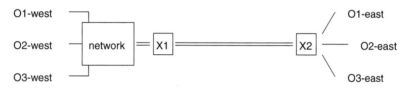

The simple fair queuing technique presented in the previous paragraph is applicable only if the cost of the link has been shared evenly between the organizations. Now, suppose that in our example O1 paid one-half of the cost, O2 one-third, and O3 one-sixth. It would be absolutely unfair to serve each queue with one-third of the capacity. One must implement a policy that reflects the respective contributions.

One possibility is to implement a "weighted round-robin" algorithm, visiting more often the larger contributors. In our example, we could visit the three queues according to the following pattern: first O1, then O2, then O1, then O2, then O1, then O3. If the queues are all active, this will result in allocating precisely one-half of the capacity to O1, one-third to O2, and one-sixth to O3. This weighted round robin policy is very simple to generalize. One has to first choose a sufficiently large number N, the size of the "pattern," then allocate slots within that pattern to the various queues, so that the number of slots of a queue divided by N will be equal to the corresponding share. The visiting of the queues is directed by an index within the pattern. If the queue corresponding to the indexed slot is active, then the packet is transmitted; otherwise, the next slot is considered.

In fact, the classification of the traffic "per organization" is not sufficient. There are many different ways to separate traffic into classes and to associate weights to the different classes for harmonious link sharing. In addition to the sharing by organization, we can also police the traffic by protocol, by class of machines, and by class of application.

Company networks are often used to carry several protocols, such as IP, Novell's IPX, IBM's SNA, DECnet, and Appletalk. These protocols may have very different dynamics and very different requirements. SNA, for example, is used mostly to support transactional applications that require very stable response times and thus would react very badly to a situation of congestion.

TCP-IP has a different problem. It incorporates congestion avoidance algorithms and reduces immediately its transmission rates in case of congestion. In a multiprotocol backbone, this means that TCP users will politely leave the playground to the bullies while SNA users will complain bitterly of poor response time. The weighted fair queuing technique can be used to control the share of the link that is allocated to each protocol.

We have seen that the simple fair queuing performed badly when several different classes of machines such as personal computers and mainframes were present in the network. We could use the weighted fair queuing technique to allocate a fixed share of the resources to each class, maybe 40% to the mainframes and 60% to the PCs.

Network managers may also want to classify the traffic as "real time," "interactive," or "batch," where real time corresponds to audio and video connections, interactive to remote logins and terminal attachments, and batch to file transfers and job submissions. Once traffic has been separated into classes, it becomes feasible to specify usage targets, such as 25% for real time, 25% for interactive, and 50% for file transfers. This classification by application profile yields better management than the alternative of using priorities or preferences. Stating, for example, that audio has priority over file transfer is very dangerous, for it would allow excessive audio traffic to exclude all file transfers from the network. One problem here is that the application is not identified in the IP header. One has to look at the protocol type (TCP or UDP) and at the source and destination ports, which are placed in the first bytes of the payload. Most application servers use fixed and predictable ports, for example, 21 for "telnet," 23 for "FTP," or 25 for "smtp"; using this information for classification is relatively easy.

In fact, the general model has to take into account multiple classifications. For example, one may want to allocate a 50% share to the IP protocol in a corporate backbone, and then enforce a sharing within this 50% share of 40% for interactive traffic and 60% for file transfers. Van Jacobson and Sally Floyd proposed a "hierarchical" organization of the classes; their model is called "Class-Based Queuing" (CBQ). In a corporate network, we could, for example, have the following hierarchy:

```
Link  ┬── 25%  ─  SNA
      ├── 25%  ─  IPX
      └── 50%  ─  IP  ┬── 20%  ─  telnet
                      └── 30%  ─  ftp
```

To each class, we associate a nominal fraction of the link's bandwidth, or an "average rate," ARi. The resource used by each class is monitored by a mechanism similar to the virtual clocks. For each class, we memorize the "nominal end of transmission date" (Fi) of the last packet processed in the class. This date is computed by adding to the real packet arrival time the "virtual duration" of transmission of this packet on a link of rate ARi. We compute for each class an "average idle period between arrivals" (APi), or an exponentially weighted moving average, using the following formulas:

$$IM_i = (1 - a) \times IM_i + a \times (t - F_i)$$

$$F_i = t + \frac{P}{AR_i}$$

where t is the packet arrival time. If the average period is positive, the queue is "overlimit"; it is negative if the queue is "underlimit." The computation will be done for all the levels in the hierarchy. The underlimit classes will be visited first, following a prioritized round-robin fashion. Packets from overlimit classes will be transmitted only if they can "borrow" resources from the classes above them in the hierarchy of classes.

The CBQ mechanism has been implemented by Ian Wakeman, Atanu Ghosh, and Jon Crowcroft, following the specifications of Jacobson and Floyd, in order to control resource allocation on the "UK fat pipe" that links British research networks to their American partners. In theory, the mechanism is compatible with the fair queuing or virtual clock techniques. We may want to use these mechanisms to share evenly the resources that are available within one class of traffic, to specify the policies that can be applied within a given class. For example, in the case of mainframes and PCs, we may want to specify different policies for each class.

```
Link    ┬── 40%  ─    mainframes: fifo
        └── 60%  ─    PCs: fair queuing
```

The mainframe's traffic is handled in a first-come, first-served fashion, while the PC's traffic is regulated by a fair queuing algorithm, within its allocated share of 60%.

14.2.4 A Theorem on Queuing and Delays

Shortly following the above mentioned work, A. Parekh and R. Gallager proved that, if a flow's data rate is confined by a "token bucket" and if it gets a sufficient service rate, then the propagation delays are bounded [3, 4]. The most interesting aspect of their demonstration is that it does not make any assumption on the network's topology, nor on the source behavior. It simply assumes that the service rate is no less than the bucket's token generation rate. The maximum delay depends on the "jitter" that will occur in each intermediate router. They demonstrate that end-to-end controls such as "token buckets" that simply limit the source data rate are not sufficient to bound the maximum delay at intermediate routers. They propose that the routers implement a policy which they name "Packetized General Processor Sharing"—which is, in fact, a variant of the Demers, Keshav, and Shenker scheme [1] they invented independently. A separate queue is defined for each specific flow for which delays have to be guaranteed.

14.2.5 A Definition of Integrated Services

Parekh and Gallager's result was exploited in a proposal by D. Clark, S. Shenker, and L. Zhang to develop a new architecture for "Integrated Service Packet Networks" [5]. The goal is to complement the traditional best-effort service of the Internet by defining new services to suit the needs of real-time applications, using "resource reservation." The basic idea is if users need real-time services, they ask the network to reserve the corresponding resources. This reservation is subject to "admission control." The network must check that the resources are available and may refuse to allocate them if there is not enough capacity left. More specifically, two different classes of reservations, "guaranteed" and "predictive," are introduced:

☞ Within the guaranteed service, one must check that, whatever the behavior of the other users, the requested quality of service will always be maintained. This service provides absolute guarantees; the resources to be reserved are computed according to the results of Parekh and Gallager.

☞ The predictive service provides "statistically predicted" guarantees. One gambles that the traffic load in near future will be very similar to that of the recent past. Instead of comparing the request to the sum of the other accepted requests, it is compared to the average availability, as measured during the past seconds or minutes.

To put it briefly, the guaranteed reservations operate on the maximum rate or peak rate of the sources and guarantee that the quality of service will be maintained even if all sources operate at peak rate simultaneously. The predictive service, on the contrary, is based on the idea that the sources are not correlated, that some will be silent when others will be emitting at peak rate. The resources used for the predictive service are related to the average bit rate of the aggregate flows rather than to the sum of their peak rates.

The model implies a third class of service, the traditional datagram or best-effort service. Once reservations are in effect, we obtain a natural prioritization of the packets. Those that belong to a guaranteed session have an implicit priority over those that belong only to a predictive session. The packets that do not belong to any of these reserved sessions will be forwarded according to the best-effort rule. A weighted fair queuing mechanism can be used to regulate the corresponding traffic.

An "Integrated Services" working group of the IETF was set up in 1994 to investigate this new architecture. After three years the group produced a set of documents that detail the definition and control of flows that request resource reservations over the Internet [RFC2211-2216]. This set of definitions is collectively called "Integrated Service" definition, or intserv in short. To actually deploy intserv, we will have to develop resource reservation protocols such as RSVP, which we will present in the next section.

14.3 A Reservation Protocol

Reservation protocols are used to signal to the network, or more precisely to the intermediate routers, the needs of the users and of their applications. Traditional reservation protocols such as ST-2 [8] tie together the reservation of resources and the establishment of a virtual circuit. This is not compatible with the datagram service of IP. In fact, ST-2 must operate by layering a virtual circuit service on top of IP. This effectively cuts the ST-2 users from the Internet. They cannot use their reservation protocols for normal applications.

RSVP [9] operates with a different paradigm. The reservation messages are sent "in parallel" to the IP packets and describe to the routers the packet profiles for which resources are reserved. This allows reserving resources without even modifying the application and can be introduced gradually into the Internet. In this section, we will discuss the principles of RSVP, its design, the way it operates, and then the issues that are yet to be resolved.

14.3.1 The Principles of RSVP

The key assumption of RSVP is that resource reservation must suit the needs of multicast applications such as high-speed video transmission. These applications have some peculiar characteristics, like a large number of receivers who may be experiencing very different transmission conditions and who also belong to different domains.

It would be impractical, with these large audiences, to have resources reserved at connection setup. For one thing, the notion of connection is not obvious when a large number of users decide at random intervals to switch to one or another video channel. On the other hand, letting the receivers decide is very natural. Just imagine a video transmission over the Internet. If the user is in a well-connected area where the network is lightly loaded, the transmission will just come through—no reservation will be needed. Suppose then that the network becomes overloaded. The delays will increase, and some packets will be dropped or will arrive too late. The image will from time to time be blurred; the sound will start featuring undesirable crackles. This is, in fact, exactly what the user paid for—in the absence of reservation, he gets the default service, just like on an overloaded freeway on a Friday afternoon.

Now, there is a slot on the side of the video receiver (nobody is going to call this a TV set anymore). If the user inserts a credit card in that slot, a reservation packet is sent to the network: "Please guarantee that I receive a crispy image and a clear sound." Many networks will be happy to do just that, for a reasonable price. And this is exactly what the RSVP model does. The receiver decides, and the receiver will be charged. This model works very well for large "multipoint" groups; point-to-point connections are treated merely as a "degenerate case."

The second design decision of RSVP is that reservation is not tied to routing. Routing protocols evolve over the course of time. We have described several versions of BGP; we have shown that the multicast routing protocols are still far from being stable standards. The RSVP protocol simply sends the reservation packets along the route that is used for the corresponding data flows.

The third design decision is to use "soft states." Reservation, by itself, installs states in the network, which is somewhat contrary to the end-to-end principle of the Internet architecture. RSVP tries to retain some of these principles. It does not assume, for example, that the routers should be trusted not to fail or that the routes will remain stable. Instead, the reservation is controlled by end hosts through repeating the requests at regular intervals, as long as the credit card remains in the slot.

Yet another important design decision is to make RSVP behave as a simple messenger that dutifully carries signalling information along data flow paths as "a bag of bits." The precise interpretation of those bits is left to the clients of RSVP to define. For example, when used to support integrated services, RSVP carries the resource specifications as defined by intserv in the way defined in RFC2210 [19]. It is conceivable that RSVP can readily serve as a signalling protocol for other purposes by carrying a different bag of bits. This possibility has been explored in the recent development of MPLS protocol, where RSVP is used to set up state for traffic flows across backbone providers.

14.3.2 Sessions, Flows, and Filters

RSVP enables a receiver to reserve resources for a "session." An RSVP session is identified by a destination address and a 32-bit "reservation identifier." Generally this identifier is made of the transport protocol type and port number. In cases where it is infeasible, or even impossible, for routers to look into transport protocol headers, such as the case of IP with security enhancement, a "virtual destination port" can be used instead [16]. A receiver requests a reservation by specifying the parameters of the session, i.e., the destination address, a "filter" that specifies a subset of the packets bound to the destination, and a "flow specification" that specifies the resources to be reserved for the session.

The destination is either the multicast address of a group to which the receiver subscribes or one of the host's unicast addresses. There can be many packets bound to that address, such as packets from different sources or for different applications. The filter is used to distinguish the packets that belong to this session; it contains the specification of the source address and source port number, e.g., to distinguish video transmissions and file transfers. The filters can be specified in the following three ways; in RSVP terminology they are called three different "reservation styles."

1. A receiver may make a reservation for a particular data flow. This is called a "fixed filter" style reservation. This is typically used when subscribing to a "movie" or to the Internet equivalent of a cable TV channel. The resources are reserved for that channel alone.

2. A receiver may want to reserve resources that are common to all sources of a multicast group. This is called a "wild-card filter" style reservation. This is typically used for audio conferences, where in practice only one participant speaks at a given time. The resources are reserved for "the group" at large.

3. A receiver may also specify a number of channels to which the same reservation applies. This is useful for videoconferences, where only a limited set of cameras is active at a given time. For example, if the videoconference organizers always validate the cameras of the current and previous speakers, the recipients will need to reserve resources for two channels. These filters are called "shared explicit" style.

In addition to select data flow from a specific application, one can also use the filter to select the precision of the data when the source uses hierarchical coding. For example, a video source may organize its emission into three different streams, corresponding to increasing levels of quality and also increasing throughput requirements, e.g., home-video quality compressed at 64 kbps, broadcast quality compressed at 1.5 Mbps, and high definition at 5 Mbps. The receiver will select the level of service according to the local connectivity and financial conditions. Various applications may have very different requirements; RSVP avoids application dependencies by specifying the filter as a simple "test under mask" to be applied to the packet.

The resources reserved for the session are described in the flow specification, which normally includes assertions about throughputs and delays as defined in RFC2211 and RFC2212 [20,21].

There is indeed no guarantee when a receiver tries to reserve some resources that the reservation will succeed. Merely waving a credit card does not suddenly increase the capacity of optical fibers. RSVP has to include admission control decisions, where each router compares the requested resources to what has already been allocated and either accepts or refuses the reservation.

14.3.3 Paths and Reservations

The second design principle of RSVP is to be independent of the routing protocols. One must, however, make sure that the resources are reserved on precisely those routers that will forward the session's data packets. Given that RSVP lets receivers set up reservations, the receiver has to know from which router the session's data come, and that router has to identify the previous relay, and so on.

RSVP solves this problem by using path messages. These messages are sent by the session's sources at regular intervals toward the session's destination address. In fact, they are not sent as plain data packets; instead, they are specially marked as RSVP packets which carry the address of the node that last examined the packet. The source sends a path packet to the next hop in direction of the destination, or to the next hops if the destination is a multicast group. Each of the next-hop routers will note the previous hop of the message, replace that address with its own, and then relay it farther toward the destination. As a result, the path messages will be received by all the RSVP-capable routers that participate in the multicast group, and that are members of the "multicast distribution tree" for that source.

Once the path has been marked, the routers are ready to process reservation requests. When they receive an "resv message," a reservation request, from a receiver, they will use the path information to identify the previous router to which they should relay the request. In fact, we will have different behaviors, depending on the style of the filter.

1. If the session uses a wild-card filter, the reservation request must be forwarded toward all the active sources, i.e., all the routers from which the local router has received a path message for that session.
2. If the session uses a fixed filter or a shared-explicit filter, the reservation request should be sent toward the sources that are listed in this filter, i.e., to the routers from which the local router has received a path message for that session and the source of that path message is listed in the filter.

There are cases in which several receivers listen to the same sources and several sources use the same paths. Let's use a very simple example network that includes two sources (S1 and S2), two routers (A and B), and two receivers (R1 and R2):

R1 and R2 are two receivers of the same multicast session; S1 and S2 are two sources within that session. R1 and R2 will both send reservations, but these reservations will specify the same session, the same destination address, and the same filter. Router B will have to "aggregate" these reservations so that only one request is sent toward A. If the two reservations are identical, we will have to properly manage only refresh intervals and lifetimes. The refresh interval on the link between B and A will be the lowest of the values received from R1 and R2; the lifetime will be the larger of the two values.

If the two values are not identical—if, for example, R1 requests more resources than R2—we will try to reserve the larger of the two values. It may well be that this larger value is not available. We will have to send an error notification to one of the receivers, and we will try to allocate the values requested by the lesser bidder.

Path messages are specifically designed to support receiver-initiated reservations. They also have a desirable side-effect of facilitating incremental deployment of the protocol. When a path message is forwarded downstream toward the receiver, if the next hop router does not know RSVP, the message will look just like a regular IP packet and will simply be forwarded to the next router en route. When the message reaches an RSVP-capable router, the previous hop address carried in the message identifies the previous RSVP-capable box upstream. The current router will jot down this address for later use in forwarding reservation requests. As a result, path messages and reservation requests cross all non-RSVP router clouds transparently.

14.3.4 Soft States and Synchronizations

The path messages are used to "mark" the network. This enables the users to send their RSVP requests toward the sources and to reserve the resources that they deem necessary. However, this mechanism requires two types of synchronization, one with the routing process and another between the "arrival" process of sources and receivers. RSVP solves this by using a soft-state mechanism.

The path that a session uses is not fixed. We have seen in previous chapters that the routing procedures are constantly trying to update the routing tables so that the packets are guaranteed to follow the shortest paths, whatever the changes in the topology. It may well happen that the session's path changes, for example, because a link breaks. The marks resulting from the previous path messages will not be followed anymore; the reserved resources will not be used. Somehow we have to synchronize reservations and routing updates.

The second synchronization requirement has to do with dynamic changes of senders and receivers in a multicast group over time. When a path message is sent to a group, it will reach all members of that group. It will propagate along the current multicast distribution tree for that source and that group. However, it will reach only the existing members—those who have already subscribed to the group. There is no way to mark paths that would lead to "potential receivers" that have not yet joined the group. Similarly, when a receiver sends an RSVP request, that request will "climb" up the multicast tree toward only the active sources. There is no way to reserve resources for a source that has not yet started to send.

RSVP solves these synchronization problems by the soft-state mechanism. Path messages and reservation requests are repeated regularly, every "refresh interval." If the routing tables have been updated, the next path message will follow the new routes; the new paths will be followed by the next reservations. Because the reservation state is "soft," the reservations along the old path will timeout and be deleted. If a new receiver joins the group, the next path messages will mark the branch leading to that receiver and will enable it to reserve resources. If a new source becomes active and sends path messages, the next repetition of the reservation messages will reserve additional resources for that source.

The combination of soft states and periodic refreshes will also act as a protection against transmission losses. If a message does not reach its destination, the next one will correct the error. In fact, we will associate to the path and reservation messages a refresh period (R) and a time to live (T). The router that receives a message creates a "local state," marking the path or reserving resources. This path will remain valid for the TTL (T). The refresh period (R) is chosen much smaller than T so that transmission errors will not cause the state to disappear prematurely.

If we merely rely on soft state to remove the reservation after a session finishes, the reservation may outlast the session's lifetime for as long as T, even if the reservation is not refreshed further. In those situations, RSVP uses "teardown" messages to expedite the freeing of resources. In fact, we will have six different message types in the RSVP protocol.

☞ Path request
☞ Path error, to be sent in response to a path request
☞ Path teardown
☞ Reservation request
☞ Reservation error
☞ Reservation teardown

The path requests and reservation requests are repeated at regular intervals by all the sources and all the receivers. Such periodic refreshes serve the purpose of keeping consistent RSVP reservation state along data flow paths. This simple approach, however, suffers from a major drawback: its overhead grows linearly with the number of active RSVP sessions. A common method to reduce the periodic refresh overhead is to use a longer refresh period. A longer refresh period, unfortunately, would lead to longer delays in resynchronizing state. Recently a "state compression" mechanism has been proposed to improve the efficiency of RSVP's soft-state protocol in its communication behavior, as described below.

14.3.5 Soft-State Overhead Reduction by State Compression

Instead of sending one message per refresh period per session, one way to reduce this overhead is for a router to compress the state of all its RSVP sessions to a single digest, which can then be sent to neighbor nodes in place of all the "raw" refresh messages. To this end we need an algorithm that can produce a mapping from the given set of RSVP state to a digest with a low enough probability of collision. Two compression algorithms have been suggested so far, CRC-32 and the MD5 algorithm. In the following discussion we assume either one can be used for the purpose.

Because the set of RSVP sessions a node has in common with one neighbor is different from the set it shares with another neighbor, in order to compute a digest an RSVP node must first group all RSVP sessions by neighbors, compute the digest, and then send to the corresponding neighbor node. It organizes all the sessions shared with each neighbor node in a hash table. Assuming the hash table has M slots, each RSVP session is hashed into one of the M slots. The hashing is done over some fixed session fields (e.g., the session ID). If multiple sessions hash to the same slot, they create an ordered linked list, following the increasing order of IP address, protocol ID, and port number of the sessions. The next step is to compute, for each of the M slots, the signature of the RSVP session states hashed into that slot.

After obtaining the M signatures that represent the state of all the RSVP sessions shared with a particular neighbor, a node could simply send to the neighbor node periodically this set of state signatures, which already represents significant overhead reduction compared to repeating periodically the "raw" RSVP messages. However one can do even better by further compressing the M signatures into one digest message. This can be achieved by building a signature tree on top of the hash table. Assuming the hash table size is 1000 slots, one can group each of 10 slots together and compute a signature for the group to get 100 level-2 signatures. We can repeat the same step to further group each 10 of these 100 signatures and get 10 level-3 signatures. Generally speaking, these 10 level-3 signatures can fit comfortably into one IP packet to be sent to a neighbor. The best we can achieve is to reduce the refresh overhead to one refresh message per refresh period per neighbor.

Whenever state inconsistency is detected (the digests of two neighbors disagree), a node can walk down the signature tree to detect which branch caused the inconsistency and quickly nail down specific RSVP sessions. Raw RSVP messages can then be transmitted to resynchronize the state.

As a further optimization, an acknowledgment message (ACK) has been proposed as an addition to the RSVP protocol. As we noted earlier, although periodic RSVP message transmissions tolerate occasional losses, recovery delays are inevitable. For example, when a new receiver joins a session, if its first reservation request is lost, it will have to wait for a refresh period R until the next request is sent to set up the reservation. To minimize such setup delay, a node can request an ACK for each RSVP message that carries state-change information, and promptly retransmit the message until an acknowledgment is received. It is important to note that the use of ACKs is to assure quick delivery of time-sensitive messages; RSVP still relies on periodic refreshes to correct any potential state inconsistency that may occur, even when messages are acknowledged—for example, state inconsistency due to undetected bit errors during transmission or undetected state changes inside a node.

14.3.6 A Few More Words for the Evolving Protocol

RSVP became an Internet proposed standard protocol during the summer of 1997. Since then it has gone through further enhancement in functionalities. Among them the overhead reduction and the addition of acknowledgment messages are the most significant. Other enhancements include the addition of protocol diagnostic capabilities, support for reservation over IP tunnels, and cryptographic authentication to prevent corruption and spoofing of RSVP messages. At the time of this writing the above mentioned changes are all in the process of becoming proposed standard.

Meanwhile the public perception and acceptance of the protocol have gone through a few ups and downs. At the same time the protocol became the proposed standard, various doubts were expressed regarding its scalability, and more fundamentally, the need for such a signalling protocol in the Internet. The diminishing interest in the protocol took a sharp upward turn with the recent development of Internet telephony. To assure the quality of telephone calls carried by IP packets, it is suggested that RSVP be used for resource reservation for individual calls. The reservation may not necessarily be made between the two ends, but instead it can simply cover the edge path between the clients and the border gateway of the backbone network. From that point on, the network provider can merge individual reservations into aggregate traffic classes of differentiated services. The protocol seems to be evolving into an integral piece of the overall resource management architecture.

14.4 Do We Need Resource Reservation?

The popular belief behind some of the resource reservation theories is that, in order to carry "isochronous" traffic such as audio or video, one absolutely needs an isochronous network—one that guarantees constant bit rates and constant delays. In fact, even the reservation approach does not result in a strictly isochronous service. The various packet queues introduce jitter. Reservation guarantees that the delay will never exceed a bounded maximum, but packets will arrive faster if the network is lightly loaded. The jitter has to be compensated by a "resynchronization" procedure at the end points.

In this section, we will describe how resynchronization works. Then we will explain why there is, in fact, no such thing as a fixed-bandwidth requirement. Real-time signals can be digitalized at variable data rates, using variable "compression ratios." If the emitter is capable of continuously sensing the available throughput, it can tune the compression ratio accordingly. We will show that this results in an optimal usage of the network resources.

14.4.1 Real-Time Applications Are Flexible

Transmitting real-time applications such as voice or video over the datagram service of the Internet poses three problems:

1. Packets encounter various queuing delays, and thus do not arrive at regular intervals.
2. Some packets may be lost due to transmission errors.
3. There is no guarantee that the requested bandwidth will be available.

One way to solve this problem is to require that the network changes its service, that it starts providing "quality of service guarantees." However, another approach is to reverse the design logic, and to design the application for the network, instead of designing the network for the applications. Recent years have seen the development of several systems and standards for doing exactly that.

Out of the three problems listed above, the first one is the easiest to solve. The various packet queues cause a "delay jitter" that, if not compensated, would result in serious sound distortion or in a very shaky video rendering. To compensate it, standard protocols such as RTP [24] place a timestamp T in each sound or video packet. The time stamp indicates the instant at which the sound or the video was captured. The packet will arrive after a delay (d), i.e., at time $T + d$. Now, if the recipient knows the maximum value of the delay (D), it suffices to store the packet in memory between T + d and T + D, and to pass it to the rendition device at that precise time. By introducing a variable queuing delay in the reception process, we compensate the delay distortion induced by the network, resulting in a smooth signal transmission. The problem is indeed a bit more complex when one does not know the maximum delay. It is however possible to estimate it by a statistical analysis of the effective transmission delays, i.e., the difference between the emission time carried in the packet and the reception time measured by the receiver. Well-designed applications will try to constantly estimate that delay, and will adjust the "play out" delay during silent intervals in the voice stream or through gradual increase or decrease of the intervals between video frames.

Dealing with the transmission errors essentially requires a careful choice of the compression and packetization algorithm, so that errors only affect a small fraction of the image and get corrected by successive transmissions in the case of video, or only affect the speech signal for a short time in the case of voice. Audio packet losses can be concealed by interpolation techniques, reconstructing a plausible signal from previous and consecutive packets.

Like many of my colleagues, I used to believe that the real-time applications mandated strong quality-of-service guarantees. In fact, I believed that until we had the opportunity to actually develop our own small-scale videoconferencing application. Our team at INRIA specialized in the study of network control protocols. Controlling multimedia applications is one of the areas that we research. For several years, we conducted theoretical studies, using numerical models of the audio or video sources, e.g., modeling the voice channel as a succession of silences and talk spurts and the video channel as a succession of images that were sent at a fixed rate but had a variable size due to compression. But, in fact, it is possible to adapt the network usage in real time, either by choosing a different audio compression algorithm or by tuning the coding parameters of video compression algorithms such as H.261 or MPEG.

In a communication to the 1994 SIGCOMM conference [10], Ian Wakeman, Jean-Chrysostome Bolot, and Thierry Turletti presented the point-to-multipoint sensing algorithm that they integrated into the IVS video-conferencing software. By measuring the frequency of acknowledgments, the source builds an estimate of the number of receivers; it uses this estimate to build up a mask, whose number of bits is proportional to the number of recipients. Each packet that solicits acknowledgments carries this mask and a random number; each recipient draws a different random number. The recipient has the right to send an acknowledgment if the masked bits of its own number match the packet's random number. This is equivalent to sampling the network conditions on a small number of recipients. If the sample set is randomly distributed and variable in time, we will obtain a statistically significant estimate. The algorithm enabled them to estimate the prevailing packet loss rate, and then to adapt the transmission rate so that it mimics the transmission rate of a TCP connection experiencing the same loss rate. A different sensing algorithm has been incorporated in RTP, or rather in the control protocol, RTCP, that comes with RTP. RTCP enables participating stations to discover the current value of the jitter, transmission delay, and packet loss rate. "Polite" sources can then adapt their behavior to match that of TCP sources.

In fact, most real-time applications could probably be made "network-conscious." Such network-conscious applications adapt their behavior to the prevalent network conditions, so as to deliver the best service given these conditions. The particular adaptation will vary: voice, video, and network games do not have quite the same requirements and will not use the same algorithms. The adaptation is also limited to a range of values—for example, to bandwidth varying between a few kilobits and a few hundred kilobits for voice transmission.

14.4.2 The Economy of Reservation

Scott Shenker is probably the first to have correctly analyzed the economy of resource allocations. Procedures like the one we described in the previous paragraph allow operation at variable bit rates, with variable quality. We can plot a curve that relates the "quality indicator" to the corresponding data rate. Indeed, the unit of quality is entirely arbitrary. To simplify, we will assume that it is expressed in a monetary unit—the price that the user is willing to pay for a signal of that quality.

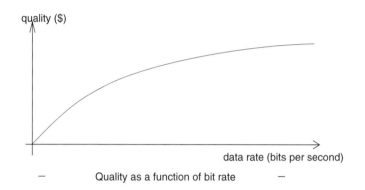

Quality as a function of bit rate

We have implicitly assumed the existence of such a curve in section 14.4.1. This curve, simple as it is, helps us respond to two important questions—choosing the bit rate for an application and understanding the economy of reservation and sharing.

Suppose that we want to select a bit rate for a specific application. If all resources were free, we would simply pick the maximum throughput that the network can provide and get the maximum value. But networks, especially long-haul networks, have a cost. Reserving twice the data rate is likely to cost twice the price. Then, if transmission is expensive, we can use the opposite reasoning: why not always use the maximum compression ratio and pay less? Economic theory tells us the solution. We must pick a data rate in such a way that an increase in the data rate will cost more than it yields, and vice versa. If we operate at rate d and obtain the quality q, it makes sense to increase the rate to d' only if the difference in quality $q' - q$ is larger than the cost of $d' - d$. If the quality curve is continuously derivable, it means that the equilibrium is found when the first derivative of the quality curve equals the unit price of transmission capacity.

Let's come back to the case where the resource appears to be "free" to the users—for example, when the infrastructure is paid by a yearly subscription and the charges don't depend on the actual usage. The network will probably use a combination of end-to-end controls and fair queuing in the routers to ensure that the bandwidth is shared evenly between the users. If only one user is present, this user will get the whole capacity; if two are present, each will get one-half, and so on. As a result, they will get variable qualities.

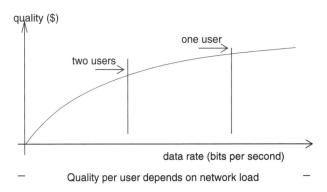

Quality per user depends on network load

In most cases, the law of diminishing returns applies—the quality increases when more data rate is available, but it does not increase linearly. If the single user gets the quality qa for the data rate d, each of the two simultaneous users will get the quality qb for the rate $d/2$, so that qb is larger than qa/2. Now, if we consider the global satisfaction in the system, it has risen to 2*qb, which is larger than qa. Mathematicians will tell you that, if the satisfaction function is "convex," the more you divide it, the more satisfaction you get.

In this situation, there is no need to reserve resources. That would actually be counterproductive. If we allowed the first user to reserve an amount d of resources, we would be forced to deny access to the second user. The total satisfaction would have stayed at the lower-level qa. This result, however, is contingent on the convex property of the satisfaction curve. If this curve was not continuous or had a stiff inflexion point, Scott Shenker points out that admission control is necessary.

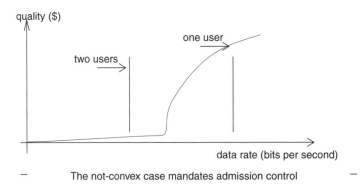

The not-convex case mandates admission control

In the "not-convex" case, dynamically sharing between many users does not work, because the quality obtained with half the rate can be much lower than the previous quality. The classical example is voice. The best vocoders today require at least a few kilobits per second. Suppose we have reached the point where all stations operate near this rate, and we suddenly add more users, so that each of them obtains only 500 bps. This is entirely insufficient to carry the signal, and the overall quality drops to 0! Obviously, we would have been better served by a combination of reservation and access control.

Whether reservations are mandatory or not depends, as we just learned, on the precise shape of the satisfaction curve. This shape depends on the hardware and software that are available. I personally believe that in most operational cases the law of diminishing returns applies. Applications like voice or video are extremely flexible. Their data rates can vary from a few kilobits to several megabits. If we pick an operation point that corresponds to 64 kbps under nominal load, we need to multiply the number of users by 30 before we reach the "nonlinear" part of the curve. In fact, even that is dependent on today's technology. One might in conditions of "bandwidth starvation" apply innovations, such as asking users to "speak more slowly" so that the compression algorithm becomes more efficient; one may even resort to written communication. If this is true, then reservations will be required only in a very limited number of cases, e.g., to get access to very specific services such as "video on demand." This is probably the real market for resource reservation protocols such as RSVP.

In any case, deploying resource reservations outside of an experimental environment requires that one charges users for the bandwidth they require. Otherwise, nothing would prevent Joe Random from simply bidding for "umpteen gigabits per second," with interesting consequences for his fellow users. This type of "charging per bandwidth" is quite alien to today's Internet philosophy. Charging for resources supposes in any case that the network can authenticate the reservation requests, which probably implies that these requests carry a digital signature. It probably also implies some form of contractual relationship between the user and the various network providers that are conducting the reservation.

14.5 Differentiated Services

Although the Internet offers only a simple datagram delivery service, it has gone through sustained exponential growth over the last several years. The previous section shows that even multimedia applications, which are generally considered performance sensitive, can run quite well on top of datagram services by adapting to varying network conditions. Thus one would naturally ask the question: Does the Internet need any service other than datagram delivery?

The answer is a firm yes. The fundamental reason is not whether particular applications can or cannot perform adequately with datagram services; rather, it is because certain classes of Internet *users* demand higher quality service. And they will pay for it. Ever since the invention of the World Wide web, the mainstream business has found the Internet to be a useful tool extending its market reach, and has been gradually moving its business onto the Internet. Rather than adjusting their applications to fit into the available resources, many business applications demand the best service possible, as long as they can make a big enough profit margin from using that service.

The exact road leading to that desired level of service control, however, did not lay itself clearly in front of network engineers. Intserv represented a first attempt, which did not receive the expected adoption from the market. Another IETF effort started in 1997 to define *differentiated services*. This readjustment of direction got many people confused: What are the fundamental differences between the intserv and diffserv? We will explain in this section.

14.5.1 QOS Support Seen from 10,000 Feet

Although it seems a great challenge to guarantee QOS over a statistically shared system, such as the Internet, the basic approach is actually straightforward and can be described in four simple steps. Consider the fact that an end-to-end delivery path is, generally speaking, made of multiple hops.

1. The first thing one must do is define the service class a packet should receive at each switch or router, similar to defining the service class on an airplane.

2. Once the number of classes and the service for each class are defined, one must allocate to each class a certain amount of resources that are needed in forwarding data packets in that class. On an airplane the resource is the space and number of seats for each class; in packet switched networks, it is the bandwidth and buffer space.

3. After these first two steps, one is ready to sort incoming packets into different service classes. This is not much different from sorting passengers to their seat classes. How to sort packets is an interesting question that we'll touch on later.

    However, notice that one cannot assign more passengers to the first-class cabin than the number of seats available. So:

4. If one wants to guarantee the service quality, one must also control the amount of traffic admitted for each class to be strictly no more than the allocated resources.

    The above four steps assure that important packets can receive corresponding QOS treatment at *one* hop. However, what the customers care about is how good a service the application can get from a client to a server (or vice versa). Thus,

5. One can guarantee end-to-end service if the above four steps are done at *each and all* the routers along the paths, or at least at those routers that have the least capacity. We call these *bottleneck* routers.

This is where the intserv effort started, that is defining coordination of all the routers along a specific path to provide QOS for a specific application's data flow. Diffserv, on the other hand, focuses on the first three steps. Whether one starts with or without the inclusion of Steps 4 and 5 above makes all the difference between intserv and diffserv.

14.5.2 Intserv

The performance received by applications is called a *service*. Intserv defines end-to-end services and specifies the set of protocols and mechanisms to realize such QOS service definitions for individual data flows.

What is the best way to identify data flows for individual applications remains an open research issue; for the time being we can assume that flows can be uniquely identified by the addresses and port numbers carried in IP packets. Sorting packets in such a way is called *multiple field* filtering, or *MF* for short. Implementing MF requires that a router establish and maintain the address and port number information for each of the application data flows passing through it, and be able to sort packets, at the wire speed, by the multiple fields in the header.

It can be considered either unexpectedly or inevitably that as the specifics of intserv definition were laid out, various people started voicing concerns about complexity, scalability, and incremental deployability. One worries about complexity because, from the above description, one can immediately tell that supporting intserv requires a router to keep a great deal more information about data flows than it does now for the current datagram delivery, which needs nothing but a forwarding table to dispatch packets in the right direction. The number of data flows that may make a reservation can be a large one, thus the concern about scalability. Furthermore, all the routers along a delivery path must coordinate with each other to assure the end-to-end quality, which implies that supporting intserv requires a flag day when all the routers on the Internet switch on the new capability, a requirement that is plainly unreachable. Given that the market is demanding new services right away, something else must be done.

14.5.3 How and How Much Diffserv Differs from Intserv

The market demands simple mechanisms that can be *quickly* and *incrementally* deployed to provide differentiated data delivery. Diffserv sets the goal of defining packet treatments at *individual* components, called per-hop behavior (PHB), as opposed to intserv's target of defining end-to-end services.

Recall the five simple steps for end-to-end QOS support. Supporting PHB still requires that one first define packet classes at a hop, but now one has the flexibility of having both globally and locally defined classes. One still needs to control the amount of resources allocated to each class, but now because the concern is on individual hops, manually configured allocation is not only a feasible starting point but also provides controllability by the network administrators. On the contrary, end-to-end QoS support requires end-to-end signalling. And one still needs to sort packets into their corresponding service classes at each hop; but, because one is only concerned with how the packets in the same class get treated at *one hop*, not the performance received by each application data flow, this sorting can be easily done by a class tag on each packet, without worrying which data flow it belongs to or how the delay at this one hop affects the overall end-to-end delay.

It is not to say that diffserv can be immune to the need for admission control or the need for signalling to assure the delivery quality along entire paths. Rather, diffserv simply *decouples* packet forwarding treatment from the state setup that controls the forwarding treatment. The former is a piece of well-understood technology, which can be implemented by queue service disciplines and/or queue management disciplines as discussed earlier, while the latter contains the more challenging, and largely open, research issues regarding the mechanisms that perform admission control, and especially mechanisms that configure the forwarding paths. The Internet today is made up of independently operated network domains, such as campus networks and ISP backbones. Supporting PHB in a single domain is a readily tangible goal, while enforcing end-to-end reservations is not—it is simply impossible to have everyone turn on QOS support in the near future, or ever, let alone the many authentication, accounting, charging, and scaling issues that remain unresolved. Separating the functionality to forwarding treatment and control plane management provides diffserv with the much needed incremental deployability as well as extensibility. In short, the per-hop behavior defined by diffserv provides a fundamental building block, rather than an all-in-one solution, in the Internet QOS support.

In fact, this approach is not new. During the early days of the Internet a decision was made to separate the packet forwarding and routing components. Packet forwarding is a relatively simple task that needs to be performed on a per-packet basis as quickly as possible. Forwarding uses the packet header to find an entry in a routing table that determines the packet's output interface. Routing sets the entries in that table and may need to reflect a range of transit and other policies as well as keep track of route failures. Routing tables are maintained as a background process to the forwarding task. Further, routing is the more complex task, and it has continued to evolve over the past 20 years.

Next we describe the few basic mechanisms in supporting diffserv.

14.5.4 Basic Mechanisms

Diffserv requires *traffic conditioning*, which is a collective term that includes the tasks of classifying, metering, shaping, and policing of flows. The first step is stamping each packet with a tag in the packet header that can be used to sort packets into treatment classes. A standard tag format has been developed in RFC-2474 [22] that uses the second octet in the IP header to indicate the treatment class. The definition also took great care to assure backward compatibility with the current usage of the octet as a "Type of Service" indicator.

Recall that intserv distinguishes packets from individual data flows and allocates resources accordingly; if a user attempts to send more packets than he has reserved for, the network is still able to assure other flows with their reserved resources. Diffserv-capable networks, on the other hand, do not distinguish packets by individual users or applications; thus, controlling the total amount of packets entering each treatment class becomes critically important. If more packets are marked for a class than the amount of resource allocated for, all applications in that class will suffer.

To prevent overload, diffserv performs packet policing at various boundary points. For example, if a campus network has subscribed 5 Mbps expedited forwarding service (EF) from its ISP, the entry router (called ingress router) to the ISP will measure the traffic by some well-established mechanism—for example, a token-bucket filter—to assure that no more than 5 Mbps worth of packet flow can be marked with EF class. Depending on the agreement between the campus and the ISP, excessive packets can be either discarded, or forwarded after readjusting the agreement (and the payment as well).

Such policing puts a big responsibility on the campus traffic control. First of all, the campus network administrator must control which or whose packets should be marked with the EF tag to assure that the total amount stays below the 5-Mbps limit. Furthermore, as the last step of assurance before the traffic leaves the campus, the network administrator must also install a control mechanism at the exit router from the campus (called egress router). The egress router checks the eligibility of all the packets carrying the EF mark, and shapes the aggregate outbound traffic flow to be within the subscribed limit. To stop excessive data flows at the earliest possible places, the campus administrator may also decide to police packets from hosts at their first-hop routers based on some fine granularity parameters, such as host addresses and transport port numbers that correspond to individual applications.

As mentioned earlier, the Internet today is made up of independently operated network domains. This is one single important fact that all the protocol designers today must take into account, because money changes hands across domain boundaries. By defining *component* behavior in service differentiation, the diffserv WG has laid out a framework that well suits the segmented Internet world. Internet service providers can extend the defined per-hop behavior to per-domain forwarding behavior as a way to differentiate network services they provide to customers. ISPs can keep all the control complexity at the edges, where they negotiate contract agreements, settle charging models, and set up the traffic conditioning parameters used for packet marking, shaping, and policing. Within a domain, one has all the freedom to pick whatever mechanisms deemed desirable, as long as the externally observed delivery performance matches the contract agreement.

One could stay with the simple FIFO forwarding as long as sufficient resources are available. One could also implement sophisticated MPLS mechanism for tight control if that is deemed necessary.

14.6 Future Internet Services

The deployment of any resource reservation mechanism in the Internet has proven to be a very elusive goal, despite a very high level of activity in the research community and also a large participation to standardization efforts. The current consensus seems orientated toward a two-tier model, distinguishing backbone and access networks.

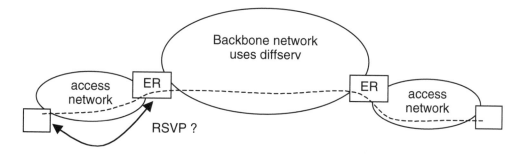

The backbone networks will typically use very high-speed transmission technologies and handle a very large number of relatively low bandwidth flows. In this environment, using techniques that require per-flow state is not practical. The backbones are likely to use the simpler "differentiated service" technology. The access networks will probably evolve from the current low-speed modems toward higher-speed technologies, such as the one provided by Digital Subscriber Loops or by cable modems. Bandwidth is likely to be more limited there, specially on the upstream channels of cable modems. Also, the number of flows is likely to be much more reduced. As a consequence, we are likely to see edge-routers enforce an access policy between the access networks and the backbone. Edge routers will identify flows and decide which packets enjoy this or that "differentiated class of service." The decision may be based on static configurations, such as subscription data. If there is a demand for dynamic configuration, we will need a signalling protocol. RSVP could well be used to that effect.

This architecture, however, is not fully understood. It is unclear, for example, whether the particular structure of RSVP, which relies on end-to-end PATH messages, is adequate in an access control protocol. It is also unclear whether a simple classification of packets is sufficient, especially at bottleneck points such as connections between provider networks or transoceanic links. There may be a need to implement some form of fair queuing within a differentiated class of service. A particularly interesting design, proposed in [25], would be to tag the packet with sufficient information in the edge routers, so that backbone routers could make queuing decisions equivalent to fair queuing without maintaining per-flow state.

All of the techniques presented in this chapter can be applied equally well for IPv4 and IPv6. The differentiated service classes are encoded in the Type of Service octet of the IPv4 header and in the Traffic Class octet of the IPv6 header, using the exact same bit pattern. RSVP can be used in conjunction with either IPv4 or IPv6, albeit the "flow label" gives an advantage to IPv6: flows can be identified by looking only at the IPv6 header fields, without having to worry about the use of encryption.

References

1. A. Demers, S. Keshav, and S. Shenker, "Analysis and Simulation of a Fair Queuing Algorithm," *Journal of Internetworking: Research and Experience*, 1, pp. 3–26, 1990. Also in *Proc. ACM SIGCOMM '89*, pp. 3–12.

2. L. Zhang, "Virtual Clock: A New Traffic Control Algorithm for Packet Switching Networks," *ACM Transactions on Computer Systems*, Vol. 9, No. 2, pp. 101–124, 1990. Also in *Proc ACM SIGCOMM '90*, pp. 19–29.

3. A. Parekh and R. Gallager, "A Generalized Processor Sharing Approach to Flow Control—The Single Node Case," *Technical Report LIDS-TR-2040*, Laboratory for Information and Decision Systems, Massachusetts Institute of Technology, 1991.

4. A. Parekh, "A Generalized Processor Sharing Approach to Flow Control in Integrated Services Networks," *Technical Report LIDS-TR-2089*, Laboratory for Information and Decision Systems, Massachusetts Institute of Technology, 1992.

5. D. Clark, S. Shenker, and L. Zhang, "Supporting Real-Time Applications in an Integrated Services Packet Network: Architecture and Mechanisms," *Proc. SIGCOMM '92*, Baltimore, MD, August 1992.

6. R. Braden, D. Clark, and S. Shenker, "Integrated Services in the Internet Architecture: An Overview," work in progress, October 1993.

7. S. Shenker, D. Clark, and L. Zhang, "A Service Model for an Integrated Services Internet," work in progress, October 1993.

8. C. Topolcic, "Experimental Internet Stream Protocol, Version 2 (ST-II)," RFC-1190, October 30, 1990.

9. L. Zhang, S. Deering, D. Estrin, S. Shenker, and D. Zappala, "RSVP: A New Resource ReSerVation Protocol," IEEE Network, September 1993.

10. J. Bolot, T. Turletti, and I. Wakeman, "Scalable Feedback Control for Multicast Video Distribution in the Internet," ACM SIGCOMM '94 Conference, London, September 1994.

11. L. S. Brakmo, L. L. Peterson, and S. W. O'Malley, "TCP Vegas: New Techniques for Congestion Detection and Avoidance," ACM SIGCOMM '94 Conference, London, September 1994.

12. ISO/IEC JTC1/SC29, "Generic Coding of Moving Pictures and Associated Audio Information (MPEG2)," CD 13818, December 1993.

13. CCITT, "Video Codec for Audiovisual Services at p*64 kbps," Recommendation H.261, 1990.

14. T. Turletti, "H.261 Software Codec for Videoconferencing Over the Internet," *INRIA Research Report 1834*, January 1993.

15. R. Braden, Ed., L. Zhang, S. Berson, S. Herzog, and S. Jamin, "Resource ReSerVation Protocol (RSVP)—Version 1 Functional Specification," RFC-2205, September 1997.

16. L. Berger and T. O'Malley, "RSVP Extensions for IPSEC Data Flows," RFC-2207, September 1997.

17. A. Mankin, Ed., F. Baker, B. Braden, S. Bradner, M. O`Dell, A. Romanow, A. Weinrib, and L. Zhang, "Resource ReSerVation Protocol (RSVP)—Version 1 Applicability Statement: Some Guidelines on Deployment," RFC-2208, September 1997.

18. R. Braden and L. Zhang, "Resource ReSerVation Protocol (RSVP)—Version 1 Message Processing Rules," RFC-2209, September 1997.

19. J. Wroclawski, "The Use of RSVP with IETF Integrated Services," RFC-2210, September 1997.

20. J. Wroclawski, "Specification of the Controlled-Load Network Element Service," RFC-2211, September 1997.

21. S. Shenker, C. Partridge, and R. Guerin, "Specification of Guaranteed Quality of Service," RFC-2212, September 1997.

22. K. Nichols, S. Blake, F. Baker, and D. Black, "Definition of the Differentiated Services Field (DS Field) in the IPv4 and IPv6 Headers," RFC-2474, December 1998.

23. S. Blake, D. Black, M. Carlson, E. Davies, Z. Wang, and W. Weiss, "An Architecture for Differentiated Service," RFC-2475, December 1998.

24. H. Schulzrinne, S. Casner, R. Frederick, and V. Jacobson, "RTP: A Transport Protocol for Real-Time Applications," RFC-1889, January 1996.

25. I. Stoica, S. Shenker, and H. Zhang, "Core-Stateless Fair Queuing: A Scalable Architecture to Approximate Fair Bandwidth Allocation in High Speed Networks," ACM SIGCOMM '98 Conference, Vancouver, September 1998.

Toward the New IP

The Internet has evolved a lot since the first days of the Arpanet. During the presentation of its routing protocols, we have mentioned several of these changes: the separation of networks into subnets, the organization of the Internet as a confederation of autonomous systems, and the distinction between internal and external routing protocols. We have seen how OSPF was designed to replace RIP, how EGP was replaced by BGP.

15.1 The Internet Lives

The imminent death of the Internet has been announced at regular intervals. The last episode mentioned three possible causes of death—exhaustion of the class B-addresses, explosion of the routing tables, and depletion of the address space. In short, the Internet would be a victim of its own success.

But we saw in chapter 10 that the development of CIDR solved the first problems. The class-B exhaustion was supposed to occur in March 1994. We are past that date. The routing tables increased dangerously, but BGP-4 is now deployed. It enables "routing table aggregation," which is expected to solve the routing table explosion.

The "address depletion" death is supposed to occur when the last remaining IP address is allocated. It will be impossible to connect any new clients without giving away the "uniqueness of addresses." But the network would then stop being entirely connected and would "destroy itself under its own weight."

The address depletion scenario is largely exaggerated. It is often the ultimate argument of the proponents of alternate technologies, in particular those who tried to push the OSI architecture through various bureaucratic exercises. In any case, address depletion will not arrive tomorrow. According to the most common estimate, we can wait at least three or four years. This will leave some time for deploying IPv6.

15.2 Address Depletion

Back in 1978, when the first draft of the Internet protocol was published, 32 bits looked like plenty. Indeed, some researchers issued words of warning, saying that the choice of a fixed address size was shortsighted. But, like those of Cassandra, their warnings were ignored. The convenience of an address that could be stored in a standard 32-bit memory word as well as the programming efficiency of a well-aligned header were too attractive. In fact, the argument has two sides. It is certainly partly because of the shortsighted "easy-to-program" header that the Internet protocol could be implemented in a lot of devices, allowing the Internet to grow so large. A more complex format would have no problem of growth—because it would not have attracted as many followers.

The estimations of how long the address space will last before the last address is allocated vary widely. A simplistic back-of-the-envelope computation shows that:

☞ There were almost 60,000,000 connected computers by the summer of 1999.

☞ Thus we need at least 26 bits of address (log2[60,000,000]).

☞ Because we are doubling every 1.5 years, we need one more bit per 1.5 years.

☞ This would leave us at most 10 years before 32 bits are entirely used.

This would mean that the address space will be exhausted by 2009. But this kind of reasoning suffers from a number of imprecisions. First, the address space is only sparsely used. Very few class-A networks connect more than a few hundred thousand hosts; very few class-B networks connect more than a few thousand. 50% of the address space is currently allocated, but only 3% of the allocated space is used. The best usage rate is observed in the class-C space, where the usage rate reaches almost 7%. If nothing changes, we can easily double the allocation rate, from 50% to 100%, and we can also hope that CIDR will help us reach the usage rate of 7% over all classes. This will allow us to connect 280 million hosts, a number that could be reached within three to four years if we continue doubling every 1.5 years.

The four-year figure supposes we succeed in more densely populating the address space—which is, in fact, happening with CIDR. As users get "exactly the number of bits they need," there is much less wasted address space. However, this increased usage rate is only achieved through a great amount of pain, as corporations cannot really get enough addresses to easily manage their networks. In parallel, we are observing a trend toward increased address demand. Users that switch from telephone modems to permanently connected cable modems or other broadband services also switch from "leasing" an address a few hours per day when they are connected to using an address in permanence. In addition, a broadband connection is an invitation for connecting all sorts of new Internet devices besides the PC, such as Internet telephones or Internet appliances.

In short, we are again facing a crisis. We must either deploy IPv6 or risk a strange evolution of the Internet toward a set of disconnected networks.

15.3 Preparing for IPv6

The making of IPv6 is now a matter of history. There were several proposals, such as TUBA, based on CLNP, or PIP, which provided innovative routing. The process eventually converged to the current specification of IPv6, for which standards are now ready.

We only have a limited time available to actually conduct the transition. If we judge by the last effort to modify the Internet Protocol, the deployment of Multicast, we may very well wonder if we will ever have enough time. Multicast deployment started in 1992, and it is hardly achieved today! The IPv6 parallel to the deployment of the MBONE in 1992 would be the deployment of the IPv6 "6BONE," which started in 1996. This leaves us some hope to complete deployment within four years. Indeed, the longer we wait, the more we will have to implement interim solutions such as address translation boxes, which contribute to isolating parts of the Internet and also introduce limitations to the set of applications that can be deployed.

On the other hand, the good news is that whether we transition to IPv6 or not, the main protocol of the Internet will be a version of IP, and the routing protocols will be those that we have studied—RIP-2, OSPF, BGP-4.

Index